Sports
in
Dayton

A Bicentennial Retrospective

By Ritter Collett

Landfall Press
Dayton, Ohio
1996

Sports In Dayton
A Bicentennial Retrospective
by Ritter Collett
Copyright © 1996, Landfall Press, Inc.
All rights reserved. Printed in the United States of America. No part of this
book may be used or reproduced except for brief quotations embodied in
reviews or articles without written permission of the publisher, Landfall
Press, 5171 Chapin Street, Dayton, Ohio 45429
ISBN 0-913428-78-7
Library of Congress Catalog Card No. 96-075102

Dedication

This book is dedicated to the several hundreds of people I have worked with on three Dayton newspapers over the last half century. They were for the most part competent professionals, many of whom became my good friends. My wife of many years is Jean Ragon, working the news desk at the old *Journal* when I proposed in 1948. Our son Jerry worked at the newspapers in the summertime when he was in college. The *Journal*, *Journal Herald* and the *Dayton Daily News* provided the structure of what has been a very pleasant lifetime.

Acknowledgments

This book could not have been written without the cooperation of many individuals.

The most important pledge of full assistance to go ahead was from J. Bradford Tillson, publisher of the *Dayton Daily News*, who made available the reference library and other facilities of the newspaper.

Ray Marcano, news manager/sports, and his editorial assistant, Lisa Weaver, come next. Lisa was invaluable in pulling out stories and columns from the electronic library.

Longtime sports staffers Bucky Albers, Mark Katz, Chick Ludwig, Greg Simms, Dave Long and Leal Beattie were helpful with background from the sports they cover. Outdoor writers Jim Robey and Jim Morris had material from the Grand American Trapshoot.

Reference library director Michael Jesse and his staff -- Nina Butler, Dean Koolbeek, Charlotte Jones, Bob Alliare, Yvetta Keenan and Sasha Stanley -- saw so much of the author they must have felt he was part of their group.

Nancy Horlacher of the Dayton and Montgomery County Public Library opened the historical files for inspection.

Carl M. Becker, retired professor of history at Wright State, is into research on the origins of professional football in southern Ohio and has published a number of articles. He has been a valuable source of information and direction.

Bob Denny, athletic director of the Dayton Public High Schools, and his secretary, Julie Vestal, got the author started off in the right direction.

Wright State sports information director Bob Noss, along with Matt Zircher and Bernadette Vielhaber, contributed material on the Raiders.

Doug Hauschild, Penny Smith and Katina Banks from the UD sports information office came through as usual. Retired administrator Gene Schill is a valuable source of UD information.

Flyer football history is being kept alive in the only book written on the subject by James Whalen Sr., who was known as Rocky Whalen when he played football at Oakwood High School.

Much of the material on Oakwood football was provided by Whalen and Johnny Sauer, whose role in football history is in the text.

In amateur baseball, Ted Mills, Dick Tatem, Junior Norris, Jack Schlemmer and Bill Fisher provided background material.

Chester A. Roush is the ultimate authority on the history of Fairmont High School football. Centerville athletic director Bernie Witzmann and Northmont AD Gene Eyler were helpful.

Bob and Jack Margolis, Ted LeVeris and Pat Schwab contributed to the golf section. Nick Ungard, himself a member of the Golf Hall of Fame, is custodian of that information.

George Freiberger and Sonny Mantia provided material on boxing.

Russ Clendenen and Mutt Anderson, a pair of youthful octogenarians, went into their memory banks on auto racing. Johnny Vance can't match them in age, but likewise knows the speed sport and provided material. Tim Wourms got us into motorcycling.

Lefty McFadden shared his knowledge in auto racing, ice hockey and several other sports.

Maureen Hopkins, the fulltime secretary of the Dayton Bowling Association (men) and Mary McCray, who has the same duties with the Dayton Women's Bowling Association, updated the Hall of Fame lists. Gary Manos, Christ Zavakos and Joe Poelking, Jr. were helpful in that category.

Assistance in many different ways came from Wilbur Curtis, Norm Feuer, Jack Brennan, Bob (Obie) O'Bryan, Dick Pendry, Ron Anello, Stan Shively, Lois Schmidt and Hy Shumsky.

Publisher's Foreword

Late in his life, my father became a baseball fan. Before that, like many of his generation and background, he considered most professional sports a colossal misuse of time, effort and energy.

When he thought about it at all, he felt that life was a serious business in Depression America, and games such as baseball were best left to children and others not concerned with making a living.

Specifically, he became enamored of the post-World War II Brooklyn Dodgers and he followed the exploits of Duke Snider, Gil Hodges, Dixie Walker and, of course, Jackie Robinson and the rest. I don't think he had ever gone to a ball park until I took him to Crosley Field.

Despite their move to Los Angeles, he remained a loyal Dodger fan for the rest of his life although he also rooted for the Cincinnati Reds. He'd let me know when the Dodgers were in town and some of our best times together were spent at Reds-Dodgers games in Cincinnati. Rooting for both sides was no hardship; it was the game itself and how it was played that counted as much as who won or lost.

That was almost 30 years ago and although much has changed in American sports, Dayton continues in its enviable position of contributing to and enjoying the best of many sports. Major league professional sports are but a short drive away; our college teams are nationally ranked as are many of our athletes. Some, notably Mike Schmidt and Edwin Moses, have achieved great distinction. Our high school teams consistently rank among the best in the state.

Participation in sport, mainly in golf, softball, bowling and bicycling continues high although, as James Michener pointed out, student physical education in most schools suffers because of the emphasis on winning teams in the major revenue producing sports.

And in this day of big-money, must-win pressure, the often touted character building aspects of sports are seriously in question.

Sports and games throughout human history have been an integral part of growing up. It has been so from the most primitive societies to the most complex. Through play are learned most lessons of life.

The transformation of sports into big business with its attendant greed and violence, its spectacle over substance, unseen since ancient Rome, is a relatively recent development in the long history of games. The conflict between the Roman Coliseum and the Greek Olympic ideal is the overwhelming sports issue to be resolved in the new century.

Perhaps we can never return to the simpler age when a team truly belonged to a city, when kids could come to a ball park on their own and get in for small change, or when heroes played mostly for the love of the game and spent a career with the home team instead of changing uniforms as often as some movie stars change spouses.

Baseball is the oldest established sport in Dayton, almost as old as the game itself. Starting with the Dayton Reds, the Old Soldiers, the Vets, the Wings and the Indians, baseball has been played here on sandlots, ball parks and city-owned fields. Major league teams and barnstormers, established stars and youngsters on their way up, have played here.

The present hiatus is the longest since the game began that the city has been without a team -- almost 50 years. Given today's attitudes, baseball's franchise monopoly may soon be a thing of the past opening the door again for teams in cities like Dayton and in leagues like the old Central.

Wouldn't it be a boon to the entire metropolitan community if one day a blighted unused section of west of the river downtown Dayton was transformed into an attractive, productive, state of the art multi-purpose facility owned by the city?

Alexander Kaye
Dayton, Ohio
January, 1996

Introduction

Dayton owns a rich history in the athletic world with the advent of its third century just down the road.

A community that produced the greatest hurdler in the world in Edwin Moses and the greatest all-around third baseman in major league baseball in Mike Schmidt has a lot to talk about.

Moses and Schmidt came out of the same high school less than a decade apart but that is getting ahead of our story.

In observing our Bicentennial in 1996 sports in the first 100 years can almost be written off.

The first 50 years had little sports and none as we know them now. In the beginning, in the first decade of the community named for Jonathan Dayton, the physical activities of our forefathers were confined by necessity to the back-breaking labor of clearing the land for plowing, building cabins and the never-ending search for food.

As our town began to be more than a small clearing in the woods between the Great and Little Miami Rivers, young men growing up occasionally wrestled and ran foot races for recreation just as did one of their peers born a little to the south and west, named Abraham Lincoln.

Biographies of the 16th President shed more light on what it may have been like for a teenager to mature into an adult as the frontier rapidly shifted westward toward the Mississippi than we have available in the limited archives of the time in our area.

The more recognizable history of sports in the Dayton area happened in the 20 century, but there was a beginning in the last three decades of the 19th century, although much of the information is sketchy.

This effort to produce a historical record of local athletic competition and its impact on the world beyond has been compiled from many sources.

How many of the followers of the Bengals and the Browns, for example, are aware that a Dayton team was a charter member of the NFL? How many contemporary golfers, for another example, are aware that Dayton was once the center of golf club manufacturing g in the United States?

How many boxing fans are aware that Jack Dempsey and Joe Louis scored knockout victories in Dayton enroute to their heavyweight championships? How many automobile racing enthusiasts know that the biggest names in their sport regularly drove at the Dayton Speedway in the 1930s and were still coming here in the years right after World War II?

It is important to emphasize what this book does and doesn't do.

This is not an encyclopedia listing the score of every football, basketball or baseball game played in Montgomery County. It would require a lifetime of tedious research to compile something of that nature. And what would you do with it once you had it?

There is no way to pay tribute to every golfer who has scored a hole--in-one. But the history of Dayton's country clubs and public courses is described plus accounts of the four national tournaments played here.

There is no way to list every bowler who rolled a 300 game nor the individual triumphs of the thousands upon thousands who have participated in sports throughout the years. But the various Halls of Fame are here and so are many of the memories that make sports so important locally and in America today.

In the late fall of 1995 every news story on the Balkan peace negotiations involving Bosnia, Croatia and Serbia carried a Dayton dateline. This world-wide attention did us proud even though the ultimate fate of the peace agreement hammered out here is yet to be played out on the world stage.

Every summer the Associated Press files stories on the Grand American Trapshoot with a Dayton dateline that go into newspapers around the country.

The easiest chapter in this work for the author involved the University of Dayton basketball program. He had previously written the UD story in *The Flyers*, having been on the scene for the triumphs and heartaches of the Tom Blackburn and Don Donoher eras.

Many Flyer followers of recent vintage may find it difficult to imagine how much favorable attention the Dayton teams received in the New York media when the Flyers were appearing in the NIT in Madison Square Garden almost every year in the 1950s nor understand the impact the teams had on the Dayton psyche.

This, then, is a chronicle of the highlights in Dayton's sports history, sport by sport.

Ritter Collett
Dayton, Ohio
January, 1996

Contents

GOLF

The first golf club, Dayton Country Club, opens clubhouse June 18, 1910.

Two of yesteryear's best known golfers, Harry Schwab (left) and Ock Willoweit, relax after each shot a 69 to tie as top qualifiers in the 1954 Max Schear Qualifier to the Dayton City Championship.

1

Playing the Game

There is no precise history of when golf crossed the Atlantic from its roots in Scotland, England and Ireland into the United States. The "game of gentlemen" did have its beginnings in America in the last quarter of the 19th century.

There is, however, a precise location for the beginning of golf in the Dayton area although the timing is a tiny bit uncertain in the records of the Dayton Country Club -- without argument the area's first course.

DCC members like to say their club was one of the first courses west of the Allegheny mountains, which may be a stretch in that Chicago was the site of some of the earliest U. S. Opens.

When the DCC celebrated its 80th anniversary in 1976, its printed history reported the Dayton Golf Club (as it was first known) was established in 1896 although the earliest "minute books" in possession of the club are dated 1897.

Whatever, for the next half century the DCC played a pivotal role in the lives of Dayton's establishment civic, political and social leaders.

Our overview of golf will be done in five areas: the development of country clubs and public courses; Dayton's role in the manufacture of golf clubs by the MacGregor Corporation; the four major national tournaments held in Dayton; the players enshrined in the Dayton Golf Hall of Fame and the list of the winners of the men, women and professional championship events.

DAYTON COUNTRY Club: The legendary John H. Patterson, the founder of National Cash Register and generally acknowledged as the most important Daytonian of them all, laid out six holes on his property just north of Oakwood in the early 1890s before a group of men formed the Dayton Golf Club.

The first officers were R. C. Schenck, president; H. C. Lowe, vice president; George H. Wood, secretary; Valentine Winters, treasurer; George H. Mead, captain and H. E. Talbott, captain.

The club was formed and initial play was on Patterson property between Brown and Main Streets known as Rubicon Farm. It was then just south of the city limits. The holes were "for the enjoyment of family and friends." Within a few years more greens were developed on the Talbott estate in Oakwood and play expanded to two locations.

In 1908, with W. H. Carr then president, the DGC purchased a 100-acre tract of land to the west once later described as "in the back pocket of Oakwood" and voted itself out of existence to establish the Dayton Country Club. The land, with its sweeping view toward Carillon Park and the Great Miami River, remains the site of a greatly expanded DCC today.

Over the years the membership has included so many family names linked to Dayton's status, wealth and progress: Schenck, Crane, Winters, Andrews, McMahan, Lowe, Stoddard, Love, Talbott and Mead.

The area also provided a great view of the growing NCR offices and factory. The name NCR of blessed memory became synonymous with golf in Dayton.

The land had been the site of what was known as the Kramer Winery and Pleasure Garden, operated as an outdoor restaurant. The vineyards had to be removed to lay out the original nine-hole golf course.

The first golf professional was Willie Hoare, hired in 1898. Hoare was available because of his association with the MacGregor factory which we will discuss later.

Hoare competed in the American Open Championship in Wheaton, Illinois in 1899 and won the longest drive contest with an effort of 269 yards, one foot and six inches.

In 1910 the elegant clubhouse was opened and the original design has been maintained despite a damaging fire in 1929 and a number of necessary expansions.

In its earliest years the DCC was the site of a sizeable stables and riding club with stables manager King Tullis building a reputation as a riding instructor. The club was also the site of some of the city's earliest tennis tournaments.

The club swimming pool was turned into a year-round facility with the addition of a removable "bubble" canopy.

Tommy Bryant, one of the area's legendary club pros, began his career at DCC in 1927 as an assistant to Jock Collins, a Scotsman who ran the shop through 1931 before Bryant took over. Bryant left in 1942 to take over at Moraine. He was followed by Massie Miller (1943-1952), Dave Caroline (1953-1954) and Norm Butler, who held the position from 1954 through 1967 when he was succeeded by Jim Gilbert, the present pro.

COMMUNITY GOLF COURSE: In 1917, the always civic-minded John H. Patterson deeded 325 acres of land in the Hills and Dales section south of Dayton "as a playground and recreational area for the citizens of Dayton."

It was known in the beginning as the NCR golf course and was operated by NCR personnel until the city administration took over through the Department of Parks and Recreation. It was also called Community Country Club for a time, something of a stretch in regard to its limited facilities other than golf.

It was from the beginning two 18-hole courses, originally known as the Hills and Dales, but became better known as the hilly "outside" and the relatively flat and shorter "inside" courses.

The dedication under its present name occurred in 1954 with the completion of the new and finer clubhouse. The quality of the more difficult Hills course was such that as early as 1924 it was selected by the U. S. Golf Association to host the third ever U. S. Public Links Championship.

It is safe to say that more rounds of golf have been shot over the two Community courses than anywhere else in the area.

Two of Dayton's finest golfers literally grew up on the course. Earl Shock was the longtime club manager and lived in a house on the grounds where his son Don and daughter Janet (more on them later) learned the game walking outside their front door.

Harry Schwab, a fine all-around athlete who made his mark in Dayton sports in many ways, was the longtime pro. He retired at the end of the 1969 season and was followed by Kevin Must, the present pro.

MIAMI VALLEY GOLF CLUB: The first golf course and country

club on the north side of Dayton was the dream of Walter and Georgeana Kidder. On a Sunday drive in 1915 that carried them up Salem Avenue from their residence at the Grand Avenue intersection past the city limit into Harrison Township, they were struck by the beauty of the tree-lined open area to the north.

Slowly acquiring title to the land on the south and east bounded by Philadelphia and Hillcrest Avenues, they eventually acquired the 153 acres that comprise the club, surrounded these days by commercial development.

The Kidders hired Donald Ross, one of the key course designers of his day to plot the layout. The Kidders recruited the membership while generously donating the land to the club.

The course was dedicated on June 3. 1918 with Walter Kidder driving the first ball off the tee. James M. Cox, publisher of the *Dayton Daily News* and a lifelong golf enthusiast, took time off from his preparations to run for president of the United States, to drive the second ball.

The 335 original members utilized a temporary clubhouse until the present one came into being in 1931. In that year, the great Robert Tyre (Bobby) Jones, winner of the U. S. Open and U. S. Amateur and the same two British titles, played a charity exhibition on the course. Other celebrated golfers of the past who played the course were Babe Didrickson Zaharias, Patty Berg, Walter Hagen and Jimmy Demeret.

Gene Marchi was the long-time pro, putting about 40 years at the club before retiring at the end of the 1969 season. He was succeeded by his brother Frank, who was pro until 1983. Chris Hale was next, followed in 1985 by the present pro, Ray Rash.

The club hosted the PGA Championship in 1957 and netted a profit of $35,000, not an inconsequential sum at the time.

MEADOWBROOK COUNTRY CLUB: This club was founded in 1924 by a group of business men who found themselves unable to join any of the established clubs because of the prejudice against Jewish people that existed in our society at the time.

The organization meeting was held in the dining room of the Egry Register Company. There were 35 original members who took part in planning a golf course and complete country club for their co-religionists.

The site selected was a 127-acre area of what was known as the Lightner Farm off Salem Pike. A nine-hole course was designed by the same Alex (Nipper) Campbell who designed Moraine at a cost of $25,000 and the clubhouse cost was pegged at $44,000. Campbell was the club's first pro, followed by Dick Sage and Fred Ebetino.

Meadowbrook's first president in 1925 was Milton Stern, president of Egry Register, followed a year later by Chester Adler. The third president was Elmer Rauh, the general manager at Egry.

Meadowbrook was just coming into its own when the great Depression struck and the club barely survived. Only a small group of the original investors remained, and there were only 32 members in 1934. Ock Willoweit, the pro for many years, stayed on without salary, earning only greens fees and lessons. The greenskeeper's salary was reduced to $20 per week. An emergency fund drive raised money to stall off foreclosure.

A membership drive and reorganization in 1935 saved the club then but another crisis occurred during World War II when the clubhouse was closed for a period. Charles Goldswig stayed on as president through the troubled war years.

A second rebirth took place in 1952 when a swimming pool was installed and the golf course expanded to 18 holes. Professional since 1990 is Dan Howard, who succeeded Tom Tise (1980-1989) and Norm Kidd, who served from 1945 to 1979.

The club has since prospered with much credit going to longtime manager Ted LaVeris. LaVeris retired in 1986 after 30 years but several times was pressed back into service when problems developed.

The club roster over the years has carried the names of many well-known Jewish families in Dayton: Matusoff, Office, Kantor, Thal, Schear, Soifer, Finn, Margolis and Donenfeld among others. Over the years since World War II the club opened its doors and the 1994 roster contained the names of more than 150 non-Jewish persons among its 330 members.

MORAINE COUNTRY CLUB: The founders of this club in 1927 represented many of Dayton's legendary leaders of industry and society.

They include Colonel Edward A. Deeds, Charles F. Kettering, Frederick Rike, Governor James M. Cox, Robert Patterson, John C. Haswell and William Keyes -- men who shaped and pioneered Dayton's future.

The area selected was a portion of *Moraine Farm*, property of Col. Deeds who, along with Kettering, founded Delco Products.

The land was so named because of the formation of the earth by glaciers during the ice age. The base of the land was a gravel formation so that natural drainage made it perfect for a golf course.

Designer Alex (Nipper) Campbell used the theory of retaining the natural terrain to replicate some traditional world class holes. Moraine's number two is based on the Rasden hole at North Berwick in Scotland and the 10th is similar to the ninth hole at Prestwick, Scotland, one of the world's oldest courses and frequent site of the British Open.

A strong NCR influence developed at the club with Robert S. Oelman and S. C. (Chick) Allyn becoming dominant figures in bringing the 1945 PGA to the club, the first major national held here.

The club still has the most limited and thus the most exclusive membership and remains low key in its operation.

WALNUT GROVE COUNTRY CLUB: This club on Dayton's eastern edge was founded by Alva Wenrick, who had 150 acres of farm land which he attempted to turn into a health club in 1928.

With the financial backing of E. P. Larsh, head of Master Electric, he formed the Greenmont Country Club. But with the collapse of the stock market in 1929 the project failed and Larsh withdrew.

Wenrick still believed his property had a future as a golf course but he was barely able to develop it through the early Depression years. In 1935 the land was purchased by Milton H. (Dick) Simmons and B. H. (Abe) Senart, who incorporated it under its present name.

Simmons served as president for 15 years retaining Wenrick as superintendent and the club began turning a profit with the prosperity of War II years. Wenrick died in 1964 at the age of 87.

The 136-acre course straddles the Montgomery and Greene county lines and has enjoyed success as a second level operation in the elite country club world. Ken Tipton became the pro in 1970.

NCR COUNTRY CLUB: The celebrated twin courses opened in 1954 and presumably will carry the name NCR into the 21st century as the venerable institution that played so great a role in Dayton's business and civic history.

The North and South courses represented a $2 million contribution by the company carrying out the tradition of John H. Patterson.

"Mr. Patterson was one of the country's first industrialists to realize the importance of good relations between management and employees," said S. C. (Chick) Allyn, the company president in an interview at the time.

"When I came to work at NCR 40 years ago (around 1914), the work week was 54 hours," Allyn went on. "When the work week gradually shortened, Mr. Patterson always felt that it was part of the company's responsibility to have happy employees outside the plant as well as in."

That philosophy led to the creation of the Old River park, providing picnic grounds, a huge swimming pool, a canal for boating, softball diamonds and wooded areas for employees.

Allyn, who was mainly responsible for bringing the 1945 PGA to Moraine as a member of the PGA Advisory board, took a great personal interest in the development of the new courses. He personally selected Dick Wilson, operating out of Philadelphia, as the designer of both courses, one of which was to be of championship caliber and the other less challenging for the average golfer.

The locker rooms were as spacious as any in your average private club and the quality of food in the clubhouse was to be first rate.

The South Course, rated among the top 100 in the United States, served as the site of the 1969 PGA and the 1986 Women's Open.

One of the last NCR corporate contributions to golf was extending a sizeable loan to the NCR Employees Benefit Association, which was used to rebuild and modernize the clubhouse in 1994-1995.

The course continues to operate under the employee association and remains profitable. Tim Walton was the incumbent pro in 1995.

SYCAMORE CREEK COUNTRY CLUB: Although located in Warren County a few miles south of the booming Dayton Mall area, the membership of this club, opened in 1959, consists of a majority of Dayton and Montgomery County residents.

The golf course was designed by Jack Ortman, the club pro who retired in 1994 after a 35-year tenure. His replacement is Pat Delaney from Springfield.

Over the last 15 years the club has been the site of the annual one-day AIM for the Handicapped celebrity tournament of Nancy Lopez, a national ambassador for the Dayton-based organization.

MADDEN PARK AND KITTYHAWK GOLF CENTERS: The city of Dayton operates these two properties as municipal courses open to the public. They were created in response to the heavy demands on the Community courses.

Madden Park is located on Nicholas Road at what was the western city limit at the time. The course was designed by Don MacKay, a native of Scotland who came to this country in 1910 and settled in Dayton in 1923.

MacKay was on the staff at Community in 1927 when he was given the assignment of laying out what was originally called Fairmount for its hilly terrain. It was renamed in honor of William Madden, the construction supervisor.

MacKay later opened a driving range under his name on North Main Street and was operating it when he died in 1953 at age 74.

Because of its west Dayton location, Madden became the course of choice for many African American residents.

The Fairway Golf Club, made up of African American golfers, hosted an annual tournament at Madden for a number of years, attracting many national celebrities including the legendary heavyweight champion Joe Louis.

Myron Coleman, one of the Fairway group, organized and ran free golf lessons for youngsters well past his 75th birthday. Onetime University of Dayton basketball player Charles (Benny) Jones has since picked up the instruction program. Golf professional since 1981 is Pete Brown.

The newest municipal courses make up the Kittyhawk Golf Center on the east side of Wagner Ford Road.

The two full length courses were designed similar to Community, the longer one to accommodate the low handicap players and a shorter one for the more casual players. The Hawk course opened in 1961 and the Eagle followed a few years later.

The 6,619-yard Eagle course rates up with the competitive aspects of most of the better courses in the area. In addition to the shorter Hawk, there is an 18-hole par three known as the Kitty.

The road into the complex is named Chuck Wagner Drive for the pro who took over in 1964 and died of a heart attack in his clubhouse in 1981 at the age of 60.

Wagner had replaced Tom Blackburn, better known as the coach who elevated the University of Dayton basketball program to big time. Blackburn had earlier been a pro at Madden. Current professional is Steve Yung, named in 1989.

THE COUNTRY CLUB OF THE NORTH: Opened in 1993, this

upscale course designed by Jack Nicklaus is being looked at by some as Dayton's golf club of the future. The 42,000-square-foot clubhouse and the $30,000 initiation fee tell the story.

As for golf, in 1994 it became the home of the Star Bank LPGA Classic, a regular stop on the women's tour, won in May of 1995 by Chris Johnson. The first tournament was won by Maggie Will. Lee Rinker is the current pro.

HEATHERWOODE GOLF CLUB: This 18-hole public course located in Springboro opened in 1991 with Bill Kumle as pro. The course was designed by Dennis Griffiths.

Clear Creek meanders through the 190-acre course on both sides of state route 741, joined by an underpass under the highway. Seven lakes and mature timber provide beauty and a challenge.

In 1993 the course became the site of an annual stop on the Nike Tour, sponsored locally by the Victory Wholesale Grocery Company.

SUGAR VALLEY, THE MILITARY BASES AND THE REST: There are a number of other golf courses, public and private, in the immediate Dayton area that need mention.

On the Wright-Patterson Air Force Base is the Wright-Patterson Golf Club with an 18-hole West and an easier nine-hole East course. Membership is restricted to active and retired military and civilian personnel at the base.

The Twin Base Golf course has the same membership restrictions but is much less expensive. The best way to define the dividing line is to refer to one as the Officer's Club and Twin Base for the rest.

Sugar Valley is a country club built in Bellbrook in 1969 and the Greene Country Club, just east of Fairborn, opened in 1960. Both have many Dayton members and may expect a greater demand as home building booms in that area.

Miamisburg, which operated its nine-hole Mound Course for many years, introduced the new 18-hole Pipestone in 1993. Cassel Hills in Vandalia and Larch Tree in Trotwood are also public courses in Montgomery County.

The area's newest course, opened in the spring of 1995, is Centerville's Yankee Trace, Brian Hughes, pro.

Moraine's Tommy Bryant

Among Dayton's golfing greats are Janet Shock Beardsley (left) and Ruth Pickrel (above).

Included with Dayton golf immortals are Diana Schwab (left); Norm Kidd (above), Gene Marchi (above, right) and Jack Ortman (right)

2

The MacGregor Company

As golf grew in popularity and participation into the 20th Century, Dayton became the hub of club manufacturing in the United States, a position it retained until 1946 when MacGregor Golf Inc. moved into a larger and more modern plant on Spring Grove Avenue in Cincinnati.

That production and design of golf clubs came into being in Ohio rather than the east coast where the game first took root is a testimony to the business acumen of one Edward Canby.

The company that became MacGregor dates back to 1829 when Archibald and Ziba Crawford, brothers from Saratoga Springs, N. Y., settled in Dayton. They founded the Dayton Last Company to manufacture the wooden forms over which shoes were shaped as well as repaired. It was the only company of its kind west of the Allegheny mountains at the time it was founded.

By 1896, the company was in the hands of W. S. Crawford, a descendant of the original owners, along with two partners. The firm was then Crawford, McGregor and Canby. John McGregor, a native of Scotland, had become an investor. He did not have the "a" in his name. When the incorporation papers came back with the "Mac" spelling, the use of MacGregor was adopted to give a more Scottish authenticity to the golf products.

Edward Canby, the third original. partner, acquired his wealth in Logan county, but his son Harry moved to Dayton to manage the plant and lived in an impressive home on Belmonte Park North on Grafton Hill. The residence is preserved and listed on the Dayton historical homes register.

Thus Crawford, Macgregor and Canby came into being with production facilities eventually completely shifted to manufacturing golf equipment.

It was on a business trip to England sometime in the early 1890s that Edward Canby became interested in a suggestion from a business associate that he consider producing wooden golf club heads. The idea was to keep his employees busy in the periods producing shoe lasts was slow.

Although Canby was not a golfer himself, he liked the idea and could see how wooden club heads could be made utilizing the same lathes that formed the shoe lasts.

In England the club heads were made from beech wood, but those trees were not plentiful in this part of the world. The CM&C company had been making its shoe lasts using persimmon, a hard wood that was abundant in southern Ohio and adjacent states to the south.

Golf heads had been mostly hand produced prior to Canby's experiment in mass production, which proved to be eminently successful.

MacGregor marketed the first persimmon heads in 1896. Three years later, CM&C was shipping 100,000 of them annually to England.

Then the company was asked to produce shafts for the heads. At the time shafts were spliced around the outside of the neck of the clubhead and held in place with glue and strong linen thread.

By the turn of the century, CM&C began making woods with sockets into which the shafts were placed. Eventually the company manufactured irons using a drop forging method on the club heads.

MacGregor solidified its position against competing sporting goods companies by hiring Will Sime as its chief engineer. Sime, who grew up in Scotland as did nearly all golfing pioneers in this country, had been making clubs for Harry Vardon, the premier golfer of his time.

Sime gradually streamlined the shape of the woods close to current design. Earlier, drivers had looked more like hockey sticks.

It wasn't until 1926 that the U. S. Golf Association approved the use of steel shafted clubs, but MacGregor had them in its catalogue three years earlier. Within four years, wood shafts were obsolete, a change which MacGregor had not fully anticipated.

In 1916, the company built a nine-hole golf course located just east of what was then the city limits. In providing a course for the benefit of the clubmakers in the company, Edwin Canby was in step with John H. Patterson and the NCR golf legacy of providing recreation for employees.

The course also provided a testing ground for the clubs, and long-hitting Clyde Mumma became the pro who tested many of them over the years with his massive drives.

On his way to the 1926 U. S. Open in Columbus, famed sports writer Grantland Rice stopped off for a round of golf at the MacGregor course and wrote a complimentary column entitled *The Golf Course That Surprised Me.*

MacGregor hosted the city amateur championship in 1926, 1927 and 1932. In 1937 Dayton Power & Light purchased the course for its employees. Because it was not possible for expansion as a golf course its use diminished and in 1987 most of the land was used in the development of a 130-acre office-park complex.

When it belonged to MacGregor, the relatively small course was good enough for company pros to practice and play. Tommy Armour, the first international golf star to represent the company, found it a reasonable challenge.

Going back to when CM&C got into golf, W. S. Crawford was one of the first sports merchandisers to recognize the value of having a star athlete endorse its products.

The first pro hired by the company was Willie Dunn, runner-up in the U. S. Open in 1896. He was followed by Willie Hoare, the first Dayton Country Club pro, and John Harrison, who toured the country pushing the company's products.

It was Armour, however, who made the biggest impact representing the Dayton firm in national circles just prior to World War II. Nicknamed the "Silver Scot" because of his prematurely gray hair, he was born in Carnoustie, home of one of Scotland's legendary courses. He had won the British and U. S. Opens and the PGA championship. The company marketed a set of high quality clubs under the Silver Scot label.

Clarence Rickey, who had taken over the MacGregor marketing operation, signed Armour in 1936, hiring him away from business rival Spaulding. Rickey was changing the company's market strategy to target upscale country clubs and pro shops and stress a quality product. It was a shift from the mass marketing that had marked the CM&C success in earlier times.

When Edward Canby died in 1936, MacGregor was sold to the P. Goldsmith Co, a Cincinnati sporting goods firm and the company became MacGregor-Goldsmith.

When Clarence Rickey moved his family from Chicago to Dayton, his son Bob Rickey was 14. Bob eventually succeeded his father and his name became virtually synonymous with golf in the Cincinnati-Dayton area in the years following World War II.

Young Rickey remembers eavesdropping on the stairs of the family residence on Volusia Avenue in Oakwood as his father was negotiating with Armour to join MacGregor.

Just as important in the long run as Armour's presence was the hiring of Toney Penna, who had been Armour's assistant pro at Chicago's Medinah Country Club, to represent MacGregor on the PGA tour. Toney would offer young players whom he pegged as rising stars free clubs and get them familiar with MacGregor early in their careers.

The senior Rickey was astute enough to sign Byron Nelson, Ben Hogan and Jimmy Demeret within a brief period around 1938. They became MacGregor representatives for a mere $1,500 a year and in 1939 Nelson won the U. S. Open at Toledo's Inverness.

The younger Rickey learned to play the game on the old MacGregor course under pro Obie O'Bannon.

During the World War II years nearly all the sporting goods manufactured were consigned to the armed forces, but there was little emphasis on golf equipment.

MacGregor's sales rep in the Dayton area in the 1930s was Oscar "Ock" Willoweit, who became a familiar and well-liked presence in Dayton golf. Ock was a pro himself and an adept teacher and story teller.

Clarence Rickey was killed in an automobile accident in 1945, just two months prior to the national PGA at Moraine, which was won by Nelson playing for Rickey and the Dayton-based company.

The last MacGregor manufacturing plant in Dayton was located on Cincinnati Street just southwest of center city. When the plant moved to Cincinnati, Bob Rickey went with it but remained a visible figure around golf events in southwest Ohio.

Rickey, a graduate of Northwestern University's Journalism School, had been briefly a part-time sports writer on the *Dayton Daily News*. He was very good at giving reporters writing tips, aimed at presenting the positive side of golf. Later just as his father had signed so many great players to MacGregor contracts, Bob Rickey signed Jack Nicklaus to his first contract. Earlier, he had been linked to the likes of Arnold Palmer.

Although golf club manufacturing has passed through the Dayton scene, it is interesting to note the change in club terminology in the MacGregor catalogs.

The clubs listed from 1930 to the present time stack up like this:

1930	1995
Driver	No.1 wood.
Brassie	No. 2 wood.
Spoon	No. 3 wood.
Cleek	No. 4 wood.
mid-iron	No.2 iron
mid-mashie	No. 3 iron
Mashie-iron	No. 4 iron
Mashie	No.5 iron
Spade-Mashie	No.6 iron.
Mashie-niblick	No.7 iron
Niblick	No.9 iron

Jane Geddes blasts out on her way to winning 1986 U. S. Women's Open at NCR; tense moment at Moraine's 1945 PGA, first of four major tournaments in Dayton.

3

The Majors

The 1945 PGA at Moraine

With World War II ended in Europe and victory inevitable in the Pacific, excitement ran high locally and nationally for the tournament.

The local excitement surrounding the community's first national major was obvious.

Nationally, the excitement surrounded Byron Nelson, then putting together the streak even now accepted as "The Greatest Feat in Golf." In 1945, the stylish Texan put together a streak of 11 straight Tour event victories, the ninth of which was the championship here.

No pro golfer has ever dominated the game as Nelson did in 1945. He entered 30 official PGA events and won 18 of them, finishing second in seven others. He had 79 rounds in the 60's and 93 rounds under par. His worst official score was a 75.

Nelson was not in the military, being classified 4-F because he was almost a hemophiliac, his blood taking five times the normal time to clot. He was never far away from clotting medicine, having to worry about even a slight nick while shaving. The condition did improve with age.

Nelson had won eight of his events, starting with the Miami Four Ball, which he won teamed with Jug McSpaden over the team of Denny Shute and Sam Byrd. Then came seven medal play tournaments making the PGA his only head-to-head match play challenge.

McSpaden was second on the money list to Nelson coming in.

Oddly McSpaden's 4-F classification was that he was also a "free bleeder" as well as having severe allergy problems.

Other stars included Byrd, the onetime New York Yankees and Cincinnati Reds outfielder. In his playing days in New York, Byrd was nicknamed "Babe Ruth's caddy" not for anything on the links but as a defensive replacement for the aging Ruth in the late innings.

The defending PGA champion was Pvt. Bob Hamilton, who was given leave to compete from his Fort Lewis base near Seattle. Another military participant was Sgt. Dutch Harrison, stationed here in Dayton at Wright-Patterson.

A distinguished national press gallery attracted the likes of Grantland Rice and O. B. Keeler, the biographer and lifelong friend of Bobby Jones.

Nelson showed he was in top form by tying Johnny Revolta in the 36-hole qualifying medal round with 138s. Lord Byron sank a 30-foot putt for an eagle on the 455-yard, par five 17th hole to catch Revolta.

In the first round Nelson was a 4 and 3 winner over the veteran Gene Sarazen despite the latter winning the first two holes. Nelson was a slow starter all through the Dayton event.

There were two major upsets in the first round, Clarence Doser of Hartsdale, N. Y. knocked off McSpaden with relative ease, 5 and 4, while Texan Jack Grout disposed of defending champ Hamilton, who played in a military T-shirt.

The classic match of the entire tournament was Nelson's narrow escape over Mike Turnesa in the second round. Turnesa was a member of a well known golfing family playing out of White Plains, N. Y.

Both men shot superb golf through the morning round with Turnesa 1-up at the break. He held that lead through the first nine of the afternoon round and upped it to two with four holes to play.

The spectators and the media swarmed around to catch the finish. All Lord Byron did was go 2-3-2 (birdie, birdie, eagle) to take the lead into the final hole, where his par was good for the match. The eagle was on the same hole that earlier had earned him the co-medalist honors.

Nelson was 68-66 for the day while Turnesa was 68-69. "It was my greatest round ever," Nelson said.

Turnesa's comment was, "I was seven under par and still lost. How in the hell are you supposed to beat this man?"

The rest of the tournament was almost anti-climatic until the final day. The unknown Doser scored upsets over Toney Penna, representing the Dayton MacGregor interests, and Ky Laffoon, a popular Kentuckian who had a sizeable gallery.

It came down to Doser vs. Byrd and Nelson vs Claude Harmon in Saturday's semifinal, a day the course was pelted with intermittent rains. Doser's magic ran out early and the former baseball player ended the match easily, 7 and 6.

Nelson had little trouble disposing of Harmon, 5 and 4, after shooting 37 in the morning round.

The gallery was definitely pulling for the underdog Byrd when the Sunday round began. Sammy gave them encouragement when he shot a sizzling 67 to Nelson's 69 for a two-stroke edge at the halfway point.

The pressure was on Nelson once again when Byrd went 3-up on the third hole of the afternoon round.

Then Byrd got a bad break when his drive struck a woman on the arm and dropped dead at the edge of the rough. It took him three to make the green while Nelson birdied to pick up the hole.

Lord Byron won both the 7th and 8th to even the match and then took a one-up lead on the 11th. Sammy never challenged again and Nelson closed it out on the 15th hole for a 4 and 3 triumph.

O. B. Keeler, who liked to write about Nelson as if he was the English naval hero, started his story, "A sweeping breeze out of the north blew away the shadow of Trafalgar for Lord Nelson."

Nelson's victory earned him $5,000 in war bonds while Byrd had to settle for $2,000, likewise in war bonds.

Nelson, who had received treatments for an ailing back from Tom Smallwood, a therapist at the Dayton YMCA, announced he was off to Rochester, Minn. where he would play an exhibition and have his back examined at the Mayo Clinic.

Nelson eventually ran his streak to 11, winning the Tam O'Shanter Open in Chicago and the Canadian Open before the string ended in the Memphis Open where Lord Byron finished six strokes behind amateur Fred Haas, Jr. who later turned pro.

In Dayton, host pro Tommy Bryant announced total attendance at 30,000 with 3,000 for the final round, a huge turnout by standards of the time.

The 1957 PGA At Miami Valley

This was to be the last golf major played in the traditional match play format. The decision was made to accommodate rapidly increasing television coverage as well as reduce the gruelling week in which the eventual champion had to survive seven matches including consecutive two-a-days.

Defending champion Jackie Burke, Jr. led the entry list and the cast represented the new generation of post-war era pros who hadn't been involved in the 1945 Moraine event.

Masters winner Doug Ford and U. S. Open champ Dick Mayer were there as well as the veteran Sam Snead. Other top names included long-hitting Mike Souchak, Claude Harmon and Ted Kroll.

Also in the field were brothers Jay and Lionel Hebert, as well as a rising player with a strong Ohio background, Dow Finsterwald. Dow had advanced to the semi-finals of the tournament in 1956 before bowing to Burke.

Jay was by far the better known of the Heberts. Lionel, the younger brother at age 29, was only a part-timer on the tour and had never won an event. Host pro Gene Marchi tabbed Ford and Snead his best bets to win, basing his judgment on their skills around the nearly flat but still challenging course

First round casualties included onetime U. S. Open champ Ed Furgol and former PGA winner Jim Turnesa . Favorites Ford, Snead, Burke and Souchak advanced as expected.

Snead got things off to a rousing start with an eagle on the opening hole and polished off a young pro named John Serafin from Pittsburgh. Snead had eliminated Serafin's father, Sammy, back in the 1938 PGA.

Young Finsterwald almost bowed out early, struggling to beat Dick Sleicher of historic Gettysburg, Pa., where he served as the host pro at the club where President Dwight Eisenhower played while staying at his vacation cottage.

Tommy Bolt, assuming the tournament started on Thursday as nearly all PGA Opens did rather than Wednesday, arrived for a practice round and almost missed his tee time for his first match.

In the second round Thursday, Snead shot a 65 in the morning to knock out Al Watrous and went on to beat John Thoren in the afternoon. Meanwhile, Lionel Hebert won his two matches over Marty Furgol and

Charles Farlow while Finsterwald breezed in his two events over Bud Williamson and Joey Kirkwood.

Heavyweight champion Rocky Marciano was a spectator during Friday's round which featured a match between Snead, playing in his 17th PGA championship, and young Finsterwald.

It turned out to be strictly "no contest" as Slamming Sammy was 4 down before he won his first hole on the 14th. "I just couldn't stay out of trouble," lamented Snead. Lionel Hebert was beginning to attract some notice when he disposed of the better known Souchak and Harmon to move into the semi-finals.

This set up an interesting angle in that Lionel would be going against Walter Burkemo who had knocked Jay Hebert out of the tournament. Burkemo had thus thwarted a possible semi-final showdown between the Hebert brothers. Finsterwald's opponent in the semis would be Don Whitt, a Californian who had racked up a string of upsets.

Those semi-final pairings of Lionel Hebert vs. Burkemo and Finsterwald vs. Whitt offered convincing testimony as to why television would not be interested in match play tournaments.

Lionel Hebert avenged his brother's loss with a 2 and 1 conquest of the more experienced Burkemo. Whitt meanwhile added excitement with a hole-in-one on the 13th in his match with Finsterwald, carrying the Ohio U. standout to the final hole.

The weather had been sizzling hot all week, cutting down on potential attendance and sapping the energy of the contestants. Sunday's championship found both players shooting fine golf despite the heat-related exhaustion factor. They finished the morning 18 dead even although Finsterwald was a stroke up in score, 68-69.

Hebert, from deep in the bayou country of Louisiana, started the afternoon as if he would bury Finsterwald, firing three straight birdies to go 3-up. But Finsterwald, the gallery favorite, steadied quickly to win the next two holes and bring the match back within reach. He drew even at the 11th. Hebert went back into the lead with a birdie at 13 and it stood that way going into the 16th where the match was decided.

There is a small creek guarding the green on the 423-yard par four hole. Hebert drove long and far down the middle, in position to use a six-iron to the green.

Finsterwald hooked his tee shot into the deep rough, causing his six iron come up short, ending up in the water. But he got a break of sorts because the ball was under a pedestrian bridge, lodged in a tile drain. He was given a free drop within the hazard but his pitch to the green went 18 feet beyond the hole and it took him two putts to get down for a bogey.

Hebert safely two-putted for his par and enjoyed a 2 hole advantage with two to go, When they halved the 17th, it was all over.

It was Hebert's first tournament win and, as it turned out, his only major. "Winning those first three holes in the afternoon gave me a world of confidence," he said. "I thought they would be margin for error. As it turned out they didn't provide that, but I was still confident."

Hebert earned an $8,000 first place check. But he didn't have the cash to tip his caddy and had to mail the young man a check.

The 1969 PGA Championship At NCR

This tournament will be remembered more by the disruptive actions of civil rights protestors rather than Ray Floyd's victory which made for a less-than-spectacular finish after an impressive beginning.

The protests that led to the arrest of 11 people were primarily aimed at South African Gary Player because of the apartheid in his native country. There were warnings of potential trouble early in the week when a group of mostly white college students and black activists calling themselves the Ad Hoc Civil Rights Coalition presented a list of 27 demands to the Dayton Area Chamber of Commerce threatening to disrupt the tournament if their demands were not met.

The demands, much too broad to be met on short notice, centered on better housing, education and job opportunities for the poor. Probably to link the tournament to the protests, there was a demand for 3,000 free tickets for the poor.

The Chamber responded by getting a court restraining order against five known activist groups to bar them from disruptive actions. The three black players in the tournament, Lee Elder, Charley Sifford and Pete Brown, who later became pro at Madden Park, went ahead with plans to compete.

There was no trouble on the first two days and play got off to a rousing start on Thursday when nine players, including Floyd, tied for the first round lead with 69s. A PGA opening day record crowd of 17,425 had plenty of golf to cheer about but were keenly disappointed when Arnie Palmer, bothered by a hip injury, shot 82 and withdrew.

Host pro Jim Rudolph demonstrated how difficult the NCR South can be at times in an embarrassing way. He took nine strokes on the third hole and wound up with an 87, then further disqualifying himself by not signing his score card. Mike Podolski, the former assistant pro, predicted his course record of 66 would fall before the tournament was over.

On the second round Player proved him correct by coming in with 65, but Gary's record didn't last out the day. Don Bies, a 31-year-old from Seattle, posted a. sizzling 64.

At the end of the day Floyd, who shot a 66, held a one stroke lead over Player, two over Bunky Henry and three over a trio including Bies, Jack Nicklaus and Orville Moody.

The protestors made their move on Saturday when Player, dressed as usual in black, was paired with Nicklaus. On the fourth tee, someone threw a bulky 230-page souvenir program at Player and was taken into custody by security men.

But the major scuffle of the day occurred on the 10th hole. On the tee, a youth threw a cup of ice in Player's face. Until then, the actions had been by individuals but when the golfers reached the 10th green, the main group made its move. A bearded youth charged out of the crowd as Player lined up his putt, calling him a racist. Then a group of black and whites charged the green, bringing all the security men into action. A large black man moved toward an angry Nicklaus who drew his putter back as if to defend himself.

Golf fans in the gallery were enraged, some yelling "kill them" as the protestors were led away.

Player, obviously shaken, managed to finish the round with a 71, which in retrospect cost him his chance to win the tournament. "I had to keep playing," the South African explained. "The man called me a racist. You can hardly call me a racist. I love all people, white, black and yellow." He declined to answer questions asking if he was afraid. Nicklaus conceded he had been unnerved by the incident, but refused to use that as an alibi for his third round 74 which dropped him 10 strokes off the pace.

Floyd, meanwhile, fired a strong 67 and took a five stroke lead going into the final round over a trio including Player, Bunky Henry and Bert Greene. Although not in contention, Miller Barber matched the new club record 64 during Saturday's action

Floyd and Player were paired as the final duo to go off Sunday, setting up a dramatic pairing and considerable concern by NCR officials and local police agencies involved in providing protection. A record crowd of 23,543 paid its way into the Sunday session.

The security, in uniform and plain clothes, around the two players was obvious. Host pro Rudolph carried a putter with him.

Player was the obvious favorite of the huge gallery for his cool and calm action for what had happened on Saturday. Floyd at that point in his career was not the fan favorite that he became in later years as he matured and got better with age.

The smallish South African made a gallant and gutsy try to overcome what seemed an insurmountable lead. He birdied the first hole to tremendous applause. He barely missed birdie putts on the 8th and 9th, commenting, "just a blasted 'arf inch."

Floyd's concentration didn't seem up to its usual standards as he won his title with a round of 74, hardly championship caliber. He safely two-putted on 18 to make off with the $35,000 winner's share while Player, who shot a final round 70, settled for $20,000. Greene finished third for $12,000, more money than Lionel Hebert had earned for winning the same tournament 12 years earlier.

The 1986 U. S. Women's Open At NCR

This is the tournament that nearly didn't come off. Rain storms, lightning and heavy winds have always been regarded as unavoidable natural problems for sponsors and directors of golf tournaments.

But white clouds of poisonous phosphorous gas?

Late Tuesday afternoon when many of the players were doing practice rounds on NCR South, a southbound freight train on the CSX line derailed in Miamisburg, four miles to the west, and created an emergency situation that led to the immediate evacuation of 16,000 area residents.

Just one car carrying the dangerous chemical exploded and burned, but it was enough to threaten people living and working in Miamisburg as well as in Moraine and West Carrollton.

With the prevailing westerly wind flow in the direction of the course, NCR was immediately closed and women ordered off the course. Tourney officials had take a wait-and-see attitude until the environmental crisis could be dealt with.

Despite a second explosion involving another of the overturned tank cars, and with 800 or more Miamisburg residents temporarily homeless, it was decided that the tournament could start on Thursday as scheduled. Meanwhile, heavy rains created serious problems in the parking lots for spectators, turning unpaved areas into mud holes. The threat of rain haunted the event all week.

The youngest player teeing off in the tournament was 18-year-old Jamie Fischer of Centerville, whose mother everyone knew as Andy Fischer, had spent some time on the women's pro tour.

Andy took Jamie along when she went to Pittsburgh in an attempt to qualify for "one more Open" but it was Jamie, with a 78, who made it, while mother's 82 reduced her to the role of caddy for daughter. Not surprisingly, the pressure of going off in the Open got to the recent high school graduate who soared to an 88.

Beth Daniel fired a 70 to take a one-stroke lead in the first round and matched it on Friday but dropped back for the final two rounds. Betsy King and Judy Dickinson of Akron each shot 72, two strokes behind Daniel on Thursday and matched each other with 71s on Friday to take the halfway lead over a soggy course with 143s.

Sally Little, who would wind up in a rare 18-hole playoff on Monday with Jane Geddes, was two off at the halfway point, but three shots better than her eventual conqueror.

Meanwhile the weather problems mounted. Friday's round was stopped twice by rain and not everyone finished.

Head groundskeeper Jack Hart, then in his 32nd year with NCR, and his staff worked all night in a valiant effort to have the course playable for the necessary early Saturday start. The same group had to do it all over again Saturday night.

Ayako Akamoto, the diminutive Japanese golfer, was the only one to break 70 in Saturday's round, her 69 matching her same score of Friday and moved her into second place, a stroke behind Betsy King, whose steady 72-71-70 moved her into the lead.

It was King (213), Akamoto (214), Little and Dickinson (217) with Geddes and Amy Alcott (218) going into the Sunday showdown.

Geddes and the veteran Pat Bradley were the only ones to break 70 on Sunday and the bogey-free 69 was good enough to get Geddes into the playoff with Little.

The South African native didn't fold, turning in a 70 herself. King did fade, coming in with 75 and wound up in a deadlock with Akamoto at 288, a stroke behind the playoff-bound duo.

With favorable weather and most of the strain of the hectic week behind them, Geddes and Little battled it out Monday. The issue was in doubt going into the final hole where Geddes finished with a 71. Little's score went into the books at 73. The win netted Geddes a $50,000 check while Little's figure was half that.

The victory was the first on the tour for Geddes, but her career took off immediately and she won her next tournament, the Boston Five Classic. She ended the year with $221,255 for fifth place on the LPGA money list and has remained a prominent figure on the tour.

4

The Golf Hall of Fame

There have been many excellent golfers on the sports scene over the years as a perusal of the list of members of the Dayton Amateur Golf Hall of Fame will attest.

But you will get little argument from most followers of the game when you put up Bob Servis as the best of the male players and Diana Schwab as the finest of the women.

Servis, a talented all-around athlete who gave up competitive golf at the comparatively young age of 33, was a five-time Ohio State amateur champion. Born in 1915, Servis swung his first golf clubs at age nine in 1924 on the private six-hole layout on the John H. Patterson property in Oakwood, where golf was first played in the Dayton area.

By the age of 13, while in the seventh grade, Servis played on the team representing Oakwood High School and defeated Eddie Hamant of Dayton Catholic (later Chaminade) High School. Dayton Catholic protested and Oakwood was forced to forfeit all the matches in which Servis played because he was not yet a high school student.

Servis also did well in basketball, baseball and bowling and gave up football to concentrate on golf. At age 14 he qualified for the city men's amateur and the Ohio amateur and in 1932 won the state high school championship for Oakwood.

At the age of 18 he played an exhibition match teamed with the legendary Walter Hagen against Jim Noble and Bob Kepler at Miami Valley, the country club he would be associated with the rest of his life.

Servis won the city match play championship in 1933 competing against the better older golfers and won it once more in 1935. He never again entered the tournament but spent hours on the course practicing all of his shots over and over.

He won the Ohio Amateur in 1933, 1936, 1939 and 1940 before going into World War II military service. He came back to capture his fifth Ohio Am in 1947 and a year later announced his retirement from competitive golf. He had played in the U. S. Open and U. S. Amateur and won a number of amateur events around the midwest.

There is a memorial stone tablet honoring Servis that greets Miami Valley golfers on the first hole at the club. It was dedicated in 1993, five years after his death.

The Servis family had been in the restaurant business in downtown Dayton for many years. He helped manage and late in his life served as maitre d' in the Miami Valley club dining room.

Diana Schwab came along much later than Bob Servis but the 14 city women's championships she accumulated rise over the achievements of a formidable list of earlier standout women golfers.

By winning the 14th of those city events in 1993, she captured championships over four decades. The most remarkable aspect of that record is that she passed up the tournament many times.

City women's play earlier was dominated by Janet Shock Beardsley and Ruth Pickrel, who between them won 12 city titles. Mrs. Beardsley won the state women's championship on three occasions.

Schwab was also a fine bowler and served as an official (referee) in basketball, soccer and field hockey. As this was researched, she was coaching the women's golf team at Fairmont High School where she is a tenured teacher and where she coached men and women's golf teams to Western Ohio League championships.

At age 53, she accepted an invitation to play in the Star Bank Classic, an LPGA tour stop taking root at Country Club of the North, in 1995.

Asked how she would like to be remembered, she responded "as a woman with dignity, who played sports with integrity; a consummate competitor."

Her husband is Tim Schwab, son of Harry, the longtime Community pro, and her brother-in-law is Pat Schwab, who has played on the tour and been a club pro in the south and east.

Two other Daytonians came out of local courses to play on the PGA tour: Bob Zimmerman and Bob Wynn. Wynn enjoyed modest success on the tour in the 1970s, winning one tournament and qualifying for the Masters. Both later played the Senior PGA tour.

Andrea Fischer, known as Andy, played on the women's LPGA tour and has been a volunteer teacher of handicapped persons and a presence in women's golf.

The Hall of Fame members cover the rest of the story.

The Dayton Amateur Golf Hall Of Fame

Charter members inducted Nov. 5, 1979:
JANET SHOCK BEARDSLEY - Has won the Dayton City Women's title five times and was runner-up seven times. Won the Ohio State championship three times. Mrs. Beardsley also won the Ohio State Seniors.

VINCENT K. HILTON - Winner of the first city championship in 1919 who captured four of the first five tournaments. Was club champion at both DCC and Moraine.

ROBERT H. KEPLER - Also a four-time Dayton City champion and the 1931 Ohio State champion. Bob Kepler turned professional and was the golf pro at the Ohio State University courses for 28 years before he died in 1975.

ROBERT W. SERVIS - A two-time Dayton city champion and a five- time Ohio State champion. An outstanding all-around athlete out of Oakwood High School, he was rarely challenged on the golf course in his home town.

Other honorees include:
ANDY AUGAITIS - Medalist in the Dayton City Championship in 1940, 1952 and 1953 and champion in 1952. Also champion of the DAGA Open in 1955 and 1956.

BETTY LEE BOREN WOOD - Won the Dayton City Women's title four times before leaving Dayton for California where she became an LPGA Master Professional and teacher.

JOHN BLESI - Dayton city men's champion in 1956 and runner-up in 1957 and 1959. Blesi was a many-time qualifier for the National Public Links Tournament.

DON SHOCK - Won the Dayton City Championship in 1946 and 1947. Turned pro and served the Columbus Country Club as home pro for more than 30 years. Brother of Janet Shock Beardsley and son of Earl Shock.

JOE HIGGINS - A two-time winner of the city men's championship in 1937 and 1942. He was very active in local events before World War II.

PAT SCHWAB - Standout high school golfer who learned the game from his father, Harry, at Community. Starred in collegiate golf at University of Florida, turned pro and played on the tour before going into club work. He has served at various clubs in the east and south.

RUTH PICKREL - Dominated city women's golf from 1957 through 1966 as she won the tournament seven times in that 10-year span

JACK ZIMMERMAN - Three-time Dayton city champion, two-time Ohio Public Links champion and runner-up in both the Ohio Amateur and National Public Links tournament.

JOE ZOTKIEWICZ - Won the Ohio State High School championship in 1932 and three Ohio Intercollegiate championships in 1936-37-38 playing for the University of Dayton. Also won the city championship in 1938.

DAVE WILSON - Captured city championships in 1966, 1972 and 1976 and was medalist in 1965 and 1969. Qualified for National Public Links five times and was a six time Fairway Open champion.

DIANA SCHWAB - Dominated the local women's scene with an incredible 14 city women's championships and was the National Public Links Medalist in 1977 and runner-up in 1978.

FRANCES (FRAN) EMERSON - Four-time city women's champion, 1950-51-59-60. Has won club championships in three states, eight times at the Dayton Country Club, three times in Florida and once in North Carolina.

NICK UNGARD - The founding father and past chairman of the Dayton Golf Hall of Fame project. A highly competitive player over a 30-year span, he was medalist (1960) and city champion in 1969. Has been involved in promotion of junior events.

CARL YUNG - No Dayton golfer ever matched Yung's string of success in 1963. Nicknamed "Mr. Golf," he won the city championship and was National Public Links medalist. Teamed with George Welsh to win the Klockson, an annual Community feature, and with Andy Augaitis to win the Blackburn at Madden. He shot 65 three times that year and was the Carling Amateur Golfer of the Year. Was Community champ in 1961, 1962 and 1974.

GEORGE WELSH - As a player he won the city title in 1969 and was runner-up in 1966. He served as President of the Dayton Amateur Golf Commission and was active in junior golf promotions. He won the Ohio Public Links Senior title in 1984. Was club champion in native Zanesville before moving here.

JAMIE WISE - Won DWGA championship in 1975 and the Dayton City Women's Amateur in 1978, 1981 and 1984. Twice qualified for the National Public Links and later became a teaching pro.

GORDON (COWBOY) WALDESPUHL - Started as a caddy at DCC. Played for Stivers High School golf team. Won the 1959 city match play championship in dramatic fashion with upsets over defending champion Jack Zimmerman in the semifinals and former champ John Blesi in finals. Later turned pro.

BILL WHEELER - Began as a caddy at Madden Park where he won the caddy championship at age nine. Wounded four times in Europe in World War II. Won the 1955 match play tournament with victory over Jack Zimmerman and Alex Pietrzak. Madden Park champ in 1958.

ALEX (NIPPER) CAMPBELL - He was born in Scotland and came to this country sometime around the turn of the century. He played in over 20 U. S. Opens but his greatest fame was as a designer and course builder. He designed Moraine, Meadowbrook, Mound and Madden park courses. Served as pro at each of them as well as a stint at Miami Valley. He died in 1942, a true pioneer legend in Dayton golf history.

MARTHA HOLBROOK PLATT - Was city women's champion five times, 1934, 1938, 1939, 1940 and 1946. Was club champion at DCC nine times and later won the same championship at Moraine.

BOB ZIMMERMAN - Youngest person to win the city men's championship at age 16 in 1957. He turned pro at an early age and had some limited success on the tour.

JIM FLYNN - Medalist and city champion back in 1936. Medalist in the 1931 Public Links and represented Dayton in the national tournament in 1931 and 1932. He was later club champion at Walnut Grove.

MYRON COLEMAN - He is the first Hall of Fame inductee without a playing championship to his credit. He was an average golfer with a great interest in developing youth golf.

ALICE BURTON - Best known for running the City Women's Amateur Tournament from its inception in 1978 through 1992. An avid golfer, she served on the City of Dayton Golf Commission for nearly two decades.

PAUL GENUNG - Led Fairview High School to the 1934 Ohio High School championship and won back-to-back City Amateur Match Play titles in 1939 and 1940. Qualified for the national Public Links tournament many times, reaching the quarterfinals in 1937 in San Francisco.

RICHARD HAIRE - Won five city amateur championships after he was 60 years old, winning in match play in 1983 and 1987 and in medal play in 1984-86-87. He was a pro much of his life but was reinstated as an amateur when he was 57.

BENNY JONES - His ticket into the Hall of Fame came for his service to young golfers as youth director of the Fairway Golf Club for 12 years and as founder of the Dayton Youth Golf Academy in 1989.

MARGE WENDEL BERRY KEENOY - Known as Marge Wendel and was still in Oakwood High School when she started her golfing career at Miami Valley under pro Jim Noble. She was club champion at both Dayton Country Club and Moraine. She won DWGA championships 10 years apart - in 1942 and 1952 and was runner-up two other times.

WALTER "BUD" LAW - Began playing golf at age six. His teacher was his grandfather E. B. O'Bannon, builder and greenskeeper at the MacGregor Golf Course. He was club champ over the years at NCR, DP&L and Sugar Valley. Won the city match play crown in 1973 after losing the 1970 match to John Fisher in 37 holes

EARL SHOCK - Followed his son, Don, and daughter, Janet, into the Hall. He was supervisor of Community Golf Course for 37 years, beginning in 1919. During his tenure the courses were expanded from nine to 36 holes. He conducted the local Public Links qualifier for years

MIKE ZIMMERMAN - He was a member of Fairmont High School's state golf championship squad and a runner-up in the national Public Links before turning pro. He was a four-time winner of the Miami Valley PGA Match Play championship and a two-time winner at medal play. He was killed in a 1988 automobile accident.

48

City Men's Amateur Match Play Championship

1919   Vin Hilton def. Walter Lanfersieck, 8 and 7

1920   Vin Hilton def. Jim Kelly, 10 and 9

1921   Vin Hilton def. Jim Kelly, 6 and 5

1922   Howard Jordan def. Walter Lanfersieck, 3 and 2

1923   Vin Hilton def. Paul Morgan, 1-up

1924   Jack Parrott def. Harold Jordan, 7 and 6

1925   Paul Morgan def. Rube Kreatz, 1-up

1926   Jim Herr def. Harry Fackler, 6 and 5

1927   Harry Lindsay def. Lt. Harold Barton, 2 and 1

1928   Ralph Brown def. E.J. Livesau, 7 and 6

1929   Bob Kepler def. Paul Stoppleman, 5 and 4

1930   Bob Kepler def. Clyde Mumma, 5 and 4

1931   Bob Kepler def. Clyde Mumma, 4 and 3

1932   Bob Kepler def. Carl Genung, 14 and 12

1933   Bob Servis def. Ralph Routsohn, 9 and 8

1934   Lt. Ken Rogers def. Bob Servis, 3 and 2

1935   Bob Servis def. Bob Kepler, 2 and 1

1936   Jim Flynn def. Paul Bohardt, 4 and 3

1937   Joe Higgins def. John Sendral, 8 and 7

1938   Joe Zotkiewicz def. Alex Pietrzak, 5 and 4

1939   Paul Genung def. Bob Randolph, 1-up

1940   Paul Genung def. Mel Lehr, 7 and 6

1941   Lt. Ben Schriever def. Mel Lehr, 2 and 1

1942   Joe Higgins def. Mel Lehr, 7 and 6

1943 - 1944 - 1945 - No tournaments

1946   Don Shock def. Dick Tang, 3 and 1

1947   Don Shock def. Fred Hussey, 1-up

1948   Dick Tang def. Willy Knopp, 5 and 4

1949   Jack Zimmerman def. Norman Lapp, 4 and 3

1950   Denny Walters def. Norman Lapp, 2-up

1951   Jack Cleary def. Maj. Robert E. Lee, 7 and 6

1952   Andy Augaitis def. Jack Cleary, 3 and 1

1953   Pat Schwab def. Hugh Howard, 8 and 6

1954   Jack Zimmerman def. Pat Schwab, 1-up

1955   Bill Wheeler def. Alex Pietrzak, 1-up

1956   John Blesi def. Bob Finke, 7 and 6

1957   Bobby Zimmerman def. John Blesi, 4 and 3

1958   Jack Zimmerman def. Bobby Zimmerman, 4 and 3
1959   George Waldespuhl def. John Blesi, 5 and 4
1960   Dudley Kircher def. Don Leedom, 9 and 8
1961   Jim MacFadyen def. Walter Law, 2 and 1
1962   Nick Ungard def. Jim Watson, 7 and 5
1963   Carl Yung def. Stu Nolan, 5 and 4
1964   Barry Baumgardner def. Don Leedom, 1-up
1965   Danny Robison def. Bob Mills, 3 and 2
1966   Dave Wilson def. George Welsh, 3 and 1
1967   Al Lewis def. Carl Yung, 8 and 7
1968   Ted Ritter def. Eddie Brown, 6 and 5
1969   George Welsh def. Jimmy Robinson, 2-up
1970   John Fisher def. Walter Law, 1-up
1971   Bob Shawen def. Bob Shivers, 3 and 2
1972   Dave Wilson def. Robert Grier, 3 and 2
1973   Walter Law def. Gene Folkerth, 1-up
1974   Jim Shively def. Bob Moore, 6 and 4
1975   Asey Jackson def. Nick Ungard, 1-up
1976   Dave Wilson def. Jim Awsumb, 3 and 2
1977   Jim Awsumb def. Jim Shively, 6 and 4
1978   James Snow def. Dave Novotny, 4 and 3
1979   Jim Neff def. Don Halloran, 3 and 2
1980   Mike Glendenning def. Bob Forth, 6 and 5
1981   No tournament
1982   Mike Glendenning def. Harold Farney, 13 and 12
1983   Richard Haire def. Larry Heil, 9 and 8
1984   Jim Neff def. Brian Hodgson, 10 and 9
1985   Dave Eby def. Chuck Licher, 2 and 1
1986   Brian Hodgson def. Jim Shively, 8 and 7
1987   Richard Haire def. Jesse Norris, 7 and 6
1988   Jim Shively def. Mike Dempsey, 5 and 4
1989   Mike Dempsey def. Don Block, 5 and 4
1990   Mike Dempsey def. Heath Wassem, 2 and 1
1991   Don Block def. Ben Stewart, 4 and 3
1992   Mike Suttman def. Don Block, 5 and 4
1993   Carl Bidwell def. Gabe Knight, 2-up
1994   Bob Jones def. Mike Suttman, 5 and 3
1995   Bob Jones def. Brian Blair, 2 and 1.

Dayton Women's Golf Association Champions

1933	Mrs. George Smith def. Rose Rubenstein, 10-and-8
1934	Martha Holbrook def. Janet Shock, 2-and-I
1935	Janet Shock def. Martha Holbrook, 8-and-7
1936	Janet Shock def. Martha Holbrook, 8-and-7
1937	Janet Shock def. Rose Rubenstein, 10-and-8
1938	Martha Holbrook def. Janet Shock, 3-and-2
1939	Martha Holbrook def. Janet Shock, 5-and-4
1940	Martha Holbrook def. Janet Shock, 3-and-2
1941	Helen Sumpter def. Marjorie Wendel, 4-and-3
1942	Majorie Wendel def. Mrs. W. M. Niswonger, 3-and-I
1943	Betty Lee Boren def. Irene Shofman by default
1944	Betty Lee Boren def. Jean Davis Harwood, 9-and-8
1945	Betty Lee Boren def. Mrs. W. M. Niswonger, 3-and-2
1946	Martha Platt def. Marjorie Berry, 7-and-6
1947	Helen Goldick def. Mrs. Lionel Mincer, 8-and-6
1948	Betty Curtner def. Mrs. Floyd Hull, 10-and-9
1949	Betty Lee Wendahl def. Marjorie Berry, 11-and-10
1950	Fran Emerson def. Jane Platt, 10-and-9
1951	Fran Emerson def. Sally Price, 5-and-4
1952	Marjorie Berry def. Eunice Schwab, 5-and-4
1953	Janet Shock Beardsley def. Nancy Walters, 10-and-8
1954	Janet Shock Beardsley def. Ruth Pickrel, 5-and-3
1955	Evelyn Brown def. Helen Goldick, 2-and-1
1956	Evelyn Brown def. Fran Emerson, 2-and-1
1957	Ruth Pickrel def. Mrs. Robert Murphy, 10-and-9
1958	Ruth Pickrel def. Fran Emerson, 7-and-6
1959	Fran Emerson def. Ruth Pickrel, 8-and-7
1960	Fran Emerson def. Janet Shock Beardsley, 2-up
1961	Martha D. Bush def. Ruth Pickrel, 1-up
1962	Ruth Pickrel def. Janet Shock Beardsley, 10-and-8
1963	Ruth Pickrel def. Diana Reichert, 6-and-5
1964	Ruth Pickrel def. Janet Shock Beardsley, 3-and-I
1965	Ruth Pickrel def. Diana Schwab, 11-and-9
1966	Ruth Pickrel def. Janet Shock Beardsley, 6-and-4
1967	Diana Schwab def. Sandy Krug, 6-and-5
1968	Sandy Krug def. Phyllis Beardsley, 6-and-5

1969   Diana Schwab def. Florris Fortune, 7-and-5
1970   Diana Schwab def. Kay Kennedy, 4-and-3
1971   Becky Uritus def. Janet Shock Beardsley, 5-and-3
1972   Diana Schwab def. M. J. Donnelly, 13-and-12
1973   Diana Schwab def. Kay Kennedy, 1-up
1974   Diana Schwab def. Phyllis Beardsley, 6-and-5
1975   Jamie Wise def. Cathy Kronauge, 8-and-6
1976   Diana Schwab def. Jamie Wise, 8-and-6
1977   Cathy Jefferson def. Diana Schwab, 2-and-I
        Tournament abandoned.

City Women's Amateur Golf Championship

1975   Diana Schwab def. Jamie Wise, 1-up
1976   Diana Schwab def. Jamie Wise, 7-and-6
1977   Kay Kennedy def. Daryl Nels, 11-and-10
1978   Jamie Wise def. Florris Fortune, 6-and-5
1979   Diana Schwab def. Cathy Jefferson, 1-up
1980   Diana Schwab def. Joan King, 10-and-9
1981   Jamie Wise def. Cathy Jefferson, 1-up
1982   Michele Miller def. Susan Justus, 6-and-5
1983   Diana Schwab def. Cathy Jefferson, 6-and-5
1984   Jamie Wise def. Cathy Jefferson, 4-and-3
1985   Michele Miller def. Cathy Jefferson, 3-and-1
1986   Michele Miller def. Cathy Jefferson, 5-and-3
1987   Diana Schwab def. Sue Stump, 7-and-5
1988   Jamie Fischer def. Sue Stump, 3-and-2
1989   Cathy Jefferson def. Diana Schwab, 5-and-4
1990   Cathy Jefferson def. Debby Clark, 13-and-12
1991   Cathy Jefferson def. Diana Schwab, 5-and-4
1992   Cathy Jefferson def. Diana Schwab, 4-and-2
1993   Diana Schwab def. Gwen Hoover, 8-and-6
1994   Susan Justus def. Cathy Jefferson, 4-and-3
1995   Cathy Jefferson def. Winnie Wheeler,

Miami Valley PGA Medal Play Champions

1938	Ock Willoweit (MacGregor)
1939	Clyde Mumma (MacGregor)
1940	Steve Zappe (Springfield CC)
1941	Al Marchi
1942	Ock Willoweit (MacGregor)
1943	No tournament
1944	Ock Willoweit (MacGregor)
1945	Tommy Bryant (NCR)
1946	Harry Schwab (Community)
1947	Ock Willoweit (MacGregor)
1948	Ock Willoweit (MacGregor)
1949	Ock Willoweit (MacGregor)
1950	George Shafer
1951	Tom Foree (Troy CC)
1952	Ock Willoweit (MacGregor)
1953	Jim Rudolph (Community)
1954	Tommy Bryant (Moraine)
1955	Jim Rudolph (NCR)
1956	Jim Rudolph (NCR)
1957	Ock Willoweit (MacGregor)
1958	Jim Rudolph (NCR)
1959	Jim Baker (741 Driving Range)
1960	Jack Ortman (Sycamore Creed)
1961	Jim Lucius (Troy CC)
1962	Jim Rudolph (NCR)
1963	Jim Baker (741 Driving Range)
1964	Jack Ortman (Sycamore Creek)
1965	Chuck Licher (Greene)
1966	Dale Fetter (Brown's Run)
1967	Bobby Wynn (Walnut Grove)
1968	Bobby Wynn (Xenia CC)
1969	Bobby Wynn (Xenia CC)
1970	Jack Ortman (Sycamore Creek)
1971	El Collins (Reid Park)
1972	El Collins (Reid Park)
1973	Mike Podolski (Troy CC)

1974   Jack Ortman (Sycamore Creek)
1975   Mike Zimmerman (Sycamore Creek)
1976   Joe Krug (Northwood Hills)
1977   El Collins (Reid Park)
1978   Mike Zimmerman (unattached)
1979   Larry King (Sycamore Creek)
1980   Joe Krug (Northwood Hills)
1981   Jim Lawrence (Dayton CC)
1982   Pete Brown (Madden)
1983   Pete Brown (Madden)
1984   Pete Brown (Madden)
1985   Ted Kauflin (Kittyhawk)
1986   Mike Glendenning (Wright-Patterson)
1987   Roy Carmichael (Brown's Run)
1988   Larry King (Wildwood)
1989   Tim Walton (NCR)
1990   Bobby Zimmerman (unattached)
1991   Roy Carmichael (Wildwood)
1992   Jim Awsumb (Jamaica Run)
1993   Pat Delaney (Springfield CC)
1994   Mike Glendenning (Twin Base)
1995   Tim Walton (NCR)

Miami Valley PGA Match Play Championship

1961   Jim Baker (741 Center) def. Jim Rudolph (NCR), 2-up
1962   Tom Ritter (Wildwood) def. Chuck Wagner (Kittyhawk), 4 and 3
1963   Jim Lucius (Troy CC) def. Chuck Licher (WPAFB), 4 and 3
1964   Chuck Licher (WPAFB) def. Jim Rudolph (NCR), 4 and 3
1965   Jack Ortman (Sycamore) def. Dale Fetter (Brown's Run), 3 and 2
1966   Jack Ortman (Sycamore) def. Jimmy Gilbert (DCC), 2 and 1
1967   Mike Podolski (Troy CC) def. Chuck Licher (Greene), 2 and 1
1968   Jack Ortman (Sycamore) def. Bobby Wynn (Xenia CC), 4 and 3
1969   El Collins (Reid Park) def. Bobby Wynn (Xenia CC), 3 and 2
1970   El Collins (Reid Park) def. Mike Podolski (Troy CC), 8 and 7
1971   Mike Podolski (Troy CC) def. Bob Bedinghaus (Piqua CC), 10 and 9
1972   El Collins (Reid Park) def. Chuck Licher (Greene), 8 and 7

1973	Chuck Licher (Greene) def. El Collins (Reid Park), 9 and 8
1974	Chuck Licher (unattached) def. John Kurzynowski (Miami Valley), 2 and 1
1975	El Collins (Reid Park) def. Ron Schneck (WPAFB), 1-up
1976	El Collins (Reid Park) def. Mike Zimmerman (Rollandia), 7 and 6
1977	Mike Zimmerman (unattached) def. El Collins (Reid Park), 6 and 4
1978	Mike Zimmerman (unattached) def. Jim Lawrence (DCC), 4 and 3
1979	Jack Ortman (Sycamore) def. Larry King (Sycamore), 7 and 6
1980	Larry King (Sycamore) def. El Collins (Reid Park), 4 and 3
1981	Mike Zimmerman (River Bend) def. El Collins (Reid Park), 3 and 2
1982	Larry King (Wildwood) def. Ray Rash (DCC), 5 and 4
1983	Pete Brown (Madden) def. Chris Hale (Miami Valley), 7 and 6
1984	Pete Brown (Madden) def. Ray Rash (NCR), 4 and 3
1985	Mike Zimmerman (Kittyhawk) def. Jeff Steinberg (NCR), 2 and 1
1986	Mike Glendenning (WPAFB) def. Larry King (Wildwood), 4 and 2
1987	John Marchi (Cassel Hills) def. Bobby Zimmerman (unattached), 3 and 2
1988	Roy Carmichael (Brown's Run) def. Larry King (Wildwood), 4 and 3
1989	Rick Cherubini (Reid Park) def. Mike Glendenning (WPAFB), 1-up
1990	Roy Carmichael (Wildwood) def. John Marchi (Cassel Hills), 6 and 5
1991	Randy McGohan (Miami Valley) def. Chip Fox (Hole Hunter), 8 and 7
1992	Roy Carmichael (Wildwood) def. Mike Glendenning (Twin Base), 8 and 7
1993	Lee Rinker (CC of North) def. Pat Delaney (Springfield CC), 7 and 6
1994	Jim Awsumb (Jamaica Run) def. Tom Saathoff (PipeStone), 4 and 3
1995	Tim Walton (NCR) def. Mike Glendenning (Twin Base) 1 up.

Daytonians in the U. S. Open

1956	Pat Schwab, Oak Hill, Rochester, 73-81, missed cut
	Ock Willoweit, 74-83, missed cut
1957	Pat Schwab, Inverness, Toledo, 72-WD, missed cut
1958	Pat Schwab, Southern Hills, Tulsa, 75-75-79-80, T-49
1960	Pat Schwab, Cherry Hills, Denver, 83-83, missed cut
	Gordon Waldespuhl, 84-81, missed cut
1962	Bobby Zimmerman, Oakmont, Pittsburgh, 77-75, missed cut
1965	Bobby Zimmerman, Bellerive, St. Louis, 75-79, missed cut
1966	Bobby Zimmerman, Olympic, San Francisco, 80-74, missed cut
1967	Bobby Zimmerman, Baltusrol, Springfield, N. J., 73-75-72-77, T-48
1968	Pat Schwab, Oak Hill, 76-70-75-69, T-24
1980	Greg Hickman, Baltusrol, 74-78, missed cut
1982	Brian Fogt, Pebble Beach, CA, 79-78, missed cut
1984	Greg Hickman, Winged Foot, Mamaroneck, N. Y., 75-78, missed cut
1985	Brian Fogt, Oakland Hills, Detroit, 81-75, missed
1987	Brian Fogt, Olympic, 77-80, missed cut
1989	Brian Fogt, Oak Hill, missed cut
1992	Randy McGohan, Pebble Beach, 76-79, missed cut

FOOTBALL

UD immortal Jack Padley (top) thrilled the fans. So does Keith Byars, OSU and pro star.

Fuzzy Faust, legendary Chaminade coach, and son Gerry, future Notre Dame mentor, check game films (above). Moose Krause and Gene Mayl enjoy a light moment (below).

The Dayton Triangles at their 35th reunion in 1951. They are (left to right seated) George Kinderdine, George Zimmerman, Norb Sacksteder, Brig. Gen. Nelson Talbott, Lawrence Dellinger and Ralph Hathaway. Standing, Lee Fenner, George Roudebush, Peck Reiter, Carl Thiele, Al Mahrt, Francis Bacon, Harry Cutler, Ernie Duncan, Dr. Dave Reese, Hack Abbott, Ed Sauer and Hugh Sacksteder.

5

The Game of Football

Red Blaik, Johnny Sauer, Fuzzy and Gerry Faust, Harry Baujan, Keith Byars, Jack Padley, Jim Katcavage, Howard Brown, Nelson Talbott, Chris Ward, Dave Reese and Chuck Noll -- these names leap out at you as you go down Dayton's football memory lane.

They represent coaching success as well as All-American athletes and only scratch the surface of those who played important roles as the sport matured.

The history of high school football, from the long-gone Steele-Stivers rivalry, is covered separately along with a special section about the elder Faust who went 12 years without losing to a city league rival.

Padley, Baujan and Katcavage are in the section devoted to Flyer football and Byars, probably the finest football player from our town, is covered in looking back at Daytonians who are part of Ohio State's history.

Deserving of special mention are incumbent NFL players Marco Coleman and Martin Bayless, who played with high school teams that were only marginally successful. Linebacker Coleman came out of Patterson to Georgia Tech and Bayless made the jump from Belmont to Bowling Green enroute to his pro success.

In the category of native Daytonians who achieved their reputation elsewhere, first up is Col. Earl R. Blaik, a member of the National Football Foundation Hall of Fame, who is perhaps better known by his nickname.

Born in Dayton in 1897, he played at Steele High School and went to Miami University where he played four years (1914-1917). He is the earliest member of that school's coaching legends. Moving on to West

Point, he played two more years during World War I and was third team All-American in 1919. He also played basketball and baseball as he had at Steele.

After a brief stay in real estate with his father in Dayton, he went into coaching as a longtime assistant at Army before becoming head coach at Dartmouth from1934 to 1940, where he was 35-15-4 including a 22-game unbeaten streak.

He jumped at the opportunity to take over at West Point in 1941, inheriting a team that had gone 1-7-1 in 1940. His first team went 5-3-1 and he never turned back. In his 18 seasons at West Point, he coached five undefeated teams, three national champions and had an overall record of 166-48-12.

From 1944 through 1947 he won or tied 32 consecutive games. Felix (Doc) Blanchard and Glenn Davis were the stars of the 1944-1945 undefeated championship teams.

Blaik coached 33 All-America players and 24 of his assistants, including Vince Lombardi, went on to become head coaches. One of his personal thrills was coaching his son Bob, who ran back a punt 75 yards for a touchdown against Michigan in 1950.

The National Football Foundation awarded Blaik its top achievement award, the Gold Medal, in 1966.

John Sauer's coaching career is closely tied to that of Blaik as the onetime Oakwood standout entered West Point in 1943 in time to be a part of those great wartime Cadet teams.

"I'm proud to say that Col. Blaik told me while I was finishing my senior year as a player that he wanted me to eventually be on his staff," Sauer says.

After fulfilling his active duty requirements, during which he was tailback on the Fort Benning National Service Champion teams, Sauer did go back to the Academy in 1947 where he spent three years working with Blaik. He left to become backfield coach at the University of Florida under Bob Woodruff in 1951-52 and then the next two years as backfield coach of the Los Angeles Rams in the NFL.

His head coaching opportunity came in 1955 when he took over at The Citadel, where he was also the athletic director. After two years at the South Carolina military school, he returned to Dayton to go into commercial real estate and launch a broadcasting career on the side. He had a daily sports program over WING radio for several years.

But he wasn't through with coaching as Otto Graham invited him to be on the College All-Star coaching staff to prepare that team for its one-game season, taking on the NFL champions in the *Chicago Tribune* sponsored charity benefit game every August.

After seven years, coaching the offensive backfield four years and three more on defense, he was named head coach of the All-Stars for two more seasons.

Sauer's broadcasting career included being an analyst on CBS national NFL telecasts. He ended his broadcasting as a longtime play-by-play man on radio for the University of Pittsburgh.

Chuck Noll enrolled in the University of Dayton in the fall of 1949 as a 17-year-old, 185 pound guard candidate out of Cleveland's Benedictine high school.

He became a three-year starter, grown up to 195 pounds, at left guard as a sophomore and was used on defense as a linebacker.

The 1951 Flyers became the only UD team to ever play in a Division I Bowl game and Noll was a factor in the 7-2 regular season and the close 26-21 setback at the hands of Houston in the Salad Bowl, the forerunner of the Fiesta Bowl in Phoenix.

Drafted by Paul Brown, he made a name for himself in his home town as a "messenger guard" -- the way Brown sent in plays to the Browns. He became an assistant coach under Sid Gillman with the San Diego Chargers (1960-65) and Don Shula with the Baltimore Colts (1966-68) before becoming head coach of the Pittsburgh Steelers in 1969.

His first year record was 1-13 but he quickly turned the inept Pittsburgh franchise into a powerhouse, winning four Super Bowl championships with the Steelers, 1973-74-78-79.

Although Gerry Faust's five seasons at Notre Dame did not turn out as well as the energetic coach had hoped, he is proud that he had the opportunity to make a lifetime dream come true.

By his own admission, Gerry wasn't ready for the many pressures that went with the head coaching job under the Golden Dome when he was invited to take over in 1981.

His fantastic success in creating a high school dynasty at Moeller High School in Cincinnati did not give him the necessary experience to put together a collegiate coaching staff and it certainly did not prepare him for the demands on his time from media and especially Notre Dame's national alumni following.

Faust moved on to coach eight seasons at Akron before retiring to go into the fund-raising operation of that northern Ohio university.

Two members of the Ankney family, one with many ties to different sports in Dayton, became head coaches at the Division 1 level.

Because of family moves, Pete Ankney played his high school football at three different schools: Roosevelt, Oakwood and Fairmont before enrolling at Miami University. After one year, he transferred to Dayton and graduated in 1956.

His high school coaching career parallels that of Gerry Faust in that he was quite successful. He started as an assistant at Xenia under his brother Ben and then served three seasons as an assistant at Fairmont before getting the head job in 1959, going 17-2 in his two seasons there. He was offered the head job at Canton McKinley, a northern Ohio powerhouse, spending two years there before the opening at his alma mater brought him back to Dayton.

Pete resigned after two seasons (4-14-1) but remained in the community in business and is an active supporter of the UD program.

Howard (Moe) Ankney is Pete's nephew and the son of Ben Ankney. He was water boy when his father coached Northridge to its state basketball championship back in 1945.

Moe started playing in high school at Xenia where his father was coaching. He finished at Fairmont under Pete and was an All-Ohio quarterback before going on to Bowling Green where he had a fine career. After being an assistant at Ball State, Tulane and Arizona he returned to his alma mater, serving five years as head coach of the Bee-Gee Falcons.

The late Sarah Ankney was married to Bobby Colburn, who figures in different sports covered in this book starting with the great Stivers basketball teams of the 1928-29-30 era.

His son, Bob Colburn Jr., was also a Bowling Green quarterback and later a Big Ten football official. Another son, Jim Colburn, played at Minnesota.

West Milton native Carl Brumbaugh is remembered as the first T-formation quarterback in the NFL. Brumbaugh played his college football at Florida before joining the Chicago Bears when that pioneer team was installing the new offensive system.

After his playing days were over, Brumbaugh was an assistant coach at several top level colleges and for a while was a broadcast analyst of UD Flyer football after he came back to this area.

Gene Mayl won letters at Notre Dame in 1921-22-23, a starter his last two years. He thus played with the Irish's legendary "Four Horsemen" although he graduated a year before Grantland Rice coined that phrase about the 1924 national championship team. Mayl, who died in 1986, became a prominent Dayton attorney.

Two prominent college and pro players came to Dayton in later life as successful businessmen.

Al Bart was one of Fordham's "Seven Blocks of Granite" in the 1930s. He was Al Babartski then, playing alongside Vince Lombardi. Bart later was a standout lineman in the NFL with the Chicago Cardinals and Chicago Bears.

Jack Doolan, who played at Georgetown and with the Cardinals when that franchise was still in Chicago, came to Dayton as a sporting goods salesman until he retired.

Ernie Green, a standout running back for the Cleveland Browns (1962-68) established residence in Dayton and is a partner in an investment firm. He is active in civic affairs, including service on the board of WPTD, Dayton's public television station. Green played his college ball at the University of Louisville.

Byars and the Buckeyes

In the twilight of Oct. 13, 1984, Keith Byars put on the greatest individual ball-carrying performance ever seen in the venerable Ohio State University concrete oval along the banks of the Olentangy.

With a national television audience glued in because of a late start dictated by the World Series game in Detroit that afternoon, Byars rushed for 274 yards and scored five touchdowns to spark a marvelous Buckeye comeback and a 45-38 victory over Illinois.

The powerful 230-pound Dayton native's performance outdid anything ever accomplished by any of the legendary Buckeye running backs of the past: Chic Harley, Hopalong Cassady, Archie Griffin -- any of them.

To recall anything remotely like his performance you would have to turn the clock back to 1940 when Michigan's Tom Harmon -- shown with torn jersey flapping on the cover of *Life Magazine* in a picture shot by *Dayton Journal* photographer Bob Doty -- ran wild in a 40-0 romp against the Buckeyes.

The highlight of Byars heroics came when the big but elusive Daytonian broke loose on a dazzling 67-yard scoring gallop minus a shoe which had come off as he made a cutback at the line of scrimmage. The Illini had built a 27-0 lead and the Buckeyes never got ahead until Byars carried the ball into the end zone from three yards out with 36 seconds left.

You will never convince many Daytonians -- and Ohio State partisans -- that it was a miscarriage of justice that Boston College's Doug Flutie beat out Byars for the Heisman trophy.

It was not for that memorable afternoon alone that Byars was a unanimous All-America selection. He was the MVP of the team and had a 99-yard kickoff return against Pitt in the Fiesta Bowl. Add his full decade of top level pro play with the NFL's Philadelphia Eagles and Miami Dolphins and you have an athlete with credentials hard to equal let alone top.

Byars came to Columbus out of Dayton Roth high school, where he transferred after his freshman year at Trotwood-Madison. Keith's high school coach at Roth, Tom Montgomery, laughs in recalling that Keith was originally a tight end.

"You'll see the Eagles used him as much as a pass receiver as a runner," Montgomery says.

Playing defense in high school, he acquired the nickname of Boomer for his jarring tackles. When he graduated from high school, he was a *Parade Magazine* All-American and the Division AA Player of the Year in Ohio as selected by the Associated Press.

It took him until the third game of his sophomore year to convince OSU coach Earle Bruce that he should be a starter. He became the second sophomore runner in Buckeye history to rush for more than 1,000 yards, the other being two-time Heisman trophy winner Archie Griffin.

Chris Ward is the only two-time Ohio State All-American from Dayton, (Patterson), the big guy achieving that honor in 1976 and 1977 before moving into the NFL with the New York Jets.

To this point, only Derrick Foster, another Patterson alum, has joined Byars as a four-season letterman. Ironically, when OSU recruited Foster, they passed up his teammate, Marco Coleman, who went to Georgia Tech and is enjoying an NFL career. Foster was plagued by injuries through much of his OSU career.

Three Dayton area quarterbacks have directed the Buckeyes. Donald Unverferth (Chaminade) lettered in 1963-64-65 followed by Bill Long (Stebbins) who started in 1966-67 but as a senior in 1968 had to yield to sophomore Rex Kern on one of Woody Hayes' best teams ever.

Centerville's Kirk Herbstreit, a three year letterman, took over in 1992, his senior year. Another Centerville passer, Gary Alders, earned three letters but never attained No. 1 status.

Doug France (Colonel White) was an All Big-Ten selection who went on play tackle for the Los Angeles Rams and Jeff Graham (Alter) was a fine pass receiver who went into the NFL with the Pittsburgh Steelers.

Tim Williams (Waynesville) closed out a brilliant career as the placekicking specialist with 39 out of 39 conversion attempts in 1993.

Dan (Big Daddy) Wilkinson, the 300-pound defender from Dunbar opted to turn pro at the end of that 1993 season and was drafted by the Cincinnati Bengals.

One of the more interesting stories in OSU history involves Greenville native Myers A. (Algy) Clark. He was a quarterback in the years before the T formation and a standout performer in 1924-25-26. It was his misfortune to miss the conversion attempt when Michigan edged OSU 17-16, the only loss the Buckeyes suffered in his senior year.

Many OSU followers never forgave Clark for that missed kick, overlooking his many positive contributions. More than that, reflecting a downside of sports in our culture, a few people never stopped reminding him of the incident.

Algy lived out his years in Dayton, carrying that piece of emotional baggage to the grave.

On the happier side, three time All-American halfback Lew Hinchman, a native of Columbus, moved to Dayton and was a voice of UD basketball for a number of years before he died. Hinchman and Stivers alum Carl (known as Carley) Cramer were halfbacks in the OSU backfield in 1931-32.

Other earlier Stivers stars who played at OSU include Ollie Klee, Joe Cox, Max Padlow and Herbert "Red" Schear.

Among the others from the Dayton area who wore Scarlet and Gray were Doug Whitmer, Gary Miller, Robert Koepnick and John Mummey.

Deron Brown, who played his high school football for Bob Gregg at Centerville, earned his Ohio State letter in 1992 as a member of special teams, those modern warriors who have unusual but vital job descriptions.

An unusual testimony to fine linemen produced in Dayton took place in the OSU stadium during the 1980 season when UCLA came into Columbus and silenced OSU partisans in a stunning 17-0 upset.

The Bruins had Erv Eatman (Meadowdale), Larry Lee (Roth) and

Joe Gemza (Chaminade) in their lineup. Eatman and Lee both went on to profitable careers in the NFL.

The Dayton Triangles

The Dayton Triangles of long ago are recognized as charter members of the National Football League beginning in 1920 and carrying through 1929 when they ended up an 0-6 season and passed into history.

But the story of the Triangles goes back nearly a decade before that to a period when numerous semi-pro and amateur teams, usually representing neighborhoods, were competing against each other around the city.

In his research for a paper on the Triangles he prepared for the Montgomery County Historical Society, Steven L. Presar found in Dayton newspaper reports teams named Wolverines, Miamis, Westwoods, Oxfords, McKinleys and Nationals competing against each other.

There was also a strong team known as Rosie's Corner, named for a bar in a long-gone Hungarian ethnic neighborhood in what is now part of West Dayton. The black population in West Dayton exploded during the years leading up to and through World War II when plentiful blue collar jobs were luring African Americans north.

These sandlot teams played at various parks including Westwood Field on Western Avenue, later Sucher Park, an outdoor arena for weekly pro wrestling bouts promoted by John Collins. Other sites included Highland Field on Wyoming Street, McKinley Field on Forest Avenue, River Field along what is now Riverview Avenue and NCR Field along what is now Patterson Boulevard.

The roots of the Triangles are closely tied into the early University of Dayton basketball teams known as the St. Marys Cadets, teams that made a great reputation covered in the basketball section of this history.

Upon graduation in 1912, the Cadets members formed the football team, using the same name as they had as undergrads.

The coach of the 1913 team was Lou Clark who also coached the UD football, team. Al Mahrt was the captain. George "Babe" Zimmerman and the Sacksteder brothers, Hugh and Norb, were standouts. One of the players who had no UD background was Carl "Scummy" Storck, who was to be associated with the NFL all his life.

By 1915, the team had changed its name to the Dayton Gym Cadets and a year later the name Triangles came into use

Industrialists Edward A. Deeds and Charles Kettering purchased a tract of land from the Edward Best estate to develop as a home field for the football team made up of their employees. It seems logical to assume that Deeds and Kettering may have been influenced by John H. Patterson of NCR in his development of recreational facilities for his workers.

The land was at the confluence of the Great Miami and Stillwater Rivers, which gave it a triangular shape. But chances are the name might have come from the three factories run by Deeds and Kettering which became part of Dayton's General Motors operations.

The 1916 team, the first under the Triangles name, went 9-1 defeating teams from Cincinnati, Detroit, Toledo and Pittsburgh. The Canton Bulldogs, with Jim Thorpe as the star attraction, claimed the world's pro football championship but ignored a challenge for a game from the Dayton team.

In 1917, the Triangles roster first included the name of Dr. Dave Reese, who was to become one of the city's best-known sports figures in his long life. Reese was a standout all-around athlete at Denison University who was hired as the "company dentist" at Delco.

Nelson "Bud" Talbott, a member of one of Dayton's prominent families, coached the team that year. Talbott had captained the 1914 Yale team and was named an All-American end by Walter Camp, who invented and made the All-America selections.

The 1917 team went 6-0-2 at what is today the site of Howell Field, Dayton's major baseball facility.

Mike Redelle, who in later life managed the Victory Theater, was hired by Delco as the team's secretary to handle all travel and other business arrangements. When Redelle went to war in 1918, Storck took over, getting his start in the administrative side of sports.

In July of 1920, four fledgling pro teams from Ohio and one from Rochester, N. Y. met in Canton at Ralph Hay's Hupmobile auto agency to try to get some organization into the chaotic condition among pro teams in the midwest.

That meeting has been recognized for years by the league itself as the formation of the NFL.

What the group did at that first meeting was to form the American Professional Football Conference. At a second meeting, again at the Hupmobile agency a month later (Hay was sponsor of the Canton Bulldogs), Jim Thorpe was named the first league president, but it was the use of his name the group wanted. Four additional teams, the Decatur Staleys (later to be the Chicago Bears), Racine Cardinals, Hammond Pros and Muncie Flyers joined. When the APFC membership was finalized, the Columbus Panhandles were admitted.

The first game between two league opponents was played Oct. 3, 1920 at Triangle Park when the Dayton team entertained the Panhandles. The Triangles made off with a 14-0 victory, the touchdowns scored by Lou Partlow and Francis Bacon, who had starred at Ohio Wesleyan. George "Hobby" Kinderdine kicked the first two extra points. He later would be elected sheriff of Montgomery County.

Partlow grew up in West Carrollton and had no collegiate experience, but was a productive and hard-hitting back who remained a Triangle to the end.

That 1920 team roster included Dick Abrell, Francis Bacon, Harold "Foos" Clark, Harry Cutler, Ed Davis, Larry Dellinger, Gus Early, Lee Fenner, Russ Hathaway, Earl Hauser, George Kinderdine, Al Mahrt, Lou Partlow, Dave Reese, George Roudebush, Norb Sacksteder, Carl "Dutch" Thiele, Glenn Tidd and Charles Winston. Talbott was the coach.

The high point of the 5-2-2 season was a 20-20 tie with Thorpe and the Canton Bulldogs at Triangle Park. The legendary Thorpe drop-kicked 45 and 54 yard field goals to enable the visitors to get the tie.

The Akron Pros, with an 8-0-3 record, won the first championship of the 14 teams that competed.

When the league planned its second season, Joe Carr was elected president succeeding Thorpe, who had never been more than a figurehead. The Columbus native set up what was to be the NFL headquarters in the Ohio city where it remained until Carr died in 1939. Carl Storck was secretary.

The change from the AFPA to the NFL was voted on June 24, 1922. By coincidence the same day the Decatur Staleys became the Chicago Bears.

In 1921 there was an incredible number of 21 teams participating in the league, the Triangles going 4-4-1. The most noteworthy playing addition was Eddie Sauer, a Stivers alumnus who played at Miami and is in that university's Hall of Fame. He was Johnny Sauer's father.

One of the highlights was Talbott inviting one of Yale's immortals, Frank Hinkey, who played in the 1890s, to come to Dayton to spend some time as a volunteer coach.

The Triangles began to slip back as early as 1922 when they still had a winning season, 4-3-1, but the focus in the league was changing from using homegrown talent to the hiring of big name college standouts who could be lured into the game. Dayton never went that route.

The Triangles were also having financial problems, even though the payroll by league limit was once as low as 16 players.

Over the next three years the Triangles were big losers on and off the field. They weren't coming close to filling their 5,000-seat stands in Triangle Park even with a low $1 general admission charge.

After the 1923 season, original Triangle standouts Al Mahrt, Dr. Reese and Dutch Thiele dropped out. Mahrt, who had been player-coach for two years, put in 13 seasons of hard-nosed action.

New talent was filling gaps in the ranks. Among that group was J. Mack Hummon, a Wittenberg graduate who was hired as a teacher-coach at Oakwood High School where he was to spend a productive life. Hummon later became a well-known football and basketball referee.

Oakwood High's football stadium is named Mack Hummon Field in his honor.

Hummon came along about the same time as Jack R. Brown, who played at the University of Dayton and later spent much of his working life in the UD athletic administration in marketing and ticket management.

It was on one of the Triangles' trips to New York City where Brown asked a cab driver to take him to a "historic place." The cabbie dropped him off at Trinity Church in lower Manhattan where in the churchyard cemetery, he spotted the tomb of Alexander Hamilton and other historic figures from the days of the American Revolution.

From that one visit to a historic cemetery, Brown made a lifelong hobby of visiting the graves of every American president and most of the Civil War generals. His sizeable collection of American history matter was turned over to the University after his death in 1991.

One of the Triangles gate attractions in 1927 and 1928 was "Sneeze" Achiu, the Hawaiian-Chinese running back who had played at UD. Because of their attendance problems at home, the Triangles played most of their games on the road, travelling in a rented Pullman car which served as their sleeping, dining and dressing room.

Luxury for travelling teams was any kind of a locker room with running water. Most pro players of the 1920s held "regular jobs" which made getting back to Dayton after Sunday games very important. There was enough rail travel in those days to attach the rented Pullman, although one wonders about how they fared often without a shower.

The salary rate for the Triangles in the 1920s was a basic $75 to $100 per game with deductions made for travel and other expenses. Fay Abbott was the coach of the team in its final seasons. At the end, only Partlow and Fenner were left from the 1920 team, the first in the league.

Fenner, a 150-pound end, had been a star at Stivers and played 14 seasons (1916-1929) without ever missing a game.

The first of four Dayton players recognized as all-league selections was guard Russ Hathaway in 1923. Hathaway played college ball at Indiana. Following him were center Hobby Kinderdine and tackle Eddie Sauer, both in 1925. The last was guard Al "Pup" Graham in 1928 and 1929. West Carrollton native Graham went on to play several more years with other teams in the league.

Dayton native Storck was the salaried NFL secretary for 18 years, then was interim president for two years until the league named Elmer Layden, one of the Notre Dame Four Horsemen, its first commissioner and moved the league offices to Chicago in 1941.

Dayton, thus, was involved in the NFL for over two decades.

The Fuzzy Faust Era

Gerald A. "Fuzzy" Faust created an enduring legacy of success both on and off the field in his coaching tenure at Chaminade High School.

The overall won-loss record (132-50-10) and 11 league championships in Faust's 21-season coaching career at the all-boys school doesn't tell the story of how Chaminade's green-clad Eagles dominated the Dayton city scene, starting with their first championship in 1940 through Fuzzy's second and final retirement after the 1956 campaign.

Following a 13-0 loss to Roosevelt in 1944, a Faust-coached team never again lost to a league opponent through his remaining nine seasons.

Born in Buffalo, N. Y. in 1907, his family moved to Cleveland where he grew up and played high school ball at Cathedral Latin. He enrolled at the University of Dayton in 1927 but a back injury cut short his playing career. Harry Baujan started him in coaching by letting him direct the prep school team the university operated at the time.

Faust graduated magna cum laude in engineering and excelled as a classroom teacher, never letting that responsibility take a back seat to his coaching. His teaching career lasted 52 years and he stayed on the Chaminade faculty long after giving up coaching.

His first coaching job started in 1930 with a year at Cincinnati Purcell, followed by two at Cathedral Latin, before coming to Dayton in 1933. Chaminade was known in the beginning as Dayton Catholic High School, fielding its first team in 1927. Through its first few years, the coaches were "on loan" from the University of Dayton.

Faust's first team went 3-4-1, opening with a 26-0 victory over Oakwood but losing to Stivers, Fairview, Steele and Roosevelt, but enjoyed a 13-7 victory over Kiser. Those five schools plus the Eagles made up the league referred to as the Big Six by the city's three newspapers.

Faust's first winning season was a 6-1-1 record in 1935, the lone loss being to Stivers.

The Eagles suffered through losing seasons in 1938 and 1939, but were coming of age for 1940, when they went 6-2-1 and captured the first of Faust's league titles. One of the losses that year was to Fairmont, the suburban school flexing its muscles building up to a strong era of its own.

Chaminade clinched the title on a bitterly cold November night at Athletic Field, the long gone "Smoke Bowl" adjacent to Kiser High School, with an 18-0 victory over Roosevelt.

Earlier that day, the Kiser Panthers had been upset 3-0 by Fairview on their home field, opening the door for the Eagles to take the crown. Kiser and Chaminade had played to a 7-7 tie earlier. Kiser was to be the primary city challenger to the Eagles through Fuzzy's years. In later years, Faust referred to the undefeated 1941 team as the one that gave him the most satisfaction because it set the standards for his other teams to follow.

This was long before free substitution made its way into high school ranks and the starters went both ways. The 1941 lineup had Jack Brennan and Bill Yahle at ends, Bob "Truck" Madden and Al Angerer at tackles, Jim Cochrane and Ed Stoermer at guards with Frank Maloney the center. Howard Neff called signals from his quarterback post with Bob O'Bryan at fullback. Faust did rotate his halfback trio of Jack Miller, Don "Doke" Hungling and Bart Mariscalco.

Opponents scared only 19 points against the physically strong Eagles and the only close call was a predictable 6-0 struggle with the equally physical Kiser Panthers. The only score came in the third period when sophomore tackle Angerer blocked a Kiser punt and Brennan fell on it in the end zone for the touchdown.

The Eagles regular season schedule called for eight games, but sensing an opportunity to score a financial success, a Thanksgiving Day game was arrange between Chaminade and 8-1 Miamisburg, which had tied Xenia for the Miami Valley League championship. Admission was 55 cents.

Chaminde rolled to a convincing 26-6 win to end the 9-0 season. The direction of the game became apparent early when the Vikings drove to the Chaminade eight yard line but were stopped, forcing a field goal attempt that missed. Although statistics weren't kept then, newspaper accounts told of fullback O'Bryan ending his career pounding huge holes in the Viking line.

Much of Faust's success as a coach came from his strictly enforced code of discipline. Despite being a deeply religious man, he meted out harsh punishment in practice for players who made mental mistakes.

Football trousers do not have belts, but Faust wore baseball pants on the practice field and would whip off his belt and yell out the name of an offender who would dutifully assume the position to absorb his penalty whacks.

"They weren't easy whacks either," laughed guard Stoermer in talking about the coach at the team's 50th reunion. "We ran a play and he yelled at me 'you missed your block' and I knew what that meant."

The 1942 team slipped to 5-2-1, bowing to Fairview and the always tough Kiser Panthers. Wilbur Wright scored a 7-0 win over the Eagles in 1943 as the team went 7-2.

Roosevelt fielded a powerful team in 1944 that knocked off the Eagles 13-0 with Jack Mackmull and Wilbur Sizer starring for the Teddies. Mackmull went on to play at West Point and eventually retired as an army major general.

The 1945 Eagles posted the second undefeated season rolling to an 13-0 record that ended with a 19-18 victory over previously unbeaten Piqua on the latter's home field.

In the immediate post-war years, the Eagles upgraded their schedule, first taking a trip to Massillon in 1946. The up-state Tigers were year in and year out one of Ohio's best, the dynasty having been created by Paul Brown.

A special train was arranged to carry Chaminade supporters to Massillon, but it wasn't a victory special, Massillon winning 35-12. Otherwise the season was a cakewalk as the Eagles scored 20-plus points in each of their seven wins. John Schneider clicked in the tradition of power running backs so dear to Fuzzy's heart.

In 1947, the Eagles paid a hefty guarantee to bring nationally-ranked St. James of Port Arthur, Texas to UD Stadium. A turnout of 12,000 watched the Texans make off with a hard-fought 22-13 victory, the only blemish an another 8-1 record.

Junior tailback Bob Koepnick rambled to five TD's in 68-0 crushing of outmanned Oakwood. The 1947 team had a number of players who went on to enjoy fine collegiate playing careers, including Jerry Smith who went to Wisconsin and on to the NFL. Koepnick played at Ohio State. Tony Kramer and Jim Raiff went on to play at Dayton.

Scatback Eddie Hess, who had a 43-yard scoring dash against Stivers, went on to a different fate. Fighting in an infantry unit in the bitter winter in the Korean war, he was taken prisoner and his status remains as missing in action.

Center Lee Falke went on to become a long-serving Montgomery County prosecutor.

The winning beat rolled on the next two seasons. The Eagles went 7-2 and 6-3 but were undefeated in the City League, as the newspapers referred to it.

In 1951, Fairmont scored what was regarded as an upset 7-6 victory over the Eagles in the opener for both schools. The other seven games were easy as the Eagles rolled up awesome scores against city opponents: 43-6 over Stivers, 40-0 over Kiser, 73-0 over Fairview and 42-0 over Roosevelt.

In 1952, Chaminade brought Chicago's Mt. Carmel High School, coached by Terry Brennan, to Dayton. The Eagles rolled up eight straight wins before bowing to Mt. Carmel, 28-21. A wild 27-27 tie with Cincinnati Purcell ended the 8-1-1 season after which Faust announced his retirement from coaching.

Bob Jauron stepped aside after one year as Faust's successor and alumnus Bucky Weaver took over. But two shaky seasons ensued and Faust was called out of retirement for the 1956 season.

The record was only 7-4, but none of the old city league rivals could handle his team.

His second retirement was for keeps with Ed Regan taking over in 1957 and the Eagles got back on the winning track. Eventually, the school became Chaminade-Julienne when the all-boys school merged with the former all-girl Julienne, enlarging the Chaminade school on South Ludlow.

The school known as C-J would have further athletic success, but the Faust era holds a unique place in the city's athletic history.'

Fuzzy was in his final illness as the 50th reunion of the undefeated 1941 team rolled around. The reunion was centered around the C-J game with Alter, then its archrival.

The players from the 1941 team were to be introduced and honored at halftime of the football game Friday night and attend a dinner Saturday night.

As fate would have it, Fuzzy's well-known son, Gerry, had an open date at Akron and received NCAA permission to come to the high school game, hoping to take his father there. But the old coach was too far gone and he died surrounded by his family Sunday afternoon, Nov. 3, 1991 at age 84.

"A coach can be a positive influence at the most impressionable period of your life," said Frank Maloney, paying tribute to the coach as did dozens of his former players. "He went about his job as the greatest high school coach in the world and he was all of that. He had complete control of your life and you didn't want to ever screw up."

Faust never apologized for using fear as one of his best motivational tools. The many stories of his resorting to corporal punishment reflect a way of teaching that is no longer accepted in society.

But it worked and hundreds of his former players who stayed in Dayton or moved elsewhere attribute much of their success in life to what their old coach stood for and taught them.

Son Gerry operated on his father's philosophy building a dynasty of his own at Cincinnati Moeller, the development of which was similar in many ways to the elder Faust building his program in Dayton.

Unfortunately, it did not work for Gerry at the college level.

6

The University of Dayton

The University of Dayton football program traces its origins back to 1905 when the school was known as St. Marys Institute.

In 1954 sports historian Deke Houlgate published a *Football Thesaurus* which referred to games as far back as 1894 by a midwestern St. Marys team he assumed was the forerunner of the University of Dayton, but that was an incorrect conclusion.

The best and only thoroughly researched history of UD football was published in 1993 by James Whalen Sr., a Dayton graduate and football enthusiast. Whalen published the book on his own as a limited edition that would be invaluable to a serious UD follower.

Whalen points out that Brother Elmer Lackner, then vice president of University Relations and a sports enthusiast himself, wrote to the publishers of the Houlgate book pointing out the inaccuracy.

Although the St. Marys teams are recognized as part of the UD program, it wasn't until 1920 that the name of the school was changed.

In University records, the modern era commences with Harry Baujan taking over in 1923. The first 18 seasons before Baujan were played without a full-time salaried coach, the last of these being Van F. Hill in 1922; Baujan had signed on as an assistant under Hill.

The original 1905 team played a modest three-game schedule, the opponents being Riverdale A. C. and Tippecanoe, which probably was an independent club made up of former high school athletes in that community, now known as Tipp City. In the first road game at Tipp City, the St. Marys men absorbed a 36-5 lathering.

The coach and captain was William Schoen, who figures prominently in the football and early basketball history of the school. The lineup included ends Pat McKenny and Floyd Foster, tackles Joe Mayl and Earl Smith, guards William Kroemer and Joe Schaefer, center Paul Wenigman, quarterback Bill Ryan, halfbacks captain Schoen and Bernard Topmoeller and fullback Rex Emrick.

Football of the time was a vastly different game with touchdowns counting five points, the forward pass was not legal and there was no such thing as licensed officials.

Things were much better in 1906 when the team, with 17 players again under Schoen, went 5-0-1 including a 36-0 win over Wittenberg, the first collegiate level opponent. Tippecanoe disappeared from the schedule forever.

Things quickly went bad in 1907 when the team lost all four games including its first ever meeting with Xavier, 17-5. The Saints, as they were first known, rebounded a year later to go 7-0-1 with Brother Matthew Hill as coach.

The 1911 season was eventful as the first of two years when Rollie Bevan, a native of Berne, Ohio and a graduate of Bucknell, came to Dayton as a physical therapist. He later became a successful high school coach at Dayton Steele, Youngstown Rayen and Toledo Woodward.

Bevan's greatest fame came as a trainer under Col. E. R. (Red) Blaik, first at Dartmouth and then West Point, where he was part of the great Army teams featuring Doc Blanchard and Glenn Davis during World War II.

The 1911 season also found Alphonse "Al" Mahrt, the first of four brothers to make their mark in UD athletic history, making his debut as starting quarterback at age 16. At that time students in SMI were able to take accelerated courses calling for long hours of study but enabling them to graduate at an early age. When Al's brother Armin came along four years later, he was playing college football at age 15.

Development of the football program was slowed by World War I with only two games played in 1918 and four in 1919. In these early days the teams were known as Saints and Hilltoppers, but the nickname of Flyers, with its obvious connection to Dayton's history as the birthplace of aviation, was officially adopted by the school in 1920 .

Revival came in 1920 when Nelson "Bud" Talbott took over the program but with no intention of making coaching a career. Talbott, a member of a prominent Dayton family, was a consensus All-American and captain at Yale in 1914. He had been coaching the Dayton Triangles as a sideline while getting involved in the family's industrial operation.

He took the school role because he thought it would consume less of his time than with the pro Triangles. Talbott directed the team to a 2-4 record and in 1921 was a co-coach with Charles Way before giving up football entirely because of business pressures.

The 1922 season turned out to be pivotal when Van P. Hill was named a salaried head coach. Harry C. Baujan, who had been a starter on Notre Dame teams in 1914-15-16 was hired as Hill's assistant.

Baujan, a native of Beardstown, Illinois, was contacted by sports writer Francis Powers, then a UD board member, about the job. The Illinois River was flooded around his home town and Baujan had to get out by crossing the flood in a rowboat to meet Powers in St. Louis.

The 1922 season plays a prominent role in another phase of UD history. Halfback Walter "Sneeze" Achiu arrived as a freshman from Honolulu. The Society of Mary, the religious order that founded and still directs the University, operated a secondary school in Honolulu known as St. Louis College.

Achiu, the son of a Chinese rice plantation owner and a Hawaiian mother, played his football at the Marianist school. He was the first of a number of Hawaiians who came to Dayton and helped Baujan build the football program to a level where it would be accepted by the more established state university programs around Ohio.

Achiu was followed from Hawaii a year later by Augie Cabrinha, Sam Hipa and Jim Spencer. Later, Raymond "Ducky" Swan arrived with Joe Cabrinha.

Baujan's football knowledge and Notre Dame background convinced the powers that be on campus that he should be head coach and Hill departed the scene. Turning the program over to Baujan was probably the best move in UD history.

No coach ever had an easier debut than Baujan as his team slaughtered a hopelessly outmanned Indiana Central squad 161-0.

Although Harry's first team finished with a 4-5 record, it was obvious that community interest in the school was growing.

Baujan, who had played three years of pro ball in Canton and Cleveland, called on his old coach at Notre Dame, Knute Rockne, for early organizational advice and got it.

The 1924 team, losing its opener 14-3 to Carnegie Tech, then an eastern power, went on to a 7-3 season. Arthur (Dutch) Bergman, another former Notre Damer and a Baujan teammate, came in as backfield coach. Lou Mahrt was the quarterback, teaming with 195-pound tackle Bill Belanich, Achiu and Cabrinha to make headlines.

Going into 1925, the university opened the new campus stadium which after World War II became known as Baujan Field. The stadium was built at a cost of $125,000 and could seat up to 9,000 spectators.

Knute Rockne himself attended the Oct. 17 dedication at which Archbishop John T. McNicholas of Cincinnati blessed the structure. William A. Keyes, president of the lay board of trustees presented the stadium to Rev. Bernard P. O'Reilly, the university president.

On the field, the Flyers celebrated with a 17-0 victory over John Carroll, which had come onto the schedule two years earlier. Jack McGarry kicked a field goal for a 3-0 halftime lead. The second half touchdowns came on a one-yard plunge by Augie Cabrinha and a pass from McGarry to Herb "Skeeter" Eisele who later became a highly successful coach at John Carroll.

The university enrollment at the time was 527 full-time students but the crowd of 7,500 gave testimony that Flyer football was accepted by the Dayton community as well as by a loyal alumni organization.

The 1925 season found team captain Louis R. Mahrt bowing out after a distinguished four-year career. His touchdown pass to Cabrinha late in the season accounted for the score in a 6-2 win over the Haskell Indians. At that time, the Indian school was considered one of the strongest nationally respected opponents the Flyers had defeated.

Al and Lou Mahrt are charter members of the University's Athletic Hall of Fame. Brothers Armin and John wore the red and blue with distinction.

Baujan turned out winning teams over the next four seasons as the schedule was gradually upgraded, Miami edging the Flyers 7-6 in 1927 in the first of many eventual clashes with the Oxford school just 45 miles away. The series with Cincinnati started in 1924 and in 1928 Detroit came aboard.

Boston College defeated the Flyers 15-6 in 1930, as Baujan and a group of active alumni supporters began lobbying to get UD accepted into the highly regarded Buckeye Conference.

In 1931, the Ohio University Bobcats won their third straight Buckeye Conference title. Other members were Ohio Wesleyan, Cincinnati, Miami, Denison and Wittenberg. Baujan played an 11-game schedule in 1932 at a time when nine games was the norm and the 9-2 record was the most wins in school history.

The Buckeye Conference was down to five schools in 1934, Wittenberg and Denison having dropped out, unable to remain competitive. The first game with Ohio University came in 1934, the Bobcats winning 17-0.

The Flyers had a three-man full-time coaching staff in 1934 with Joe Holsinger and Lou Tschudi hired as assistants.

The Flyers were admitted to membership in the Buckeye going into 1935, and went 2-2-1 against league opponents. There was a 26-0 loss to the Bobcats, who went unbeaten on a schedule that included a 6-0 win over Illinois. Baujan's men lost to Cincinnati 29-0 but tied Miami at 6-6 and scored wins over Ohio Wesleyan and Marshall. Cam Henderson, who achieved a degree of notoriety as Marshall's football and basketball coach, was in his first season at the Huntington school.

The Flyers suffered a 4-5 losing season in 1936, the last and only the third in Baujan's 21 seasons. But UD came back strong in 1937 with a 7-2 record that included a memorable 6-0 victory over Don Peden's Ohio U. Bobcats, who had beaten Dayton in their first three meetings.

Ohio had not tasted defeat in its home stadium since it was dedicated in 1926 and the game seemed destined to end in a scoreless tie with time running out. But the Flyers got possession at the OU 35-yard line with five seconds remaining. Bob Reidel unleashed a long pass which Jack Padley, then a sophomore halfback, took at the goal line for the upset.

Coming back a week later before an overflow crowd of 12,000 in UD Stadium, the Flyers knocked off Western Reserve, which hadn't been defeated in a string of 28 games.

The crowd was not only the largest in Dayton history, but it was the first Flyer game broadcast on radio, the announcers working from a window in St. Joseph Hall which overlooked the field. The press box at the time was too crowded and noisy to accommodate broadcasters.

Baujan unveiled a brand new backfield in 1937 nicknamed the "The Quaker State Express" because all four were Pennsylvania natives. Quarterback Joe Thomas, halfback Jack Padley and fullback Ed Marre were from Philadelphia with Coley McDonough, the other halfback, from the Pittsburgh area.

A year later the Flyers shared the Buckeye Conference title with the Bobcats, but had the satisfaction of handing them a 13-0 defeat enroute to a 7-2 season that included wins over Cincinnati and Marshall. Padley, lineman Ralph Nieuhas and Paul Wagner were first team All-Ohio choices by the Associated Press.

Tony Furst and Duncan Obee, later to enjoy pro careers with the Detroit Lions, made that 1938 forward wall one of the best in Flyer annals.

The Flyers slipped to a 4-4-1 record in 1939 but UD partisans look back on it as a special season because it involved a cross-country rail trip to the West Coast for a game with the highly regarded St. Mary's Galloping Gaels. The junket was the first time a UD team came close to national exposure.

The Gaels were coached by Elmer "Slip" Madigan, a Notre Dame graduate whose team was recognized as a national power in the 1930s. St. Mary's had defeated Texas Tech 20-13 in the Cotton Bowl at the end of the 1938 campaign.

The Flyers were considered a three touchdown underdog but managed to gain 6-6 tie. Padley scored the Dayton touchdown from four yards out in the opening quarter, setting it up with a 48-yard sweep.

Padley, a first team All-Ohio selection along with Furst, is considered one of UD's all-time greats. His 22 career touchdowns and 132 points were school records at the time.

Padley went on to a distinguished military career in the Marine Corps during World War II and again in the Korean War. He retired as a full colonel in 1959. After his death in 1989, he was buried in Arlington National Cemetery.

Dayton had strong teams the next three seasons (6-3, 7-3 and 8-2) before World War II forced a three-year layoff. Jim Carter came on the scene in 1940, the former Purdue star replacing Holsinger as backfield coach as well as serving as head basketball coach.

Beno Keiter, co-captain of the 1941 team with Pat Ryan, later became sheriff of Montgomery County and a highly respected community figure. He and Jerry Westerndorf, captain of the 1942 team, are in the school Hall of Fame.

During the time Baujan was bringing the football program to a level with other Ohio schools except for Ohio State's Big Ten position, the University did not have a salaried athletic director, members of the Marianist order serving in that capacity.

There was, however, a group of alumni and friends who worked tirelessly on ticket sales, publicity and other organizational duties that Baujan didn't have time to handle. Prominent among that group was Jack R. Brown, Hank Malloy, J. Ellis Mayl, Bob Payne (not to be confused with football player Bob Payne, a member of the UD Hall of Fame), Leo Spatz, Harry Mack, Bill Lemhaus and Merle Smith.

The revival of football in 1946 turned out to be Baujan's last season as he put together a team made up of more than a dozen military service veterans and a talented incoming freshman crop.

A 35-0 lathering at the hands of Miami in the second game shocked UD partisans, who were unaware of the awesome powerhouse Sid Gillman had going for him. The Redskins included the likes of Ara Parseghian, Paul Dietzel, Bill Hoover and Mel Olix part of two-deep offensive and defensive units.

After the 6-3 season, the administration decided that Baujan should give up coaching to become the school's first full-time athletic director. The man his former players affectionately called "the Blond Beast" resisted the idea but had to accept it.

Joe Gavin, a onetime Notre Dame basketball captain who had been a highly successful high school football coach at Cleveland Holy Name (84-47-13), was the choice to take over. His initial 6-3 season was considered a success because he had gone to a more wide open offensive style. He installed the T-formation which Baujan had resisted in favor of retaining the Notre Dame single wing.

In the third game of the season, the Flyers edged the strong Cincinnati Bearcats 26-21 in UC's Nippert Stadium in what many observers (including the author) consider one of the greatest wins in UD history.

Former Chicago Bear standout Ray Nolting was UC's head coach and his team had whipped the 1946 Flyers 19-0. Cincinnati's star halfback Roger Stephens returned the opening kickoff 90 yards for a score to put the Flyers in an immediate hole.

But the Flyers fought back in the see-saw battle. Gavin's choice as his first T-quarterback was Ed (Chief) Toscani, who threw scoring passes to Art Bok and Dale Babione. Bok dueled with the highly regarded Stephens all night. It took an interception by UD's Ray Munger in the final minute to preserve the upset before 24,000 emotionally drained spectators. A scuffle on the field involving Baujan, Nolting and Cincinnati halfback Alkie Richards led to a four-year interruption in the series.

The 1948 season found the Flyers at their peak of community support. There had never been a sellout in the expanded UD Stadium but an overflow throng of 15,000 was on hand for the visit of the Miami Redskins, coming off an undefeated 1947 season and a win over Texas Tech in the Sun Bowl.

A touchdown pass from Toscani to Bok was the only score in Dayton's 7-0 victory, ending a 16-game Miami winning streak. For whatever the reason, the Flyers couldn't sustain the emotions of that Miami win. A great defense anchored by Gus Shroyer, Fran Kilbane, Bob Wagner, Pop Dunn and Don Mills had racked up five straight shutouts including that of the high powered Redskins.

But a 13-13 tie with Oklahoma City a week later and a season ending 21-6 loss at Chattanooga diminished the enthusiasm of a 7-2-1 season.

Gavin's stock began to slip despite a 6-3 season in 1949, being marred by a 53-20 beating at Miami and two losses to rival Xavier. The two games with the Musketeers represented an effort by both schools to combat scheduling problems.

The Flyers slipped to 4-6 in 1950, Gavin's first losing campaign but they came back a year later to earn their only Bowl trip as a Division I program. Dayton was invited to play in the Salad Bowl, the forerunner of what is now the prestigious Fiesta Bowl in Phoenix. Dayton took a 7-2 record west, with perhaps its strongest showing in a 21-20 home field loss to Miami. The Flyers had held a 20-7 lead going into the final period but couldn't stop Miami's great ground game featuring shifty John Pont.

Bobby Recker, a scatback from Toledo, along with quarterback Frank Siggins, provided Dayton's offense in the 26-21 bowl game loss. Siggins completed scoring passes to Recker and burly Jim Curran while Recker went over from seven yards out to finish a 67-yard first quarter Flyer drive.

Chuck Noll, the future pro guard who coached the Pittsburgh Steelers to four Super Bowl championships in the 1970s, was a standout lineman on that team which included a number of fine athletes who remained in Dayton, establishing themselves as solid citizens. Among them were Tony Kramer and Jim Raiff who went from Chaminade to UD a year apart and who tragically died a few months apart in 1994.

Others who stayed in the Dayton community include Captain Lou Cannarozzi, Russ Johnson, Pat Maloney, Dick Durbin and quarterback Siggins. In 1952, former players Frank Maloney, Jim Raiff and Siggins joined

Gavin's staff as volunteers trying to bring the working group up in numbers to most schools on the schedule.

When the Flyers lost their first three games in 1953, Gavin announced he would resign at the end of the season, citing self-inflicted pressure and saying he wasn't under fire from the administration. After the resignation was announced, the team stabilized a bit but there wasn't much to cheer about in the 3-5-1 season.

Gavin remained in Dayton and prior to the start of the 1955 season was shot and killed by a crazed gunman in the lobby of the Third National (now Society) Bank in downtown Dayton.

Enthusiasm was running high for UD football when it was announced in January that Hugh Devore would be the new coach. Devore, like Baujan and Gavin, was a Notre Dame man, class of 1933. He had a long coaching record including a one-year stay in 1945 as interim head coach of the Fighting Irish during the war.

Ironically, he was available because St. Bonaventure and New York University, his last two coaching posts, had given up football for economic reasons. He came into the Flyer picture with a new staff including Herb Dintaman, who had been a lineman under him with the Bonnies. Dintaman was destined to stay on in Dayton in a number of athletic jobs into the 1990s.

The Flyers opened what was to be a 5-5 season with three straight losses, but finished strong, including a 20-12 win over the Parseghian-coached Miami team in Oxford. It was UD's first win over the Redskins since the memorable 1948 meeting.

The changes in NCAA rules restricting free substitution found the game swinging back to two-way players.

Devore's 1955 team slipped to a 3-6-1 record on a very difficult schedule including a 53-7 loss at Tennessee. But the amiable coach, well liked in the community, had accepted a new three-year contract when the Philadelphia Eagles came offering him their head coaching job. The UD administration released him from his contract.

Jim Katcavage, who played both ways in Devore's two year tenure, was headed toward a highly successful pro career as a member of the New York Giants "Fearsome Foursome" defensive unit featuring Andy Robustelli, Rosey Grier and Dick Modzelewski.

Devore's successor turned out to be Bud Kerr, another Notre Dame man who had earned some All-American notice as an end in 1939. The

NCAA announced that Dayton now was officially a "major school" on the strength of its schedule.

Kerr's four-season tenure started off with a 4-6 mark and jumped to 6-3-1 a year later, the first UD winning season in five years which included a 13-13 tie with Cincinnati and victories over Xavier and Miami in the unofficial "backyard rivalry."

End Fred Dugan was selected as a first team All-American in 1957 on the team picked by the Football Writers Association of America and *Look Magazine*. He was second team on the AP All-American. Gerry Faust, the future head coach at Cincinnati Moeller, Notre Dame and Akron, alternated at quarterback with Don "Butch" Zimmerman.

In 1958 Kerr's team slipped to 2-8, starting a run of eight straight losing seasons while the school began to absorb heavy financial losses in an effort to restore the program to its former level.

Oddly, in that losing period some excellent individual athletes performed in UD uniform including Emil Karas, Bob DeMarco and Mike Ciccolella, a trio who enjoyed NFL careers, and Bill Korutz, who played in the East-West Shrine game.

Stan Zaidel's coaching tenure produced identical 2-8 records in 1961-62 although attendance started each year strong with Jack R. Brown, now the salaried ticket and promotions manager, staging special reduced rate nights. Pete Ankney, a Dayton native with a successful high school coaching career, tried his hand at reviving the team in 1963-64 without success. He resigned after two seasons.

The University made a very significant move early in 1964 naming Thomas J. Frericks athletic director to succeed Baujan. Frericks' role in UD history is discussed in the basketball section of this history.

New head coach John McVay, a native of Canton who as a Miami lineman had competed against the Flyers, took over in 1965 when the program hit rock bottom in a 1-8-1 season in which a total of only 26 points were scored, being shutout in seven games.

But McVay had put together a great coaching staff that included George Perles, Tom Moore, Joe Eaglowski, Ed Youngs and Wayne Fontes. Perles, Moore and Fontes later coached in the NFL, as did McVay himself.

Perles, a defensive specialist who later joined head coach Chuck Noll with the great Pittsburgh Steeler teams, forged a strong group that included Jim Place, Bob Print, Barry Profato, Bob Shortal and Pete Richardson.

The Flyers rebounded in 1966 with a surprising 8-2 season that represented the high mark before the program was dropped to Division III a decade later.

McVay's team enjoyed a 6-3-1 mark in 1967 with a running back attack featuring Billy Mayo, Bernie Kress and Bob Madden. The Flyers had to settle for a 5-5 season in '68.

Gary Kosins, destined to be one of the great power running backs in the nation, made his debut in 1969 in an all-new backfield and a rebuilt offensive unit. The team lost its first five games and finished 3-7.

Although the overall record in Kosins' three seasons wasn't that good, the slashing 210-pound graduate of Chaminade High School established national recognition as a workhorse, setting an NCAA record of 38.2 carries per game in 1970. Unfortunately, the Flyers never generated a passing attack to supplement Kosins on the ground.

When he finished his last season, Kosins had smashed all existing UD rushing records, 2,812 yards in 779 carries and 41 touchdowns for 246 points. Those records survive from UD's Division I play. His scoring record was broken by kicking specialist Mike Duvic with 327 points (all kicks) in 1986-89. Gary was MVP of the Senior Bowl, played in the Blue-Gray and three seasons with the Chicago Bears.

McVay's seventh and last season ended 4-6-1 in 1972 as he was moved up to athletic director, a post he gave up a year later to become head coach at Memphis in the short-lived World Football League. John then became head coach of the New York Giants and later general manager of the San Francisco 49ers in years they were racking up Super Bowl victories.

Ron Marciniak, a onetime NFL linebacker and an assistant coach at Northwestern, was hired as McVay's replacement. Former Flyer stars Joe Quinn and Bill Lange, members of the athletic board, resigned in protest when former Flyer captain Bill Gutbrod, who had a great winning record at Cleveland's St. Joseph High School, was passed over by the search committee.

Joe Quinn had come to Dayton as a player in the 1930s, stayed on as an assistant coach, and two of his sons, Dan and Tim, played on later teams. Lange was a standout lineman (1946-49) who went on to a six-season career in the NFL and was a member of the Los Angeles Rams who won the championship in 1951, defeating the Cleveland Browns.

Marciniak was well liked in the community and by the media, but the problem of recruiting Division I talent was becoming more difficult all the while. At the same time, the administration was getting apprehensive over the financial drain on the budget. Longtime rival Xavier gave up football after the 1973 season for economic reasons.

The final meeting of the two schools resulted in a 28-28 tie in Marciniak's first year and the long series ended with Xavier holding a slight 27-21-4 edge over the Flyers.

Starting in 1974, the Flyers began to play their home games in the newer Welcome Stadium, signing a 25-year lease agreement with Montgomery Country, the City of Dayton and the Dayton Board of Education, the three of them holding title to the land. Baujan Field was on its way into history.

Welcome Stadium is across the Miami River from the main campus and adjacent to the UD Arena, which opened in 1970 for the basketball program.

The new home wasn't much help to Marciniak's team which went 3-8, giving up 310 points. There was slight improvement a year later, but major changes were in the works.

Going into the 1976 season, it was announced that starting a year later there would be no more football grants-in-aid (scholarships) and future scheduling would be in Division III. Players on the team who had scholarships would continue to enjoy them until their eligibility expired if they cared to stay.

The new coach was Rick Carter, a Dayton native who had been a three-sport star at Kettering Fairmont high school and who had 11 years of coaching at the Division III level, six at alma mater Earlham and five at Hanover.

"I've been recruiting for 11 years at Division III," Carter said at his first media conference. "We have one of the finest Division III stadiums in the country, we have an excellent academic program and a great city." Although he didn't predict a national championship by his fourth season, that's precisely what he produced.

The Flyers astonished most football experts with an 8-3 record in Carter's first season, playing five Division I opponents. The Flyers were edged in their opening game at Miami, 26-23. The Redskins barely escaped being tied when Fred Johnson kicked a 26-yard field goal with time running out. Later, Carter's men scared the daylights out of Iowa State on the latter's home field before bowing 17-13.

86

Miami was the lone strong Division I team remaining on the 1978 schedule and the Flyers earned a 10-10 tie to terminate the long series between the two old rivals. Miami has a 29-10-3 overall edge in the record book, but there were many great games along the way.

UD rolled to a 9-1-1 regular season, qualifying them for the post-season Division III playoffs for the first time. Unfortunately, Carnegie-Mellon knocked them off 24-21 in overtime in Pittsburgh.

One of the standouts on the 1978 team was tri-captain and line-backer Rick Chamberlain, a Springfield native who became a longtime assistant when Mike Kelly launched his highly successful tenure.

In Carter's third season, the Flyers went 8-2-1, still unable to get its full schedule down to its proposed level. There was I-A Bucknell and four Division II teams to be dealt with.

The dream season turned out to be 1980 when the Flyers soared to a 14-0 record and the national championship. Carter had put together an offensive juggernaut that functioned behind a fine forward wall. No opponent came close to challenging the Flyers in the 11-0 regular season and they opened the playoffs with an impressive 34-0 romp over Baldwin-Wallace, a perennial Division III power in northern Ohio.

A trip to Chester, just outside Philadelphia to face Widener, produced what clearly stands out as the most remarkable Flyer comeback victory ever. Widener built up a 24-0 halftime lead as the Flyers stumbled around under the first real pressure of the season. But they did respond, winning 28-24, stunning the home team and its followers.

Senior quarterback Jim O'Hara completed a 15-yard scoring pass to Al Laubenthal to get Dayton on the board and the Flyers drove for another third quarter score with Gerry Smith carrying it over.

Then came the most amazing aspect of it all; quarterback O'Hara was knocked out of the game with a head injury. Sophomore Jon Vorpe came off the bench to direct the Flyers to two TD's, utilizing the option play to carry the final two scores over himself. The winning drive was set up when Tim Tepe blocked a Widener punt with three minutes on the clock.

The trip to Phoenix City, Alabama for the Amos Alonzo Stagg Bowl championship was almost as astonishing. The Flyers could do nothing wrong in manhandling a previously undefeated Ithaca, New York, team, 63-0, obviously setting a championship game record.

In season stats, tailback Gradlin Pruitt, a Hall of Fame inductee in

1994, rushed for 1591 yards in 323 carries, an average of 4.9 per carry. Gerry Smith was next with 465 yards and UD had six more carriers over 100 yards.

O'Hara passed for 1446 yards, 883 to Laubenthal, who scored eight touchdowns. Meanwhile, the defense limited the opposition to 46 points in the regular season and 70 overall, allowing for Widener's 24.

Carter was voted College Division Coach of the Year by the American Football Coaches Association and was offered a head caching job at Holy Cross College. The opportunity to move to the Division I school was too good to turn down.

Tom Frericks, then vice president for Athletic Programs and Facilities, was renamed AD and on Dec. 23, a week after Carter announced his resignation, named defensive coordinator Mike Kelly the new coach.

West Milton native Kelly had been an outstanding all-around athlete at Manchester, a small Indiana college. He was a four-letterman in both football as quarterback and baseball as a catcher. After five years in high school coaching, he joined Carter's staff at Hanover and came to Dayton with him.

Kelly started his head coaching tenure with three full-time assistants, quarterback coach Dave Whilding, who also came to UD with Carter, former standout linebacker Rick Chamberlain and offensive coordinator Keith Jordan. Chamberlain and Whilding were still with the head coach going into the 1995 season.

It would be an understatement to say that Kelly's record is exceptional. A string of 14 consecutive winning seasons has him percentage-wise up among Knute Rockne and Frank Leahy as the all-time winning coaches. His 137-24-1 record (through 1992) moved him past Baujan's 124 victories. There were four trips to the Stagg Bowl before an NCAA rules change forced the Flyers to go back to the lowest rung of Division I in the 1993 season.

Mike's first team in 1981 went 10-1 in the regular season, losing to Division I-AA Eastern Kentucky. Qualifying for the Division III playoffs, the UD contingent easily handled Augustana (19-7) and Lawrence (38-0) before facing Widener again at Phoenix City.

This time Widener avenged the stunning loss in the semi-finals the year before by edging the Flyers 17-10. This time it was Dayton's turn not to hold the lead, UD being up 10-0 at halftime. The Pioneers made a defensive adjustment that shut down the Flyers. They sacked quarterback Vorpe nine times, resulting in two fumbles that turned the game around. Defensive back Doug Conley was first team All-American.

If Kelly had a down year, it would have been the 6-4 record in 1982 when the Flyers lost close games to 1-AA Bucknell, Division II Ashland and strong Wabash and Baldwin-Wallace. The scheduling problem that was never solved in UD's Division III years was evident in a 71-0 romp over Jersey City and 62-0 over Maryville. Neither team was capable of competing, and Kelly made no attempt to run up scores.

Following a 7-3 season in 1983, the Flyers got back into the post-season picture in 1984 with a regular season 10-0 mark, only to be edged 14-13 by Augustana, the Illinois school that has been a Division III powerhouse. This first round struggle was waged in Welcome Stadium and Augustana was enroute to the second of four straight Stagg Bowl triumphs. In a streak from 1983 through 1987, Augustana would amass an incredible 59-0-1 record that was destined to end in Welcome Stadium.

Kelly's men missed the playoffs in 1985 and that season triggered a tragic event that shocked UD followers and the entire Dayton community.

Rick Carter's Holy Cross team had struggled to a 4-6-1 record, only his third losing season in 20 years of coaching. On Sunday Feb. 2, 1986, the 42-year-old coach committed suicide at his home in Boylston, Massachusetts. As best can be determined, the death of his father, serious illness of his mother and the Holy Cross decision to de-emphasize to an Ivy League, no-scholarship program, combined to trigger Carter's unpredictable decision.

Kelly was terribly shaken by the death of his close friend, but went about the business of getting his team ready for another unbeaten regular season in 1986. The campaign opened with a 17-16 squeaker against Butler, but the rest was relatively easy. This was the year Baldwin-Wallace, the strong Division III school in suburban Cleveland, dropped Dayton from the schedule, alleging the UD program had too many advantages to be a true Division III entry. Kelly tried every year to get more Ohio schools on the schedule, but the B-W sentiment expressed the feelings of many other coaches and AD's around the state.

Mount Union defeated UD in the first round of the playoffs in a wild 42-36 battle in Dayton. The Purple Raiders had a great passing game built around quarterback Scott Gindlesberger who connected on 16 of 29 passes for 302 yards and three touchdowns. Dayton's strong running attack of Tim Norbut and Jackie Green piled up 362 yards, but it wasn't enough.

Kelly's quest of taking his team to the Stagg Bowl a second time became a reality in 1987. Regular season losses to Butler and St. Joseph's of Indiana threatened Dayton's hopes of making the playoffs, but a 24-0 win over Ithaca in the season's finale got them over the hump. The shutout was Ithaca's first in 73 games, dating back to that Stagg Bowl humiliation at the hands of the Flyers.

In the first playoff game in Welcome, UD jumped off to a 52-28 win over Capital, the Ohio Conference champions. Quarterback Kevin Wilhelm connected on two early scoring passes to Tim Ewbank and Randy Cummings to got things going.

The Flyers were confronted with Augustana in round two. Coach Bob Reade's team was undefeated and ranked No. 1 in the country with that long undefeated streak on the line. Dayton was a 38-36 winner, as strange as it sounds in view of the score, hanging on with a strong defensive game in the fourth quarter.

Senior tailback Dave Jones of Newark, Ohio carried the ball for 219 of Dayton's 369 yards on the ground. The passing combo of Wilhelm to Ewbank was good for two touchdowns, including a 50-yarder in the fourth quarter that was the margin of victory.

Given a third straight playoff date at home, the Flyers knocked off Central Iowa 34-0 and set sail for Phoenix City once more, this time facing Wagner, an independent located on Staten Island, N. Y. The Seahawks turned out to be bigger and stronger than the Flyers and clearly deserved their 19-3 championship triumph.

The UD travelling party was stunned to see the high powered offense unable to produce one touchdown. Senior tailback Jones set three single season records rushing for 1,803 yards, 160 points and 26 touchdowns. Kelly was voted Ohio Coach of the Year in an annual poll by the *Columbus Dispatch.*

A year later, Butler beat Kelly's men, 34-17, in a 9-1 regular season that opened with a 35-0 romp over ancient rival Wittenberg in Welcome Stadium. The UD administration was delighted that the Tigers had come back on the schedule, the two schools not having met in the regular season since 1938. An excellent crowd of 9,511 turned out for the game.

And who should turn up as UD's first playoff opponent -- those same Tigers from Springfield who stunned Kelly's men in a 35-28 two-overtime thriller.

Kelly's dream of his first national championship and the second for the program came to pass in 1989. His teams had made the playoffs four times and twice advanced to the Stagg Bowl.

The season opened with a 28-3 conquest of Wittenberg on the Tigers' home field. A 13-13 tie with Butler in the third game was followed by an 11-game winning streak carrying them all the way. A string of one-sided regular season victories was followed by playoff wins over John Carroll, Millikin and St. Johns of Minnesota before the title game against Union, another eastern opponent.

Union marched 67 yards from the kickoff to take a 7-0 lead, but this time the Flyers managed to snap back. Quarterback Dan Sharley scored two touchdowns on keepers and Tim Duvic kicked the field goal for a 17-7 victory. Dayton's defense was great. Linebacker Randy Mason was named MVP of the game. Defensive captain Lou Loncar was a standout all season as the Flyers wrapped up the 1980s with a tremendous 99-19-1 overall record.

The Flyers, coming off that 13-0-1 championship season, ran their unbeaten streak to 25 in 1990 sailing back into the playoffs after still one more undefeated regular season. Formidable rival Augustana fell 24-14 to start the post-season but Allegheny ended the streak with a 31-23 victory at the Pennsylvania school's home field in Meadville.

There was one more jaunt to the Stagg Bowl before the Flyers were forced to bow out of Division III. The 1991 Flyers ripped off 13 games in a row before bowing in the championship game to Ithaca, 34-20. The Stagg Bowl had been moved to a new site in Bradenton, Florida after its years in Phoenix City. In their last year in Division III, the Flyers followed their pattern of an undefeated season but then came a 27-10 loss to Mount Union in the playoff's first round.

The NCAA legislation that changed the Flyer program dictated that a school must compete its full athletic program at the same level. In Dayton's case, the basketball program is the breadwinner, forcing the entire program to the I-A level.

The Flyers joined the Pioneer League, a non-scholarship grouping at the low end of the Division. The charter members were Dayton, Butler, Evansville, Drake, Valparaiso and surprisingly, from the West Coast, the University of San Diego.

Kelly promptly got off to a 10-1 year to win the first championship of the circuit and shared it with another 10-1 season in 1994. The 1995 Flyers went 9-2, finishing second in the league.

A young Tom Frericks becomes UD AD in 1964 suceeding Harry Baujan (above); first UD coach Harry Solimano (right).

Baujan bids farewell to the UD field that bears his name (top).

Current UD coach Mike Kelly drills the defense (left). The Flyers under Kelly have an impressive winning record.

7

High School Football

The history of high school football in Dayton evolved from intramural games dating back to when Central, the city's first high school, was located at the corner of Fourth and Wilkinson Streets.

A research paper under the title of *The Earliest Days of Dayton High School Football* by Charles Lloyd Lindenwald is in possession of the Dayton and Montgomery County Public Library and also of the athletic office of the Dayton Board of Education.

The study eventually involved the long-gone rivalry between Steele and Stivers High Schools which dominated the picture until 1939.

Before Steele high school was constructed in 1892-93, Central was the only school with grades 9-12.

A publication known as the *High School Times*, published by the Philomathean Society of Central, and dating back to Volume 1 in 1882, provided much of the material for Lindenwald's well-researched paper. It refers to games between the Reds and Blues on Thanksgiving day.

Lindenwald also found an article in the *Dayton Daily Democrat* of Nov. 10, 1879 of a game between high school teams from Dayton and Cincinnati. But that game had to have been played under rugby rules as football rules for scholastic teams had not yet been drawn up.

When the high school students moved into the new Steele building in 1893, football was more of a student-run than administration-run operation and continue so for several years.

In 1895 the *Dayton Evening Herald* reported an 8-6 Steele victory over Xenia in the first mention of the Steele team playing another high school team. By 1899 the Lions played a six-game schedule and won five, tying Cincinnati Walnut Hills in one of two games with that school. There was a 10-0 road win over Delaware High School, which had claimed the southern Ohio championship the year before.

Steele enjoyed considerable success against such as Troy, Piqua, Springfield and several Cincinnati schools over the next five seasons.

The opening of East High School in 1906 provided the Lions with their most celebrated rival. When the new building was finished in 1908, Stivers was located on East Fifth Street, where it still serves as a middle school. The name wasn't changed to Stivers until 1908, but the Steele-Stivers series began on Sept. 28, 1907 when Steele handed the young Stivers-to-be team a 38-0 beating.

The *Dayton Daily News* reported a crowd of only 400 on that Saturday afternoon. Eventually the series attained the status of a classic and became an annual Thanksgiving Day attraction climaxing the high school season.

The lineups from that first game included for Steele: Zehring and Deeter, ends; McCartney and Oelman, tackles; Kiefaber and Caton, guards; Whitmore center; Rice, Lytle, Wise and Stover, backs. For East: Winn and Hartner, ends; Bryant and Ulen, tackles; Kohr and Conklin, guards; Schneyer, center; Hall, Banta, Walters and Marquardt, backs.

Steele rolled just as easily in 1908 with a 43-0 victory and won again a year later by a more respectable score of 16-6.

Stivers, the "new kid on the block" scored its initial win in 1910, and was enroute to three decades of overall excellence in football, basketball and other sports. What made the series memorable for the community was the excitement stirred up by the student bodies of both schools.

The Steele lion, the bronze statue of the King of the Jungle, which stood by the steps of the architecturally classic old Steele building at Main and Monument, was often painted orange overnight in the week before the game. By the same token, the Stivers building would find itself festooned with red and black streamers.

Beyond that, for well over 30 years up to World War II, most native Daytonians grew up attending one or the other of the schools and the Steele-Stivers rivalry was a topic of conversation involving doctors, lawyers, teachers and businessmen well into the 1960s before their sons and daughters started attending suburban schools.

A partial listing of Steele athletes who made headlines over the years includes Earl Blaik, later to be the famous Dartmouth and West Point coach; Tom Sharkey, a sprinter on the 1932 Olympic team while attending Miami University; Dick Johnson, who died on the infamous Bataan Death March in World War II and Art Valpey, who went on to play at Michigan. Add to the list of familiar names those of Ollie Klee, Jack Keefer, Eddie Sauer, Harry Zavakos (victim of a famous unsolved Dayton murder), Clyde (Chief) Gehring, Dr. Tish Hoerner, Horace Lytle, Walter Oelman, Bob Metzger and E. J. Reynolds.

The Stivers list includes Carley Cramer and Joe Cox who went on to Ohio State; Horace "Hawk" English who later coached both basketball and football at Stivers and the captain of that first team, Willard Marquardt, whose sons Bill and Dick coached in the city system with Bill becoming the top athletic administrator. There were also family performers: the three Schwab brothers, Harry, Harvey and Vernon, known as Bum; the Schear brothers; the Supensky brothers and Toby and Gifford Leap. Other familiar names include Ray Otto, Max Padlow, Kick Ramby, Harry Fenner, Pete Tidd, Bob Worst, Marty Armbruster, Sam Hermann, Jim Hanby and Herman Raiff among others.

Before the final game in 1939, the two schools had met 33 times with Stivers capturing 19, Steele 11 with three ties.

The rivalry began to get one-sided in its later years when enrollment at Steele declined with the likes of Roosevelt, Fairview, Kiser and Wilbur Wright High Schools draining the downtown school's enrollment.

The winner of the game could naturally claim the city championship in the early years but in 1934, Kiser broke through as champion.

Steele's last city championship is recognized as 1936 when the Lions defeated the Tigers, 7-0, with Harry "Tuffy" Brooks breaking away on a 73-yard off tackle play. After playing at Indiana University, Brooks came back to Dayton and spent his life in the sporting goods business, his firm still operative as this was being written.

The year before Brooks' dash, Steele had also won by the score of 6-0 with the touchdown scored by Jim Thornton on a 30-yard run. The *Dayton Daily News* described Thornton as "a colored sophomore halfback."

One of the memorable earlier games occurred in 1923 when Stivers went into the game 9-0 and Steele 8-0-1. Rol Bevan was the Steele coach and Harry Wilhelm directed the Tigers. Some 8,000 fans overflowed Triangle Park despite a steady rain. Stivers emerged an 8-6 winner.

Harry L. Kennedy, writing in the *Dayton Journal*, said the playing field resembled a lake. Steele scored first for a 6-0 lead but Stivers got on the board with a safety when Whitmore was tackled in the end zone. In the final quarter, Ray Otto, the Stivers quarterback, scored on a touchdown pass from Ken Stiles, the play covering 23 yards. It needs to be pointed out that in those days the signal calling quarterback was a blocker rather than a ball carrier or passer.

The captain of Steele's 1923 team was Russ Young, who starred in three sports and made professional baseball his career choice. He made it to the big leagues as a catcher with the St.Louis Browns in 1931. Neither team knew the 1939 meeting would be the last, the announcement that Steele would be closed wasn't made until the spring of 1940.

Carl "Dutch" Davis, whose father had played for Stivers years before, was the hero in a 13-0 game played before 6,500 people in the UD Stadium. The Tigers had been clear favorites and were expected to win by a bigger score.

Kiser's intrusion as the first acknowledged city champ other than the Steele-Stivers duo came after a hard fought 13-9 conquest of the Tigers in the 1934 season. The week before the game coach Dutch Lee's Panthers had shown offensive power in a 25-7 conquest of Chaminade in Fuzzy Faust's second year. Kiser captain Ray Reeder returned the second half kickoff 85 yards for a touchdown and later scored on a 29-yard run.

Joe Bryan was the Panther tailback and threw a scoring pass to the other halfback, Julius Galas in that game. In the upset over Stivers a week later, Galas reversed his role on a trick play and threw a touchdown pass to John Gaylor.

Some confusion exists in the way the high school records define city champions in the 1940s and 1950s.

Chaminade's dynasty under Fuzzy Faust is treated separately in this history. In those years the Eagles competed regularly against the city's public schools and were considered a member of what was known in the newspapers up to World War II as the Big Six.

As new schools were added it became the Big Seven, then the Big Eight and finally the Dayton Public League. But most of the time the newspapers referred to it simply as the City League although that was never an official designation. It wasn't until the early 1960s that the records in the athletic office of the Dayton school system dropped any reference to Chaminade as a league member.

For example, Kiser is listed as the city champion in a five-year stretch (1945-49) but the Panthers lost to Chaminade in all five of those seasons, as did the other city schools. Kiser football, however, was top caliber all through the 1940s under coach Bill Stover, who eventually became principal there.

In 1946, four Kiser standouts made the All-City team: Roy Hortman, Russ Johnson, Joe Horvath and Ron Brookey. Brookey, who lettered four years in three sports, later became the first football and longtime baseball coach at Meadowdale.

Kiser's home football field, formally designated Athletic Field, is remembered by veteran football followers as the infamous "Smoke Bowl." Situated between the school building and the north-south railroad tracks of the B & O railroad, fans in the stands were often showered by soot from the coal-burning locomotives of passing trains. At times under certain wind conditions, play had to be halted to permit the smoke to blow away.

Going back to the start of the Big Six, Roosevelt started its athletic programs in 1926 with Paul "Putty" Nelson as the first coach. One of Roosevelt's early stars was Alex Rado, who played his college ball at New River State in West Virginia then played on the original Pittsburgh Steelers team in 1933. Rado became a familiar figure wearing a striped officiating shirt in both football and basketball in later years.

Fairview under coach Roy Mayberry got started in 1933 with a bang with a memorable upset of Stivers. Fullback Joe Keller scored both Bulldog TD's. But Fairview didn't get a whiff of the title until 1937, sharing it with Roosevelt before winning it outright in 1939. Both Rado and Mayberry died in 1995 as this book was being written.

Mayberry's Bulldogs developed strong teams in the late 1930s around a remarkable family: the seven Brown brothers, all close in age, who played from the mid-1930s through 1943. The best of the group and one of the finest players who ever came from Dayton was Howard (Goon) Brown. The nickname was from a comic cartoon character of the time in the Popeye strip.

Brown was a punishing fullback on offense and played various defensive positions in high school. When he turned up at Indiana in the fall of 1941, he was converted into a two-way lineman and played as a freshman under Bo McMillin. Drafted into the army as a combat infantryman, he fought in the European theater and was wounded three times.

He returned to Indiana with a medical discharge to play on the undefeated 1945 team, the only one in IU football annals. He captained both the 1946 and 1947 Hoosier teams and then played four years in the NFL, following coach McMillin to the Detroit Lions. He returned to his alma mater in 1951 as freshman football coach, staying on the staff under six different head coaches until he died of a heart attack in 1976. His plaque in the IU Hall of Fame refers to him as "Mr. Indiana."

The other six Browns included fullback Bob, a 1942 Fairview grad who was killed in the war, George, Clarence Jr., Lloyd, Don and Fred. Four of that group went on to play college football.

Fairview had a unique offensive weapon for the time in kicker Bill Seremetis, who surely was the first soccer style placekicker in Dayton. Described in the *Dayton Daily News* as "a ponderous, swarthy tackle who learned to kick on the soccer fields of his native Greece," he kicked four field goals in the 1940 season: three of them were game winners in 3-0 scores over Kiser, Stivers and Cincinnati St. Xavier.

After World War II, a great social and demographic change was in the works in America and the face of high school football in Dayton drastically changed. In the process, all of the original Big Six members lost their old identities.

Steele, of course, disappeared. Stivers, Fairview and Kiser became middle schools. Roosevelt had a new role as a multi-purpose building shared by the board and the city recreation department. Chaminade remained a high school but was combined with the former all-girl Julienne.

Fairmont had come on strong just before the war but the post-war growth eventually split the Kettering district school into two high schools. The population shift and growth led to the likes of Centerville, Wayne, West Carrollton, Beavercreek, Vandalia-Butler and Stebbins becoming top level competitors. Alter and Carroll joined Chaminade as parochial high schools.

Within the city Dunbar, previously denied league membership because of the racial segregation policies, became a league member and new high schools like Meadowdale, Belmont, Colonel White and Roth emerged. Because of population shifts and busing, the changes never completely subsided as Roth went back to a middle school and Colonel White's status changed back and forth.

Biggest Crowd - Biggest Game

It was the development of the Colonel White Cougars in the late 1950s that led to the biggest crowd ever to see a high school football game in southwestern Ohio.

The clash between Jim Eby's Cougars and the Chaminade Eagles on November 19, 1960 attracted 17,822 paid admissions into Welcome Stadium, which had a listed capacity of 12,000. The stadium, named for Perc B. Welcome, an administrator who headed the city schools athletic operation, had been dedicated in 1949 during an East-West All-Star game, a Thanksgiving Day feature for a few years. Bill Marquardt, who had replaced Welcome as administrator of athletics, verified the overflow crowd by the number of tickets sold.

The emotional tempo for the game represents the zenith of interest in local high school football. College football on television was limited at the time and professional football had not yet come to Cincinnati.

Chaminade had continued to field strong teams after Ed Regan replaced Fuzzy Faust. Regan compiled a 52-23-5 record and won league titles in 1957 and 1958. Leading up to that showdown with Colonel White, the Eagles had announced their intention to drop out of the city league to play an independent schedule.

The week before the game, the Eagles added fuel to the emotional fire with an 88-0 blasting of Stivers, the worst defeat that once proud program ever suffered. It might have been worse had not the Chaminade third team played the fourth quarter.

Followers of other city schools, weary of losing to the Eagles, were overjoyed at the prospect of the Cougars being favored to thwart Chaminade's bid for one final league championship.

Colonel White had fielded its first team in 1956 and in only four years the softspoken Eby had built a powerful team that ranks among Dayton's best ever. Although Roosevelt had knocked off the Eagles earlier that year, it wasn't a case of Chaminade coming down to Colonel White's level, it was the Cougars building up to the Eagles level.

Colonel White was led on offense by its great tailback Jimmy Ratliff and slick quarterback Bill Gaines, running an option "belly series" attack. On the offensive line the Cougars had George Pavlakos, John Weaver and Pat Langley with Mike Hershey and Butch Baldasarre passing targets for Gaines when he wasn't handing off to Ratliff or carrying himself. Terry Meyer, Dick Bodey and Bob Klein were key defenders along with Baldasarre, who played both ways.

Colonel White fulfilled the expectations of their city-wide enthusiasts with a 32-12 win that really was never in doubt. Gaines helped set up the first touchdown with a 44-yard run deep into Chaminade territory and later threw two touchdown passes. No high school game since has come close to attracting that kind of attention or coverage. The *Journal Herald* had three staffers involved.

Colonel White's 10-0 was the first "perfecta" in city league competition since the Eagles had turned the trick in 1945. There wouldn't be another until Meadowdale put together consecutive 10-0 seasons in 1976-1977 under coach George Kellar, who had been a backup player with Colonel White that historic night in 1960.

"I learned a great deal playing for coach Eby," Kellar said, looking back on his own coaching achievements.

Quarterback Jim Johnson who directed the 1976 Meadowdale offense so capably, did not play college football but went to Tennessee on a baseball scholarship. Fullback Tim Campbell went on to play at Marshall University, Fred Motley played at Michigan and tackle Denver Smith starred at Indiana. Smith met a tragic end, fatally wounded by police in a domestic struggle near his apartment on the Indiana campus.

Kellar retired from coaching to go into business, having achieved a 51-16-1 record in seven seasons. Pat Masters came on to have a successful 17-year run at Meadowdale. His teams won the league title nine times and his overall record was 98-50-2.

"I'm more proud of the fact that 52 of my players earned Division I scholarships," Masters said. One of those was defensive back Sheldon White, who played at Miami and had eight years in the NFL. Linebacker Derrick Bunch became a regular at Michigan State and also went into the pro league.

The Dunbar Experience

The high school named for Dayton's famous poet, Paul Laurence Dunbar, opened in 1933 for Negro students at a time segregation was sadly a part of our way of life. At the time, the descriptive word black was considered insulting and it took a half century for the term African-American to come into use.

In the beginning, there was no athletic competition with white high schools either in or out of Dayton for the school on Summit Street. The street name was later to changed to Paul Laurence Dunbar Avenue.

Frederic C. MacFarlane, Dunbar's first principal, designated Stanglaws Slater as coach of all three school sports: football, basketball and track. This sentence from the program observing Dunbar's 50th anniversary describes conditions,

"Athletes of the era wore hand-me-down uniforms and travelled hundreds of miles to get to games, using any means of transportation available."

Games were played against segregated schools in Covington, Ky, Louisville, Evansville, Cleveland, Cincinnati and Indianapolis.

Dunbar's first football team included Luther Craft, Charles Stokes, Theodore Christian, John Clark, Ernest Crawford, Russell Brown, John Pullins, Edward Rice, Bill Farrell, Elmer Sallee, Joe Clark, Bill Woods, Carvin Crowe, Lofton Hill, Dog (correct) Brown, Sterling Brown, J. H. Regulus, Randolph Blackburn, S. D. Johnson, John Twiley, J. C. Young, James Green and others. The same athletes made up the roster in the other two sports plus M. Lucas.

The first real breakthrough to get Dunbar into the high school mainstream occurred when David D. Albritton, a former Ohio State Olympian and 1936 silver medal winner in Berlin, joined the faculty and was soon to build his reputation as a track coach.

In May of 1947, the athletic board of the Board of Education granted Dunbar a membership in the league and that fall Fairview and Wilbur Wright played the Wolverines in football for the first time. Albritton's 1948 track team won the state championship (covered in the Track and Field chapter) and in 1949, the Dunbar basketball team won the city league championship.

Coach Jack Hart's football team shared the Public League championship with Roosevelt in 1950 and Dunbar went on to make its mark as one of the successful high school programs over the years.

The story of Tom Montgomery, the Dunbar coach going into the 1995 season, sheds some light on the shifting of coaching personnel that makes it difficult for people to follow Dayton high school sports over the last 30 years.

Montgomery came to Dayton from Anniston, Alabama in 1971, hired by Thomas Webb, the Roosevelt principal and administrator who believed that athletic participation can be a useful tool in the education process. The Teddies were 20-14 in the four seasons the Alabama native was head coach (1971-74) including a share of one league title.

"I rank my 1972 team as one of my four best ever," says the man who went on to coach at Roth before assuming his present role.

"There were 12 players off that team who went on to college, not all of them played football. I'm proud of that group" Montgomery put it. The all-city players from that team included Bobby Packnett, Roosevelt Kelley, Sidney Beck, Charles Sandrick, Michael Ramey and Tozell Franklin.

When it was announced Roosevelt was closing in the spring of 1975, there was a coaching shuffle which found Montgomery assigned to Roth, where he was an assistant coach to Dave Henderson for two years before taking over as head coach in 1977. Mike Haley, who was to coach four state basketball champions, moved to Roth at the same time as did the late Don Mitchell, an outstanding track coach.

"In my last year at Roosevelt, the senior class voted me Teacher of the Year," Montgomery said, emphasizing teacher rather than coach.

Keith Byars, the future Ohio State star, was a sophomore in Montgomery's first year (as a transfer from Trotwood-Madison) and was the tailback on successive 10-0 teams his junior and senior seasons. Cedric Manuel was voted the MVP of the 1980 team and went to Ohio State at the same time Byars did, but as a track man not a gridder.

"Then when it was announced that Roth was going to be a middle school, it marked the second program I'd closed down. None of the other coaches wanted to follow me to Dunbar," Montgomery said with a laugh. But he took over in the unusual combination of head football and girls basketball coach, and enjoys coaching the latter as much as the former.

In his decade there, he coached seven league champions and shared another, but is most proud of starting the study table for the athletes.

"I can look back on my players and they fall into three general categories, those who went on to college, those who wound up in the streets selling drugs or those who were killed on the streets," the coach says.

He rates his 1972 Roosevelt, the 1980 Roth and the 1986 and 1990 Dunbar teams as his favorites although a couple of others had better records than the 1986 team that lost the city title to Meadowdale.

South Suburban Football

Oakwood, West Carrollton and Fairmont started their football pro-grams with pickup games in the early 1920s. Fairmont was situated then in Van Buren Township long before the city of Kettering was established with the population growth after World War II.

In 1924, Fairmont fielded its first organized football team with a publicized schedule. It was coached by William (Bill) Ramsey, later a pro-fessor at Miami University and Dwight L. Barnes, who went on to serve 42 years in the school system, eventually as superintendent of the Kettering city schools. In the late 1920s, Fairview, then not yet a Dayton city school, competed against Oakwood and Fairmont is what was called the Little Three Suburban league.

Fairmont's early success was under Chester (Pop) Warner, who in his 18 years compiled an 85-58-18 record. Coach Warner won three league championships including an undefeated/untied season in 1939. By then Fairmont had joined the newly organized Miami Valley League, the other charter members being Greenville, Miamisburg, Oakwood, Piqua, Sidney, Troy and Xenia.

Hadley Watts coached Dragon football for six seasons starting in 1942 and later became principal, then Superintendent, of Centerville schools. Fairmont's high watermark years on the grid came when Chester A. (Chet) Roush took over in 1948. He had launched his coaching career with two successful seasons at Randolph High, which became part of the Northmont system.

Roush's teams won two MVL league championships and enjoyed a perfect 1951 season before he went into the administrative side. He later served 17 years as superintendent of the Kettering system and was a mem-ber of the state Board of Education.

From 1952 through 1963, Fairmont fielded strong teams under a parade of coaches: Jack Fouts, Dave Puddington, Pete Ankney, Jim Hoover and Bob Hildreth, all of whom moved into college coaching. Ankney's undefeated 1959 team finished third in the state Associated Press rankings.

In 1963, Fairmont formed two high schools, Fairmont East and West. The two schools were partially responsible for the formation of the Western Ohio League which also included Beavercreek, Fairborn, Wayne, Stebbins, Springfield North and Xenia. Eventually Centerville and Spring-field South joined.

After 20 years the two Fairmont high schools were consolidated. Fairmont East's finest season came in 1972 under coach Doug Schmidt when they captured the WOL title. Fairmont West won the league in 1974 with a perfect record under coach Dick Hoppe. The East's Firebirds also won the title in 1967 and 1975.

Fairmont's stadium was dedicated Oct. 1, 1937 with Federal funds provided by the Public Works Administration of the Great Depression years. It was gradually expanded over the years. The last major change came in 1970 on a $40,000 grant from the Foreman Family. Charles (Bo) Foreman had been a Fairmont player in the 1950s. The stadium is called Foreman Field in his memory.

The biggest crowd in stadium history is believed to be the 8,000 who saw the Fairmont and Troy teams battle it out for the WOL title in 1951. Both were undefeated going into the game and Fairmont won, 19-0.

The Dragons, as they were known then, built up a fine rivalry with Chaminade and the Fairmont-Chaminade game in 1951 drew 14,000 fans into the new Welcome Stadium. It was a battle of coaching giants, Roush and Fuzzy Faust. Fairmont was the 7-6 winner, the edge provided when the Dragons blocked the Chaminade point-after-try late in the fourth quarter.

Many fine athletes played for Fairmont over the years. One of the best was defensive back Chet Moeller, a 1972 graduate who went on to the Naval Academy and earned consensus first team All-American honors in 1975. Earlier, Jim Irons had played at West Point and retired as a general.

The school produced two Little All-Americans in Tony Hall (1959), a running back at Denison and Rodney Miller (1963), a wide receiver at Wittenberg. Hall is the long-time congressman representing Ohio's Third District.

John Roush (1967) was a first team Academic All-American fullback at Ohio University. A number of Fairmont players made it into the NFL including Calvin Withrow, Bruce Puterbaugh, Jack Micklos, John D. Hoke, Rob Taylor and Kyle Kramer.

The Lumberjacks Of Oakwood

Oakwood launched its football program back in 1923 with only modest success until the arrival of Ed Cook in 1930. Cook, a Michigan native, had shared the Olympic pole vault gold medal in 1908 with fellow American, A. Gilbert at the height of 12 feet and 2 inches.

Cook coached the Lumberjacks into the war years and in his 12 seasons had three undefeated teams, the first coming in 1935 with a record of 9-0-1. Powerful fullback Bob Stein was the headline maker.

Oakwood had a strong team in 1940 led by Chris Stephen, one of the school's finest all-around athletes. He went on to play at Ohio University and to enjoy a successful career in high school coaching and administration. Other big names over the years at Oakwood were Wid Worthington and Rod Boren.

It was Cook's 1942 powerhouse that arguably was the best ever. With Johnny Sauer at quarterback, the team averaged 46 points per game, amassing 417 points to a mere 13 for the opposition on their 9-0 cakewalk. They were clearly the dominant team in the region that year.

"We were never challenged," says Sauer looking back. Tailback Gates Thruston along with Connie Vanderberg and Bud Sorensen made up the backfield with Sauer. Thruston scored three touchdowns in the 27-0 conquest of archrival Fairmont.

"Sorensen, one of my best friends, took an appointment to the Naval Academy," recalled Sauer, who went to West Point and played on the great teams led by Doc Blanchard and Glenn Davis. "Navy converted him to offensive center. Every year before the big game (Army vs. Navy) we shook hands out there before all those people."

Sam Andrews of Stivers basketball fame replaced Cook as Oakwood coach for the next six years. The area to the south (Van Buren township) was exploding in population during the war and Fairmont began to dominate the traditional rivalry. Oakwood was taking its lumps from other teams in the Miami Valley League and in 1953 withdrew from the circuit, dropping Fairmont from the schedule among others. With an easier schedule, coach Ed Wysocki's team surprised everyone by going 9-0.

Jim Schindler captained that 1953 team and Doug Teegarden was the passer. He connected with Frank Sargent for the TD in 7-0 win over West Milton. The Lumberjacks gave indication of what kind of a year it would be with a 7-0 upset of Fairborn in the second game of the season with Skip Waltz scoring the touchdown. Later, Waltz ran for all four touchdowns in a 27-0 homecoming victory over Trotwood-Madison.

Other standouts on the team included Pete Davidson, Brad Boen, Bill Oelman, Dave Greer and Charles Keck. The perfect record wasn't equalled until 1985 when Howard Sales coached the Lumberjacks to a 10-0 record and a spot in the state playoffs.

The Centerville Story

When Bob Gregg was a 140-pound running back at Centerville back in 1950, the school was small enough to be in class B and there was open country between the new suburb of Kettering and Centerville. The area grew up quickly, but the Centerville football program didn't really grow up until it hired alumnus Gregg to take it over in 1973. Gregg, who had played college football at Wilmington, was coming off successive 10-0 seasons at Jefferson, also a class B school to the southwest of the city.

In a dozen years at Jefferson, Gregg compiled an 82-27 record, won seven league championships and built a reputation as a no-nonsense disciplinarian. When he returned to Centerville, friends warned him he would have to soften his hard edges, that the young men from affluent Centerville would have to be handled differently than those with whom he had worked from blue collar backgrounds.

As for becoming more diplomatic with his rivals, the media, his rival coaches, parents, officials, whoever, Gregg had one way of direct response, "I'm not a phoney, I say what I think. That's part of my personality."

Before his first season opened, Bob was quoted in the *Journal Herald* about coming into the strong Western Ohio League, "There ain't no National Trails in this league," he said. The reference was to the Preble County school just getting into football that Gregg's Jefferson team had beaten 71-0 and 61-0.

In his first season, the Elks went 3-7 and then improved to 4-6 as Gregg started to weed out the candidates who didn't want to toughen up. The coach was on record he patterned himself after Vince Lombardi and the iron discipline Lombardi exercised over the professional Green Bay Packers.

The turnaround became evident in Gregg's third season. The athletes from up-scale families who drove to school in their own cars began to pay the physical price to get into Gregg's hit 'em hard style. The highly successful soccer program had to share the spotlight in the fall months. By 1976, the Elks achieved the first of Gregg's four 10-0 seasons and were into a run of 10 straight years when they either won outright or shared the WOL championship.

In 1977, he was voted Coach of the Year in his division by the Ohio Associated Press. By 1980 he was the first Dayton area coach to schedule

Cincinnati Moeller when Gerry Faust's powerhouse was towering over the rest of Ohio prep football. The Elks lost their first meeting to Moeller, 20-14, the year before Faust moved up to Notre Dame. The two schools opened the 1981 season in a game that drew an overflow crowd of 7,840 in the Elks stadium. Moeller won that game, 21-7, on a rainy night, converting five fumbles and two interceptions into their scores.

In 1984 the Elks gained a victory over Moeller in the playoffs but lost to eventual Division I winner Toledo St. Francis DeSales in the semifinal. Dunbar knocked them out of the playoffs in 1986 but they got into the championship game in 1991, losing a 24-21 struggle to Cleveland St. Ignatius. Moeller knocked them out of the playoffs in 1993.

Gregg's overall record at this writing is 265-77 for a 77 per cent average. His Centerville record for 22 seasons is 181-47 for 79 per cent.

Two of his quarterbacks, Gary Alders and Kirk Herbstreit, went to Ohio State with the latter leading the Bucks to an 8-3-1 season in 1992. Other standout athletes from Gregg's tenure include Jeff Felton, Andy Harmon, Matt Cravens, Kent Bruggeman, Matt Bradley, Chris Forgy, Greg Wofford, George Reinke, Bill Price and David Morrell.

The Schneiders Of Miamisburg

Henry (Hank) Schneider was born in Miamisburg in 1917 and went through the school system in that community. He quarterbacked Miamisburg High through a 28-game winning streak and went on to the University of Cincinnati on a football scholarship.

World War II interrupted his college stay and he spent three and a half years in the service before returning to UC where he played his senior year. He started a 40-year coaching career as an assistant at Miamisburg in 1947. Two of Hank's four sons went into coaching.

Son Dave became head coach at Cincinnati Withrow. Son Mike started as an assistant to his father, then became head coach at Miamisburg (1976-1980) before moving on to Wayne where he has established the Warriors as a power in the tough Western Ohio League. All told, 42 of Hank's former students and players went into coaching.

During his tenure as Miamisburg head coach (1952-1960) he was 50-23-3 and his 1952 team won the MVL championship.

Hank replaced Ed Regan at Chaminade in 1961 before moving on to Waynesville for two years before his final stop at Stebbins (1971-77) before retiring. He is a member of the Ohio High School Coaches Hall of Fame.

Some of his better known players from Miamisburg include Jim Dickey, who went on to play at Michigan and is into high school coaching in that state, Doug Schmidt who has been a high school coach at Miamisburg, Fairmont East and Fairmont High Schools. Jack Van Buren and Doug Rice played at UC and both went into high school coaching.

At Chaminade he coached Gary Arthur who was an all-MAC pass receiver at Miami and played in the NFL with the New York Jets, plus Mike Clark who went on to captain the U.S. Naval Academy team.

Going into the 1995 season, Mike Schneider owned a 110-32-3 record at Wayne, including six league championships. In his 14 years there, the Wayne-Centerville game has decided the league title in 11 of those seasons. The rivals stood 7-7 when these figures were put together.

Among those who played for Mike at Wayne are Greg Shackleford, an academic All-American and team captain at Ball State, Roosevelt Mukes Jr., who became the all-time career pass reception leader at Cincinnati, and Eric Dixon who played at Southern California.

Ned Booher And The Rest

Northmont built a strong program when Ned Booher launched a 24-season run as head coach in 1962. His first team went 8-2 and then jumped to 10-0 the next year, winning the Southwestern Buckeye League championship. This was the first of Booher's five 10-0 perfect season teams, winning him championships in three different leagues.

The three leagues are part of the shifting patterns. Booher's 1963 team was quarterbacked by Eddie Swope and featured John Kelly as its standout lineman. Darvin Marshall later became mayor of Phillipsburg, one of the communities that once had its own high school but is part of the Northmont consolidation.

Booher's second perfect season came in 1970 and one of its players, tight end Eddie Kain, went on to Ohio State and played in three consecutive Rose Bowls.

Four Swafford brothers, Don, Dan, Doug and Darrell played for the Thunderbolts at different times. Don went to the University of Florida and played pro football in Canada, Doug was a regular at Indiana and Dan played for Mike Kelly at UD. Dave Palsgrove, Stan Hunter, Mark Lucas,

Steve Magateaux and Phil Nussman are other familiar names from the T-Bolt tradition.

Coach Booher moved to California and coached football at Notre Dame High School in Riverside before giving up coaching to become athletic director at this writing.

Alter started its football program in 1964 under coach Bill Rankin and it was nearly as successful as the basketball program. When Rankin's Knights knocked off Chaminade in 1965 in an 8-2 season, their fans knew the program was on solid ground.

Jeff Graham, who went on to Ohio State and went into the NFL with the Pittsburgh Steelers and more recently the Chicago Bears, might be Alter's most prominent football grad. But brothers Tim and Dan Quinn, who went on to play a lot of football at UD, also played for the Knights.

Among the other coaches who had lengthy tenure around Dayton were Jack Hollon at Vandalia, Bill Fredrick at Wilbur Wright, Ron Bradley at Fairview and Lloyd (Punky) Williams at Fairborn.

Jim Place, onetime standout UD lineman, is the most recent coach to continue the winning tradition at C-J. He also coached at Stebbins and Middletown.

Boys Football City Champions

YEAR	SCHOOL	YEAR	SCHOOL
1930	Stivers	1964	Roth
1931	Stivers	1965	Belmont
1932	Steele	1966	Belmont
1933	Steele	1967	Dunbar
1934	Kiser	1968	Dunbar
1935	Stivers	1969	Belmont
1936	Steele	1970	Patterson,Roth,Belmont
1937	Fairview, Stivers	1971	Dunbar, Patterson, Wil-
1938	Fairview		bur Wright
1939	Kiser	1972	Meadowdale, Roth
1940	Fairview	1973	Roth, Belmont
1941	Fairview, Roosevelt	1974	Belmont, Fairview
1942	Kiser,Roosevelt	1975	Belmont, Roth
1943	Fairview,Wilbur Wright	1976	Meadowdale
1944	Kiser,Roosevelt	1977	Meadowdale
1945	Kiser	1978	Meadowdale, Belmont,
1946	Kiser		Roth
1947	Kiser	1979	Meadowdale
1948	Kiser	1980	Roth
1949	Kiser	1981	Roth
1950	Dunbar, Roosevelt	1982	Dunbar, Meadowdale
1951	Kiser	1983	Meadowdale
1952	Stivers	1984	Dunbar
1953	Roosevelt	1985	Meadowdale
1954	Stivers	1986	Meadowdale
1955	Roosevelt	1987	Dunbar
1956	Roosevelt	1988	Dunbar
1957	Dunbar, Roosevelt	1989	Dunbar
1958	Roosevelt	1990	Dunbar
1959	Colonel White	1991	Dunbar
1960	Colonel White	1992	Meadowdale
1961	Dunbar	1993	Meadowdale
1962	Dunbar	1994	Meadowdale
1963	Roth	1995	Dunbar

The Steele - Stivers Rivalry

1907	Steele 39	Stivers 0
1908	Steele 45	Stivers 0
1909	Steele 16	Stivers 6
1910	Stivers 13	Steele 0
1911	Stivers 12	Steele 0
1912	Steele 7	Stivers 7
1913	Stivers 13	Steele 7
1914	Steele 9	Stivers 7
1915	Stivers 44	Steele 0
1916	Stivers 27	Steele 10
1917	Stivers 0	Steele 0
1918	Steele 10	Stivers 6
1919	Steele 33	Stivers 0
1920	Steele 28	Stivers 0
1921	Steele 26	Stivers 6
1922	Steele 0	Stivers 0
1923	Stivers 8	Steele 6
1924	Stivers 49	Steele 0
1925	Stivers 28	Steele 0
1926	Stivers 6	Steele 0
1927	Stivers 13	Steele 0
1928	Stivers 13	Steele 0
1929	Stivers 25	Steele 0
1930	Stivers 6	Steele 0
1931	Stivers 19	Steele 0
1932	Stivers 6	Steele 0
1933	Steele 9	Stivers 0
1934	Stivers 26	Steele 0
1935	Steele 6	Stivers 0
1936	Steele 7	Stivers 0
1937	Stivers 13	Steele 6
1938	Stivers 32	Steele 0
1939	Stivers 13	Steele 0

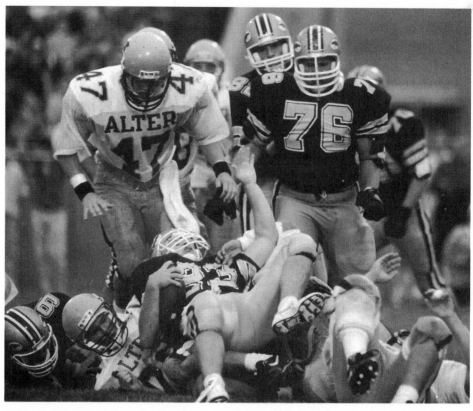

Fairmont back Pat Burke (with football) against suburban rival Alter (above).

Three outstanding high school football coaches: Bob Gregg of Centerville (left); Fuzzy Faust of Chaminade (center) and Chet Roush of Fairmont.

BASEBALL

8

Mike Schmidt

On a gorgeous summer afternoon that was picture perfect for baseball, Michael Jack Schmidt stood at the podium looking out over a sea of red, the biggest throng ever to witness a Hall of Fame induction ceremony.

This was July 30, 1995 at Cooperstown, New York and the sea of red was clothing and banners from Philadelphia Phillies followers who came in 200 chartered busses to pay homage to their greatest third baseman and greatest home run slugger.

Even though Cooperstown is 670 miles from Dayton, it was also the ultimate success story of our town's baseball history.

Mike Schmidt's journey to baseball's Valhalla began in tiny Ridgecrest Park on Pinecrest Drive in the Ridge-Siebenthaler area where Jack and Lois Schmidt raised their son, Mike, and their daughter, Sally.

Along the way, Mike hammered 548 home runs, putting him seventh on the all-time list. The six legendary sluggers ahead of him, Henry Aaron, Babe Ruth, Willie Mays, Frank Robinson, Harmon Killibrew and Reggie Jackson preceded him into the baseball shrine.

Dayton's greatest player did more than hit the ball out of the park.

The all-around athlete out of Fairview High School won ten Golden Gloves for his defensive heroics at third base. He was quick enough to steal 174 bases during his career and he drove in 1,595 runs. He holds numerous Philadelphia club and National League records.

In the beginning, Jack Fenner, Mike's first Little League coach, concedes he didn't detect the potential in the 10-year-old redhead. Bill Braley, who coached quarterback Schmidt on the Loos school 7th and 8th grade football teams, never gave Mike's baseball skills a second thought. Nor did Ron Bradley, the Fairview High School football coach, who was grooming Schmidt to play a role as a sophomore backup quarterback and safety.

That promise never developed when Mike, making his debut as a punt returner, fielded his first kick in a pre-season exhibition. He took two steps forward, stopped to make a cut, his knee gave way, and he crumpled in a heap underneath two tacklers.

The damage to his anterior ligament was sufficient to require surgery and he spent the next two months in a full leg cast.

By spring, he was a candidate for the baseball team where coach Dave Palsgrove saw potential, but certainly not at the Hall of Fame level. Nor did Lefty Gilliland, the veteran amateur pitcher who coached Fairview's summer league team.

Schmidt obviously had good all-around ability as evidenced by his basketball play his junior year under coach Don Barger, but he damaged his other knee that season. The mishap wasn't nearly as serious as the earlier injury, but it also required surgery.

As a senior with two gimpy knees, Schmidt passed up football and basketball in favor of baseball under coach Bob Galvin, who had taken over for Palsgrove.

The Fairview athlete attracting attention from pro scouts in the spring of 1967 was catcher Ron Neff. Future big league slugger Schmidt hit only one home run, but it decided the city league championship game.

There were no college scholarship offers coming Mike's way but enter Dr. Dave Reese, one of Dayton's legendary sports figures and at the time commissioner of the Mid-American Conference.

Reese, a friend of Mike's maternal grandfather, John Philipps, helped arrange for Mike to enroll at Ohio University, which had a great baseball program under outstanding coach Bob Wren.

Mike himself had not given up on the idea of trying his hand at all three sports at the college level. He was immediately disqualified in the physical examination for football because of his knees but he did play freshman basketball.

It didn't take Wren long to see Mike's true potential, and trainer Larry Starr was directed to set up a year-round exercise and conditioning program to strengthen the surgically repaired knees.

Starr, who left OU at almost the same time as Schmidt to begin a 20-year tenure with the Cincinnati Reds, made Mike a year-round project and Schmidt went on full scholarship going into his sophomore year.

"What we worked on was not just strength, but flexibility with good lateral movement," explained Starr, who was the trainer of the Florida Marlins as this was being written. "What we were thinking was not just getting Mike ready to play baseball, but to enable him to go through life without his knees giving him trouble," Starr summed up.

Later, during his days with the Phillies, Mike looked back on the OU program with gratitude. "I had one doctor tell me early in my pro career that I might have trouble walking by the time I was 50," he said. But he plays golf so well in his retirement that he has talked about taking a crack at the PGA Seniors Tour when he turns 50 in September, 1999.

When Mike returned to Dayton after his freshman year, he needed to get with a top level team in the DABC (Dayton Amateur Baseball Commission) to continue his development. But there were only four teams and league managers, remembering him as a very ordinary high school performer, showed no interest.

If going to OU was the flash point starting Mike on his way to the majors, the second jump start came from Ted Mills. Mills, who for several years had been coming up with the best area college players for his Parkmoor Restaurant team, had won the national NABF title the year before.

"Mike kept showing up at our practice with his spikes and glove, even though I told him we didn't have room for him," Mills recalled. "He was really so determined that I found a spot for him. Some of our older players thought I was crazy and my guy who had been playing shortstop quit the first time I put Mike in the lineup at that position," Mills went on.

What impressed Mills, as it did Wren at OU, was Mike's willingness to work on the weak spots of his game. Back at OU he had to be warned not to play on his fraternity (Beta Theta Pi) intramural teams. He was established as the Bobcat shortstop going into the Mid-American Conference season and quickly began to show himself as a premier player.

"Mike had that awesome God-given power and I'd never had a player with that much of it," said Wren, who had sent several other players to the majors including Rich McKinney (White Sox), Dick Murphy (Reds), Terry Harmon (Phillies) and Steve Swisher (Cubs).

In Schmidt's junior year, the Bobcats became the only Mid-American Conference team ever to make it into the NCAA College World Series. Schmidt wasn't the only Daytonian on that team. His good friend and roommate Tom Smith (Kiser) was the first baseman and Malcolm Smoot (Northmont) was the catcher.

If there was one flaw that tormented Mike about his game it was his tendency as a free-swinger to strike out. Coach Wren worked on that with varying success. "I wanted to convince Mike that he didn't have to pull everything to get his hits. By the time he was a junior, once in a while I'd give him a hit-and-run sign on certain counts even if no one was on base. The idea was, I wanted him to make contact.

"One day, on a 3-and-1 count in that situation, I gave him the sign. The pitch was outside, wasn't close to being a strike, but he drove it to right center over the trees back there."

Wren and the Hall of Famer have their own mutual respect society. "I might not have made it to the Hall of Fame if I hadn't come under the influence of Bob Wren," Schmidt said in a talk at the 25th reunion of the 1970 team.

"Players like Mike made me a winning coach," said Wren, who after his retirement at OU worked as a minor league instructor in the Philadelphia, Cincinnati and New York Yankee systems.

Even though Mike was a collegiate All-American as the 1971 summer draft approached, the history of his knee surgeries made a number of big league teams cautious about making him a first round selection.

Unfortunately, that included the Cincinnati Reds, who had a file on Mike that went back six years. The Reds first round selection in the 1971 draft was an infielder who never made it to the majors.

Schmidt's biggest booster was Tony Lucadello, a veteran scout for the Phillies who lived in Findlay, and had first seen Mike in high school, then watched his development at OU. Mike was the first player taken in the second round of the 1971 draft by the Phillies.

When Lucadello came to the Schmidt residence with the club's offer, including a modest $25,000 signing bonus, Jack Schmidt hesitated and wanted to negotiate a bit more of a bonus. Mike, who had to overcome so many early obstacles on his way, was anxious to get going and let his father know he was ready to sign. Mike and friend Tom Smith had gone to Cincinnati a week before the draft and trainer Larry Starr showed them the spacious Cincinnati locker room, whetting Mike's appetite to get into that environment.

Schmidt made his pro debut with the Reading, Pennsylvania farm team where in 74 games, he batted only .211 and hit eight home runs.

His solid college experience led the Phillies to let him skip the lowest two rungs in the farm system to play his first full season (1972) at the triple-A level at Eugene, Oregon in the Pacific Coast League. He hit 26 home runs and was promoted to the big league club in September, where he went to bat 34 times and savored his first home run off Montreal's Baylor Moore, September 16, 1972.

The Phillies had not yet determined his best defensive position, as he played at least one game in all four infield positions. In the 1973 season, his numbers weren't all that impressive: a .191 average and 145 strikeouts. But there were 18 home runs, a barometer of things to come.

When Reds manager Sparky Anderson watched him take batting practice in Riverfront Stadium the first time, he asked the front office, "How did this fellow from our backyard get away from us?"

Reminded of the scouting reports critical of Schmidt's tendency to strike out, Anderson retorted, "You don't see the kind of raw power this kid has without taking a chance."

Settled in his role at third base, Schmidt became a headliner quickly in 1974 when he led the NL in home runs for the first time with 36. He made the first of his 11 All-Star game appearances as a back-up selection.

The Phillies had been moribund as a franchise when Mike joined them, but they were slowly climbing into contending status with Schmidt an important factor.

In 1976 they won the NL Eastern Division but were wiped out in three straight games in the LCS (League Championship Series) by the Big Red Machine, then at its dominating best.

That division championship was the first of three in a row for the Phils, but they never got into the World Series, bowing twice to the Dodgers after their 1976 loss to the Reds.

As the club's attendance climbed, Schmidt was getting involved in a love-hate relationship with the emotional and often critical Philadelphia fans. They cheered his home runs but they booed his strikeouts and infrequent errors.

Mike's somewhat introverted personality was a factor in the problem. Always a low key individual, he often came across as an aloof or distant figure to Philly fans who tend to be emotional and like their heroes to display more enthusiasm than they saw in Schmidt. But the boos and media critics had no adverse effect on his performance.

Schmidt, perfectionist that he remained in setting his standards and judging himself, never seemed to be having fun in the eyes of his detractors.

The Phillies made a major financial investment in 1979 when they won the bidding war to sign free agent Pete Rose.

Schmidt believes the addition of Rose gave the club and himself the mental impetus to finally become World Series winners.

"I had watched, admired and respected Pete for years before I got to playing high school ball," Schmidt explained. "When I got to know him after I came up with the Phillies, I began to respect him even more.

"But I really never knew what he could mean to a team until he came to the Phillies. I learned a long time ago his hustle was for real, that he was always willing to be helpful to players on the other teams and that he enjoyed playing the game. But you have to be on the same team with him to really appreciate him.

"They put Pete on first base, which wasn't his normal or best position. But day after day you could see him taking ground balls with that built-in energy and enthusiasm. If he can do those things at age 40, I can put that much energy into helping myself. He gave us the example of what it takes to believe you can be the best," Schmidt summed it up.

The motivation certainly worked for Schmidt, who had the best year of his career in 1980 when the Phillies made it into the World Series after a 30-year struggle to duplicate the 1950 championship.

Mike had the greatest year of his career, leading the NL in home runs (48) and RBIs (121) and the World Series triumph over Kansas City. Mike batted .381, homered twice and had seven RBIs in the six-game series. That earned the Dayton native the first of his two league MVP awards, the other coming in 1986 when he again led in both of those prime offensive categories.

When the Phillies got back into the Series again in 1983, Mike had a strong year with 40 home runs and drove in 109 runs. But his bat went cold along with those of most of his teammates as the Baltimore Orioles ran over the Phils, winning the Series four games to one.

In the aftermath of that disappointment, Schmidt should have gained more respect from his media critics. Even though he had only one single in 20 at bats, he remained at his locker to be interviewed as long as any writers were around. Some of his teammates who had been critical of him in the past ducked into the medical rooms, off limits to the media. The post-season play in 1983 was to be the last for the Phillies during Mike's remaining active years.

There was only a slight drop-off in Mike's production through the next four seasons (1984-87) and he again led the league in home runs (37) and RBIs (119) in 1986. He hit his 400th home run in 1984 off Bob Welch of the Dodgers and his 500th in 1987 off Pittsburgh's Don Robinson. But there was a very noticeable decline in his play in 1988, the summer he turned 39. His average dropped off to .249 and his long ball production to 12, the lowest ever.

"I should have made my decision to retire in that off-season," he said later. But he went through a rigorous off-season conditioning routine and went through a punishing spring training. But the snap in his wrists as he swung the bat was never the same and after struggling through 42 games into the 1989 season, he announced his retirement.

It was Mike's typical way. He called it quits on the road, while the team was in San Diego. That decision made him wait an extra year to qualify for the Hall of Fame because a player must be retired for five seasons before his name appears on the ballot.

Schmidt was an easy first-time winner when the Baseball Writers Association, which conducts the vote, made its announcement in January, 1995.

Although he advised the Phillies he was interested in going into the front office, he was disappointed that no offer was made. Likewise, his offer to come to spring training to serve as a batting instructor for the minor league players wasn't accepted.

He lives in comfortable retirement in Jupiter, Florida in an upscale housing complex with wife Donna, daughter, Jessica, and son, Jonathan, who were 16 and 15 respectively watching their father go into the Hall of Fame.

It will be a long time, if ever, before a better third baseman shows up in Cooperstown.

Hall of Famer Jesse Haines when he pitched for the St. Louis Cardinals.

Hall of Famer Mike Schmidt of the Philadelphia Phillies.

9

Jesse Haines

"People said I'd become a bum, that I'd never amount to anything playing baseball."

That dire warning back in 1914 did not turn out to be accurate for Jesse Joseph Haines, the first Dayton-area native to reach the baseball Hall of Fame.

Haines, born in the village of Clayton in northwestern Montgomery County, July 22, 1893, pitched for the St. Louis Cardinals from 1920 through 1937 and later had a remarkable 28-year tenure as Montgomery County Auditor, an elective office.

He carried a lifetime 210-157 record when he was inducted into the Cooperstown shrine in 1970, the year Mike Schmidt became an All-American at Ohio University. At an even 6-feet, 190-pounds, Haines was considered a big athlete by the standards of his time.

He never lived anywhere but in the immediate area of the farm where he was born. He used his check from the winning share of the 1926 World Series ($5,584.71) to build a large white frame house "in town" -- along the main street of Phillipsburg.

To say that he held and lived by strong Middle American values would be an understatement.

There was no community high school to attend when Jesse finished grade school not long after the turn of the century so he was doing odd jobs when, despite his young age, he started to play with the older fellows on the town baseball team.

In the summers from 1911 through 1913 he pitched for teams in Dayton's loosely regulated semi-pro competition. Newspaper clippings show him pitching for the Standards, NCR and the Lilly Brews. Elmer Redelle, business manager of the Central League Dayton Vets, signed him to pitch the final game of the 1913 season.

Jesse's pro career really began in 1914 when he pitched for Saginaw in the Michigan State League. The next year this league folded but he had a tryout with the Detroit Tigers, who optioned him to Springfield in the Central League.

In an interview in 1965, he described pitching batting practice to Ty Cobb, the crusty veteran who rarely had a kind word for anyone. "As he walked out of the batting cage he said to me, 'Kid, you throw a ball that's hard to follow. You might go places later on'." He was referring to Haines' version of the knuckle ball.

Wearing a Springfield uniform, he pitched in 1916 and 1917 against Dayton's entry in the Central League, winning 43 games in those two seasons. He was expecting the Tigers to call him up, but they mailed him a one-sentence letter releasing him.

Given a tryout with the Reds, he pitched five scoreless innings in a game in 1918, but as he recalls it, "the man who signed me called me in afterwards and gave me my release," which again made him a free agent.

It was back to the minors, but the Cardinals purchased his contract from Kansas City of the American Association for $10,000 going into the 1920 season. The deal was engineered by Branch Rickey, who had been hired to handle the Cardinals in 1919.

At the time, the St. Louis club was the perennial doormat of the National League, never finishing higher than third place. The Cardinals were 54-83 in Rickey's first year as manager and the former catcher knew he needed pitching and had personally scouted Haines.

Rickey was just getting started in his brilliant career as an executive and, as it turned out, he kept Haines on the active roster until 1937 when Jesse was 44 as an influence on younger players, especially the pitchers.

Rickey was also starting to set up baseball's first farm system in the early 1920s. "He was the sharpest baseball mind it was my privilege to play for and get to know," Haines said often in later years.

The raw-boned Ohioan quickly moved into the starting rotation and worked 301.2 innings in his rookie season, posting a 2.98 ERA. But he had to settle for a 13-20 record with the weak club on the field behind him. An exception was young second baseman Rogers Hornsby. "The best hitter I ever saw," was Jesse's tribute to the controversial Texan.

A year later, in 1921, Haines was 18-12 and gaining respect as one of the quality pitchers in the eight team league.

He pitched a no-hitter against the Boston Braves July 17, 1924 in which Casey Stengel, then near the end of his career as a player, became the 27th out. It was the first Cardinal no-hitter in the 20th century.

By 1926, Rickey had assembled a team that won the first of what were to be many Cardinal pennants. Hornsby had taken over as player-manager as Rickey devoted his attention to the front office. It was a season in which Haines had some arm problems, but the Cards had solid pitching and a 20-game winner in Flint Rhem. They also acquired Grover Cleveland Alexander, then in his 16th season.

The 1926 World Series between the Cardinals and the New York Yankees, early in their climb to greatness, is regarded as a classic.

The series opened in Yankee Stadium with New York ace Herb Pennock (23-11) against St. Louis lefty Bill Sherdel and winning, 2-1. Haines pitched a scoreless eighth after Sherdel had been lifted for a pinch hitter.

Alexander pitched the Cards to a 6-2 victory in Game 2 and after a day off the series resumed in St. Louis on Tuesday, October 5. Haines not only pitched a five-hit shutout, but hit a two-run home run off loser Dutch Reuther for a 4-0 victory.

The Yankees won the next two games sending the series back to New York with the NL team down, three games to two.

Alexander came back with his second complete game victory to even the series at three games each and legend has it that Old Pete, as he was called by his teammates, celebrated that night as was his custom, confident he was finished with any further pitching responsibilities. Alexander's problems with alcohol were well-known, later documented in a motion picture in which he was portrayed by President-to-be Ronald Reagan.

Haines drew the starting assignment for the final game, matched against Waite Hoyt, later the long term radio broadcaster of the Cincinnati Reds. St. Louis held a 3-2 lead going into the last of the seventh, one of the Yankee runs being a homer by Babe Ruth.

Haines developed and broke a blister on his index finger from his knuckle ball grip. After manager Hornsby inspected Haines' pitching hand, to the surprise of everyone in the park including Alexander himself, Old Pete was summoned from the bullpen.

Alexander, nursing a king-size hangover, walked to the mound facing a two-out, bases loaded situation and struck out young Tony Lazzeri in what has become one of the game's enduring legends. Before Alex slipped the third strike past the Yankee second baseman, Lazzeri had missed a grand slam home run by a few feet on a smash that curved foul into the left field seats.

Alexander finished the game, preserving Haines' second series victory. The game and series ended when Ruth was caught stealing second base with two out in the last of the ninth.

Haines came back the following year with his best numbers ever, a 24-10 mark, but the Cards were edged by the Pittsburgh Pirates for the pennant.

St. Louis won again in 1928 and again faced the Yankees. This time the powerhouse Yankees, who had swept Pittsburgh four straight in the 1927 World Series, did the same thing to the Cards. Haines was the starter and loser in the third game.

Haines had what he considered his greatest World Series outing in 1930 against Connie Mack's Philadelphia A's. It came in the fourth game when he was matched against Lefty Grove, who had won 28 games that year and had beaten the Cardinals in the series opener.

"That was my career victory," Haines said often in later years of his 3-1 triumph. "My control was a little off and they left seven men on base. They had a great hitting lineup with Jimmy Foxx, Al Simmons, Mickey Cochrane and the other guys and I was pitching against the greatest pitcher in the game. I never saw a better pitcher than Grove in my years in the game."

At that time Haines was 37 and near the end of his regular spot in the starting rotation. New manager Gabby Street had strong and younger pitching depth in 1931 and Jesse became a spot starter. Still he compiled a 12-3 record but appeared in only 19 games. He was stepping into the role envisioned for him by Rickey. He was the pitching coach by example but without that designation.

In 1932, Jay Hanna Dean, soon to be known as Dizzy Dean, blazed on the scene like a whirlwind, destined to post winning totals of 18, 20, 30, 28 and 24 in the next five seasons.

"He was my first pitching coach," said Dean of Haines when he came to Dayton to speak at a banquet in 1969. "Of course, he wasn't a pitching coach because we didn't have one. But he was a rare one in that he tried to help the kids coming along. In those days veterans didn't do that. You were on your own. But Pop was different. He'd go out of his way to help you out."

Despite their differences in age and temperament, the veteran Haines and the youngster from deep in the Arkansas backwoods became good friends. "As hard as he threw, he didn't need much help," was the way Haines referred to Dizzy.

The Cardinals rebounded from two years in the second division by surging to the pennant in 1934 when the team was dubbed the "Gas House Gang." Dizzy won 30 games that year (30-7) and kid brother Paul, known as Daffy, won 19. Pepper Martin, the "Wild Horse of the Osage," and Joe "Ducky" Medwick helped make the Cards a colorful team.

Manager Frankie Frisch had no plans to pitch the then 41-year-old Haines, but used him for two-thirds of an inning in a 10-4 loss in the fourth game of the World Series against Detroit. The Cardinals won the seventh game and the series in a stormy 11-0 triumph pitched by Dizzy.

Haines remained an active pitcher on a limited basis for three more years and retired as owner of the club record for pitching victories with 210, later broken by Bob Gibson. In 1938, one of Jesse's good friends, former pitching standout Burleigh Grimes, was managing the Brooklyn Dodgers and offered his old friend a job as pitching coach.

Haines went to spring training in that role but D. C. Brower, then the kingpin of the Montgomery County Republican party, visited him with an interesting proposition. Would he consider running for County Auditor against a longtime Democratic incumbent?

The temptation to be closer to home was too great to resist and Haines left the Dodgers late in the season to come home and campaign. Brower guessed correctly that Haines' reputation from his long baseball career and his solid character would make him a winner at the polls.

The incumbent, Joe Lutz, who had held the job for 16 years, never knew what hit him. Haines won the election by 10,000 votes and launched his own long incumbency. In his victory statement he said, "My ambition is to outlast my baseball days," which he certainly did.

He conducted his office in a no-nonsense way and there was never a hint of scandal. Somehow the voters never looked upon him as one of the regular politicians.

In 1951 Dickson T. Burrows, then president of the Dayton Amateur Baseball Commission (DABC) which oversaw amateur baseball, pushed for setting up teams and leagues for younger boys. The franchised Little League program had just come into being but it was too limited to accommodate the number of youngsters who wanted to play.

So the new Jesse Haines League for the 9 to 12 age group was inaugurated. The program proved very popular and by 1963 there were 218 teams in the Haines program involving as many as 10,000 youngsters and 654 managers and coaches. The program still carries on, providing places to play and supervision for hundreds of Dayton youngsters every year.

Haines was voted into baseball's Hall of Fame at Cooperstown by the Veterans Committee at its meeting in March, 1970 and he was inducted in July. His wife, Carrie, their daughter and her husband, their two sons and other family members attended.

It was in his induction speech that Jesse made reference to his long gone neighbors who worried that he might turn into a bum.

As one might expect, Haines had problems relating to the changes in baseball brought about by free agency and the salary spiral.

In July of 1975, Jesse and Carrie celebrated their 60th wedding anniversary. He died August 5, 1978 at the ripe old age of 84 and was buried from the same church where he and Carrie were married.

The funeral was from the Phillipsburg United Methodist Church, right next door to where Jesse and Carrie had built their first and only home.

10

The Big League Contingent

More than three dozen players with either Dayton roots or Dayton connections have made it to the major leagues.

A number of them, including familiar names like Steve Yeager, Fred Scherman, Bob Borkowski and Ron Nischwitz, had careers of some duration. Others had very brief appearances in box scores such as William (Dutch) Ussat, who had one at bat with the 1925 Cleveland Indians and came back two years later for four games at third base.

Ussat came out of Dayton's east end and was an athlete at Stivers. In his case, as well as well as others who had a brief moment at the top, making it is an achievement not to be dismissed.

If you go by the official *Baseball Encyclopedia*, which lists every man who played at least one game in the majors, there are some arguable Dayton connections.

The *Encyclopedia* correctly lists Dayton as the birthplace of Boston Red Sox standout pitcher, Roger Clemens. Clemens spent his early years in Vandalia and played Little League baseball in that community.

But the Clemens family moved to Texas the year before the big pitcher entered junior high. Roger became a standout high school athlete in Houston and went on to become an All-American at the University of Texas. He considers himself a Texan and does not volunteer information about his Ohio background.

Jack Rowan, born in New Castle, Pennsylvania in 1887, pitched for four different teams prior to World War I and later became a policeman here and spent the rest of his life as a Daytonian.

Former New York Yankee slugger Chris Chambliss was born in Dayton in 1948 when his military father was stationed here. Duffy Dyer, who had a long career as a catcher with the New York Mets, was born here but the family moved away before he started school.

Pitcher Dave Burba, obtained by the Reds in a trade with the San Francisco Giants in July 1995, was indeed born in Miami Valley Hospital. But the family lived in Fairborn at the time and the big guy grew up in Clark County.

Dodger catcher Steve Yeager was born in Huntington, West Virginia in 1948 but the family moved here before he started school. He grew up and earned a reputation in Dayton as a standout all-around high school athlete (1964-67). Counting Yeager's 15 seasons of drawing major league pay, he is the most durable of the Dayton contingent except for Hall of Famers Schmidt and Haines.

Ron Brookey, Yeager's coach in both football and baseball at Meadowdale High School, says he was one of the best all-around athletes and the most competitive athlete he has seen in his years here.

"He also played basketball and never missed a game in the four years he was at Meadowdale," Brookey recalled. "It's possible he never missed a practice. He just loved competition."

Yeager's four years at Meadowdale paralleled Mike Schmidt's at Fairview High School and naturally they were rivals. But the media attention at the time was focused on the more outgoing Yeager.

Schmidt conceded in a book he wrote on his development as a hitter that he felt intimidated in the batter's box with the talkative Steve behind the plate. "After I would swing and miss or take a called strike, he would hold up the ball as if he were going to shove it in my face," Mike wrote, referring to his own need to be more aggressive.

"Steve loved to hit people on the football field," Brookey said, laughing at the memory. "We used him both ways and he was probably a little better as linebacker, but he was also a good quarterback. In defensive practice, he'd yell at Paul Palumbo, our backfield coach, to send the best runner at him."

Yeager had the skills but not the grades to attract a lot of college scholarship offers and he wasn't a high pick in the baseball draft. But he wasted no time signing with the Dodgers who drafted him.

During Schmidt's four years on campus at OU, Yeager was climbing up through the Dodger farm system to their top AAA club, Albuquerque. Both men started the 1972 season in the minors, Yeager being called up in mid-season and Mike in September.

By 1974, Yeager had become the Dodgers starting catcher and was in the first of his four World Series. His reputation as a competent handler of pitchers and a fine defensive player was established. His career batting average of .228 illustrates why he was always low in the batting order.

One of his personal triumphs in his first season as a regular was beating the Reds with a grand slam home run one night in Dodger Stadium. Tom Lasorda, who replaced Walter Alston as manager in 1977, was especially fond of Yeager as their competitive natures were a good mix.

While the Dodger front office kept hoping to develop a catcher with more offensive punch, the athlete from Dayton just kept going and going and despite his low average never was an easy out in the clutch.

Steve was particularly proud of the fact he hit better than his average in the four World Series in which he played, the last three against the Yankees. His Series average was .298 and he hit four home runs, contrasted with a career total of 102 for his 14 seasons with the Dodgers.

He finished his 15th and last season with the Seattle Mariners in the American League, retiring after the 1986 season. He had played in 1,269 major league games.

Yeager pretty much severed his connections with Dayton once he got up with the Dodgers and continues to make his home in Los Angeles. He has been hosting a call-in radio sports show in recent years.

Extending The Borders

Through the careers of "nice guys" Wally Post, Harvey Haddix and Brooks Lawrence, Dayton baseball fans, and those of the Reds in particular, regarded these three area athletes as "locals."

Post, the St. Henry native who died of cancer in 1981, came up through the Reds' system following World War II and went on to a 15-year career, much of it in Cincinnati.

He came up to the Reds in 1951 and was traded to the Phillies after the 1957 season only to return to Cincinnati in 1960 in time to be a member of the National League champions of 1961.

The muscular Post hit some of the longest home runs in Crosley Field and his career total was 210. He also had a strong throwing arm, having been signed originally as a pitcher.

But it was his friendly, outgoing personality and his presence at so many activities in the area north of Dayton that made him a hero.

Clark County native Haddix spent only one of his 14 seasons in the big leagues with the Reds, in 1958 when he was only 8-7. The smallish lefthander broke in with the Cardinals in 1952 and a year later had his best season, 20-8. He was traded to the Phillies who traded him to Cincinnati.

Gabe Paul, the Reds general manager, made what he later referred to as "my worst trade" when he sent Haddix, third baseman Don Hoak and catcher Smoky Burgess to the Pittsburgh Pirates for slugger Frank Thomas and three marginal players. Thomas was a failure as a power hitter in Cincinnati while the three ex-Reds helped the Pirates to their 1960 World Series triumph over the Yankees.

Haddix is the only pitcher in the history of the majors to have pitched 12 perfect innings. He performed the feat in 1959 against the Milwaukee Braves but still lost. His teammates hadn't been able to give him even one run and the Braves finally broke through for a hit and a run in the 13th to win the game.

Like Post, Haddix always returned to his home area once the baseball season was over and was a popular figure in this part of the world. He died of emphysema in a Springfield hospital in 1994.

While Haddix actually grew up on a farm in South Vienna just outside Springfield, Brooks Lawrence was a native son of that city.

Lawrence was born a few years too early to think of a pro baseball career until Jackie Robinson and the Dodgers broke the color line in 1947. The hard-working righthander earned the nickname "The Bull" from his first manager Eddie Stanky after coming up to the Cardinals in 1954 at age 29. He nearly died from a misdiagnosed bleeding ulcer a year later and had a poor 1955 season, after which he was traded to the Reds.

Back in solid health, he won 13 straight for the Cincinnati club in 1956 and had a 19-10 record. He was 13-8 a year later, his two strong seasons in a delayed career. Lawrence has continued to live in Cincinnati and for several years coached the Wilmington College baseball team.

Back To The Beginning

We will get to Dayton's other big leaguers in chronological order starting with Dan Bickham, brother of the publisher of the *Dayton Journal*. Fresh out of Princeton, Bickham pitched and won his only start for the Reds in 1886.

Oliver Caylor, born in Dayton in 1849, managed the Cincinnati

Reds in 1885-86 when they were in the American Association. He died in 1897 in Waynona, Minnesota.

Steamboat Bill Otey, born here in 1886, pitched briefly for Pittsburgh in the NL and Washington in the AL. He died in Dayton in 1931.

Ducky Holmes was in nine games for the St. Louis Cardinals in 1906. Monroe Swartz had an 0-1 record pitching for the Reds in 1920.

Howard (Ty) Frigeau, born in Dayton in 1902, broke in with the Cardinals in 1922 and was a teammate of Jesse Haines. He played seven years, also serving with the Cubs, Braves and Dodgers. He was a drowning victim in Chattanooga, Tennessee in 1932.

Ollie Klee, a star at Stivers high school, was in three games with the 1925 Reds. Russ Young, another Stivers standout, caught 16 games with the St. Louis Browns in 1931.

Clyde Engle, born in Dayton in 1884, broke into the American League in 1909 and played seven years including a season in the Federal League. He died in Boston in 1939.

Berly Horne pitched briefly with the 1929 Chicago Cubs. He died in Franklin in 1983.

Oris Hockett, an Indiana native, was an athlete at Roosevelt High School in the 1930s. He came up to the majors in 1938 with the Dodgers and later played with the Indians. He died in Torrence, California in 1969.

Bernie Hungling, a lifelong Daytonian (1896-1968) had a long career in the minor leagues but caught for the Dodgers in 1922 and the Browns in 1930.

Robert Vilarian Borkowski came out of the Polish enclave of what is now called Old North Dayton. The ethnic neighborhoods of the area produced many fine athletes many of whom, including Borkowski, played for Kiser High School.

He carried his high school nickname of "Bush" all through his baseball career which started in the Chicago Cubs organization in 1946. In his third minor league season, he hit .376 and wasn't even the leading hitter on his team, the Nashville Vols. The Nashville team played in a famous minor league park known for its short outfield fence.

Called up to the Cubs in 1950, Borkowski was traded to the Reds along with catcher Smoky Burgess going into the 1952 season. The Daytonian had a strong area support group during his three-plus seasons in Crosley field. He retired after being traded to the Dodgers in 1955 and returned to his home town where he lives in retirement.

Lloyd Gearhart, born in New Lebanon and an all-around athlete at Dixie High school, spent only one season in the majors, but was part of a historic achievement by the New York Giants. Taking advantage of the short distances down the foul lines in New York's Polo Grounds, the Giants hit 221 home runs in 1947 for a National League team record.

Gearhart enjoyed a long career in the high minor leagues, which in those days provided a livelihood for many good baseball players at a time when there were only 16 major league teams, contrasted to the 28 in the 1990s. Gearhart later scouted for the New York Mets and in 1995 is the proprietor of his own baseball museum and novelty shop in Waynesville.

Cal Hogue, a graduate of Roosevelt High School, made his way to the big leagues as a pitcher through the Pittsburgh Pirate farm system starting in 1952. He returned to Dayton and operated a contracting business until his retirement.

Bob Durnaugh, a Beavercreek High School grad, had a taste of the big leagues with the Reds in 1957.

Dick Johnson, an Oakwood High School athlete, made his way up to the Chicago Cubs in 1958 as an outfielder-pinch hitter.

Ron Nischwitz, a Fairview standout, went on to Ohio State where he starred as a lefthanded pitcher, becoming the strikeout leader in the Big Ten in 1961. His battery mate there was John Edwards, who caught for the Reds from 1961 through 1967.

Nischwitz signed with the Detroit Tigers in 1961 and spent four years in the majors. He spent time working as a pitching instructor with the Mets but his biggest impact on baseball in Dayton was yet to come.

When Wright State started its baseball program, Nischwitz took over the coaching job on a part-time basis and built the Raiders to a contender in NCAA Division II and then in Division I. With his amateur status restored, he continued to pitch in the DABC summer leagues beyond his 50th birthday in 1987.

His enthusiasm for the game survived a personal tragedy in the accidental death of his 19-year-old son, Greg, whose pitching talents were believed to have had major league potential. Greg was electrocuted on a construction job in September, 1980.

A feature of the summer amateur program in Dayton is the Greg Nischwitz Memorial Tournament held during the July 4th holiday.

Mickey McGuire, an infielder out of Dunbar High School, was signed into the Baltimore organization in the late 1950s by Dayton resident

Jack Baker, who was a full-time regular scout with the Orioles. Baker's biggest lament is that he couldn't persuade the Orioles to get serious about an infielder playing in Dayton's summer league in 1960. That infielder, as you might suspect, was Peter Edward Rose.

McGuire had two brief stays with the parent Orioles: in 1962 and again in1967. Most of his career was spent with the Rochester, New York farm club in the International League.

Fred Scherman came out of Fairview High School five school years ahead of Mike Schmidt and made it to the majors as a lefthanded pitcher with the Tigers in 1969.

Scherman's career with the Tigers, and two National League teams, Houston and Montreal, covered eight seasons and he wound up with a 33-26 record.

Jim Fridley, a native of West Virginia, came to Dayton as an out-fielder with the Dayton Indians in 1949. He made it up to the majors briefly with the Cleveland club in 1952, with Baltimore in 1954 and again with the Reds in 1958.

He settled here and after his long career, mostly in the minors, makes his home in West Carrollton.

George Foster and Pete Rose conduct well attended baseball clinic sponsored by *Dayton Journal Herald* in July, 1972.

1970 NABF championship trophy is admired by manager Lou Albers, Ed Duckerson, Phil Morgan and Tom Fries of the winning Dayton team (below).

Ducky Holmes

Ron Nischwitz (left), builder of the outstanding WSU program, with his assistant coach, Bob Grote.

11

The Early Pro Teams

At various times through the last part of the 19th century and the early 20th century, no fewer than 40 different communities in Ohio had minor league professional baseball teams.

Such relatively small towns as Ironton, Portsmouth, Lima, Middletown, Marion, Lancaster, Chillicothe and Findlay were involved in the long ago. Dozens of players enroute to the big leagues passed through the Buckeye state enroute to the majors. Compiling a list of them prior to 1900 is an impossible research effort.

After World War I, the research is more fruitful. For example, Walter Alston, the Hall of Fame manager of the Dodgers, made his way from the family farm in Darrtown to managing in the big leagues starting in Portsmouth.

Dayton's long history in the minor leagues dates back to 1884, yet the National Association of Professional Baseball, which governs the minor leagues and handles the records, shows Dayton's entry into the Central League in 1903 as this city's first recognized minor league team.

However, thanks to researcher Jack Carlson, Dayton's professional baseball history may be available soon in considerable detail. Carlson is an engineer who came to Dayton in 1946 as a civilian employee at Wright-Patterson AFB and spent his working lifetime here.

Since his retirement, as a member of SABR (Society of American Baseball Researchers), he has spent three mornings a week in the files of the Dayton and Montgomery County Public Library on his project to trace the history of the game here to its beginnings. He intends to publish his efforts through SABR.

That first Dayton team in 1884 played in a league with Springfield, Hamilton, Portsmouth, Ironton and Chillicothe and was known as the Gem Cities. Accounts of the games in the *Dayton Herald* are sketchy. The games were played on the "Association" grounds. Carlson's effort to pin down the location leads him to believe they were in the vicinity of what later became NCR property along the Miami River.

There is a five-year gap from the Gem Cities before the Dayton Reds appeared in 1889. This team played in West Side Park, located on Williams Street. That location was described in a 1978 term paper prepared in the Wright State history class taught by Professor Carl G. Becker. It was submitted by Lisa Corley and was entitled "The Rise of the Reds, the Gem City's first professional Baseball Team."

Corley and Carlson identify the league as the Tri-State. Harry T. Smith of Springfield, Illinois, came to Dayton to organize and manage the team. The Reds finished fourth, and being $2,000 in debt at the end of the season, disbanded.

Further illustrating the lack of organization and control, was a report of the time that "shortstop Lyons spent three days in jail in August for assaulting an umpire with his bat." But he returned to the lineup without other penalty or sanction.

Two more Dayton teams played in the Tri-State League in 1890 and 1891, followed by a six-year gap before the appearance of the Dayton Old Soldiers in 1897 in the Interstate League. This league consisted of Toledo, Youngstown, Fort Wayne, Mansfield, Springfield, Wheeling and New Castle, Pennsylvania.

Outfielder Elmer Flick, a native of Bedford in northern Ohio, batted .386 for Dayton in the 1897 season and the following year went up to the majors with the Philadelphia National League team. In 1902 he was sold to Cleveland where he starred for nine seasons before closing his career with two years in Toledo in the American Association. Flick was inducted into the Hall of Fame in 1963.

He was not the only memorable personality involved in the 1897 Old Soldiers. The man who helped organize and later managed the team was William G. Armour of Homestead, Pennsylvania, near Pittsburgh. In 1902 Armour turned up as manager of the Cleveland Indians and later moved on to Detroit where he was Ty Cobb's first manager.

The home grounds for the Old Soldiers were in Fairview Park, situated where Fairview Avenue cuts off to the northwest from Main Street. At that time, the north Main trolley line ended there. The baseball grounds were part of the general amusement park there, including a dance hall and vaudeville theater.

The nickname Old Soldiers was in honor of the hospital and residence hall facilities, now run by the Veterans Administration, then and now a major community institution. The Old Soldiers were champs of the Interstate League in 1897, 1900 and 1901, and then the league folded.

The fact that the league was free-wheeling is attested by Carlson's discovery that a man named Nicholson started the 1899 season as an umpire, signed on as Dayton's second baseman and finished the season as manager at Wheeling.

In the period when Armour was involved, major league teams didn't go to Florida or Texas for spring training, but many would come to Dayton to play pre-season games.

There was no local pro team in 1902 but an American League game was played here involving Baltimore and Armour's Indians on a Sunday. At the time, local blue laws in the Cleveland area prohibited Sunday play. The Indians won that game 6-2 with Elmer Flick in the lineup. Attendance was reported at 4,876 which meant that at least half of the fans stood.

The so-called blue laws were in force in Pennsylvania until 1932 keeping the state's three major league teams -- the Philadelphia A's and Phillies and the Pittsburgh Pirates -- from playing on Sundays. The law was then amended to permit Sunday games with a 6:59 p.m. curfew which was enforced to the minute.

In the 1900 season, world heavyweight champion James J. Jeffries umpired the bases in a Dayton-Wheeling game.

Researcher Carlson is continuing into the early 20th century where the National Association records show Dayton as a member of the Central League at four different times. The initial period was from 1903 through 1917, when the league disbanded during World War I.

Dayton was out of professional baseball until 1928 when the Dayton Aviators took their place in the Central League. The team was also known as the Wings at another time after the Central League re-organized in 1932 (it did not operate in 1931).

Owner-manager Ducky Holmes took Dayton into the Central League a third time when he put the 1932 team in it. A year later, Holmes shifted the franchise into the Middle-Atlantic (1933-1942) until World War II caused a three-year break in Dayton's minor league history.

The next franchise was in the class D Ohio-Indiana League for two years, 1946-47. Although there was a working agreement with the Cleveland Indians, the team (named the Dayton Indians) was locally owned.

When the Central League was re-organized in 1948, Bill Veeck and his longtime associate, Rudie Schaefer, while running the big league club in Cleveland, took out a franchise for Dayton, jumping the classification for the local team from the lowly Class D level to Class A.

This was to be the last minor league operation, lasting four more years. The final year (1951), Veeck and Schaefer having moved to the St. Louis Browns, was the last working agreement.

When the revised Old Soldiers went into the Central League in 1903, they continued to play their games at Fairview Park.

The "new look" Old Soldiers weren't very good, spending the whole year in the second division, finishing in seventh place in the eight team league with a 58-75 record.

Four teams out of Indiana: Ft. Wayne, South Bend, Evansville and Terre Haute anchored the circuit. The eastern outpost was Wheeling, West Virginia and rounding it out was Grand Rapids in Michigan. Ft. Wayne was the league champion, finishing a game and a half over South Bend.

Newspaper clippings of that 1903 team did not carry first names of most of the players and the coverage was in a style that would be unrecognizable to current sports followers.

Evidence of the free-wheeling sports writing comes from a story on July 31, 1903 in the *Dayton Daily News*:

"The Dayton club has secured the services of a new outfielder named Selig, who is recommended by Armour of Cleveland. If he is no better than the other players Armour recommended, then he will not remain on the Dayton payroll long as President Lander is determined to have a good team."

In that same story, an unnamed player was said to have been fined $15 "for careless playing."

The account of the final game of that season began, "Dayton baseball patrons deserve better treatment than they received yesterday at Fairview. It was not so much the fault of the Dayton management as it was that of the bum umpire who made a farce of officiating at both games. Any 10-year-old schoolboy could have umpire (sic) better ball."

The apparent player-manager was Doggie Miller, who divided his time between second base and the pitching mound.

Those examples of coverage reinforce the belief that pro baseball before the first World War was not strictly regulated and often poorly organized, as with the home teams providing the umpires.

Trying to research the history of all the player movements of Dayton's teams prior to World War I is an exercise in futility. Players and managers came and went and all of minor league baseball was operated at the local level. Branch Rickey's development of the farm system didn't take shape until the early 1920s and changed all that.

The nickname of Dayton's Central League entry was shortened to the Dayton Vets and they gave Jesse Haines a tryout in 1914.

Starting with the shutdown during World War I, Dayton was out of professional baseball until 1928, but baseball itself came on strong in the early 1920s.

Golden Age At North Side

With the development of North Side Field in 1922, Dayton's baseball history for pros and amateurs entered what could be called the Golden Age in the two decades leading up to World War II.

The history of North Side Field is carefully preserved in the Dayton and Montgomery County Public Library in book and photographic form thanks to the efforts of Roland L. Larke.

The library prepared and has an oversized display of highlights from North Side which it puts on display from time to time as well as Larke's history in book form.

Larke, who died in 1993 after completing the work, dedicated it to his brother Carl, who was the salaried superintendent and groundskeeper of the park. Roland Larke was involved in working for his older brother and was witness to the appearance of Babe Ruth and Lou Gehrig here in 1928.

The project (North Side Field) was incorporated as the North Dayton Amusement Company with John P. Naas as president. Naas headed the North Dayton Business Association which was made up of various small businesses which served as the core shopping area for the ethnic neighborhoods in what is now called Old North Dayton.

In Larke's words, "The playground of youth of Old North Dayton was a natural environment for camping, fishing, hunting, canoeing and wintertime sledding and ice skating." He was referring to the need for a playing field with the city expanding outward.

Larke described the five acre area, which today is bounded by Stanley Avenue to the north and east, by Troy Street to the west as part of the "Kossuth Colony" -- a reference to the enclave once populated by immigrant Hungarian-Americans.

All the construction work was done by North Dayton businesses and the cost of the projected seating capacity of 4,000 was minimal.

Because it had to be built in the small acreage available, North Side had unusual dimensions. It was 370 feet down the left field line, dropping off to a distant 420 feet in center. Right field was a short 285 feet with a high fence to foil cheap home runs, but it was still an inviting target.

Dayton's top amateur players will be discussed in the history of the Dayton Amateur Baseball Commission, but Larke made special mention of two North Side favorites, players who came out of the North Dayton environment.

Harvey Reese and Julie Tangeman played in the park as amateurs, pros and semi-pros and finished extended careers in the park. Reese, a pitcher known for his curve ball and control, made it up to Rochester in Triple-A as a pro. He later dropped down to the Central League and came back to Dayton pitching against the Aviators -- and winning.

Tangeman was an outfielder with several pros teams including a year with the Ducks in 1933. He later pitched and managed in amateur ball for years.

From the beginning, North Side was a multi-purpose facility and was the primary field for the top level amateur and semi-pro teams, including what amounted to an All-Star team sponsored by Shroyers Sporting Goods store.

The early visits of barnstorming Negro League teams were played there but did not attract many African American fans. After Hudson Field was opened a decade later, those games were shifted to West Dayton.

Professional ball returned to Dayton in 1928 with the Dayton Aviators coming into being as a part of Branch Rickey's growing farm system with the St. Louis Cardinals. The team was managed by Everett Boos, perhaps the most inappropriate name any manager ever had, rhyming with what disgruntled fans always do.

One of the stars of the team was Mike Ryba, a Cuban who later played with the Cardinals and spent a lifetime as a minor league manager and major league coach. The team didn't win and the Cardinals shifted the franchise to Ft. Wayne going into 1929.

October of that year produced the appearance of Yankee stars Babe Ruth and Lou Gehrig. North Side's short right field was a great target for lefthanded power hitters and an overflow throng of 4,000 turned out. Gehrig hit four balls over the wall while Ruth connected only once, but it was a grand slam blast in the eighth inning sending the crowd home happy.

In 1929, Bill Knelbelkamp, the owner of the Louisville team in the American Association, entered into a working agreement with the Aviators and sent in an upbeat Cuban, Marito Acosto as manager. It was also a very young team that created much more fan following than the year before.

Future Hall of Fame second baseman Billy Herman was on that team as was pitcher Johnny Marcum, nicknamed Footsie, who later made the big leagues. Another interesting team member was Wayland Dean, who had made it to the majors with the New York Giants. Dean, who pitched very well for the Aviators, died a year later of tuberculosis at age 31.

With the Central League folded because of economic reasons, Dayton nonetheless had an exciting summer of baseball, thanks in part to John L. Shroyer, owner of a sizeable sporting goods store located near Fourth and Jefferson.

Shroyer turned promoter for his own semi-pro team, using North Side as the field to play strong teams from Cincinnati, Indianapolis and Detroit as well as games between the Marco's, Dayton's best black team, against visiting Negro League opponents.

Shroyer also booked in the House of David, then touring the midwest with a portable lighting system with poles mounted on trucks. The bearded team had as an added attraction Grover Cleveland Alexander, the Hall of Fame pitcher, whose big league career had ended. Alexander pitched one inning in the game here. Shroyer brought in major league teams such as the New York Giants who played their regular lineup and ripped the Dayton team 17-2.

The Philadelphia Phillies, Pittsburgh Pirates and Cincinnati Reds also played the Shroyer teams of the early 1930s.

Pro baseball returned to Dayton in 1932 with Ducky Holmes entering front and center, his era to follow in the next chapter. That same year, North Side hosted the NABF senior division national tournament. This is the federation to which the Dayton Amateur Baseball Commission belongs. Fisher Foods of Detroit won the tournament.

The Forgotten Marcos

The first competition between black and white teams in Dayton is generally believed to have been baseball games between the semi-pro Dayton Marcos and the Shroyer All Stars in the early 1930s.

However, there are newspaper accounts of the Marcos meeting white semi-pro teams as far back as 1915.

The Marcos were sponsored by John Mathews, a West Dayton florist, and played as much on the road as they did in Dayton because so few white teams were willing to play them. Mathews entered the team in the Negro National League in 1926, but it was a losing proposition which did not last very long.

There are no known records of the year-to-year performance of the Marcos, but they were good enough to have been better remembered if it weren't for the fact they generated little or no white media coverage or general fan attention. Among their problems was the lack of a home field.

Among the best players on the Marcos was Eddie Huff, a catcher compared by some old-timers to Josh Gibson, now in Cooperstown's Hall of Fame. Like Gibson and the great Roy Campanella, Huff was a stockily built power hitter from the right side. In later years he managed the team.

Other well known players included George (Chippy) Britt, variously a pitcher, catcher and infielder. Ray Brown was one of the better pitchers. Other names from box scores include William Marshall, Jack Becoy, Blanchard Chesters, George Brown, Otto Briggs, Rev. Walter Canady, Albert Clark and Mack Eggleston.

The Marcos did not reorganize after World War II what with Elwood Parsons bringing in teams from the Negro leagues on a weekly basis when the Dayton Indians weren't scheduled at Hudson Field.

Parsons played a unique role in the integration of major league baseball. When Branch Rickey brought Jackie Robinson and other blacks into the Brooklyn Dodger organization, he needed a black scout to travel in the deep South. This was a potentially dangerous role in the segregated South, but Parsons played it well.

"I knew my place," is the way he described his travels, staying in black hotels and eating in black restaurants. Ironically, integration eventually did away with the Negro leagues, depriving Parsons of his role of booking those teams into Dayton. Mr. Parsons died in September of 1995 at age 84, closing a phase of Dayton's sports and cultural history.

12

Ducky The Wild One

The name most easily recalled from Dayton's lengthy history in and out of minor league baseball is that of Howard Ebert (Ducky) Holmes.

The colorful and controversial Holmes was born in Dayton, July 8, 1883 and went through life with a nickname that in today's era of social and political correctness would never have appeared in print.

Ducky Holmes had a prominent nose which, as he grew older, seemed to get redder and more prominent.

Holmes started his pro baseball career as a catcher with the Saginaw team in the Michigan State League in 1902 when he was 18. He advanced to Savannah in 1905 and his contract was sold to the St. Louis Cardinals in 1906, when he appeared in nine games and batted .187.

He spent the next decade bouncing around the minor leagues and in 1913 became the owner-manager of the Saginaw team. The grandstand burned down and was rebuilt only to have the league collapse in 1915.

Ducky's initial return to Dayton was as a coach with this city's team in the Central League for a year and in 1916 he became an umpire.

He went up through the ranks and got into the American League where his quick temper built up resentment against him. He once ordered Phil Ball, owner of the St. Louis Browns and his manager, George Sisler, not just out of the game but out of their home park.

Forced back into the minors where he umpired his last two seasons, he disappeared from the game in 1927, opening a grocery store he and his wife ran in East Dayton.

The Great Depression caved in many minor league teams and leagues, eventually disposing of the Central League in 1931. But the league was reorganized in 1932 and Holmes, with modest financial backing, managed to get a franchise and formed the Dayton Wings. That name changed a year later to the Dayton Ducks.

It was in his first year in the Central League that Holmes engaged in one of his many odd escapades in what became his never-ending war with the umpires.

Ejected from a game in Fort Wayne, he wandered outside the park and spotted a ladder beside a telephone pole behind the outfield fence. He used the ladder to climb to the crossbar on the pole, and straddled it. Still in his baseball uniform, he appeared to be using signals to run the team, but it had to be more of a show trick than anything else.

Dayton attorney Fredrick W. Howell was president of the Central League and tried to keep it afloat but South Bend and Canton folded in August and only four teams, including the Ducks, finished the season.

Ducky's gang captured the championship series against Ft. Wayne, four games to one, for what was to be the last Central League championship until the league re-formed in 1948.

In 1933, Holmes took his team into the MAL (Middle Atlantic League) which was swinging west to pick up survivors of the old Central. Much of the history of the Ducks and the MAL in the Depression years is preserved in a paper by Eugene Murdock at the Montgomery County Historical Society.

Once in the MAL, nicknamed Mad Atlantic, the Dayton franchise operated in that circuit until after the 1942 season when most of minor league baseball shut down for World War II.

Zanesville, then a farm club of the Cleveland Indians, was one of the powers in the MAL in the 1930s. Other Ohio cities with franchises included Canton, Portsmouth, Springfield and Akron. Erie, Pennsylvania and Huntington West Virginia were also involved.

Holmes, with some assistance from city and business leaders. built a new $60,000 baseball park for the 1934 season. Situated off West Third Street, it was to have accommodated 4,000 spectators, but when finished, the actual seating capacity was somewhat less.

The new stadium was named Ducks Park and Depression or no, Holmes packed 60,000 fans into the park for the first 30 home games, closing out the first half of the season which was won by his team. Most minor league seasons were played in two halves, with a playoff to determine the pennant winner.

Murdock's historical paper described Holmes' stormy involvement with the umpires, a seemingly strange development from a man who had been a major league umpire.

Ducky's penchant for crowd pleasing antics reached of a zenith in 1934 when the Pittsburgh Pirates were to meet the Ducks in an exhibition in the Springfield park. The Pirates were to use a female pitcher, one Jackie Mitchell, who back in 1931 in an exhibition game in Chattanooga, Tennessee allegedly struck out Babe Ruth and Lou Gehrig of the Yankees.

The Dayton team came up with its own girl pitcher, Josephine Doak, a bearded lady with flaming red hair stuffed under her cap, wearing a Ducks uniform. Josephine turned out to be Ducky himself.

The 1934 season found an 18-year-old pitcher named John Vander Meer on the Dayton club. Four seasons later, the young southpaw, pitching for the Cincinnati Reds, became the only man in major league history to pitch successive no-hitters.

Holmes, egged on by the crowds at home and away, was ejected by the umpires June 18, July 8 and July 17. In the first episode, he got down on his knees and raised his hands as if in prayer to umpire Shannon.

Zanesville defeated Dayton in the 1934 championship playoff marred by a fight between the Dayton manager and umpire Bill Osborne.

Dan Tehan, the Cincinnati native who became one of the nation's best known football and basketball game officials, umpired a year in the MAL and in later years offered an insight into what may have been a factor in Holmes' conduct. It was well known that Ducky had a drinking problem.

"When he'd come out and hand you the lineup card before the game, he appeared to be cold sober," Tehan recalled. "Later, when he came storming out to argue, his breath might blow you away. We never figured out where he had the stuff hidden in the dugout."

Holmes was suspended for the first 90 days of the 1935 season for the fight with Osborne, the suspension being upheld by Judge William Bramham, who ruled the minor leagues. It turned out that Ducky had made an arrangement to sit in a window in a house behind the park and wig-wagged his signals to manager Riley Parker.

Among new players in 1935 was shortstop Rod Dedeaux, destined to become one of the great college baseball coaches at Southern California. Also on the team was Paul Birch from Duquesne who became an outstanding pro basketball player and Stan Kostka, an All-American fullback from Minnesota.

Dayton got much national attention as the host in December of 1935 for the minor league winter meetings. Although the formal business of the convention did not concern the major leagues, the big league club officials, usually including their managers, came to the meetings. The Biltmore Hotel was the convention center and many news stories were filed out of Dayton around the country.

Meanwhile financial woes involving the operation of the Ducks became apparent in 1936, a season in which Dayton second baseman Joe Paiement was married at home plate before a loss to Canton. In 1937, businessman Harry Mack took over the Ducks front office to oversee financial matters with Holmes deciding to confine his duties to running the team on the field.

In July, police had to be called to the field to end a bitter dispute between Holmes and a rookie catcher, Charley Schupp. After three passed balls by the young receiver, Holmes gestured his catcher out of the game, then changed his mind and a lively argument ensued. The crowd, angry that Holmes was embarrassing the young man, started throwing cushions and pop bottles on the field.

The next night a large crowd turned up and the Ducks started a winning streak leading to speculation there was often a method to Ducky's madness.

The team didn't do well in the long run and Ducky shifted signals on how the club was to be run. He would stay in the front office and a new manager would be hired. The new manager, Red Rollings, lasted only a month and Ducky was back in uniform.

A capacity crowd of over 3,000 turned out to welcome Ducky back on the field and sure enough, he was ejected before the game was over.

The country was starting to come out of the depression but financial problems were continuing to plague the Ducks. Holmes, who owned nearly all the stock, was operating in debt and a board of trustees was set up to control the spending.

The Brooklyn Dodgers, who had entered into an agreement to option players to the Ducks, were scheduled to play an exhibition game here on September 1, 1938. When the Dodgers arrived at the park, the sheriff was on hand to attach the gate receipts.

Then in early 1939, he was responsible for creating a near riot in a game in Springfield, winding up with another long term suspension inflicted by minor league boss Bramham.

Holmes was forced into receivership and the Dodgers ran the Ducks in the 1939 and 1940 seasons. The Brooklyn club announced it was pulling out and a group of business men came up with fresh capital and Holmes was back on the field for the 1941 and 1942 seasons.

The club made a comeback in 1941 and Holmes seemed to be behaving himself. A big crowd turned out July 8 for a Ducky Holmes appreciation night. But the team wasn't winning and staggered home in seventh place in the league. Holmes had given up managing in the last weeks of the season, turning the club over to third baseman Bill McWilliams.

The end of the line for Holmes and minor league baseball in Dayton for the duration of World War II made for a gloomy 1942 season. Only six teams held their MAL franchises and many players went into the military as volunteers or draftees.

Ducky hired and fired one more manager, catcher Paul Chervinko, and drew one more suspension for a fracas in Charleston.

Holmes died Sept. 18, 1945 at age 63 of natural causes. He had a varied career in the game, and he had his problems. But it needs to be remembered he did entertain Dayton fans and create interest in minor league baseball.

Among the players who wore the Dayton uniform and went on to the major leagues were Roger Wolff, Harry Eisenstat (a lefthander Holmes referred to as his best pitcher), Johnny Vander Meer, Frank McCormick, Jake Powell, Johnny McCarthy, Dick Siebert and Wally Westlake.

Baseball Returns In 1946

Minor league baseball came back to Dayton in the spring of 1946 with a new ownership and was greeted and supported well in the media and by the fans.

Dr. Warren O. Bradford and Hy Shumsky purchased the franchise for $7,500 from Mrs. Ducky Holmes and entered it in the Ohio State League, a class D circuit, the lowest in pro ball. This was baseball at its lowest level ever in Dayton. The cities involved were Middletown, Springfield, Marion, Lima, Newark, Zanesville and Dayton in the Buckeye state with Richmond, the Indiana entrant.

Dr. Bradford was an osteopathic physician and sports fan who was also the doctor for the Fairview High School football team. Shumsky had come to Dayton in 1939 to manage the concessions at Ducks Park. A native of Springfield, Massachusetts, he was hired by the Jacobs-owned Sports Service firm of Buffalo, New York which had a near monopoly in managing concession business throughout pro baseball.

"We entered into an agreement with the Cleveland Indians, who were to provide us with players," Shumsky recalled. "On their recommendation, we signed Frank Parenti as manager before we had a single player under contract."

The Indians sent scouts Laddy Placek and Wally Laskowski down to Dayton to conduct a two-day tryout camp at Hudson Field. An indication of the quality of this first post-war team came from the fact that half the team which opened the season came out of that camp.

Two of the signees were the Burton twins, Carroll and Farrell, Chaminade high school athletes who opened the season as catcher and third baseman. The starting pitcher opening night was Joe Jackson, a Darke County native who was signed out of the camp.

The league got a bit of national publicity when an 18-year-old umpire was signed to be on the regular staff. The young man, Henry McGowan from New York City, turned out to be no more of a major league prospect than most of the players on the Dayton roster.

The owners got off to a good financial start with an exhibition game between the Cincinnati Reds and Detroit Tigers which lured an overflow crowd into Hudson Field.

"It was snowing the night before, and we were going crazy," Shumsky said. "If the game couldn't be played, there was no way we could get the teams back. But the sun was shining, the temperature went up to 70 degrees and we packed the park."

Shumsky conceded, "We didn't have a very good team, finishing seventh in the eight team league. But we had a lot of promotions and drew people."

The team was much better in 1947 under Ival Goodman, but attendance was down to 40,000 on the season and the owners knew they had to find a higher level league. The opportunity came with the reorganization of the Central League at the Class A level, which meant the Dayton team would need more experienced players. The makeup of the six team league included Muskegon, Grand Rapids, Flint, Saginaw, Ft. Wayne and Dayton.

Most Dayton followers assumed the new franchise was owned by the Cleveland Indians. The year 1948 is the most memorable in the history of the Indians when the club won its last world championship and set a major league attendance record. But Bill Veeck and Rudie Schaefer, running the big league club, owned the Dayton team on their own with Dr. Bradford retaining some stock.

The Indians named Joe Vosmik, former Tribe outfielder, as manager and stocked the franchise with solid players. Outfielder Joe Morjoseph led the league in home runs with 32 and the starting pitching was solid behind Joe Pennington, Charley Sipple and Joe Payne, who pitched a no-hitter that season.

Dayton and Flint battled all season for the league lead. The Michigan entry won out by five and half games in the regular season, but Dayton came back to capture the four-team playoff series. The last weeks of that season were notable for the arrival of the then unknown Orestes (Minnie) Minoso. The hard-hitting Cuban, and pitcher Joe Santiago, joined the Indians late in the season.

Minoso was actually 26 years old, but the Indians introduced him here as being only 21. Whatever his age, Minoso tore up Central League pitching with a vengeance. In 11 games he hit .525 (21 hits in 40 at bats). He had seven hits in a doubleheader including four doubles and a triple.

A writer asked Vosmik if Minoso would be a good hitter in the majors and Vosmik replied, "He'd be a prospect to hit if there was a league higher than that." Minoso went on to an outstanding major league career, identified for much of it with Bill Veeck.

The 1948 Dayton Indians enjoyed a home attendance of 170,000, the highest up to that point and the high water mark of baseball in Dayton.

Manager Vosmik and superstar Minoso were promoted in the off season and the Cleveland organization sent in Oscar Melillo, who had a 12-year career as a big league infielder, to take over as manager.

Charleston came into the league replacing Ft. Wayne and proved to be a drawing card because the West Virginia team was a farm club of the Cincinnati Reds. Joe Nuxhall was one of the pitchers on that squad.

Dayton's prominent newcomers were basketball standout Sweetwater Clifton at first base, hard-hitting outfielder Jim Fridley and shortstop Ray Rakar. Fridley eventually made the big leagues with three teams: the Indians, who originally signed him, Baltimore and briefly with the Reds.

Cleveland native Rakar, facing up to the fact his chances of making the big leagues were slim, turned down a chance to join the Wilkes-Barre team in the Cleveland organization and settled in Dayton in the "real world" as he put it. He became associated with General Motors and became recreational director at what was then known as Delco Products. He remained in baseball as a coach of youth teams.

Rivals Dayton and Flint continued to battle it out 1-2 atop the standings in the Central's second season but this time it was Dayton winning the regular season championship. But they didn't meet in the playoffs because Muskegon upset the locals.

A highlight of the 1949 season was the appearance of Lou Boudreau's Cleveland club, winners of the World Series the previous year, in an exhibition game against their farmhands.

A third major leaguer, former National League first baseman Dolf Camilli, came in to manage the Dayton Indians in 1950. Although the local Tribe didn't contend for the pennant, they had a winning season (68-62) and finished in third place.

With attendance on a down curve, the Indians absorbed a serious financial blow when an exhibition game against the Reds had to be cancelled because of heavy rains which made Hudson Field unplayable.

The season came to a dismal finish when Muskegon eliminated the Indians in the fifth and final game of the playoff series. Only 382 fans paid their way into Hudson Field to see the Muskegon club score a 7-2 victory.

One of the Dayton pitchers was Ryne Duren, the hard-throwing bespectacled righthander who went on to become a fine relief pitcher with the New York Yankees.

Dayton's final year in minor league baseball, in 1951, found the Tribe affiliated with the St. Louis Browns, where Veeck was operating after a change of ownership had forced him out of Cleveland. Jim Crandall, son of Otis (Doc) Crandall, who had been a pitcher with the New York Giants under John McGraw, was the Dayton manager.

This final Dayton entry was strong enough to capture the regular season championship, but the Central League was about to sink in a sea of red ink. Charleston led the league in attendance with 92,000 and the total in Dayton was only 60,000. On Friday, two days before the end of the regular season, league president T. J. Halligan announced that the playoffs were cancelled. Halligan, who had struggled to keep the league afloat through all four years it operated, might as well have announced its disbandment.

The city of Dayton, which owned Hudson Field, tried to keep the park available for amateur team use, but that didn't last long and the property was eventually sold for industrial use.

13

Dayton's Amateur Program

Sandlot baseball in Dayton dates back at least into the 1880s, but there was never a governing body to control the teams or leagues and, more importantly youth programs, until the Dayton Amateur Baseball Commission was established in 1927.

Most of the sandlot activities prior to World War I could better be called semi-pro and there was no organized high school baseball.

In the 1920s, the major industrial plants in Dayton sponsored the stronger athletic teams. Teams representing the General Motors plants -- Frigidaire, Delco, Moraine, Inland -- formed the DIAA (Dayton Industrial Athletic Association) which offered competition in numerous sports.

National Cash Register was always in the forefront of recreational activities for its employees but it preferred to keep the leagues in all sports at company level. NCR had its own basketball and softball leagues well into the 1950s.

NCR, a pioneer in providing recreational competition for women, had, of course, the huge Old River complex along Patterson Boulevard just south of the Dayton Marriott hotel, testimony to John H. Patterson's determination to make life more pleasant for workers and their families.

Below the DIAA was a second industrial recreational organization called IRAD (Industrial Recreation Association Dayton) made up of smaller plants such as Standard Register, Duriron, McCalls, Egry Register and several others. This was primarily a basketball grouping.

In baseball, the GM teams formed the backbone of the DABC's top level teams until the decade after World War II.

Fredrick Howell, an Oakwood municipal judge and a great baseball fan, was one of the organizers of the DABC and its first president. At one time he was also president of the Central League in which most Dayton professional teams played. Howell Field, the only lighted, first rate baseball facility in Dayton is named in his memory.

The DABC has been associated with the NABF (National Amateur Baseball Federation) and sends its senior and high school age champions to the NABF tournaments every year.

Dayton has hosted the junior (high school) tournament a number of times and in 1936, the Des Moines, Iowa team featured a hard-throwing 16-year-old right-handed pitcher named Bob Feller. Feller's team was eliminated when he dropped a 1-0 decision to Battle Creek.

In 1960, the Lebanon Merchants had a young infielder building a reputation as an all-out hustler. His name, Peter Edward Rose.

The continuity of the Dayton commission's affiliation with the NABF makes the annual goal for the senior (AA) and high school (B) leagues every year. Any Dayton baseballer to play professional baseball in the last 60 years has almost certainly come out of the DABC program at some level.

The DABC's greatest service to the Dayton community is providing fields and supervision to the youth leagues. Below the class B (high school) level is class C (15-16), D (13-14) and Jesse Haines (9-12) leagues. Credit for the development of the Jesse Haines program must go to Dick Burrows, who served as DABC president longer than anyone else and who worked tirelessly to keep the programs solvent and growing.

Until the establishment of the national level Little League program in the late 1940s there had been very little thought of putting kids below their teens into uniforms and playing supervised games with umpires in organized leagues.

"The only thing wrong with Little League is that it is too exclusive. Only the more mature kids have a chanced to play," Burrows said at the time to explain his idea. "What we need is a DABC program to give every kid who wants to play, a chance to play."

The Jesse Haines program with more of an emphasis on teaching the kids how to play rather than winning was launched in 1952 and has been successful over the years.

It stands as a lasting tribute to Burrows, a charter member of the DABC Hall of Fame when it was organized in 1962. Burrows was also head of the DABC when the lights at Howell field were dedicated and installed in 1957.

The first Dayton team to win the NABF national title and arguably as good as any to ever to represent the city was the Acme Aluminum Alloy team of 1944 managed by Dick Bass.

This team won the tournament in Youngstown by beating Battle Creek in the playoff round. As it happened, Acme had to beat the Michigan entry twice for the title and did it on the same day with 1-0 and 2-0 wins. Both shutouts were pitched by the same man, Russ Wolfe.

Wolfe lived all his life in Brookville in northern Montgomery County. He had an unorthodox submarine delivery along the lines of a softball pitcher. He was 25 years old when he performed that double shutout for Acme, and continued to pitch into his 40's.

"When the team got back from Youngstown, the city threw a parade for them and I remember seeing them ride up Main Street in open convertibles," recalled Janet Weber, widow of hard-hitting Kenny Weber.

Another member of the team was infielder Buddy Bloebaum, who later scouted for the Reds and was involved in the signing of his nephew, Pete Rose. Others on the Acme roster included swift outfielder Deacon Diehl, Hal Tidrick, Bobby Colburn, Lefty Gilliland, Bobby Rowlands, Lee Ruse, Carl Kennedy, Red Probst, Johnny Fine and Dave Lucas. Teams headed for the tournament could add players and Acme added Ben Harrison and George Yadloski.

Acme dropped sponsorship shortly after the war while Frigidaire and Delco-Moraine had power-packed teams in the late 1940s. Frigidaire, managed by Earle (Pappy) Sykes, went undefeated through 36 games in 1949, but was upset in the post-season playoffs by White-Allen.

Gene Brown, a basketball-baseball standout at Stivers High School who went on to Ohio State, pitched White Allen to a 6-4 victory over Frigidaire in the first game before a big crowd in Hudson Field. In the next game, Frigidaire's Jack Bunger had a no-hitter going after seven innings.

Dick Tatem had a one-out single for White Allen to break up the no-hitter. Dick Harp followed with a single and Gene Brown came up as a pinchhitter and slashed a two-run triple down the left field line. Brown scored on a sacrifice fly and White-Allen won the 3-2 game. Frigidaire's perfect season came to a sorry end.

"The thing about it is, Moraine beat White-Allen to finish the playoffs and went to the tournament," recalled Tatem, the man who broke Bunger's heart. Frigidaire also had a strong class B (high school age) team after the war and won the national junior title in 1947. The tourney winning team included Leland (Junior) Norris, Walt Hirsch and Troy's Corky Valentine, who later pitched for the Reds. The rising costs of baseball sponsorship led to a change in policy by GM and Frigidaire pulled out of the DABC as a sponsor in 1953 and Moraine followed a year later.

The next AA powerhouse was the Wiedemann-Buds, sponsored by John T. Stanko and managed by catcher-manager Junior Norris. Norris, who had starred as a University of Dayton basketball standout, was a fine two-way athlete. The Buds were in the league only five seasons but were the dominant club and went to three national tournaments.

The most recent series of successful Dayton AA teams have been managed by Ted Mills. He was a Roosevelt high school graduate who pitched at the University of Cincinnati.

"I can talk about the first game under the lights at Howell Field because I pitched in it," Mills said. "I was 18 years old, it was a class B game, I was with the Optimist Club and Dick Poeppelmeier was the manager."

Turning to managing, his first sponsor was Parkmoor Restaurant for four years and in 1967 that team became Dayton's second (after Acme) to win the NABF national title. In 1971, Mills-managed Cassis Packing won another NABF national title and Mills had a third one in 1984 with his H. H. Morgan team.

The other DABC team to win the NABF national title was Blatz in 1970, managed by Lou Albers.

In subsequent years Mills had a variety of sponsors. Because Mills scheduled so many games out of the league, his budget ran higher than most others in the circuit. He had no trouble getting the veterans he wanted and he recruited a balance of youngsters, mostly from area colleges.

In the summer of 1968, Mills gave a young shortstop an opportunity to play at a time there was no indication he would eventually hit 548 major league home runs. Mike Schmidt had been no ball-of-fire in high school and after his freshman year at Ohio University needed a chance to play and develop. He got that chance from Mills.

In addition to the NABF tournament, Dayton teams became eligible to enter the ABC (American Baseball Congress) tournament. Mills took his H. H. Morgan team there for five straight years in the early 1970s.

H. H. (Blinky) Morgan was a man of modest means who had a small business. He had a great love of baseball and sponsored as well as coached a number of teams for kids in the 1950s and 1960s. Mills, who had played on a one of Morgan's teams, tired of struggling for sponsorships, started to sponsor his own teams in 1981 and named them H. H. Morgan in memory of the man who did so much for youth baseball.

Former big leaguers Fred Scherman and Dave Coleman played for Mills after regaining their amateur status. Ron Nischwitz is another former big leaguer who had a long active career as a pitcher in the DABC, continuing that active role after becoming the highly successful baseball coach at Wright State University.

One of the features of amateur ball in Dayton is the annual Greg Nischwitz Memorial Tournament, held over the Fourth of July holiday, to which a number of top level out-of-town teams are invited to play. Greg Nischwitz was electrocuted in an industrial accident at age 19 in 1980. He was a promising athlete and enrolled at WSU where he would have played for his father.

The story of the DABC is best told by studying the roster of players, managers, administrators, sponsors and even an umpire enshrined in the Dayton Amateur Baseball Hall of Fame. To be eligible, the player must have played five seasons in AA baseball.

The Charter Inductees, 1962

Jim Armpriester, Edward (Buddy) Bloebaum, Dick Burrows, Clarence (Pinnie) Coleman, George Harr, Wendell (Deacon) Diehl, Fredrick Howell, Ben Hudson, Willie Jones, Terry Lyons, Shorty Minzler, Howie Padgett, Bobby Rowlands, Claude (Tater) Huffer, Kenny Weber, Russ Wolfe.

The non-players include Judge Howell, Burrows, Hudson and Minzler. Hudson was a Dayton police officer killed in the line of duty for whom Hudson Field was named. Minzler was an umpire. Five players, Weber, Wolfe, Diehl, Bloebaum and Rowlands were on that 1944 Acme team.

The class of 1963 included Bobby Colburn, Tuffy Burke, Jim Boyles, Hugh Furry, Junior Norris and Roy Pfahler.

Picking them up by year:

1964: Ed Barney, Johnny Fine, Hap Grieshop, Dave Lucas, Charlie Menkel, H. H. (Blinky) Morgan.

1965: No selections.

1966: Ralph (Moody) Lamb, Joe Somuk, Bob Norris.

1967: Lefty Gilliland, Bobby Paxton, Bob Young, John McNabb.

1968: Don Bollechino, Bill Green, Johnny Shoup, Ernst Guild.

1969: Dick Aregood, Carl Ackerman, Horace English, Charley Maxton.

1970: Seymour (Kick) Ramby, Jack Chappelle, Marty Armbrister, Homer Leisz.

1971: Ray Otto, Bob Schlemmer, Emmett (Pete) Tidd, Tom Rogers.

1972: Herman Frank, Lefty Baker, Jim Murray, Jesse Haines.

1973: Carl Milby, James Brooks, Bucky Staggs, Russell Pearson.

1974: Ben Harrison, Russ Sanford, Ray Gatts, E. L. (Bud) Anderson.

1975: Lee Bordewisch, Al Burger, Don Murray.

1976: Orville Loughman, Bill Morgan, Dave Swartz, Ed Long.

1977: Ed Kruer, Bob Payne, Tony Trent, Ted Mills.

1978: Wayne Campbell, Jim Harrison, Vern Randolph, Lefty McFadden.

1979: Pete Brucken, Al Harp, Norm Schlicklin, Emil Guerra

1980: Donald Black, Charles Newcomb, Charles Zweisler, Dick Tatem.

1981: James Donnelly, Bill Frederick, Lee Ruse, John Berger.

1982: John Swisher, Joe Wilson, John Wolfe, Bill Early.

1983: Jim Hampton, Doug Huwer, Jimmy Rader, Orville Smith.

1984: Charles Barlow, Gene Brown, Joe DiMatteo, Joe (Dude) Zenni.

1985: Harold Dodson, Chuck Groves, Don Lyons, John Swain.

1986: Rod Andrew, Chuck Marr, Dick Mitchner, Tom Pequignot, Ben Waterman, Gary Wright.

1987: Bob Gohman, Nick Klein, Alkie Richards, Henry (Lefty) Tell.

1988: Fred Scherman, Bob Petri, Jess Waymer, Larry Drehs.

1989: Ton Fries, Mickey McGuire, Jack Schlemmer, Bill Warren.

1990: James Reboulet Sr., Phil Morgan, Chuck Long, Glendell Wylie.

1991: Wilbur Pytel, Ron Mason, Tom Brunswick, Bill Mote

1992: John Schlemmer, Howard Sewell, Darrell Wetzler, Fred Alves.

1993: Ken Fox, Bob Berry, Herm Schalnat, Steve Kring.

1994: Ron Nischwitz, Jim Reboulet, Jr., Theron Spence, Bill Fisher.

1995: Norb Zimmerman, Jack Hollon, Ron Duncan.

TRACK

Effort and determination are evident as Edwin Moses just beats Harald Schmid in the 400-meter hurdles of the World Track Championships in Rome in 1987 (above).

The road to Seoul and the 1988 Olympics was not an easy one for the greatest hurdler the world has ever seen. Despite age and injury he won the U. S. Trials in Indianapolis (right) and the bronze medal in Korea.

14

World Class Athlete

Because he earned world-wide headlines, recognition and respect, Edwin Corley Moses is clearly the best known athlete ever to come out of Dayton.

Because he dominated his individual sport as no track and field performer in history, his admirers can stake a claim that he can be called the best athlete ever to come out of Dayton.

The irony of those two tremendous achievements is that by the nature of his sport, he was never able to compete in his home town after he became a world figure. It wasn't until the 1988 Olympic Trials in Indianapolis, a dozen years after his first Olympic triumph, that he competed anywhere near Dayton.

Whatever else, Edwin Moses shot from obscurity in his sport to Olympic champion faster than any other performer: a mere four months.

In 1976, Moses was a junior at Morehouse University in Atlanta, building an academic reputation which helped him adapt his trim body to the requirements of his specialty, the 400 meter intermediate hurdles.

There was no hint of the incredible Moses story during Edwin's years in the Dayton school system, where he excelled in the classroom. But in track he was just an average kid in the high hurdles and the quarter mile, with an occasional go in the mile relay.

"I was always too small then," he said later in explaining his routine prep days.

He came by his intelligence naturally. His father, Irving Moses, Sr., had come into the Dayton system as a teacher. In 1976, when Edwin captured his Olympic Gold medal in Montreal, the father was principal at Fairport Elementary. His mother, Gladys, was a traveling instructor in the Dayton elementary system.

Edwin was the middle of three brothers, all of whom attended Fairview High School on the open enrollment plan then in effect. His track coach at Fairview, John Maxwell, Jr., remembers him as a 5-10, 125-pounder with average speed as a sprinter.

When Moses enrolled at Morehouse, he concentrated on improving his abilities in track and was still running the 440-yard dash and the 120-yard high hurdles. He was also carrying a 3.5 GPA in physics and math at the school from which Dr. Martin Luther King, Jr. graduated.

The real break in Edwin's approach to track came when the Rev. Lloyd Jackson became the Morehouse track coach in the fall of 1975.

Jackson, a Baptist minister and onetime national level competitor as a member of the Philadelphia Pioneer Track Club, also played pro football with the Philadelphia Eagles. He quickly turned an ordinary Morehouse track program into a contender in the SIAC, a conference of southern black schools. Moses meanwhile had added 40 healthy pounds to his frame and was on an exercise program to build his upper body strength.

Coach Jackson watched Edwin stretch his long legs on the high hurdles and suggested they try the intermediate hurdles where his ability in the quarter mile sprint could be coordinated with his stride.

"I start my move three steps ahead of the first hurdle and utilize a 13-stride pattern," Moses described the way he and Jackson theorized he could maximize his physical assets. Most intermediate hurdlers run on a 14 or 15-stride pattern.

He had never entered a 400-meter event until March 27 of the Olympic year and was never rated until the Trials. In May in the Florida Relays, Edwin was up against Harold Schwab, the defending champion in the 400 meter hurdles. At the time Schwab was a senior at Penn and was looked upon as the favorite to win a spot on the Olympic team in that event.

Schwab had to lean into the tape to edge Moses in what was to be the Dayton native's last defeat before the games.

Even after he beat Schwab a week later in the Penn Relays, not many track observers would have considered Moses a likely Olympic champion. But that was before he set an American record in the Olympic Trials at the University of Oregon, one of the few schools where track and field is a dominant sport on campus.

Edwin's performance at Oregon had the electronic experts checking their timing devices. They were astonished that such an unknown and inexperienced competitor could record that 48.30 timing. Not only was it the new American record, it was the third fastest time ever recorded. His very first race back in March was timed at 50.1, good enough to qualify him for the Trials, another unprecedented turn in his storybook career.

When he won at Oregon with that 48.30, all of a sudden the unknown Moses became the favorite in the event going into Montreal because defending champion John Akii-Bua of Uganda wasn't going to be able to compete because of a military upheaval in his homeland.

But with the world looking on, the way Moses shattered the Olympic and world record with a 47.64 timing convinced most experts that the young American would have won the gold anyway. He finished a 1.05 seconds ahead of the runner-up, American Mike Shine.

In the aftermath of Moses' triumph came what was described by this author in his *Journal Herald* column:

"In one of those rare, spontaneous moments in sports, Moses and Shine ran a 'victory lap' arm in arm to the cheers of the packed Olympic Stadium crowds of more than 70,000 people. The applause was deafening as Shine, who is white, joined hands aloft with the black Daytonian in a double victory salute."

"I couldn't believe he was pulling away from me at the end," said Shine, who had finished ahead of Moses in an unofficial warm-up race a week earlier.

The celebration with Shine provided one of the few moments in his competitive career that Moses is seen with a broad smile. He always entered any competition in a deadly intensive mood, as his post race interview attests.

"I had hoped to run a 47.5," he said, ignoring the fact he hadn't even competed in the event until that spring. "It wasn't a perfect race by any means. I was coming off the slowest start I've ever had but I made up for it in the second hundred."

This was typical of the totally unemotional way Moses analyzed every race of his fabulous career.

When he went back to Atlanta for his senior year at Morehouse, Edwin confided to Michael Mayberry, a classmate and photographer who was the first to take pictures of the youthful Moses gliding over the hurdles, that he was confident he would win at Montreal.

"He knew before he left here that he was going to win, but he's not one to get overconfident," Mayberry told an Atlanta newspaper. He was also disappointed that his Olympic victory didn't seem to be featured as one of the classic events of the 1976 Games' media coverage.

Moses left Morehouse with a dual degree in engineering and physics, doing part of his work at Georgia Tech.

Long before the Olympic rules were liberalized to permit professionals to compete, American track performers were making big money on the summer circuit in Europe. Champions like Moses were given guaranteed appearance money regardless of the competitive outcome.

When Moses went abroad in the summer of 1977 as a 21-year-old, he had not yet made the proper connections with promoters to line up appearance money and travel accommodations.

In making his entry into the European track circuit he suffered a defeat at the hands of Harold Schmid in Berlin, then launched the most remarkable victory streak in world competition in any sport. That streak carried him past his second Olympic Gold Medal in Los Angeles seven years later.

"He should never have beaten me," Moses said, referring to his loss to Schmid. "I was running all over Europe. It was the first time I was running so many meets close together. I ran three races in five days, going from Nice to Zurich to Berlin."

Moses won his event in four more West German meets following the unexpected setback that was to become the yardstick for his triumphs that followed. Back in this country, Edwin moved to California where he could engage in year-round training. He also went to work as an engineer with a major American concern.

When he went on tour in the summer of 1978, he understood the frustration of many American track and field Olympic champions in that he was better known around the world than in the United States. In the four year gap between the Olympics, track is often largely ignored by the average sports follower. Edwin's triumphs were recorded in Taiwan, Jamaica, Finland, Italy, Switzerland, Poland and England as well as West Germany.

Moses kept increasing the physical punishment of his training regimen. He became a vegetarian and approached his meals with a scientific dietary view. "I'm concentrating on taking care of my body," he said on one of his infrequent visits with his family in Dayton.

Moses explained he got the idea of eliminating meat from his diet while in a psychology class at Morehouse.

"Meat draws blood to the stomach for digestion and takes it away from the brain," he explained. "That's why people often get sleepy after a big meal."

The streak continued all through 1979 and it was apparent that Edwin was aiming for the 1980 Olympics scheduled for Moscow. The Daytonian had bettered his own world record twice since Montreal. The World Cup was scheduled in the Montreal Olympic Stadium in 1979 and Edwin returned to the scene of his greatest triumph, rising to the occasion with a 47.53 timing.

When President Jimmy Carter decided that the United States would boycott the Moscow games because of the Soviet undeclared war in Afghanistan, Moses was frustrated and openly critical of the decision. He went through the formality of competing in the Olympic Trials to be part of the American Olympic team and then had another busy summer on the world circuit.

A clue to some of Edwin's strong feelings about the Olympic boycott can be found in his comments about his own frustration over what he considered a lack of respect for his achievements.

"I'm definitely the best track and field athlete in the country," he told the *New York Times*. "Yet I can't get any kind of recognition."

It was obvious he felt a second gold medal would have helped in that respect. As it turned out, he had to wait four more years.

He was never better than in the summer of 1981 when he set himself on a limited schedule to be at his peak, running twice in June, three times in July, twice in August and four times in September. At a time when only two other men, Akii-Bua and Schmid had run under 48 seconds, he did it six times in seven of his events between June 21 and Sept. 4.

By this time Moses was engaged in many off-track activities, serving on the President's Council for Physical Fitness and was one of two athletes sitting in at the U. S. Olympic meetings. In business., he was on the boards of two electronics engineering firms.

After sitting out the 1982 season, he went back to work in 1983, obviously timing toward the 1984 Olympics in Los Angeles.

The streak was approaching the 100 mark with the Olympic Trials coming up, and there was no one on the horizon to challenge him.

He wasn't really pressed when he won his second gold in the Los

Angeles Coliseum in a race he had dedicated to the memory of his father, who had passed away the year before.

He was comfortably ahead of teammate Danny Harris, who won the silver and old rival Schmid who had to settle for the bronze. It was his 90th consecutive championship victory and the 105th counting qualification heats.

Tranel Hawkins, a graduate of Trotwood Madison High School and a two-time NCAA Division II champion in the Moses specialty, qualified as a member of the U. S. team but was beaten out by Schmid for the bronze medal.

Harris, a defensive halfback on the Iowa State football team, had told the media before the race that Moses could be beaten. Afterwards, he smiled when asked about the statements. "Edwin did what he had to do," he said in the press conference. "But I'm going to be around and there will be other times."

For his part in the post-race Olympic media session, Moses sat on the platform with his German-born wife, Myrella, his mother, Gladys, and two brothers, Irving, Jr. and Vincent.

"I'm fortunate to have been around eight years and the fact we were not permitted to compete in Moscow in 1980 sweetens the whole thing," he said. "I'm very sorry my father wasn't here to see this. He passed away during the last year and I dedicated the race to him."

Moses also made it plain that his career wasn't over even though he was then 28, considered a ripe old age in the track and field world.

The road to the 1988 Seoul Olympics wasn't an easy one for Moses, who took most of the 1986 year off.

The streak came to an end in 1987 when Harris made good on his promise "to be around for a while" and became the first man to beat Moses to the tape after 107 consecutive Moses victories. There were indications that age and injuries may have been catching up with the greatest hurdler the world had ever seen.

But Moses showed once more his iron will and physical prowess by winning a place on the Olympic team at the Trials in Indianapolis. His race there finally afforded many Dayton area track followers an opportunity to cheer him in person.

A crowd of 11,904 watched the veteran hurdler take command with a sizzling 47.37 timing to outdistance Andre Phillips and Kevin Young, who joined him as qualifiers for the trip to Seoul. Edwin's old rival Harris, who had ended the amazing victory streak, failed to qualify, finishing fifth. Tranel Hawkins finished sixth.

"This is the best I've felt in five years," said a relaxed Moses in the aftermath.

His bid for a third gold medal wasn't to be realized however. In Seoul, he was beaten by teammate Phillips, who ran a sizzling 47.19. A Senegalise runner won the silver while Moses settled for the bronze. His time was 47.56, bettering the time of his first gold medal and an impressive showing for a man who had just turned 33.

Moses acknowledged that in the press conference. "I beat the odds by being here," he said. "I'm happy. I knew I was going against the odds."

As columnist Gary Nuhn, who covered the games, put it, "He didn't create the event, but he perfected it."

Even then Moses refused to say he was finished and hinted at trying to qualify for the 1992 Games in Barcelona when he would have been 37. If it hadn't been for the Moscow boycott, he might have captured an unprecedented three golds in the event.

By the end of his active career, Moses had become a dominant figure in his sport. He was chairman of the Substance Abuse Committee of the U. S. Olympic Committee and was instrumental in having the TAC, the governing body of international track, adopt a drug abuse policy. He's a force for the positive side of his sport.

He completed work for his MBA at Pepperdine University, the business degree putting him in a position to function both as a researcher and in the front office of international corporations.

His is a remarkable career, unlikely to be duplicated in longevity or achievement.

Bob Schul, an American Pioneer

West Milton native Bob Schul made track history as the first American to win an Olympic gold medal in distance running when he captured the 5,000 meters in Tokyo in 1964.

Prior to Schul's gold, only three Americans had won any medals in the long distance competition.

Schul got a late start in developing his talent. When he was a senior at West Milton High School under coach Bill Ginn, Bob qualified for the state meet in the mile, but finished fifth in Columbus.

Bob grew up on the family farm and it was Willard Schul's intention that all four of his sons get a college education to match that of their mother, Katherine. She was teaching English in the Tipp City school system when her son won Olympic fame.

Bob's three brothers, Norman, Larry and Dave all have graduate degrees and are or were in the teaching profession.

Bob waited a year after high school to enroll at Miami University where he showed up in 1956. He started training in distance running and dropped out of school to enlist in the Air Force after his sophomore year.

During his military stay, he got deeply involved in the concept of distance running after he encountered Max Truax, a member of the U.S. Olympic team in 1960. It was Truax who got him to seriously train for distance competition to represent the Air Force.

Schul was blessed with the seeming prototype body of a distance runner. Just over six feet in height, he weighed only 145 pounds the year he won in Tokyo -- lean, wiry and hard-muscled.

In 1961, Hungarian refugee Mihaly Igloi became coach for distance runners in California and the Air Force gave Schul a month's leave to train under him for the military games. Laszlo Tabori, another Hungarian distance runner, was in the group and in tandem training with him under Igloi, Schul began to realize what was necessary in terms of physical and mental dedication to the sport.

"We ran 16 to 18 miles every day that first week," he recalled. "At the end of a morning workout, I'd almost collapse and I didn't think I could go out there again. But they talked me into it and I would die all over again in the afternoon. But by the second week, I was used to it. At the end of the month I was taking it in stride and in the best shape of my life."

While in the Air Force, he made three trips overseas to compete in European events. But his involvement did not get much attention back in this area. When he left the military service in 1962 to return to Miami, he was one of the better distance runners in NCAA competition, but there was very little emphasis on distance events in collegiate track.

At that time he also learned a hard lesson that would haunt him in later years -- that distance runners did not rate many headlines in what little media attention track and field generates in non-Olympic years.

The Tokyo Olympics were held late in the calendar year, so he spent the summer before sharpening his endurance and strategy. He had been confined to running the mile and two mile in many Miami collegiate meets which did not have longer races on the agenda. Not many Americans then, or now for that matter, easily translate 5,000 meters into our more accepted measurements. It is three miles, 188 yards and four inches

The Dayton Athletic Club sponsored Schul's entry into the Olympic trials with modest financial backing. But Schul was on his own spending the summer in California with Igloi. The daily routine then averaged "12 miles every other day" as he learned how to pace himself.

By the time of the Olympic Trials, he was recognized in track circles as a candidate for a medal in the Games -- the first American to generate that level of attention in the 5,000 meters.

Schul qualified for the trip to Tokyo by setting an American record in the Trials at Brunswick, New Jersey, winning in 14.10.8, bettering the old record by almost three seconds.

Bob's time in Tokyo (13.48.8) was even better as he outdistanced German runner H. Norpath. American teammate William Dellinger won the bronze. It was the best day ever for U. S. distance runners as Billy Mills, an American Indian from Oklahoma, was a surprise winner in the 10,000 meters.

Schul described his race in an interview with the author after he returned to America.

"You have to remember I was slightly boxed as we started the last lap," he explained. "I was very worried at that time and had to get some running room in a hurry. I could see Jazy (Michel Jazy of France) a good 20 yards ahead out in front.

"I managed to ease past the man from Kenya and then passed the German (Norpath) and only Jazy was out ahead. With 150 yards to go, I was still 15 yards back, but I saw him tighten up. I could see his shoulders tighten and his knees sag and I knew I had him.

"I kept telling myself 'drive, drive, drive' and when I passed him I had the great fear of someone coming up behind me. Suddenly, I felt the strain myself, and my legs began to hurt, but there was only 30 yards to go and you can take anything for 30 yards.

"I was smiling across the finish line because the tension was over. My mind could relax. The mental torment was finally over."

Schul's smile was captured in a sizeable color photo of the finish published in *Life Magazine*. When he returned to this country, he and his wife, Sharon, were among a group of Olympic medalists invited to a White House luncheon by President Lyndon B. Johnson.

On a quick visit to his home town, West Milton turned out en masse to pay tribute to their Olympic champion and Mayor William O. Callaghan presented him with a gold watch. In turn, he and Sharon had a gift for the community, an engraved silver tray expressing gratitude for the support given him.

With the winter indoor track season coming up, Schul seemed in position to enhance his reputation and look ahead to the outdoor season in this country and Europe where "amateurs" were capable of profiting from lucrative expense payments. Schul also declared his intention of volunteering to conduct track clinics at youth group sessions and at high schools. He made dozens of such appearances for expenses only.

He competed well in Europe and in this country the next two years but when he went back to Miami to complete work on his undergrad degree, he found himself in the middle of a running battle between the NCAA and the AAU in 1966. The argument was over eligibility and as a result, Schul gave up collegiate competition to compete at the national and world level. As a consequence he gave up a scholarship that would have applied to graduate study after he obtained his Miami degree in 1966.

Schul encountered frustration at his inability to obtain media recognition and more to the point, an inability to cash in on his Olympic success.

"Distance runners are not the glamour boys of track," he said.

Because of his late start, Schul would have been 31 if he had qualified for the 1968 Olympics in Mexico City. But he missed out in the Trials and his career as a world class performer was headed downhill.

Looking back in 1984, he lamented, "I guess I came along 20 years too soon. Distance runners today are making a living, winning races in the same times I was capable of running back then."

But he still takes great pride in his achievement.

"Winning that medal means more to me today than it did 20 years ago," he explained. "As each Olympiad goes by, what we did seems to have more and more meaning. As Americans, we hadn't done too much in long distance running, then Billy Mills and I won the gold in the 5,000 and 10,000. I thought that was a great breakthrough for the USA but it hasn't developed that way."

He does like the idea that he was a pioneer in the sense of public acceptance of jogging, mini-marathons and just plain running as a means of staying healthy. Bert Nelson, editor of *Track and Field News*, paid him a tribute along those lines in the 1984 Olympic year.

"Schul had a great impact on distance running because he was one of the first Americans to become an established international star at any distance over a mile," wrote Nelson. "His training was revolutionary for the time. Everyone else training for distance was doing pack work (running in groups). Schul and his coach (Igloi) did individual workouts with emphasis on speed work. He was 10 years ahead of his time."

Nelson also wrote that Schul had enough success at the world level after he won the Olympic medal to prove that it was no fluke. He was still competitive beyond his 50th birthday in 1987, still running in age class events whenever possible.

Schul opened a sporting goods store in Troy in 1972 and later added an athletic shoe store in Huber Heights. The business ventures eventually failed, unable to compete with nationally franchised firms.

The Barcelona Games

Edwin Moses was out of the Olympic picture going into the 1990s but Dayton's growing reputation as a hotbed of track and field development was verified in the 1992 Games in Spain.

LaVonna Martin climaxed a decade as a world class performer with a silver medal in the women's 100 meter hurdles and Joe Greene, a Stebbins high school graduate who starred at Ohio State, came up with a bronze finishing behind the veteran Carl Lewis and Mike Powell in the long jump.

Meadowdale graduate Tonja Buford was the youngest member of the American women's team in Barcelona, where she gained valuable experience but no medals. With the 1996 Atlanta Games less than a year down the road as this material was compiled, Buford is one of the favorites in her specialty.

Roland McGhee, another Trotwood-Madison alum and more recently an alum of Middle Tennessee State, was the No. 1 ranked long jumper in the U. S. in June of 1995. Greene, with a second medal on his mind, was ranked second just behind him. Chris Nelloms' detoured dream of an Olympic medal may be realized in Atlanta.

If the name Floreal should appear on the Trials list, it would be the married name of LaVonna Martin-Floreal, who at age 27 would be battling the odds if she resumed the necessary training grind. As LaVonna Martin, her credentials as one of the area's finest athletes, are well established.

Trotwood-Madison won the team championship in the state track meet in 1983 and 1984. Exceptional individual performers frequently carry their team to such titles, but in LaVonna's case, there was no doubt. She WAS the team.

LaVonna was T-M's only qualifier. Her first place finish in the 100-meter and 300-meter hurdles as well as the 200 meter dash were enough points to win the title. Amazing enough, but to have done that in successive years stamped her as one of the legendary performers in the history of the state meets.

The groundwork for LaVonna's development began at home where her father, Harold "Lefty" Martin, played a major role. For over 30 years, Lefty Martin headed the Northwest Track Club, a program from which 46 individuals captured national youth championships. Seven went on to win individual NCAA championships and four became Olympic participants.

From high school she went on to become All-American at the University of Tennessee. During her competition for the Vols, she captured a pair of NCAA indoor championships in her specialty, the 100-meter hurdles. More importantly from the Olympic goal, she was competing in national events such as the Mobil Championships and Penn Relays as well as getting a start on the European circuit.

LaVonna earned a spot on the 1988 Olympic team that went to Seoul, where she lasted into the semifinal heat. From there she was on the European summer circuit in 1989-1990, building her reputation. At that point in time, she seemed an automatic choice to represent her country in Barcelona. But an unexpected roadblock came perilously close to wiping out her dream.

On May 5, 1991 she was handed a two-year suspension after a January drug test came up positive for the diuretic furosemide, one of 400 substances banned by the IAAF, track's international governing body. The furosemide was administered in a pair of diet pills spuriously given to Martin by then-coach Tatiana Zelentskova, who admitted she knew the substance was banned but did not advise LaVonna of that.

Martin said at the time she was suffering from flu and menstrual cramps and was retaining fluids. Martin maintained that when she had questioned the Soviet coach she was working with about the possibility of the pills having anything illegal in them, she was assured they did not.

The suspension was to last until January 1993, which meant LaVonna would miss the 1991 Pan American Games where she had won gold in 1987, the 1991 world championships and the 1992 Olympics.

The suspension sent shock waves through Dayton's track community since both LaVonna and her father had excellent reputations as church-going people who were careful to abide by all the rules. It led to a lengthy legal battle to clear her name. A third review panel finally, in March, 1992, found for her and the IAAF dropped the suspension.

That opened the door for her rebuilding process and in the words of her mother, Brenda, "It was very difficult for her, but to be truthful, Vonnie has come out of this a better young woman, a better Christian and certainly a better athlete."

In the June Trials, she qualified with a time of 12.71, the fastest in her career, exceeded only by that of Gail Devers, America's top rated competitor.

"I've never seen her so focused," said her father, observing her training in Barcelona.

She won both of her qualifying heats as well as the semifinal and was among the eight women with the opportunity to go for the gold in what turned out to be one of those Olympic events decided by an unexpected twist of fate.

Martin's start wasn't as explosive as she had hoped, and Devers, the world record holder, was in front of a Bulgarian and Greek hurdler with LaVonna fourth. Then Devers caught her knee on the 10th and last hurdle and went into a high speed stumble, almost falling toward the finish line.

Greece's Paraskevi Patoulidou took advantage of the mishap to become the first woman from her country to win an Olympic gold in track.

Martin thrust her chest across the line ahead of the Bulgarian to capture the silver. Her time of 12.29 was her career best. Ironically, she had finished ahead of Patoulidou in her three qualifying races.

Naturally the media, especially the television seen in America, concentrated their attention on what had happened to Devers and LaVonna's friends in this area were disappointed that her resurrection (from the suspension) was given very little notice.

While she may not have fulfilled her dream of a gold, she was the first Dayton-born woman to win an Olympic track medal and had come all the way back from the dark year of 1991 when her activity was restricted to training.

"Having come off the trials and tribulations I did, and being overlooked by so many people who just wrote me off, I'm truly ecstatic," she said pouring out her feelings. "My thank you's go to Jesus Christ, my family, my coaches and so many of the people back in Dayton. When there's been a great storm, my hometown has always given me shelter. That's why this night is their night too," she went on.

On that same evening, Joe Greene won his bronze in the long jump, marking the first time in Olympic competition that two athletes from Dayton had earned medals on the same day. The 25-year-old Greene gave the USA a sweep in the long jump,. The celebrated Carl Lewis, winning his third straight gold, and his perennial challenger, Mike Powell, ran 1-2 as expected and, in this instance, Greene was more than happy to join them on the platform.

Greene, a graduate of Stebbins Wayne High School, had a strong personal following in Dayton because of his participation in church activities at the United Christian Center, which sent a telegram of support the morning of the race.

In high school, Greene's best jump was a wind-aided 24.1, hardly indicative of the Olympic medalist he would become. At Ohio State, he won the NCAA, and decided the long jump was his best sport. He started his college competition in the triple jump.

Greene is a charismatic person, as he displayed in Barcelona. When walking off his steps in warm-ups, he was clapping his hands overhead, drawing attention from fans who started their own claps in accompaniment.

In the media conference that involved Lewis, Powell and himself, Greene's cheerful and positive demeanor made him a lot of friends.

"I like being in competition with Joe because he never lets you get too serious," Powell said of his friendly rival.

Talking about his high school days, he saluted Dayton over Columbus, where he went to OSU and lives.

"Dayton has it all over Columbus because Ohio State is all football," he said. "Football blots everything else out. But in Dayton they appreciate our sport. They know good track and field in my hometown."

For Tonja Buford, the Barcelona Games were her springboard into the European circuit but her ultimate goal remains a medal in Atlanta. Reaching the semifinals in Spain set her up.

The Meadowdale athlete became one of the finest women athletes ever to compete at the University of Illinois. In her junior year (1993) she won the 100 meters, the 100 hurdles,. the 400 hurdles and ran legs on the winning 400 and 1,600 meter relays.

A year later, she helped Illinois to a seventh place team finish in the

NCAA outdoor meet personally accounting for 28 points. Her 25 Big Ten victories, individual and relay events, are a Big Ten record.

Once out of Illinois, she decided to concentrate on her specialty, the 400 meter hurdles, the women's version of Edwin Moses' specialty.

She won a bronze medal at the 1991 Pan American Games in Cuba, the year before the Barcelona Games. She was fifth in the 1993 world championships in Stuttgart, Germany and the Goodwill Games in St. Petersburg. Going into the 1995 summer tour, Buford seemed to be approaching her peak. She finished second by the lean of the body to Kim Barris in the 400 meter hurdles, in the exciting time of 54.74 seconds.

Chris Nelloms Starts Early

The late 1980s were an exciting time for Dayton area track enthusiasts with the success of such standouts as Chris Nelloms, LaVonna Martin, Tony Lee, Tonja Buford, Leron Brown, Joe Greene and Roland McGhee performing at the national level.

Nelloms, who started his serious track training at age seven, flashed across the high school scene very early in his career at Dunbar.

The slender speedster, who also played high school football, wound up leading the Wolverines to the city league championship all four years he was competing.

On May 22, 1987 in the finals of the Dayton District AAA meet, as a freshman he won the 100 meters (10.7), 200 meters (21.9) and the 400 (48.4) and anchored the 1,600 meter relay team to win, his leg being unofficially clocked at 47.47.

That performance sent Nelloms off to Columbus for the state meet a week later where he captured the first of four successive 400 meter championships. Eventually, he led Dunbar to state team titles in 1988, 1989 and 1990, capturing11 individual state championships in the process.

His coach, Randy Waggoner, realized early on that he had an athlete at the same exceptional level as Craig Wallace, who led Dunbar to two state titles in the early 1960s specializing in the 100 and 220-yard dashes. In the 440, Nelloms was bettering the times of Earl Richardson, a star in the early 1970s.

Within two years, Nelloms was running in Junior Olympic events across the U. S. and Canada, into South America and Europe. *Sports Illustrated* did a story with art on him in the spring of 1989 on the basis of his performance in the Mansfield-Mehock Relays, long one of the state's premier open events.

Chris became only the fifth athlete in the history of the 57-year-old Mansfield event to win three titles at one meet. These were the 110 high hurdles and the 200 and 400 meters, the latter becoming his premier event.

In his junior year in the state, he accounted for 38 Dunbar's 56 points to win the team championship with victories in the 200 and 400 and again anchoring the 1,600 meter relay team. He finished second in the fastest 110 high hurdles ever run in the prep event in Ohio Stadium up to that time.

Although he was the only high school athlete in the country eligible to attempt to qualify in the 400) meters for the 1988 Olympic Trials in Indianapolis, Nelloms passed it up because he was just coming back from a pulled hamstring.

Competing with the U. S. Junior National team, he became the first American to win three gold medals in a world junior meet. The next summer found Nelloms winning a junior national track championship and qualifying for a trip to South America.

During his high school days, Chris' most serious rival in the Dayton area was Jefferson's Tony Lee. In Lee's senior year, he was capable of beating Nelloms to the tape in the 100 with his fast start. But Chris handled the curve better and generally prevailed in the 200. This was the case in the annual Roosevelt Memorial in 1988 when Lee won the 100 and Nelloms the 200.

Both Lee, a three-time Ohio champion in the 100, and Nelloms competed for the U. S. team in the World Junior Championships in the summer of 1988. Lee went on to compete at the college level at the University of Tennessee.

Going into his senior year, Nelloms worked hard at an earlier ambition to master the 110 high hurdles, leaving the 100 meter spots on the team to talented teammates. At the same time, he was zeroing in on the longer sprints.

At Ohio State. he was academically ineligible as a freshman, but came on like a whirlwind against collegiate competition as a sophomore. He won the 200 meter Big Ten indoors championship and was named Athlete of the Meet in the Big Ten outdoors for his success in capturing the 100 and 200 meters and running on both the winning 400 and 1,600 relay teams.

At that point the sky seemed the limit for the wiry Daytonian with his eye on the potentially lucrative European summer circuit and beyond that the 1996 Olympics. But as fate would have it, he had to survive a close brush with death.

As he was out for a late evening jog alone near his home in Trotwood in the summer of 1992, while the Olympics were going on in Barcelona, he was ambushed. A bullet nearly took his life, entering his chest two inches above his heart.

For two days he was listed in critical condition but his superb physical conditioning helped him through a difficult rehab routine. The crime has never been solved. Chances are it was a case of mistaken identity.

"All I know is that there were three guys dressed in black and nobody said anything," he was quoted. "I've heard all kinds of things why it happened. I was shot in a drug deal. I owed a drug dealer money. I was meeting with someone else's wife. None of that is true."

Chris made a rapid recovery, judging by the fact he came back that March to win the NCAA indoor 200 meter championship.

But then in May, two days before the Big Ten meet, he collapsed in practice with muscle spasms around his heart. But he surprised everyone after obtaining medical clearance by winning the 100 and 200 in the conference meet and being voted Athlete of the Meet for the second straight year.

In the summer of 1993, he was up against the world's best in Europe and he proved he belonged by finishing third in a meet in Zurich. In that top level European circuit, he finished in the top five in six 200 meter competitions.

More hard luck cropped up in his senior season for the Buckeyes. A pulled muscle that resisted treatment forced him into limited duty, running only in relays. With his college eligibility behind him, he has a degree in recreation/sports management from OSU. He turned pro in the summer of 1994 and launched his career against the best again in Europe. His goal beyond that is the Atlanta games.

If all goes well, the best may yet to be. As a matured, 5-11, 165-pounder, he turns 25 on August 14, 1996 in the last week of the Atlanta Games.

"In the back of my mind, I'm capable of world records in the 200 and 400," he declared in outlining his dreams.

Dave Albritton carries the Olympic torch in downtown Dayton in 1964 (left).

LaVonna Martin of Trotwood-Madison (below, left) wins by a hair over Centerville's Laura Kirkham.

Albritton with his OSU classmate and friend Jesse Owens (below, right).

Olympic gold medalist Lucinda Adams.

178

15

Dave Albritton's Era

David D. Albritton was born on a tenant farm in Alabama but spent the last 53 years of his life as a respected member of the Dayton community, recognized as successful in three different activities.

In between Alabama and Dayton he had grown up in Cleveland, starred in track, became an All-American at Ohio State and captured a silver medal in the high jump in the 1936 Berlin Olympic Games.

He also was involved in a life-long best friend relationship with Jesse Owens, one of America's greatest Olympic legends.

Albritton and Owens were born a few miles apart in Alabama and both families moved to Cleveland about the same time. The two of them led Cleveland East Tech to the state high school championship in 1932 and 1933.

At Ohio State, Albritton was the NCAA champion in his specialty, the high jump, three straight years, 1936-37-38, while Owens set four national records in one day in the 1935 conference meet in Ann Arbor.

Going to Berlin together was the climax of their athletic achievements, Owens winning four golds in the 100 and 200 meters, the long jump and as a member of the 400 meter relay team.

Albritton came to Dayton for a civilian position at Wright Field early in World War II. He had no inkling of what lay ahead as an educator, legislator and business man.

When he took over coaching the Dunbar track team, the all-black school was not on the schedule of the other Dayton high schools.

After the war, Albritton managed to quietly persuade several white coaches who had come to know him to send their teams against his in dual meets that attracted little attention or publicity.

His role in helping break down the segregation barriers for all of Dunbar's athletic teams to get the school accepted into the city league was a positive development in different ways. In an interview on the 50th anniversary of the Berlin Games, where Owens and fellow black Americans humiliated Adolf Hitler, Albritton put his life into perspective.

"The Olympic medal was a great moment in my life and a great experience," he said. "But I want to be remembered for a lot more than that. A lot of nice things have happened to me and I'm equally proud of some of my other achievements."

Not dwelling on his years in the state legislature or in the insurance firm that bore his name, he looked back on the racial barriers that existed when he started coaching.

"The other Dayton schools wouldn't play us in basketball or football, but when we had dual track meets with Fairview, Kiser and Stivers, I guess we proved blacks and whites could compete without causing a riot," he said.

Dunbar's big breakthrough in community recognition came in 1948 when Albritton's team captured the state class A championship.

The key performers on the team were Maceo Cofield in 100 and 440 yard runs, sprinter Sammy Mukes in the 100 and 220, Frank Kilgore in the mile and half-mile, Vernon Stroud in the high jump, Russ Henderson in the hurdles and Lynn Owens in the half-mile.

It was a memorable state tournament in that Gene Cole almost won it single-handedly for Lancaster. Cole was easily the most outstanding sprinter in the history of Ohio high school sports at that time. He went on to Ohio State and owned several Big Ten records at one time. In the meet, he set state records in winning the 100, 220 and 440 yard events, setting an American record with 48 seconds flat in the 440.

Kilgore and Owens won their distance events and the slender half-point margin that meant the championship came with Dunbar winning the mile relay with Mukes, Cofield, Owens and Henderson.

A few weeks before the state tournament, Albritton helped form what was called the Dayton Athletic Club to sponsor an AAU sanctioned open state meet on the track at the University of Dayton stadium.

Ed Dugger, who had been a nationally ranked hurdler at Tufts University, had come to Dayton to work as a technical engineer at the air base. He joined other track enthusiasts Harold Green, Norm Saettel and the author as incorporators of the DAC.

Albritton persuaded Olympic-bound Harrison Dillard, one of the top names in track at the time, and his coach Eddie Finnegan of Baldwin-Wallace, to enter the meet, sponsored by the *Dayton Journal.*

Gene Cole was also persuaded to come to Dayton for the meet, which gave area track enthusiasts a rare attractive special event.

There were no records set on the seldom-used cinder track at what later became Baujan Field, but until the national AAU meet was held here in Welcome Stadium, it was the biggest track event staged in Dayton.

Albritton's track teams at Dunbar were then getting into a string of eight straight city championships (1946-53) until Roosevelt broke the sequence in 1954.

Albritton gave up coaching to run for State Representative for the then 85th district in 1960, winning as a Republican in the year the country went Democrat as John F. Kennedy won the presidency.

Dave served in Columbus for 12 years. Although he lost an electoral bid to become Montgomery County Clerk of Courts in 1976, he remained active in civic affairs and was a driving force behind the successful bid to have a street named for Olympic track standout Edwin Moses.

The First National Meet

Dave Albritton was a vital influence in helping bring the four national AAU meets staged in Welcome Stadium. An army of volunteers, more than is necessary to stage a golf tournament, is a must for a community to submit a bid to the national AAU to host a national track meet.

The Dayton Chamber of Commerce (the official title in 1953) agreed to put up $20,000 to underwrite the event. Pledges of support came from the city administration as well as from the civic-minded S. C. Allyn, the President of NCR.

Although the 1953 meet was the 65th in AAU history, it marked the first time it was ever held in Ohio.

Many of the committee members were well-known track and field officials or enthusiasts who had helped stage the Dayton Athletic Club's 1948 invitational meet. The list included Jim Boyles, Art Shroyer, Norm Saettel, Harold Green, Ted Bailey, Wayne Yarcho (a top power walker competitor) along with Albritton and Dugger. Other members of the committee were from the business and civic side of the Chamber of Commerce.

The star-studded field of competitors included a number of athletes who had performed in the Helsinki Olympics the year before. Included were Gold Medalists Walt Davis (high jump), Parry O'Brien (discus), Sim Iness (shot put), Mal Whitfield (800 meters), Andy Stanfield (200 meters), Horace Ashenfelter (steeplechase) and silver medalist Jack Davis (110 meter hurdles).

Another headliner was Wes Santee, the University of Kansas miler, who was in quest of the then magic four minute mile. The AAU meet here wasn't metric and the mile is not an Olympic event.

Chamber officials and committee members were nervous about the crowd, but as it turned out 9,500 spectators jammed into Welcome Stadium Friday night and a turnout of 6,500 Saturday made for a total attendance of 16,000. The goal of breaking even was more than met and the slight profit made it a financial success as well.

It turned out that only 5,000 25-cent programs had been printed and more than 4,000 of them were sold Friday night. The supply was quickly exhausted for the finals on Saturday.

The headline event, and one of six AAU records set, belonged to Walt Davis, the rangy (6-foot-6) Texan who broke the world high jump record with a leap of 6-feet, 11 1/2 inches. Track hadn't been the primary sport of the 23-year-old when he was a basketball player at Texas A&M.

Among the first to congratulate Davis, a father of three children, was Albritton, who had won his Olympic silver in the same event in Berlin.

Santee made no headway against the four minute mile, but his time of 4.07.6 did set a meet record. Jack Davis of the Los Angeles AC was the only double winner, taking golds in the 110 high hurdles and the 220 lows.

Norman, Mitchell And Randy Waggoner

The changing enrollment patterns in the Dayton school system that led to the closing of Roosevelt High School in 1975 did not disrupt the strong track program that had developed there first under coach Floyd (Dude) Norman and carried on under Don Mitchell and Randy Waggoner.

The coaching staff transferred to Roth and eventually to Dunbar and kept the Dayton area in the state spotlight.

Waggoner, one of the most successful track coaches in Ohio high school history, is unique in that he does not have a college degree and started as a volunteer assistant after graduating from Roosevelt in 1962.

"As I wasn't going away to college, I asked coach Norman if I could help with the track team," Waggoner recalled about the start of his 28 year coaching span. Randy's first project was working with Alan Huff, who was the runner-up in the state meet in the 400 meters.

In 1967 Roosevelt's track standout, Leo Hayden, was better known for his football ability, going on to be a star running back at Ohio State. "He was the runner-up in the state in the high hurdles," Waggoner said.

Mitchell moved up from his role as assistant to become head coach when Norman retired in 1969, and Waggoner stayed on. The two of them had their first individual state champion in Olden Wallace, who won the 100 meters and finished second in both the 120 high and the 190 low hurdles.

Jeff Parks was selected an All-American in 1971 when he won three events in the state - the high and low hurdles as well as the long jump. Roosevelt finished second in the state meet in 1972 when John Rudd captured the trophy and blue ribbon in 120 highs and ran on the winning 400 and mile relays.

With the closing of Roosevelt, Mitchell moved over to Roth along with Waggoner and promptly directed the Falcons to the state title in AA. The top performers were hurdler Marshall Parks, middle distance man Jim Smith, who won the 800 meters, and Robert Buchanan, who captured the 400 meters, ran second in the half mile and was on the winning mile relay team.

Tragedy struck in mid-May of 1979 when Mitchell, who had been out on his own daily conditioning run before practice, came into the locker room gasping for breath. He collapsed and fell to the floor. He was dead of a heart attack before paramedics got him to the emergency room at Good Samaritan Hospital.

James Caldwell, the Roth principal, turned the team over to Waggoner and petitioned the OHSAA to approve Randy taking over the coaching role despite his lack of a teaching certificate.

"I was working at Chrysler all along and not on the school payroll," Waggoner recalled. "I was thrilled when I learned the state association gave me the opportunity."

In the next ten years Waggoner won five state championships to earn his place in the Ohio Track Coaches Hall of Fame.

The first of those championships came in 1981 when the Falcons were carried to the title by the multi-talented Deron Brown, who won the

200 and 400 meters, finished second in the 100 and ran a leg on the winning mile relay team.

"As a team we scored 62 points, the most ever in a state meet up to that time," Waggoner said.

Competing in a different division a year later, the Falcons dominated in their visit to Columbus, the site of the state meet. Brown repeated as champ in the 400 meters but had to settle for second in the 200. Cedric Manuel captured the 800 meter and football star Keith Byars contributed to wins in two relays.

"We had an awful lot of talent and our team total of 77 points was the record in AA, and hasn't been topped yet," Waggoner said in the summer of 1995.

Waggoner moved over to Dunbar just in time to find himself blessed with the arrival of Chris Nelloms. whose feats have been covered in treatment of the 1992 Olympics.

"Chris is the finest athlete I've ever had the pleasure of working with," Waggoner said of the young man who won four consecutive state titles in the 400 meters. "He's not only a world class sprinter, but a fine young man with great character and charisma."

In the 1988 state meet Nelloms qualified for the Olympic Trials with his blazing 45.8 timing in the 400. At age 17, he was the youngest athlete eligible for the trials.

With Doane Moore and Steve Ragland also contributing points, Nelloms and the Wolverines triumphed again in 1989. Chris saved his best for his senior year when he set two national high school records with a 45.5 clocking in his specialty, the 400 meters, and he went 13.3 in the 110 meter high hurdles.

Waggoner, weary of working two jobs, gave up coaching at that point and as of the summer of 1995, was in his 31st year with Chrysler.

Waggoner retired after having directed his teams to five state championships in that 10-year span. His teams won three team titles in the Mansfield Relays, one of the most prestigious high school meets in the country and he helped build the Dayton Relays into a statewide attraction.

The most successful challenges at the local level to Dunbar's superiority in the 1980s came from Patterson, coached by Craig Wallace, a star performer at Dunbar in the early 1960s. Wallace's team won three straight city titles (1985-86-87).

The 1957 Men's National

By the time Dayton went after another national AAU in 1957, there was less concern about the project breaking even.

Albritton was the meet manager as he had been in 1953 and the basic group of track officials and enthusiasts remained pretty much the same. S. C. Allyn was again honorary chairman.

The cast of competitors was considerably different, of course, but once again gold medal winners from the 1956 Games in Melbourne were in the list of entrants. All told, 10 Olympians were in the competition.

A 33-man California Striders team arrived on Wednesday. It included Charles Dumas, who had broken the world record in the high jump set by Walt Davis in Dayton and was the first man to better seven feet.

Dumas had won the gold in Melbourne at 6 feet, 11 and 1/2 half inches but wasn't able to match that in winning the AAU meet here at 6 feet, 10 1/2, under the Walt Davis height which held as a meet record.

Another big name was Dave Sime, the Duke athlete and the 100 yard champion in the NCAA. Sime won here, but his time was only 9.7 but most observers felt the track wasn't in tip-top shape. It had rained a lot during the week, and although Albritton himself supervised work keeping the track in shape, it wasn't as good as hoped for.

Glenn Davis, the Barberton native and one of Ohio State's all-time track greats, performed here and won, but his 50.9 time in the high hurdles was well off his Olympic medal time of 50.1. In the 1960 Rome Olympics, Davis bettered that time to become the first man to break the 50-second barrier. Al Oerter, who was to win four consecutive golds in successive Olympics in the discus, was a routine winner.

One of the interesting sidelights of the 1957 meet was a demonstration by Olga Connolly, the wife of Harold Connolly, at the time the American record holder in the 16-pound hammer throw. As expected, Harold Connolly won his specialty. Olga, the native of Czechoslovakia and world class standout, was not eligible to compete, but her ability with the discus, hammer, shot and javelin impressed the crowd of 6,799 and was a forerunner of the great developments ahead in women's competition.

Another headliner, Rev. Bob Richards, two-time Olympic pole vault champion and the first track man to have his picture on a box of *Wheaties*, won his event as expected.

The limited capacity of Welcome Stadium being what it is, Dayton never again had the income potential to enter a bid for a national meet as the costs skyrocketed.

The Women Come To Dayton

When the 1963 National AAU Girls, and Women's Track and Field championships came to Dayton, Dave Albritton was in the state legislature in Columbus, but the organization he helped found in 1948, the Dayton Athletic Club, was the sponsor.

The DAC, which had been staging annual open meets in Dayton, had the support of the University of Dayton, which handled the ticket sales and other business aspects.

Norm Saettel, the long-time Dayton District AAU secretary and a member of the National AAU Women's and Men's track committees, was the meet director. Jim Ehler, track and basketball coach at Fairmont East High School was the president of the DAC, and Chuck Hardin, director of Dayton Public High School track program was the games director.

Other sports figures on the Games committee included Bill Braley, Al Turner, Ray Clemens, Bill Ginn, Tom Hamlin, Jack Brown, Paul Heckman, Dan Hamrock, Gaston (Country) Lewis, the longtime coach and athletic director at Central State, and Harold Green.

There was added national interest in the meet because the first two finishers in each event would qualify for the AAU national team trip for dual meets in the Soviet Union, Poland, Germany and England. Because the meet was run in two divisions, for girls and women, the program took three days rather than two to run off.

In terms of participants, this event attracted far more entrants than either of the previous national men's meets. There were 42 registered teams along with a few individuals who had qualified to compete without affiliation.

As might have been expected, coach Ed Temple's Tennessee State teams won both division titles.

Few in the stands could have known when they watched Edith Maguire edge teammate Wilma Tyus in the 100 yard dash, both running 11 seconds flat, they were watching the 1-2 finalists in the Olympic 100 meters a year later. Only at the Games Tyus edged Maguire for the gold, but the latter captured her gold in the 200 meters.

In the broad jump here, Maguire beat out Willye White, another

1964 Olympian. White competed for the Mayor Daley Track Club of Chicago.

The competition in the girls division finals Friday night wasn't finished until 1 a.m., the last event being a long battle in the high jump, finally won by Eleanor Montgomery, competing for the Cleveland Track Club. The Ohioan edged Terrezene Brown of Tennessee State. Montgomery, 16 at the time, and Brown, 15, were both future Olympians.

Six years later, the girls and womens 1969 national championships returned to Welcome Stadium, this time sponsored by the Knights of Columbus of Greater Dayton. Saettel was again the force behind the event as meet director. Through the 1970s Saettel was involved in staging several national AAU boys meets held on the track at Central State.

The 1969 extended meet didn't look like a box office success and the national AAU tried to help out by getting several male Olympic champions to come in for a five-event added exhibition.

The headliners were John Carlos and Randy Matson. While they were in Dayton, an NCAA official tried to warn them they were risking their college eligibility by participating. After telephone conferences between the AAU and NCAA, the problem was resolved and the men performed despite threatening weather.

Eleanor Montgomery, who had won the high jump at age 16 in the girl division here in 1963, this time broke her own American record with a leap of 5-11 1/2.

Tennessee State, which won both divisions of the meet again, set a record in the 880 relay with Matteline Render, Madeline Manning, Iris Davis and Pauline Hunter participating. Manning was the winner in her specialty, the 800 meters.

Olympic sprinter Barbara Farrell slogged her way along the slow track to victory in both the 100 yard and 220 yard sprints.

The Lucinda Adams Era

The beginning of girls athletic programs in the Dayton city schools is directly related to the hiring of Lucinda Adams as a special education teacher at the start of the 1961-62 school year.

Adams came to Dayton a year after climaxing a brilliant track and field career with an Olympic gold medal as a member of the U. S. 400 meter relay team at the 1960 Games in Rome.

A native of Savannah, Georgia, Adams was one of the many great women track competitors turned out at Tennessee State under legendary coach Ed Temple.

Her first trip to the Olympics in 1956 took her to Melbourne, Australia where, as a freshman, she came back with nothing but a wonderful experience and a groundwork for future triumphs.

Within two years she was a member of the American team that competed in the first USA-USSR international meet in Moscow. She captured two golds there, in the 200 meters and in the 400-meter relay.

The U. S. team also competed in Hungary, Poland, Greece, Germany and England before returning to the USA.

Adams finished third in the 1958 voting for the Sullivan Award that goes to the top amateur athlete in the country. In the Pan American games in Chicago in 1959, she won three golds and set an American record for the 220 yard dash.

The Olympic gold in Rome ended her competitive career but not her involvement in the Olympic movement. She eventually was a member of the U. S. delegation to the International Olympic Academy in Athens, Greece in 1986. Previously, she had performed other duties in coaching and chaperoning women's teams.

Over the years Adams was to become involved in community activities in Dayton far beyond the sports scene. There was no hint of that sort of a career when she was hired into the system as an elementary instructor.

Adams spent her first decade in the elementary system where her track and field experience helped her teach physical education classes to handicapped children in special education.

But in 1972, John Maxwell, Sr., then the superintendent of the system, had her assigned to Roosevelt High School in health/physical education.

Bill Marquardt, then heading the athletic office, sent out directives that women's programs could be set up in track, volleyball and basketball.

"Until then, there had been no concern about varsity sports for women," Adams recalled. "The three coaches in the beginning, Doris Black (Colonel White), Anne Earley (Dunbar) and myself got things going. As if we didn't have enough to do in three sports, I was also to be the cheerleaders advisor."

It is interesting to remember that Doris Black became the only woman to coach a boys varsity basketball team at Colonel White.

The girls sports teams had a difficult time sharing the facilities at their schools with the men's teams.

"Naturally, there weren't many events and we had little competition," Adams recalled of the beginning. "We had to have our track meets against each other at the little track at Grace E. Greene, an elementary school."

The same problems existed when it came to basketball.

"We'd pack the girls in our cars and go where we could play. All the games were in the afternoons after school and there was little attendance and no recognition. Gradually, the other high schools started up their programs, but we were never looked on as being as important as the men."

Things began to change in 1979 when she was appointed supervisor of Athletic, Health and Physical Education in the system. By then an emphasis on girls and womens sports had become the law of the land.

Adams' role was expanded to make her curriculum consultant for a comprehensive health/phys ed, driver education and safety program. Her retirement took effect Aug. 1, 1995.

"It has been a very rewarding experience to see the girls programs develop into what they are now compared to what they were in the beginning. When we started to organize teams, we didn't know what to expect, but right away we had more kids than we could handle. This caught the attention of the principals."

Adams maintains that administrators were slow to recognize the educational benefits that can be had from participation in athletics.

"They were slow to appreciate what belonging to a team can do in motivating the girls to became better all-around students. It was rewarding to see the parents of our girls became much more involved and supportive of the whole educational process," she added.

Although the federal legislation known as Title IX applies more to college than to high school programs, Adams credits the legislation for producing benefits down the line.

"I'm sure Title IX helped us in the struggle to get the pay scale for women coaches up to those of the men," she said.

Adams says she does not intend to get too far away from the athletics scene after her retirement.

"I look back on so many great memories," she said, "even the ones that didn't seem so good at the time. Like the only speeding ticket I ever got in my life. Our Roosevelt girls were on the longest trip we had ever taken for a basketball game. We were following the Roosevelt men in their bus going to Steubenville.

"The highway patrolman seemed very surprised that he had stopped a car packed with high school girls so far from home."

Adams was honored by being voted one of the Top Ten Women in Dayton in 1987 and was a recipient of a Lifetime Achievement Award in 1994 given by the Ohio Professional/Amateur Athlete of the Year committee.

In February, 1995, she was the recipient of a Diploma of Honor from the International Committee on Fairplay in Stuttgart, Germany. The King and Queen of Norway were honored at the same event.

BASKETBALL

Tom Blackburn with Jack Sallee, Chris Harris, John Horan and Bill Uhl at NIT in 1954 (above); Don Donoher, Hank Finkel and Dave Inderreiden (left).

Dr. Elaine Dreidame, UD senior associate athletic director (above); Mortally ill Blackburn refused to quit. He's with Jim Palmer, Al Sicking and Dr. George Rau (below).

16

The UD Flyers

The history of basketball at the University of Dayton has its beginnings at about the same time as did football when the school teams were the Cadets of St. Mary's Institute in the first decade of the 20th century.

Education at St. Mary's was on three levels: elementary, covering grades five through eight; prep, covering high school grades and the college level. These levels cause some confusion in researching the earlier teams, as some of the school's better athletes played with the Cadets while they were still in grades 11 and 12.

The current university media guides list a six-game season in 1903, and there is a picture of coach George Heithaus and players Alex H. Schoen, Edward Grimes, Francis Wong Leong, Frank Biesinger and Victor Schlitzer. The media guides do not list a regular coach until 1910 when Father William O'Malley began a two-year stay, so it is safe to assume that Heithaus, the 1903 coach, was probably a student.

Newspaper clippings in the UD archives tell of a game Feb. 5. 1905 between the Cadets and Springfield High School, which is not listed in the current media guides. Another clipping states that women are welcome at the Cadet games in the old campus gym. "Comforts of the fair sex are looked after in a way creditable to the student body," a statement said. Another undated clipping tells of 75 rooters and the St. Mary's team taking the D&T traction line to Tipp City for a 34-22 victory over Tippecanoe, the same team listed as a 1905 football opponent.

Alex Schoen played on the first four SMI Cadet teams. His name is preserved on the Alex Schoen Memorial Trophy established in 1950. It goes annually to the player with the best free-throw shooting percentage and is the longest running of any of the trophies honoring UD basketball players.

Another notable name of that era is Bill Pflaum, who later became the St. Mary's game official. At that time, competing schools would designate "a representative of high principle" to be its official. Paid neutral officials didn't come into use until after World War I.

In the 1911-12 season there is a 2-0 forfeit win listed over Notre Dame, and Pflaum was the cause of it. The Irish objected to Pflaum being assigned to officiate and sent a telegram the day before the game that they were cancelling and instead going on to Oxford to play Miami.

Harry Solimano, a dominant figure in both SMI football and basketball circles and a charter member of the UD Athletic Hall of Fame, had advanced from playing to coaching going into the 1911-12 season. During this period several players were playing with the school-sponsored Saints as well as the St. Mary's Cadets playing an independent schedule.

The Cadets, utilizing a lineup of Solimano, Hugh Sacksteder, Al Mahrt, Al Schumacher and Babe Zimmerman, claimed the "World Championship" by virtue of a victory over the Buffalo Germans, a team out of the western New York city which had won 111 consecutive games in a streak between 1907 and 1910.

The Dayton-based Cadets, who also had Norb Sacksteder, Ralph Baker, Martin Kuntz, Al Gessler and Lou Rotterman on their roster, nudged the Germans, 32-31, when that group was on tour. Then to prove it no fluke, they hammered the Germans, 45-30, when the Buffalo team came back to town in 1913.

It was after that victory the Cadets claimed the world championship, a claim that probably wasn't widely recognized but which gave Dayton sports fans something to brag about.

Of that team Alphonse Schumacher was one of the most popular players and later went into the religious order and spent most of his life as a parish priest in Xenia. George "Babe" Zimmerman's son and grandson, both named Jack, played for the Flyers in later years and Jack Sr. was a top-notch amateur golfer.

The SMI Saints were undefeated on their college schedules in 1911-12-13 seasons and although they slipped to 5-4 in 1914, it was a significant season in that all nine opponents were college teams.

The first of a run of three games against Ohio State was played in

1913, the Buckeyes winning 23-16. The Buckeyes won again, 30-19, the next year before SMI won, 24-23 in 1915. That was to be the last meeting between the two schools until 1985.

Schedules up to, through and immediately after World War I were pretty much hit and miss. During that period, in 1920, the school officially became the University of Dayton and the nickname Flyers was adopted shortly thereafter.

In the 1920 season, Solimano, now a practicing lawyer, was back for one year as basketball coach, followed by Dayton Triangles football player Dutch Thiele, who also coached for one year. In 1922 when Van Hill became a full-time head football coach, his duties also included coaching the basketball team. After Harry Baujan replaced Hill the next year he coached the cage sport the next five seasons. From then on until after World War II Flyer basketball was in the hands of an assistant football coach, first Bill Belanich, then Lou Tschudi, Joe Holsinger and finally Jim Carter.

Jack R. Brown, who played on the 1922 and 1923 basketball teams and who later served as athletic business manager of the university, described the way things were, "In fairness to the men who played through those years, there wasn't much emphasis or money spent on basketball. Of course, here and there, a good basketball player popped up. But there were so many losing seasons, it got to be embarrassing and along about 1937 some of the alumni began pushing to build up basketball."

When Jim Carter joined Baujan's staff, the program finally had a coach who had basketball coaching experience at the high school level. Carter had been a star halfback at Purdue and had taken basketball coaching classes from John Wooden, then coaching Boilermaker basketball.

The first UD basketball scholarship, in 1939, went to Charles "Hooks" McCloskey of Salem, Ohio. The second went to Bob Kavanaugh, although the Springfield native had been recruited to play football. He led his team in scoring all three of his varsity seasons.

Carter's 1940 team made UD's first extended basketball trip, a five-game eastern junket which opened with a victory over Rhode Island State but wound up with losses to St. Josephs in Philadelphia, LIU and St. Johns on Long Island and Scranton. Two years later Carter's men enjoyed a 12-6 record, by far the most impressive since the days of the Cadets. The Flyers posted a winning 9-8 record in the 1942-43 season but then the war wiped out the next two seasons.

When the decision was made to start up the basketball program in October of 1945, there had been no thought of scholarships. Carter himself had been working in a war plant in Indiana and was called back to duty. There were plenty of bodies, but talent was scarce. The schedule was hastily thrown together and the 3-13 record was predictable.

One name to remember on that team was freshman Bill Ginn, who played his high school basketball at Stivers and was to be a contributor to the revival about to begin under Tom Blackburn.

A trio of former football players came back from military service and won places on the team: Gus Shroyer, Bill Knisley and Ken Boxwell. As the team staggered through a 4-17 season, the alumni began to press for a full-time basketball coach, or at least one not involved in football.

The Tom Blackburn Era

A native of Scioto County and a graduate of Wilmington College, Tom Blackburn enjoyed a decade of success coaching football and basketball at West Carrollton and Xenia High Schools before going into the Navy. Blackburn considered himself primarily a football coach but his 1942 Xenia basketball team won the state championship.

When he came out of the service, Blackburn did not want to go back to Xenia and wound up becoming the golf pro at Dayton's community-owned Madden Park, having obtained his PGA status before the war.

Actually, there was no money in the UD budget for a full-time basketball coach, but Jack R. Brown, the school's unofficial athletic director along with fellow alum Hank Malloy, the unofficial ticket manager, saw a chance to work out a deal with Blackburn. Their selling point was that he could coach Flyer basketball during his "off season" in the winter without jeopardizing his main source of income.

Blackburn finally accepted the idea and took over the UD program for a ridiculously low stipend ($1,800). While no one dared speculate on the degree of success he was to enjoy, Dayton basketball was perched on a skyrocket.

The new coach inherited a team stronger in numbers than talent. The only newcomers on that first team included former servicemen like Bobby Flynn, a smallish guard from Lexington, Kentucky whom Blackburn had known in the navy, as well as Rip West, a former Roosevelt athlete who had worked for Tom at the golf course.

The automatic choice for captain was Jim Finke, who had been on Carter's teams before the war and who wound up a decorated combat veteran from the European invasion. Charles "Benny" Jones, who had come out for basketball in Carter's last year, was the school's first black player.

The new coach's first season was 12-14 and a few UD followers began to sense a new day. "What we learned real fast about our new coach was that he was a strict disciplinarian and played no favorites," Finke recalled.

In 1948-49, the Flyers played a 28-game schedule, their most ambitious ever, and added two games in a tournament in Cleveland called the National Catholic Invitational.

During the early days of bus travel, North Carolina native Elizabeth "Libby" Blackburn made the trips and became visible with her pleasant smile and Carolina drawl through Tom's years.

The coach beefed up his lineup with a trio of players he had known in the military. Dick "Razor" Campbell, Brian McCall and Gene Joseph came to UD and helped turn the Flyers into a winner in Tom's second year, 16-14. Center McCall had only one year of eligibility but made the most of it, leading the team in scoring.

The Flyers were playing their home games in the Fairgrounds Coliseum that had only a limited seating capacity. Standees could swell a crowd to 3,000.

Blackburn's biggest step in that 1948-49 season was recruiting three former local high school stars for his freshman team. They included Chuck Grigsby, who helped Stivers to a city title in 1947, and Don Meineke, who served the same role for Wilbur Wright a year later. The third was Leland "Junior" Norris, an all-around star at Fairmont.

Pete Boyle, the first basketball recruit from the New York city area, joined them on a freshman team that was good enough to qualify for the national AAU tournament in Denver.

The Meineke-Grigsby-Norris-Boyle class made its varsity debut with a 60-36 win over Cedarville in the Coliseum. The team reeled off 10 straight wins before taking its first ever trip to Chicago, only to absorb a 69-46 wake up call at the hands of Chicago Loyola.

There was another road block in that 24-8 season. Blackburn had scheduled a four-game, four-day trip to face the best collegiate opposition in northern Ohio. The result was a four-game losing streak to Bowling Green, Baldwin Wallace, Muskingum and Kent State. The initial loss to highly regarded Bee-Gees was marked by controversial officiating and the young Flyers never had time to regroup. The coach learned a valuable lesson about scheduling.

Construction of the $600,000 Fieldhouse, begun in the spring of 1950, was scheduled for completion in time for the season's first game. The permanent seats on both sides accommodated 4,000 people. There was no indication at the outset that temporary bleachers at each end would be needed but the eventual capacity would be pegged at 5,600.

It becomes ever more amazing over the years that the team that would have the entire Dayton community buzzing by February, lost its first game on the new home court. The Flyers never adjusted to the slow tempo of Central Missouri State and were totally frustrated in the 50-47 outcome.

The Flyers suffered only four more losses all season, all on the road as they rolled to a 27-5 record that ended up in the championship game of the National Invitation Tournament in Madison Square Garden.

Blackburn's homegrown powerhouse had tremendous chemistry. The four junior starters -- Meineke, Grigsby, Norris and Boyle -- enjoyed the stability of Navy vet Campbell as the playmaker and leader

Veteran guards Gene Joseph and Bobby Flynn had productive moments off the bench as did backup center, Vaughn "Ox" Taylor, also a homegrown talent. Featuring his lefthanded hook and other offensive moves, Meineke set a new season scoring record with 660 points, a 20.6 per game average.

Norris, the roly-poly appearing guard, backed him with 374 points and became a crowd favorite. Grigsby was the third scorer and joined Boyle in playing the boards. Boyle was the team's prime defender, usually assigned to hawk the opponents top scorer. In the late stages of the season, Grigsby was hampered by a groin pull and sophomore Gene Hickey, a Toledo native, played well backing him up. By mid-season it was virtually impossible to buy tickets into the Fieldhouse and advance orders piled in for season tickets for the 1951-52 season.

When the Flyers accepted their first bid to the NIT on Feb. 27, the university promptly cancelled Friday and Monday classes around the March 10 opening game in New York against Lawrence Tech. The New York Central railroad announced a $29 round trip excursion fare for UD students and put two extra coaches on their Friday evening overnight train, the Ohio State Limited. The official UD party boarded a TWA Constellation Thursday, making its first of many eventual team flights.

Older fans and alumni also came up with plans to go to New York and a ticket office manned by Jack Brown and athletic director Baujan was set up in the lobby of the Paramount Hotel where the team was staying.

The Flyers didn't disappoint. When New York sports writers got their first look at the unknown Ohioans, they promptly dubbed Junior Norris, Humphrey Pennyworth, after the Al Capp comic strip character in L'il Abner. A year later Norris, made up as Humphrey, rode a bicycle towing an old-fashioned outdoor privy in the homecoming parade through downtown Dayton.

Dayton knocked off Lawrence Tech, 77-71, in the opener but weren't overly impressive. But then the Flyers played up to their ability as they zapped third-seeded Arizona, 74-68, with Meineke having a great night with 37 points. That pushed the Flyers into the semifinals and set off another exodus from Dayton with the rival Pennsylvania Railroad joining the Central in the excursion fare battle.

The semifinal match sent Blackburn's men against St. John's, coached by Frank McGuire, a nationally ranked team playing on what was practically its home floor. It was clearly UD's biggest opportunity for national recognition.

Dayton responded to the challenge with a 69-62 win in overtime in a solid team effort. After Meineke fouled out with 7:58 to play, Taylor came off the bench to defend against Zeke Zawoluk, the star center of the Redmen. When he left the game on fouls, Meineke joined Norris on the bench for the same reason. A makeup unit of starters Grigsby, Boyle and Campbell, plus Taylor and Gene Joseph carried the Flyers through in the overtime.

That sent Blackburn's men into the championship game against Brigham Young. The team from Utah easily handled the Flyers, 62-43. "We ran out of gas" was Blackburn's laconic comment ending the greatest Flyer season up to that point. An emotional welcome home ceremony in the Fieldhouse found a huge crowd saluting the Flyers for their successful foray into big time basketball.

The lone losses to graduation were playmaker Campbell and the popular Flynn. Replacing the slick ball-handling Razor was a challenge, but the problem was solved when freshmen were made eligible because of the Korean war.

The incoming freshman class included John Horan, the wiry 6-8 swingman from Minneapolis, Chris Harris from Floral Park, N. Y. and

Jack Sallee, standout from Springfield High School, who were to dominate the "second wave" of the Blackburn era. Available new talent also included Ray Dieringer and Jim Paxson, Sr. from the freshman team of the year before along with a 6-3 forward from Toledo, Don Donoher.

It isn't surprising this talented and deep squad posted a 28-5 record, the number of wins still being the school record as this is written.

Still, the Flyers dropped three games in December, an overtime home loss to Louisville, a controversial 61-60 loss to rival Miami on the latter's home floor and a 62-60 loss to revenge-minded St. John's in Dayton's first regular season appearance in Madison Square Garden.

But with Meineke, Grigsby and Norris being the 1-2-3 scorers, Blackburn worked newcomers Horan, Paxson and Sallee along with Boyle into what amounted to a strong seven man regular lineup. Dayton won the remaining games on the regular schedule, avenging the early season losses to Louisville and Miami.

But the streak was hardly a piece of cake. In one stretch, the Flyers edged Louisville, Toledo, Bowling Green and Eastern Kentucky by a combined total of six points. All these pulsating finishes were on the road, attesting to the maturity of the veteran team.

The last home game against ancient enemy Miami provided a dramatic farewell performance of the exceptional senior class. It was also the first meeting of the two since the December loss to the Redskins in Oxford and UD came out on top, 65-56.

With 2:19 to play, Meineke fouled out. As the tall pivot headed for the bench, the Fieldhouse exploded with wild applause and cheers that held up the game for several minutes.

"I'll always remember it," he said later. "I looked at the Miami bench and their players were clapping too." A year later Meineke was NBA Rookie of the Year with the Fort Wayne Zollners. In the final seconds, other seniors got their noisy tribute, but the Meineke reception, spontaneous as it was, remains a bright memory.

Invitation to the NIT was almost automatic, and the second exodus to New York was better planned by students, alumni and followers. Once in the big city, the Paramount Hotel was Dayton headquarters as it had been the year before, but Blackburn moved the players to another hotel to hide them from the fans who might unwittingly break their concentration. The Flyer tournament games were broadcast on all three Dayton radio stations as well as the first televised games by WHIO-TV.

The first round 81-66 victory over New York University drew an overflow Garden crowd of 18,423. Meineke responded with a 30-point night. Grigsby suffered an aggravating finger injury giving freshman Sallee more playing time and Jack had a 15-point night, indicative of things in the future.

Grigsby shook off the pain of his jammed finger for 22 points in a 68-58 win over St. Louis and Meineke keyed the 69-62 semifinal victory over St. Bonaventure. Blackburn's men went into the championship round as the wagering favorite and UD partisans were wildly overconfident their heroes would win their 21st straight game.

LaSalle had three freshman in their lineup including Tom Gola, a brilliant All-American to be. The Explorers were coached by Ken Loeffler, who had coached in the pro league the year before. He had a solid game plan to choke off the Flyer attack and UD was fighting uphill all night before bowing, 75-64.

"The most disappointing game I ever played in," Meineke was quoted 36 years later.

"Losing the year before to Brigham Young wasn't so hard to take because we made it to the championship game on our first try," Norris said. "As seniors, we expected to beat LaSalle, but on that night. they were a better team."

The disappointed Flyer Faithful hardly noticed that a week later, Dayton played in the NCAA tournament for the first time, losing to Illinois in Chicago in a game in which all five UD starters fouled out.

Meineke, the first Flyer All-American, ended his career with 1848 points, a career mark that stood until Hank Finkel broke it 14 seasons later. Monk, as he was known to his teammates, is still fifth on the all-time list. As a class, Meineke, Grigsby, Norris, Boyle, Taylor and Joseph had an overall 79-18 record, three of the losses being in post-season tournaments.

Despite losing his first great senior class, Blackburn seemed to have a good nucleus returning for the 1952-53 season. Sophomore Horan moved from his natural forward position to play center and did his best, but the team struggled to a 16-13 season and didn't get into post-season play.

But the final home game found undefeated and No. 1 nationally ranked Seton Hall coming into the Fieldhouse with a 25-0 record. The Flyers playing with five iron men, Horan, Sallee, Paxson, Harris and Donoher, scored a 71-65 upset over towering Walter Dukes and his mates.

During the season, Bill Uhl, a seven-footer who had started at Ohio

State, transferred to Dayton. Uhl grew up in Greenfield, a small town southeast of Dayton and felt overwhelmed on the huge Columbus campus. He was to become the Flyer center for three winning seasons starting in the 1953-54 opener. The importance of his presence was emphasized by Horan's ability to move back to his more natural forward position.

Uhl made his debut against Canisius in Buffalo, N. Y., in a game televised back to Dayton. The road opener was a rarity as the Flyers usually opened at home. One of the later highlights of the campaign was a triple overtime loss to nationally ranked Western Kentucky in the Fieldhouse.

They eventually fought their way back into the NIT in what was an overall 25-7 year. Paxson had been drafted into the military. Uhl, Sallee and Horan each had averages of 15-plus points in balanced scoring and the team made its third trip to the NIT in four years. This time, UD was bumped by Niagara in the second round.

Donoher, the steady swingman, graduated at the end of the season and went into the army. His unforeseen great coaching career was a decade away.

But the winning beat went on as Horan, Sallee and slick-passing playmaker Harris headed into their senior year. The 25-4 season was notable for four games against Duquesne, where the great Sihugo Green and the Ricketts brothers were having a banner year.

The Flyers lost to the Dukes in the Madison Square Garden Holiday Festival, came back to win both regular season games only to be soundly beaten in the NIT championship game.

Blackburn's 1955-56 team has been called by many observers his best ever. It could be argued the 1951-52 team deserves that accolade. Not only did both teams have great records, they had impressive depth in young players who would play key roles later.

With Paxson back from the army along with Arlen Bockhorn, who had been on the UD freshman team two seasons earlier, Blackburn picked up two strong talents to go with his big men, Uhl and a maturing Jim Palmer. With Ray Dieringer in the role as playmaker, doing what Campbell and Harris had done so well, this team got off to a great start.

Dayton had been invited to play in Adolph Rupp's prestigious University of Kentucky Invitational Tournament and took a 6-0 record to Lexington, where they were matched against highly regarded Utah. The Flyers won that game 77-73 and then stunned the blueclad home crowd by solidly trouncing the Wildcats, 89-74.

The impact of that victory over Kentucky was felt in the Dayton community. Hundreds of Kentucky natives had come north to work in this city's blue collar industries and had scoffed at UD attaining the UK level.

Capturing the tournament on Rupp's home floor in Lexington stamped the Flyer program as one that had come of age. On top of the two strong appearances in the NIT, writers and coaches took note of Dayton in voting in the polls. The Flyer Faithful were on solid ground in pointing out that UD was up there with the elite of that era.

Blackburn's men went on win 14 games before losing to strong rival Louisville in Dayton. It turned out to be the Cardinals who kept this from being UD's greatest season. Peck Hickman's UL team beat UD in the return game in Louisville and then capped it all with a 93-80 victory in the NIT title game, the fourth time Blackburn had taken his team to the championship game only to come away empty.

The other UD loss in that tremendous 25-4 season was on the road at Duquesne. Uhl, Paxson, Bockhorn and Palmer all were in double figure scoring averages.

Despite the heavy graduation losses (starters Uhl, Paxson, Dieringer and reserves Bob Fiely and Bob Jacoby) Blackburn came back with another team that made it five out of six years to the NIT. This team went 19-9 with Al Sicking at center, Palmer and Bockhorn forwards and Carmen Riazzi and Don Lane at guards. Temple bumped the Flyers in the second round of the NIT this time.

Ever resilient, the Flyers came back in 1957-58 with an overachieving small team with Jack McCarthy, at 6-7, playing center. What happened at the end of the year in the NIT made it appear Blackburn was jinxed forever in terms of winning his championship.

This 25-4 team had beaten Xavier twice in the regular season and indeed, the Flyers were dominating their Cincinnati rival all through the 1950s. The surprising Flyers took a 22-2 record into the season-ending game against the Cincinnati Bearcats and their sophomore sensation Oscar Robertson. The game set a Cincinnati Gardens attendance record of 15,011 as the Flyers gamely tried to close the gap against the favored "Big O" club but UC hung on for an exciting 70-66 struggle.

After whipping two "home" New York teams, Fordham and St. John's, the Flyers went down in overtime to the Musketeers, 78-74. A pivot shot by McCarthy at the buzzer in regulation time that rolled in and out was to haunt the UD players for quite a while.

It took four more seasons for the Dayton team to finally end the NIT jinx and give their coach his first championship on his sixth try. After missing the tournament in the spring of 1959, the Flyers made it back to New York in 1960 and 1961, but were victimized by Bradley and Holy Cross before reaching the championship level.

The nucleus of the '62 champions had been planted when Gary Roggenburk and Tom Hatton assumed starting roles as sophomores two years earlier. The slender Roggenburk and Hatton were close friends and provided the leadership when the '61 team came of age.

The big impetus came from coach Herb Dintaman's freshman team of the year before. Bill Chmielewski, a mobile 6-10 center from Detroit, Roger Brown from Brooklyn and Tom Hatton's younger brother Gordie looked ready to play. They were a star-crossed group from the beginning. Brown never played a varsity game for UD. He and Connie Hawkins, who had enrolled at Iowa, testified before a New York grand jury that they had accepted money and favors from indicted gamblers. The allegations were that the favors were to be repaid by helping control point spreads. Although Blackburn vigorously defended Brown, the university issued a statement that Brown would "not be permitted further registration."

Brown remained in Dayton for a while playing independent ball until the new ABA (American Basketball Association) said it would welcome him along with Hawkins. Both enjoyed successful pro careers but neither approached the earning level they would probably have had if not for their involvement with potential fixers before they got to college.

Gordie Hatton was to become doomed to spend his life in a wheelchair after shattering his spine in an automobile accident a decade after graduation. The third senior on the championship team was guard Stan Greenberg, a Philadelphia native who had sat out what would have been his normal senior year because of other campus activities. "I was surprised that Blackburn took me back, but he did and I'll always be grateful," recalled Greenberg, who remained in Dayton and is a partner in the law firm of Rogers & Greenberg.

Chmielewski and the younger Hatton started immediately as sophomores and junior forward Hal Schoen rounded out the lineup that eventually brought the first Flyer national title.

The team opened with a seven game win streak, then lost to Wisconsin in the Madison Square Garden holiday event. It had a rocky January, losing three road games including an 80-61 loss to Cincinnati. The

Bearcats were dominating the Flyers year-in and year-out and were also two-time NCAA champions.

It wouldn't be until 1971 that Dayton would snap that UC jinx. But the 1962 UD team really started to jell in February and won their last seven games to be invited into the NIT as an unseeded team. Perhaps weary of so many earlier disappointments, the Flyer Faithful were not all that excited about the tournament.

The initial opponent was Wichita which stressed a pressing defense the Flyers handled well with an excellent game plan. Chmielewski had a 24-point night in the 79-71 victory. Roggenburk scored only 13 points but Blackburn went out of his way to praise the all-around solid play from his rangy senior

Chmielewski was outstanding with 32 points in a 94-77 romp over Houston and that sent UD into the semis against Chicago Loyola. George Ireland's Ramblers were a year away from one of the most stunning upsets in NCAA tournament history when they thwarted Cincinnati's bid for a third straight national championship.

The Ramblers, with four starters who would face Cincinnati a year later, took a 44-41 halftime lead. But the Flyers responded with a sensational 57-point second half to win going away, 98-82. This set the stage for Blackburn's sixth shot at the championship. An old rival stood in the way, the St. John's Redmen.

The Flyers prevailed in the nationally televised game, 73-67. Chmielewski was voted the tournament MVP and the large delegation of Flyer fans rushed the floor in a wild celebration. Blackburn stood aloof from the turmoil, smiling at the victory that had eluded him for so long.

As fate would have it, the UD triumph came at the zenith of the coach's professional life. In less than two years he would be dead.

The NCAA slapped a two-year probation on the UD program partly as a result of the Roger Brown situation. The penalty also alleged that an excessive number of games were played by the freshman team.

The Dayton program was in limbo for the next two seasons for more reasons than one. Chmielewski, citing financial problems involved with his marriage, dropped out of school in October, 1963, never to return. The Flyers finished 16-10 and 15-10 those two years.

In August of 1963 doctors discovered cancerous spots on Blackburn's lung and surgery was ordered. The coach kept his illness away from the media until after the operation. He had been a heavy smoker.

Don Donoher, who had not been happy in sales work in the business world, had come back into coaching as an assistant to Tom Frericks at Chaminade High School and wound up being hired as a Blackburn assistant going into what was to be Tom's final season. Donoher's other experience had been doing most of the scouting of UD opponents for several years.

Blackburn was on his feet coaching the Flyers through that agonizing year never complaining but at times in very obvious pain. By February it was apparent that the end was near, but the gallant coach, gritting his teeth through the pain much of the time, was on the bench during a losing effort to Miami eight days before he died.

Death came March 6, 1964, only 24 hours before the last scheduled game against DePaul. It was decided to play the game which Ray Meyer's team won, 69-63. The Flyers had won their two other games under interim coach Donoher.

The Don Donoher Era

The Flyers' new coach was 32 years old with very minimal coaching experience, but Blackburn had always respected his feel for the game. The decision to give the Toledo native the job paid huge dividends with Donoher's coaching record and more so in the reputation for integrity he was to build for the college and the Dayton community.

Coincidental with the coaching change was an administrative move in the wake of the NCAA probation. During the Blackburn years, the administrative control of the program was primarily, indeed almost exclusively, in the hands of the Rev. Charles L. Coliins, chairman of the athletic board. The university's presidents rarely got involved, but things changed now as Father Raymond A. Roesch put himself and Brother Elmer Lackner, who was in charge of community relations, on a committee with Father Collins. But there was a big step to be taken beyond that.

Thomas J. Frericks, whose playing career had been cut short by back ailments, was named Athletic Director with a mandate to get the programs into compliance with NCAA regulations. It was felt that Frericks had the necessary administrative experience to handle a job that was getting more complicated by the year.

With one outstanding exception, Donoher did not inherit a great deal of talent from the last Blackburn team.

Seven-foot Hank Finkel had come into the program in a round-about way. The gangly young man grew up in Union City, New Jersey, across the Hudson River from the big city. When he graduated from high school, he wasn't a redhot prospect but did wind up at St. Peters, commuting on a city bus to the school a few miles from his home. When his father died, Hank had to go to work to help support his mother and gave up college ideas.

After a year away from basketball he was steered toward Dayton by Harry Brooks, who had played at Seton Hall but whose kid brother, Tom Brooks, was then on the UD freshman team. Encouraged by his mother to take the opportunity to get his education, he came but there was a question as to how much eligibility he would have in the UD program. Making an appeal based on Finkel's family hardship, Blackburn got the NCAA to rule Finkel could have three years of varsity eligibility.

After his sophomore season when he scored 576 points, he was eligible for the NBA draft because he was 23 years old and his normal graduation year was the spring of 1964. The Los Angeles Lakers did draft him and Donoher spent an uncomfortable off-season keeping in touch with Finkel. His mother urged him to finish his education and become the first member of his family to get a college degree. Finkel kept his word.

"Knowing his financial situation at home, there was no way I would have tried to talk him out of accepting the Lakers offer," Donoher said . "But I honestly feel that I might not have succeeded had he not stayed in school. He certainly gave us what we needed to build a winner."

Flyer fans weren't expecting a great deal from the team in Donoher's first year but the Flyers demolished Niagara, 95-64, in their opener and were on their way to 22-7 season that ended in the NCAA tournament.

Finkel's 733 points erased Meineke's single season scoring record. The big guy also led by a wide margin in rebounding. His supporting cast included Bill Cassidy, later an assistant coach, senior captain Bob Sullivan and a sophomore guard, Gene Klaus.

Taking aim at playing in the NCAA tournament, which was eclipsing the NIT, the Flyers wound up being blasted by Michigan, but it was certainly a fine debut year for Donoher.

Donoher had come up with a classic freshman class in his first turn. He had bagged Don May, a member of the Belmont High School team that had won the state tournament, as well as guard Bobby Joe Hooper, who had played for his father, Vern, in rural Clinton County. Glinder Torain, an agile 6-7 forward from Muncie, Indiana and Rudy Waterman, a guard from New York City rounded out the group.

That foursome became eligible for Finkel's senior year and the Flyers roared to a 23-6 season and qualified for the NCAA again as an independent only to be eliminated by a very strong Kentucky team, 86-79.

Finkel finished his career with 1968 points, a 23.2 average and went on to a nine-season career with the Boston Celtics in the NBA.

The big fellow was gone going into Donoher's third season but the coach had lots of other fine talent. May was enroute to an All-American season; Hooper, Waterman and captain Klaus were a trio of excellent guards and the coach opened the season gambling with the undersized Torain at center. Before long, sophomore Dan Obrovac moved into that position and the 6-10 Canton native handled it well the rest of his career.

Although the Cincinnati jinx held up and the Flyers lost twice to Louisville in the regular season, there was no doubt that Dayton was headed into the NCAA once more, and it turned into a magical moment in UD history. Because the field had been expanded to 32 teams, the Flyers played five games enroute to a championship showdown against mighty UCLA.

The Flyers were an underdog in their first tournament game, played in Lexington. Western Kentucky had enjoyed a 23-2 season and were ninth in the AP poll, but the Flyers came through in overtime on Hooper's clutch basket, 69-67.

That sent Donoher's men to the second round in Chicago where they faced Tennessee, the champions of the SEC, also rated in the top ten. But with a game plan to counter the Vols slow tempo, the Flyers came through, 53-52. May broke loose for 28 points as the Flyers followed their close win over Tennessee with a 71-66 win over Virginia Tech, sending them into the Final Four to be played in Louisville's Freedom Hall. The Flyers were to face North Carolina and ticket pressure was just as intense as it had been in the early days of the NIT in New York.

If the win over St. John's in the 1951 NIT was the watershed victory in the Blackburn era, Dayton's easy 76-62 win over North Carolina fills that role in Donoher's tenure. The UD upset was keyed by a spectacular 34-point night by May. The 6-4 junior was virtually unstoppable and he set an NCAA record by hitting 13 straight from the floor. He found time to collect 15 rebounds in what stacks up as the ultimate dominant single game performance in Flyer annals.

Although they were never in a position to win the final game, losing to the national champion UCLA Bruins by a 79-64 score, reaching the finals by way of the stunning win over North Carolina stands as the zenith of the Flyer program. John Wooden's UCLA team went 30-0 in solidifying their No. 1 ranking.

Donoher made sure all 12 members of his team had their names in the box score to "show their grandchildren," as he put it.

With a veteran team coming back, (only captain Klaus and backup forward Jim Wannamacher had graduated), expectations ran high. But a chemistry problem developed that pushed Donoher's coaching skills to the limit. For whatever reason, black players Torain and Waterman felt discriminated against and eventually took their complaints to the student newspaper and outside media. Both players had contributed much to the drive to the Final Four and Donoher was seemingly caught off guard by the developing friction.

The Flyers had an up and down December, going 4-5 with the problem starting with a home court loss to Miami. They played hard in a repeat visit to the Kentucky Invitational but lost by three points to Adolph Rupp's host Wildcats and then the next night blew a late lead in a 71-70 loss to Cincinnati. By mid-January, the Flyers knew they wouldn't be going back to the NCAA, but an amazing turnaround was at hand.

The coach settled on a lineup of May, Hooper, Obrovac, junior Dan Sadlier and sophomore Jim Gottschall, one of a pair of twins who had played at Chaminade High School. That group sparked the team to a 10-game winning streak to close the season and earn an invitation to the NIT.

Once in New York, the new combination kept rolling and defeated West Virginia, Fordham, Notre Dame and Kansas to bring home the second NIT championship to go with the one captured six seasons earlier. The 61-48 win over the Jayhawks was played at a tempo which cut down May's scoring opportunities but the likeable big kid had 22 to bring his career total to 1980, surpassing by 12 Finkel's record two years earlier.

The surge in New York lifted the Flyers to 21-9, the fourth straight year Donoher's teams had bettered 20 wins. It was a very emotional win for the coach considering all the early problems. "This team could have been the biggest joke in Dayton history," Donoher said. "Instead they fought back to make it one of the great UD teams."

By the end, Torain and Waterman had cut off all communications with their teammates. The racial split was probably a reflection of troubled times in society in general with the Vietnam War creating campus turmoil in many places. The two athletes involved in the situation left town expressing bitter feelings. The unofficial campus reaction was that they had been overly influenced by "outside sources."

In the summer of 1977, Waterman surprised the coach with an unexpected visit during which he and Donoher talked out their differences. Waterman ended his own troubled life at age 34, shooting himself Feb. 21, 1981 in New York City. He lingered in a coma until he died June 17. Donoher attended the funeral.

By the end of his first four seasons, Donoher had compiled a 91-28 record and established his reputation nationally as a competent college coach. It would be difficult to match that torrid pace, but the winning beat rolled on for the coach all through the 1970s.

Don May's younger brother Ken came along to help Donoher's teams keep up the winning pace. Ken, Sadlier, Obrovac and the Gottschall twins paced UD to a 20-7 record in 1968-1969 season, Donoher's fifth. But the season ended in a first round NCAA tournament loss to Colorado State.

A very meaningful development in the program came in December of 1969 with the opening of the new UD Arena with its 13,400 capacity for basketball. Pushed through under the leadership of Frericks, the building was financed by a 30-year $4 million bond issue backed by the Ohio Higher Education Facilities Commission.

Bowling Green, the opponent in the first game in the new building, nearly pulled off the kind of an upset Central Missouri had done in the Fieldhouse. But Donoher's men, with Ken May leading the way, won in a 72-70 squeaker. The 1969-70 season ended with another visit to Texas and a tournament loss, this time to Houston. May was the scoring leader.

The UD Arena got into the act of hosting post-season play in its very first year, welcoming an NCAA first round. Notre Dame's Austin Carr put his name into the record books with a 61-point surge against Ohio University. When the Arena was the site of first round games in 1995, it marked the 14th occasion NCAA tournament games have been played here, amply fulfilling Frerick's hopes for the facility.

After an ordinary 18-9 year in the second season of the Arena, the Flyers slipped to 13-13 in the 1971-72 season, the first non-tournament year in Donoher's tenure.

The slump was halted because assistant coach Pat Haley, who had come aboard on Donoher's staff in 1968, spent the entire spring of 1970 trying to recruit Donald Smith, who had enjoyed a spectacular career at Roth High School. When Donald went to Pittsburgh to play in the Dapper Dan Roundball Classic in June, he wound up rooming with Mike Sylvester, who was coming out of Cincinnati Moeller.

"It was an amazing thing," Donoher said later. "Here was this white kid from Cincinnati in awe of this black kid from Dayton. Mike wanted to go where Donald went and Donald had a lot of choices."

That Donald wanted to stay at home paid huge dividends for the Flyers. The year he became eligible, Donoher had two senior guards, Al Bertke and the often-injured Rex Gardecki. The latter would probably have been an outstanding player but a severe knee injury hobbled his career. Bertke is best remembered for firing the winning goal in a 70-69 decision over the Cincinnati Bearcats to end a string of 14 consecutive losses to that traditional rival.

Going into the 1972-73 season, the NCAA made freshmen eligible and the UD Invitational tournament was set up as an attraction over the Christmas holidays.

Smith and Sylvester were to run 1-2 in scoring all three years they were together. As sophomores and juniors they had to endure 13-13 seasons, but as a junior Smith went on a 52-point rampage against Loyola in the old Chicago Stadium, supplanting Meineke's old record of 49 back in 1951. He also had a 44-point night against Xavier.

Going into Donald and Mike's senior year, they were surrounded with strong talent including freshman Johnny Davis, Allen Elijah, John Von Lehman, Joe Fisher and Jim Testerman and the Flyers made it back into the NCAA tournament.

A win in the first round at Pocatello, Idaho sent them to Tucson where they were confronted by UCLA, then seeking its eighth straight championship under Wooden. The Flyer Faithful didn't have much hope, but underdog Dayton did everything but beat the Bruins before going down in triple overtime, 111-100. Sylvester led the Flyers in scoring in that near-classic upset with 33, while Smith, hobbled with a bad heel, finished his career with 26.

"Donald Smith was the best pure shooter we ever had," Donoher said, paying tribute to the smallish guard.

The next big turn in Flyer annals came from the "Detroit Pipeline" from where Elijah, Johnny Davis, Leighton Moulton, Erv Giddings and eventually Negele Knight came to UD. But the Flyers were also working on a recruiting pipeline closer to home. From Alter High School in the 1970s came Jim Paxson, Jr., Joe Siggins, Bill Frericks, Doug Harris and Jack Zimmerman.

Davis enjoyed two strong seasons before passing up his senior year to turn pro under the NBA's then hardship rule. Davis was part of Donoher's first losing season when the Flyers dipped to 13-16 in 1975. The Flyers came back with four winning campaigns before there was another losing season (13-14) in 1980.

Jim Paxson Jr. was the standout for Donoher in four performance seasons, his point total of 1945 putting him fourth on the all-time UD list. Dayton went 19-10 in both his junior and senior years, but never made it into the NCAA. They did, however, host NIT games, losing to Georgetown in 1978 and Purdue in 1979.

The finish of the 1979 season found Paxson knocked out of action with a separated shoulder late in a loss to (who else, but) the UC Bearcats. The Flyers had started the season on a 12-2 run, but were 8-8 the rest of the way.

Roosevelt Chapman, destined to become UD's all-time scoring leader, made his appearance in the fall of 1980 and was a standout performer in all four of his UD campaigns. Nicknamed "Velvet" for his smooth play by radio voices Larry Hansgen and Bucky Bockhorn, the Brooklyn native poured in a career 2233 points, well above Don May's previous record of 1980. However it must be noted, Chapman had four seasons compared to three for May and most earlier players.

In Chapman's senior year, the Flyers had another fling at glory in the NCAA post-season affair. Dayton beat LSU and Oklahoma in Salt Lake City before advancing to the regionals in Los Angeles. A win over Washington got them into the regional title game against Georgetown. The Hoyas, enroute to the championship, took the measure of the Flyers in a physical 61-49 struggle.

An important regular season victory was Ed Young's shot at the final buzzer to defeat perennial rival DePaul.

Donoher brought a great honor to his program when Indiana's Bob Knight selected him as an assistant coach on the 1984 U. S. Olympic team. The Flyer coach was very involved in the Los Angeles games where the Michael Jordan-led U. S. team captured the gold in impressive manner.

In 1985 the Flyers, with an 18-10, record had the opportunity of playing a first round NCAA tournament game on their home floor. But they lost a low scoring battle to Villanova, the team on its way to the NCAA title. As things turned out, this was Donoher's last NCAA or NIT post-season tournament.

Three straight losing seasons led to his dismissal in March of 1989, ending a 25-year tenure. Donoher's overall record was 437-275, including 15 post-season tournament appearances. There were some individual players worthy of being remembered in his final seasons including Damon Goodwin, Dave Colbert, Dan Christie and Ed Young.

After years as an independent, Dayton had made the major move of joining a conference in what turned out to be Donoher's last season. The Flyers joined the Midwestern Collegiate (MCC). They lost their last four league games and were edged by Evansville in the conference tournament.

O'Brien And The Hard Years

The new UD coach turned out to be Jim O'Brien, an assistant to Rick Pitino on the staff of the New York Knicks. O'Brien's only head coaching job had been at small school Wheeling Jesuit, but he had NCAA experience as assistant at Maryland, Oregon and St. Josephs of Pennsylvania, his alma mater.

O'Brien's name was injected into the search for Donoher's successor by Jim Paxson, Sr., who had gotten to know him through his friendship with Jack Ramsay, Jim Jr.'s coach at Portland in the NBA. Sharon O'Brien, the coach's wife is Ramsay's daughter.

Taking over a senior-laden team that had never played up to its potential, O'Brien seemed to work a miracle in his first season. The record was 10-10 going into a Feb. 10 game at Marquette. With senior guard Negele Knight turning into an offensive whirlwind, the Flyers won their last seven regular season games and then swept through three opponents in MCC play to qualify for the NCAA tournament, the irony being that UD probably wouldn't have been invited into the post-season play on a regular season 18-9 record.

Scoring more than 90 points in each MCC tournament game, O'Brien's men swept past Detroit, Loyola and old rival Xavier. They continued their magic run in the NCAA tournament with an 88-86 win over Illinois of the Big Ten before bowing to Arkansas 86-84, these games played at the University of Texas.

Knight was the catalyst to the exciting finish that had Arena crowds worked up to the kind of feverish excitement missing in recent years. The Detroit native's point average soared from 13.9 as a junior to 22.8 in his final season. But it wasn't only his scoring. He took fellow seniors Anthony Corbitt, Bill Uhl, Jr., Ray Springer, Troy McCracken and Nolan Robertson to a higher level with him.

A year later, the Flyers dropped to 14-15, the season ending in an MCC tournament loss to Xavier. The impending collapse of the program wasn't apparent as Norm Grevey, a fan favorite as a three-point shooter, closed out his career.

O'Brien's third year found the club holding together in a 15-15 season. But the university suffered a tremendous loss when athletic director Frericks died Jan. 31, 1992 after a hard struggle with cancer.

Frericks had become a powerful man in NCAA circles and had to turn down an opportunity to become president of the organization that controls college athletics because of his health concerns.

During that same season, it was announced that after only four years in the MCC, Dayton was joining the Great Midwest, a powerful basketball league with Cincinnati, DePaul, Marquette, St. Louis, Alabama-Birmingham and Memphis State.

The stronger league had something to do with UD sinking to an incredible 4-26 record in 1992-1993 but it was just as obvious that the talent level was also sinking. Only a handful of UD players, particularly Chip Hare, Alex Robertson and newcomer Andy Meyer, out of Alter, could have earned a berth on other Great Midwest teams.

Despite alumni pressure for his dismissal, O'Brien was permitted to coach the final year of his contract, which ended 6-21. In late February, it was announced his contract would not be renewed.

Athletic Director Ted Kissell, who had succeeded Frericks, headed the search group that settled on Oliver Purnell, who had been coaching at Old Dominion, his alma mater. Purnell was given a six-year contract with the mandate to get the program turned around.

Purnell's first season showed little improvement with a 7-20 record, but the new coach was popular with the fans and the media.

17

The Birth of the Raiders

How do you start a college basketball program from scratch?

John Ross found out in October of 1969.

Wright State had no organized athletic program in the spring of 1968 when the first senior class graduated. The school had started life a decade before as a jointly operated branch campus of the Ohio State and Miami Universities. The Ohio Board of Regents approved its upgrading to full four-year university status in 1964.

The school, with only one campus residence hall well into the 1970s, moved slowly towards setting up an athletic program. The board of trustees approved soccer as the first varsity sport in March of 1968. A year later, the trustees approved baseball, basketball, golf, gymnastics and wrestling as varsity sports.

Ross, who had guided Belmont to the state high school basketball championship in 1964, was the successful applicant for the basketball coaching job. The first Wright State basketball team was to play its initial season at the junior varsity status. From that humble beginning, the WSU program came of age to win a national championship in its 13th season and advanced to Division I in its 18th.

"Nobody will ever know how difficult it was," the now retired Ross said. "There was no budget to speak of. I kept our equipment in my car because we had to move around to practice in different high school or even grade school gyms when we could get the time.

"One of the reasons I got the job was because I had started the high school program at Belmont. But I had plenty of help and backing. This was different. I was by myself. We didn't have as much as a high school team had. We had basketballs and uniforms but no facility, no trainer and no equipment people."

The first practice, at Spinning Hills Junior High, attracted a turnout of 87 players.

Jim Brown, who had played for Ross at Belmont and was to become the first salaried assistant coach at WSU, started out as a volunteer helping sort out candidates who could dribble and those who couldn't. The squad was eventually pared to 15 players.

There was no way for Brown, a University of Dayton graduate, to know he was embarking on a 25-year collegiate coaching career at the institution. He started as a part-time assistant to Ross before becoming the first full-time paid assistant and stayed on through the Marcus Jackson and Ralph Underhill regimes.

So the Raiders set sail into an 18-game schedule, outmanned by most opponents, including talented freshman teams from the likes of Cincinnati and Ohio State. They finished 4-14. One of the players destined to become a part of the WSU picture in the future was Bo Bilinski, a freshman out of Stebbins High School.

Bilinski is better known for his baseball skills and became one of the area's best known amateur long ball hitters. He's been a part-time assistant to WSU baseball coach Ron Nischwitz.

Bilinski laughed recalling his first year in college basketball. "We would go out to the junior high gym and wait for the 7th and 8th graders to finish their practice. It wasn't frustrating to me, because I was just out of Stebbins and I didn't know what it was supposed to be like."

The initial varsity season found the homeless Raiders (home games were played at Stebbins High School whenever possible) with a 7-17 record. In the very first varsity game, the Raiders lost in triple overtime to Cumberland College, 82-80, on the home court of the Kentucky school.

Mark Donahue was MVP, with Bill Fogt the leading scorer. Fogt, a Piqua native, was probably the best talent in the first few seasons, lettering all four years. Ross and Brown laid the groundwork for the early success by coming up with an outstanding recruiting class going into the 1972-73 season. Bob Grote, who would become the school's first All-American, headed that group.

Grote came out of Cincinnati Elder High School where his older brother, Steve, had starred before going on to play at Michigan. Bob's kid brother, Mike, would come to WSU a decade later and be a valuable member of the team that captured the Division II national title in 19?3.

That '72 group included Lyle Falknor, Rick Martin and Mike Herr, and they helped provided the program with its first winning season, 17-5.

Athletic Director Don Mohr, who had assumed that role in April, 1971 after service as director of financial aid and coaching the baseball team, made a risky financial move to start the 1972-73 season.

The Raiders would not get into their new campus home until February. Bidding for exposure and media attention, he rented the UD Arena for WSU's first home game against a Division I opponent. The Miami Redskins breezed to an 84-59 win, but Mohr felt the crowd of over 5,000 justified the expense.

Grote eventually joined Jim Brown on the coaching staff. At the time, he looked back on his start as a freshman and compared it to the incoming freshmen he was helping recruit.

"The difference is night and day," the husky Cincinnati native explained. "I can still remember eating pickle loaf sandwiches on the way home from practice. We'd drive in vans over to Stebbins to practice, get back to the dorm three hours later, maybe hit the books and get up the next morning to go to class."

Grote also remembers the struggle for recognition in his playing years (1973-76) when the team had four straight winning seasons. By then, the multi-purpose Physical Education Building, with its 2,800 seating capacity, had been built on campus and the Raiders promptly went on a 23-game home-floor winning streak. Attendance was good from the beginning.

"Nobody respected us," he said. "That provided real motivation to keep us a very close group of guys. We had something to prove."

At the end of the 1974 season, Tim Walker had become the school's first 1,000 point scorer, starting a club that by 1995 had 17 other members. After his fifth season, by which time his record had climbed up to 65-54, Ross resigned as coach to become assistant athletic director.

Marcus Jackson took over the coaching duties in the 1975-76 season. The Raiders, sparked by the strong senior group of Grote, Falknor and Martin became the first WSU team to hit the 20-victory plateau at 20-6, qualifying for the first time for the Division II playoffs.

The excursion into post-season play found them losing to Evansville, 85-75, but they rebounded to beat St. Josephs, 72-68, in a consolation game. The next year found the bottom dropping out in a hurry toward an 11-16 season.

The victory streak in the PE building was halted when Slippery Rock upset the Raiders, 77-75. That was nothing compared to a 110-52 humiliation at Cincinnati in the fourth game of the season. Although the team got back on the winning side at 14-13 the next season, Jackson submitted his resignation under pressure, setting the stage for a rocket launch to the top of Division II.

The Ralph Underhill Era

Don Mohr's role in building the Wright State athletic program was significant in many ways, but his most lasting contribution may have been hiring Ralph Underhill to coach the school's only revenue producing sport going into the 1978-79 season.

As this was being written, the personable Kentuckian was heading into his 18th season as the Raiders' mentor. He was also dean of Ohio's active college coaches and the owner of a gaudy 342-149 record for a .697 winning percentage.

Underhill had spent the six seasons before coming to WSU as the No. 1 assistant to Ron Shumate at Chattanooga. The Mocs had gone to the finals in the national NCAA Division II tournament in 1977 and came back to capture the championship in 1978.

"When I was interviewed for the job, I'm sure my being with a team that had done so well in Division II was a factor in my favor," Underhill said. "I had recruited the Cincinnati and northern Kentucky areas, and I had a feel for how you need to go about recruiting in Division II and what that program needs for success."

Underhill had grown up in the Cincinnati area, graduating from Lloyd High School in Erlanger, one of the many northern Kentucky suburbs. He played college basketball as well as track at Tennessee Tech. He started his coaching at Ohio County High School in Hartford, Kentucky then moved up to Louisville Manual High School, spending one season there before getting the opportunity to move into the collegiate level at Chattanooga.

Jim Brown, the only full-time assistant at the time, stayed on and the new coach inherited some proven talent in senior center Bob Schaefer, whose 1,634 career points was the record until Bill Edwards broke it in

1992. Sophomore guard Eddie Crowe was an excellent floor leader. Both Schaefer (Alter) and Crowe (Franklin) were homegrown players.

Hard working Steve Hartings was a valuable sophomore contributor, becoming a four year letterman. Bob Cook and Jimmie Carter, two of the other starters, were seniors and there was some concern the seniors might have a difficult time adjusting to the coach's fast break and pressing defense.

"They worked very hard to fit into it," Underhill said, laughing when he added, "Schafer wasn't the most agile or fastest guy, but he adjusted and we got off to a good start with a 20-8 record and a spot in the tournament. "Some people thought they were overachievers, but they were just a bunch of good kids that were fun to work with," he recalled.

Schaefer was voted the team MVP for the third successive season, a record that stood until Bill Edwards came along a decade later.

A 64-63 upset of the Miami Redskins on their home court was a big win for the Raiders, still struggling to a degree for recognition.

Underhill's second season vindicated the coach's confidence that WSU could be a force in Division II. In the 25-3 season they went 18-1 at home and developed a loud student-section following which became known as the Raider Rowdies.

The arrival of Rodney Benson, a Louisville area native who had started at Wichita, was the first of a number of transfers Underhill worked into the system while trying to get the WSU name known among area high school prospects. Underhill had tried to recruit Benson for Chattanooga when Rodney came out of high school.

With Crowe as floor leader running the show with the likes of Benson, Roman Welch, Hartings, Tom Holzapfel and Mike Zimmerman, the Raiders came within a whisker of the national title in Ralph's second season. The only losses were an upset at the hands of Central State in a game played in the UD Arena, a road game to Division I Rice and a 73-64 loss in the tournament to Eastern Illinois.

The Raiders came right back with a 25-4 campaign fueled by Benson, who went over 500 points in each of his two seasons as a Raider, winding up with 1048 for his career. WSU was rated No. I in the Division II poll a good part of this season and a segment of off-campus support was beginning to build up.

Underhill's brow furrowed as he thought back to a one-point loss at the hands of Northern Michigan in the first round of the tournament.

"They had a little guard named Montgomery, a very good player who wound up beating us with two free throws at the end," Underhill recalled. "Benson put us ahead with a driving lay-up with 10 seconds left and he was fouled on the play. That gave us a one-point lead but Rodney missed the free throw.

"That could have put us up by two, this was before the three-point shot was in the rules. Montgomery came down the floor and was moving for the shot which Hartings blocked, but a foul had already been called on Zimmerman. Montgomery went to the line, sank both free throws and we lose, 70-69. I felt we had a team of national championship caliber and with both Benson and Welch voted All-American, we could have won it all."

With Benson, Welch, Hartings and Crowe leaving, it seemed inevitable there would be a dropoff, but the Raiders came back with a 22-7 season, laying the groundwork for the national title a year down the road.

Bob Grote, who had gone into professional baseball as a pitcher in the New York Mets system, had come back as an assistant coach and his kid brother, Mike, turned up as a sophomore guard. Gary Monroe and Anthony Bias were valuable pickups from junior college ranks. Fred Moore and Steve Purcell moved up to fill the other gaps. Senior Tom Holzapfel saw valuable service.

The 1982 team was knocked off in the tournament by Kentucky Wesleyan in a 76-71 overtime struggle, setting up a dramatic touch of revenge in the championship year.

Mike Cusack had been hired as athletic director to succeed the retiring Mohr in 1982. Cusack, who had been AD at Gannon College in Erie, Pennsylvania set up Wright State's first holiday tournament hoping it could help showcase the Raiders

The 1982-83 championship year went through an uneven tempo in the middle of the schedule, touched off by Central State's 89-67 victory in the championship game of that first Wright State Invitational. That was a wakeup call for a team which stood 9-0 and may have been getting a bit overconfident.

Then Cheyney State, a Division II power from the Philadelphia area, came into the PE building and handed the Raiders their second loss, 68-60. That was followed by an unexpected one point loss to Indiana-Fort Wayne and the Raiders seemed to be spinning their wheels as they took a 13-3 record into Owensboro to face Kentucky Wesleyan, the team that had beaten them in the tournament at the end of the 1982 season.

That was where the legend of "The Shot" was born. Mike Grote, the popular point guard and floor leader, is the man who launched that impossible basket which earned the Raiders a 65-64 escape and projected them toward the championship.

With the clock ticking down to one second and the Raiders trailing by one point, Grote had no choice but to get the ball in the air toward the basket. But he was double teamed, and four arms were poised to jam the ball back in his face.

Somehow, falling backward to get the ball over those waving arms, his team mates swear he was in a floating horizontal position as he released the ball. But he got the ball in the air and it swished through the hoop as the horn sounded to end the game.

"I passed to Tom (Holzapfel) and he took a shot from the top of the key that missed," Grote explained. "Normally, I don't go after a rebound because my job is to get back on defense. But this time I had to go after it and somehow got it maybe 15 feet from the hoop. But I had nowhere to go. I was pushed before I got it in the air. It seemed the whole Kentucky Wesleyan team was all over me,"

Grote's once-in-a-lifetime heroics climaxed an incredible rally that began with the Raiders down by 13 points with 4.02 to play.

"It was not only an unbelievable shot, the reaction of our guys was unbelievable," said longtime assistant Brown.

From that point on, the Raiders won 16 of their final 17 games, the only loss in that stretch at the hands of Division I powerhouse Louisville. By tournament time, Underhill was pretty much rotating a seven man unit: Monroe, Bias, Moore, Grote, Holzapfel, Purcell and T. C. Johnson.

Fate seemed to be against the Raiders because in the first game they were again confronted by Kentucky Wesleyan as the road block toward Springfield, Massachusetts, site of the Division II Final Four. A tense battle all the way, this time they didn't need a miracle for a 69-67 victory.

After victories over Bloomsburg State and Cal State-Bakersfield, Underhill's frisky kids found themselves up against District of Columbia, the defending champions and top team in the polls all season. A strong contingent of WSU students and fans followed the team to the tournament in Massachusetts, just as UD followers had flocked to the NIT in the 1950s.

To the delight of the WSU followers, the Raiders dominated their favored opponents, 92-73. They swept the boards and converted 30 of 48 shots from the floor in a brilliant demonstration of team play.

Gary Monroe wrapped up his two-year career with a 23 point performance and tournament MVP honors. He joined Bias as the top rebounder with eight, but it was a well balanced team effort. Bias contributed 16 points and Moore 15. Johnson had 12, Purcell 10 while guard Holzapfel had four. Grote ended up with eight.

Underhill made sure every Raider who was dressed got into the game, giving Eric Ellis, Phil Bensinger, Rob Sanders, Steve Purcell and Mark McCormick a chance to get their names in the championship box score. Monroe became the fourth Raider to earn All-American honors.

Some of Mike Grote's popularity with the fans had to do with his publicized struggle with Crohn's disease, a severe intestinal disorder that flared up frequently during his playing days. The problem never seemed to slow Mike's up-beat personality, which made him a great floor leader.

His teammates, who had a closer view of his problem, had nothing but great respect for him knowing that every day might become a struggle to drag himself off to practice.

The championship season lifted Underhill's overall record over his five seasons to an eye-popping 120-26 and naturally drew attention from schools looking for a coach. But he stayed on, aware that the university trustees were committed to advancing to Division I and eventually building a new arena that would ease the scheduling problem. There was no chance of bringing top-flight Division I teams into the 2,800 seat PE Building.

With Monroe and Bias having used up their eligibility, the 1984 team became Underhill's first not to reach the 20-victory plateau, but the 19-9 season would have looked good at many rival schools.

As if Grote didn't have enough physical problems to cope with going into his senior season, he suffered a potentially disabling injury. He had injured a nerve in the back of his right leg, noticing it when he was in a crouching position working on building roofs in his summer job.

The problem was serious enough to cause concern about whether he would play, his foot in danger of going suddenly "dead". Underhill was already facing a problem at guard what with Grote's roommate, junior Mark McCormick out for the season with a knee injury.

Unfortunately for Grote, who did manage to play, a different late season knee injury forced an early end to his star-crossed but courageous career.

"We would have won 20 again if we could have beaten District of Columbia in our final home game," Underhill recalled, thinking back to the tough 69-67 setback. "That loss also cost us a bid to return to the tournament, and I still think we deserved one."

In his seventh season, Underhill and the Raiders were back on familiar ground with a 22-7 mark with an unhappy ending, a tournament loss to archrival Kentucky Wesleyan in the second game.

The veteran coach looks back on the 1986 team with bittersweet memories. The Raiders that year won the same number of games with one fewer loss (28-3) than the championship team three seasons earlier. The Raiders went into the tournament under a full head of steam and polished off two familiar rivals in Kentucky Wesleyan and Illinois-Edwardsville. But they were beaten by Cheyney which went on to the national event at Springfield, earning third place in the tournament.

There were three members of the 1,000 point club on that team, Mark Vest, Andy Warner and Joe Jackson, There were two fine guards in Tyrone Joy and senior Mark McCormick, lots of talent.

Despite finishing 20-8, the Raiders didn't make the playoffs in Underhill's ninth season and final one in Division II. "There was probably a little politics there," Underhill complained.

From the very beginning, Wright State fans had been wondering about playing the Dayton Flyers, the big school across town. With the Raiders winning big after Underhill's arrival, the mood developed to a demand for UD to get off its high horse and give the Raiders a chance.

Even though WSU followers were clamoring for that opportunity, the UD administration and coach Don Donoher maintained the position that as long as the Raiders remained Division II, there could be no game. But with WSU moving to Division I status going into the 1987-88 campaign, an agreement to meet was worked out between University Presidents Paige Mulhollan of WSU and Brother Raymond A. Fitz of UD.

The meeting was scheduled for Saturday, March 5 in the UD Arena and as the game approached, the Flyers were having a losing season. That built the confidence of WSU fans their team would prove it could handle the crosstown big kids.

Don Donoher's men went into the game at 11-17 against WSU's 16-10, but the Raiders seemed intimidated by the hostile capacity crowd of 13,511. To Underhill's dismay the Raiders shot only 28 per cent in the first half. The Flyers went to their locker room with a 50-23 halftime lead and the few WSU followers able to get tickets were in a state of shock.

Although the Raiders outscored the Flyers in the last half, the issue was never in doubt with Dayton's 89-71 victory going into the record as the start of a long series expected to last well into the new century.

Corey Brown reached the 20-point level for the Raiders converting 10 of 15 free throws, but it was a disappointing end for WSU's first season in Division I.

Because the Flyers had major schedule adjustments to make going into the Midwest Collegiate Conference the next year, the rivalry wasn't resumed until the 1989-90 season by which time Jim O'Brien had replaced Donoher.

In the intervening season the Raiders had an ordinary 17-11 record on an uneven schedule as AD Cusack began scouting around for a conference for his school, just as the Flyers had moved into the MCC. Cusack and Underhill knew the odds were overwhelming against the Raiders making the Division I tournament as an independent.

Wright State's incoming class of the 1989-90 season was destined to pay huge dividends in the drive toward that first NCAA tournament four seasons down the road.

Looking for ways to help his team at the Division I level recruiting, Underhill had arranged to take the Raiders on a European trip in the summer of 1988 to play club teams over there. The trip itself was a delight for the players who made it, but the future dividend wasn't apparent to anyone except the coach. Underhill carefully cultivated relationships with European club directors and coaches.

The first European player to come to the Dayton area to finish his high school play was 6-10 Marco Pikaar at Beavercreek, who wound up at UD. But the first player to enroll at WSU was seven-foot Mike Nahar, who had played on the junior national team in his native Netherlands. Although Nahar was not ready to compete against Division I collegiate level players, Underhill brought him along slowly as a freshman, then had him sit out as a redshirt, bringing him back to be the center on the 1992-93-94 teams.

The major immediate impact in that 1990 year was Bill Edwards, a 6-8 power forward who started his high school career at Franklin and transferred for his last two years to Middletown, where he won All-State honors. Edwards either won or shared the Raider MVP in all four of his seasons and was the mainstay of teams that gave the Raiders recognition as a legitimate Division I contender.

Also making their debuts were Jeff Unverferth, a tireless 6-7 rebounder from Columbus, and Sean Hammonds, another front court performer from Louisville. Both contributed over their four years.

The most satisfaction of the season was a thrilling 101-99 verdict over the Flyers, again in the UD Arena. These were the Jim O'Brien coached Flyers who went on to win the MCC conference and defeat Illinois in the NCAA tournament. This was the highlight of the 21-7 season, and some WSU partisans felt the Raiders deserved a tournament bid, but it didn't come.

After Donoher's ouster at UD, two of his assistants wound up on Underhill's staff, now increased to four men. Jack Butler became a full-time assistant and Jim Ehler the "restricted earnings" fourth man under the tighter NCAA rules.

The historic opening of the 10,700-seat Ervin J. Nutter center began a new era in Raiders basketball. The first game in the new facility, Dec. 1, 1990, was against Tennessee State and the invaders almost threw a damper over the celebration as Underhill's men had to struggle to an 88-86 victory.

The team wound up with a 19-9 season, but was not a good road team absorbing, among other losses, a 90-60 pasting at Ohio State.

Going into the 1991-92 season, the Raiders found their first conference affiliation, joining the Mid-Continent Conference (whose initials are the same as the Midwestern Collegiate Conference, which WSU joined in the 1994-95 school year.)

The Raiders struggled to a 15-13 overall record, going 9-7 in the league and being ousted in the tournament by Western Illinois. WSU submitted a bid to host the MCC tournament, the selling factor being the size of the Nutter Center. That tournament led to the goal of getting into the "Big Dance," the NCAA tournament against the big boys.

The next regular season had its ups and downs, ending up 17-9 going into the MCC tournament. The Raiders swept Eastern Illinois, Valparaiso and Illinois-Chicago to earn the automatic bid to the NCAA tournament and their growing following was ecstatic. Not even learning their first round opponent was perennial power Indiana diminished the optimism and the excitement.

The game against Bob Knight's Hoosiers turned into a nightmare in the form of a 97-54 lathering, but *just being* in the NCAA tournament had to be looked upon as a plus.

Edwards had a tremendous season to climax his career, scoring 747 points as a senior and ending up with 2,303. That total obliterated the previous record of Bob Schaefer dating back 14 seasons, topping it by 669 points.

Edwards had to share the spotlight with Mark Woods, the point guard who ended up in the 1,000 point club and is the all-time leader in assists. The slender Woods was another Louisville native, coming from one of Underhill's longtime recruiting areas.

The second European player to join the Raiders was 6-7 forward Delme Herriman, from Manchester, England who moved into the picture as a freshman and started as a sophomore in 199?

Without Edwards, Woods and Unverferth, the Raiders were not as much a force in their third and last season in the Mid-Continent, suffering through a 12-18 campaign and an early exit in tournament at the hands of Cleveland State.

Negotiations to put the Dayton-Wright State rivalry on an annual basis were completed going into the 1993-94 season by Presidents Mulhollan and Fitz. The plan worked out was for home-and-home the first year with annual games to follow, rotating the site.

The game was to be promoted as the Gem City Jam with the *Dayton Daily News* as sponsor.

The Flyers surprised people on both sides with an easy 83-56 victory on Dec. 11, 1993 in WSU's third joust with the Flyers in the Arena. Dayton made its first appearance in the Nutter Center a month later and the Raiders evened the series at 2-2 with a 77-65 victory. Wright State took the overall lead with a 74-63 victory, again on their home court, Dec. 10, 1994.

The Raiders found the going rocky in their venture into their new league affiliation. They had, in effect, replaced the Flyers in the Midwest Collegiate and finished 13-17 overall. But in hosting the conference tournament, they pulled off one of their great upsets.

Trailing heavily favored Xavier by one point in the final minute of the tournament game, the Raiders scored a memorable upset on a rare full court pass completion from guard Rob Welch to Herriman, who turned as he caught the ball and let it fly as the buzzer sounded. The 71-70 triumph sent the home crowd into a frenzy as fans rushed the floor to join in the celebration.

There was no celebration when Wisconsin-Green Bay ended the WSU hopes for a return to the NCAA tournament with a 73-59 victory for the league crown.

The bright spot of that season and promise for the future is the presence of another European import. Vitaly Potapenko is an agile, impressive physical specimen at 6-10, who had beefed up to 305 pounds going into the 1995-96 season.

The huge young man from Kiev, Ukraine may be one of the better college players anywhere and his future, including the NBA, would seem unlimited.

Early in the 1995 season, in the renewal of the rivalry between the two local teams, an underdog Flyer team convincingly defeated the Raiders to even the series at three victories each.

The sprawling campus on the western edge of downtown belies the fact that Sinclair Community College once existed in a few rooms in the Dayton YMCA building on Monument Avenue. Even then the school had a basketball team, using the Stivers High School gym for its home games.

When the Physical Education building on the present campus opened in 1975, three years after the initial Sinclair buildings, the team finally had a home court.

Sinclair has been quite successful competing against other junior colleges in the Ohio-Kentucky-Indiana triangle. But because of the more frequent turnover of students the school has had trouble getting off-campus fan support.

The modern era men's program began in 1964 and has gone through three coaches. Larry Hamant was the first, compiling a 27-39 record in four seasons, 1964-1968.

Kevin O'Neill was at the helm from 1968 through 1980, during the era when the campus games began, and his record was a more than respectable 203-106.

Don Cundiff, who doubles as athletic director, is in his 16th season as coach with a 285-195 record heading into the current campaign.

1980 UD NCAA Division II champions (above) hoist coach Maryalyce Jeremiah in victory, Ann Meyers at right.

WSU's Ralph Underhill (right) intent on the action.

1982-83 NCAA Division II national champion WSU Raiders (below).

18

The Women Come to Play

Tracing the history of sports for women in Dayton, or anywhere else, is difficult for the obvious reason that while women have always competed in certain activities their abilities were looked upon as inferior to the men in the male-dominated American society.

In 1985, Dr. R. Elaine Dreidame, Senior Associate Athletic Director at the University of Dayton, was commissioned to do a historical survey of women's athletics at the school.

Dr. Dreidame had come to Dayton in 1970 as the coach of women's basketball and volleyball. Four years later she became the first full-time woman administrator in the UD athletic department.

Her survey dates back to 1935, the year women were first admitted as students at the all-male school.

Dividing her research into four phases, Dr. Dreidame referred to the 1935-1946 period as the Intramural Play-Day era.

That meant the women competed against other UD women except for the annual so-called Play Day which found women travelling to the University of Cincinnati campus to compete against women from other Ohio schools in basketball, volleyball, swimming and bowling.

In those years, expenses incurred were taken care of by the Women's Athletic Association (WAA), founded by Mrs. Joseph Holsinger, whose husband was a member of Harry Baujan's football coaching staff and head men's basketball coach.

Mrs. Holsinger's group set up a complete system of physical education for women students. The WAA first supported tennis and then branched into soccer, volleyball, softball, basketball, archery and paddle tennis.

In the 1937-38 school year, Mrs. Lou Tschudi, wife of another football assistant coach, headed the program. The WAA constitution was revised and a point system established to make women eligible for athletic letters.

Mary Lou Thomas was the first UD woman to be publicized as a winner of two swimming awards at the Play Day in Cincinnati.

In the 1939-40 school year the first defined intercollegiate sport for women came into being when Bill Salsinger coached 15 coeds twice a week in fencing. The team defeated Cincinnati 6-3 and 5-4.

In the 1940-41 year, the WAA created the first women's award, named in memory of one of its early workers, the Janet Breidenbach Memorial Award. The award was based on sportsmanship, scholarship, leadership and service. The first recipient was Margaret Reiling.

Women's activities went on the back burner through the World War II years, but the WAA was revived in the 1945-46 school year with Mrs. Eileen Sears becoming the first faculty advisor.

Dr. Dreidame's second phase (1946-1965) is designated the "quasi intercollegiate era" because UD teams did start to compete against other colleges. But they also counted games against high schools, alumni teams and club teams.

The typical women's team in this period averaged about two practices per week. All coaches were non-salaried volunteers and the WAA still had to fund the activities, but in the 1952-53 school year, the physical education department began contributing $200 to pay officials.

Field hockey became a popular addition to the women's programs in this era and in 1949-50 there were two active teams made up from 44 women candidates. Pat Monette coached both teams as well as the basketball team.

In 1956, Dr. Doris Drees and Mary Leonard were two new faculty members in the phys ed department. Ms. Drees played a strong, early role when the women were moving toward varsity status.

Interestingly, when the selection committee for the University's Athletic Hall of Fame first voted to admit women, the first so honored in 1978 was Susan Finke Schiller, who had excelled in basketball and field hockey. At her induction, Finke Schiller spoke of playing basketball under Pat Monette and Drees, although the sport was not on a varsity level.

"Not too many people ever saw us play," she said. "As for our program we were lucky to get gasoline money from the school to drive to Springfield to play Wittenberg or over to Richmond to play Earlham."

Finke Schiller's best sport may well have been golf, even though the links sport was not then involved in the UD women's program.

The women's basketball team in the early 1950s played very few games, the 1951 schedule included only Ohio State, Antioch and Wittenberg. The team, coached by Drees, continued to play Ohio State and in the 1963-64 school year posted a 6-0 record including a 44-42 victory over Miami, ending a losing streak against the Redskins.

The third segment of Dr. Dreidame's history (1965-74) is classified as the pre-Title IX period.

The 1965-66 school year marked the first time the women's teams had a budget of their own from the athletic department. The total was $3,506, $1,700 of which was for personnel services.

The budget covered the salaries for part-time coaches, the awards, travel (mostly gasoline for the cars of students and coaches), officials and uniforms.

The UD women's basketball media guide recognizes the 1968-69 team, coached by Judith Bowman to a 4-7 record, as its first varsity season. With this in mind, we will pick up the basketball story later and concentrate here on the general expansion of women's sports activities.

In 1971-72, with Dr. Drees as the women's athletic director, the university became a charter member of the AIAW (Association of Intercollegiate Athletics for Women.) Dayton was a charter member of the national AIAW and also of its Ohio and Midwest subsidiaries. Two years later the athletic budget under Dr. Drees was up to $7,467 with $2,500 designated for salaries and $4,967 for operating expenses.

Basic salaries at the time for Dr. Drees, Dr. Dreidame and other women coaches came from whatever educational department had hired them; in Dr. Dreidame's case, the physical education department. In her first season on campus, Dr. Dreidame was paid $250 for each of the two sports she tutored.

In the spring of 1975, the student publication *Flyer News* launched its annual Female Athlete of the Year Award, giving it to Patti Palcic.

The decade between 1975 and 1985 (when Dr. Dreidame's report ended) was described as different as night and day.

The women's athletic budget had gone from the $7,467 in the last year prior to Title IX to the $250,000-plus level in 1985. Dr. Dreidame points out that the 1995 budget for women is in excess of $1,000,000.

In 1974 the university had no full-time staff members for women's athletics A decade later, there were one full-time administrator, three coaches, a trainer and a secretary. Dr. Dreidame herself was the first full-time employee in women's athletics.

The first athletic scholarship to a women was $500 to Deirdre Kane and a Woman's Athletic Boosters Club made its appearance in 1975. Kane was the MVP of the first MAIAW volleyball tournament held on campus two years later.

The title Dr. Drees held as director of women's athletics was abolished and the salary gap that once existed favoring men over women in the same positions has been eliminated.

"The salary we pay our coaches now is based on market value," Dr. Dreidame put it, referring to the pay of Oliver Purnell and Clemette Haskins, men's and women's basketball coaches. "If you want a winning program, you hire people with the reputation to provide just that."

Female athletes are now eligible to be members of the Varsity D Club, long a bastion for football players.

In 1977, women's athletic scholarships were included in the athletic budget. Growth and expansion have been on a steady pace ever since.

Going into the 1995-96 season, there are eight women's programs, each with a salaried coach: basketball, volleyball, golf, tennis, softball, soccer, cross-country and track.

UD Women Come of Age

The way Elaine Dreidame looks at it, she has gone through the process in which women's basketball has come out of the Dark Ages.

"When I was playing at the University of Cincinnati back in the early 1960s, we had six players on a team and a guard, the position I played, was limited to three dribbles," she said.

"We played something like an eight game schedule all within a 100 mile radius of the campus and our meal money was $2 per day."

When she took over as head coach at the University of Dayton six years after graduating from UC, there was no budget for women's sports even though the men's basketball program had been a money maker for nearly two decades.

"There was really no budget for the program when I took over," she said in an interview for this book.

As the Senior Associate Athletic Director for all varsity sports she looks over the athletic program. The budget on the women's side is now into seven figures, the once fabled million dollar plateau.

There was women's basketball at Dayton prior to the 1968-69 season, which is recognized as the first season in the Flyer media guides.

But basketball on the Dayton campus was pretty much in the same loosely organized state it was at most Ohio colleges. It wasn't a varsity sport, but more of an intramural or club competition.

The first recognized women's team posted a 4-7 record under Coach Judith Bowman and the top scorer was Pam Diehl with a 7.1 average. A year later the Flyers improved to 6-3 on a schedule that included Miami, Ohio State and Bowling Green.

That's when Dreidame came to Dayton as basketball coach having been head coach at Mount St. Joseph, then a women's school in suburban Cincinnati. Dreidame's first team wound up hosting the first OAIAW (Ohio Association of Intercollegiate Athletics for Women) tournament.

"We faced Bowling Green, a team we had beaten in the regular season and they blew us away, 52-30, " Dreidame recalled. "We came back to win the next three games and win the consolation bracket." The record was 11-5 with Janet Deeters and Linda Keefe the leading scorers.

Dreidame was launched on a sequence in which she coached basketball for eight seasons, compiling a 109-63 record that included two top ten finishes in the ratings. She was even more successful in 10 years of handling the volleyball team, compiling a 309-95 record that included four state and two midwest championships.

The Flyer women -- don't call them Lady Flyers -- began slipping back a bit in the early 1970s and then started to build toward their greatest seasons ever. Sandy Johnson and Betty Burke shared honors in the 15-5, 15-8 and 9-13 seasons prior to the big breakthrough.

The Ann Meyers Era

There is no way UD followers of the men's team could agree on who was the best Flyer ever -- be it Hank Finkel, Monk Meineke, Jim Paxson, Jr., Roosevelt Chapman, Garry Roggenburk, Bucky Bockhorn or whomever.

But to this point in time at least there is no doubt as to the identity of the women's overall MVP.

Ann Meyers, class of 1980, departed the program as a three-time All-American, top rebounder and top scorer. She was the first woman player who could be referred to as a box office attraction.

When Meyers enrolled at Chaminade-Julienne that high school did not have a girls basketball team. It wasn't until her junior year that C-J fielded a varsity team and it wasn't all that well organized an operation.

With that in mind, it was undoubtedly to the University of Dayton's advantage that Meyers, a 6-1 center in her last year at C-J, wasn't heavily recruited by other colleges fielding women's teams.

"I think our biggest break in getting Ann was the fact Ohio State wasn't all that interested in her," said Dreidame, taking a candid view. "We didn't have full grants for women and were dividing partials and we got Ann some help in academics and part of one of our grants," she explained. "She was from a family of nine and needed some assistance."

Whatever the investment, it was a terrific bargain. In her four seasons, the UD women went 114-19, played in the post-season AIWA all four years, climaxing it by winning the national championship in 1980.

As talented as she was, Meyers might never have had it so good had not coach Dreidame come up with two excellent recruiting classes. Beverly Crusoe, who had played at Dunbar and was a starter at a junior college in Texas, transferred back home and finished in the class of 1980. So did Julie Johnson, a third local girl, and the daughter of Russ Johnson, a former UD football player.

A year later, in the 1977-78 season, that group had been joined by playmaking guard Tammy Stritenberger out of Colonel White. The one not from a Dayton high school was Carol Lammers of Miller City, Ohio.

In what was planned to be Dreidame's last season of coaching before moving to the administrative level, the lineup of Meyers, Crusoe, Stritenberger, Lammers and Johnson went 24-6 and won two games in the national tournament before bowing to Southeastern Louisiana.

The new Flyer coach going into the 1978-79 season was Maryalyce Jeremiah, who had been coaching at Cedarville. In the odd way women's programs were taking shape, tiny Cedarville was competing at a level the school's male team could never hope to attain.

"Maryalyce stressed an up-tempo game with emphasis on speed than had been my style," Dreidame said of her selection to replace herself.

Dreidame also handed her successor the most ambitious schedule in terms of big-name opponents than any UD team of any kind ever faced.

The UD women opened that year against Indiana and then took on in order Cincinnati, Miami, Auburn, Kentucky, Detroit, Eastern Michigan and Marshall, and beat them all. Later in the season, the UD women beat Michigan, Louisville and Purdue.

"The fact is that at the time we weren't overmatched against those schools because they weren't emphasizing their women's programs," Dreidame said. When the big schools fell into line, pushed by Title IX, the Flyers weren't in a position to recruit against them on even terms.

Despite taking a 30-2 record into the national tournament, the UD women lost out in the finals to South Carolina State, another example of the then seemingly upside-down status of the women's game.

Hosting the tournament in the UD Arena in 1980, the Flyers did get over the hump as Jeremiah led her team to a 36-2 season and the AIAW national championship. That game, played on March 24, 1980, attracted a crowd of 4,737 and the noise level was a big plus for the Dayton power-house. The tournament was the most successful in the history of the AIAW and a tribute to Dayton area basketball fans.

"We broke even on Friday night," Dreidame said of the three night affair. "Some people on campus thought we were assuming a big risk. Naturally, we think this was a real plus for our women's program, not just basketball, but all of them."

The championship game was the wrapup of Meyer's brilliant career and she responded with 40 points and 14 rebounds in the easy 83-52 romp over the College of Charleston, South Carolina. By her senior year, Meyers had added a couple of inches to her height (6-3) and had developed strong physical board play.

The women opened the tournament with a 105-88 racehorse romp over California State of Pennsylvania and then rolled over the next two opponents into the championship game.

Meyers finished her career with 2,672 points, a higher total than Roosevelt Chapman's men's record of 2,233.

The success of the program cost the women their coach as Jeremiah was offered the head coaching job at Indiana. The Big Ten opening and the opportunity to be part of the IU program headed by Bob Knight was too strong a lure to turn down.

Assistant coach Linda Makowski took over and with Stritenberger,

Lammers and reserves Kim Ramsey and Journey Beard returning, the team went 27-7 but did not survive the tournament, again played in the Arena.

In 1982, with the NCAA pushing to build up women's basketball, the Flyers played in Division II for two seasons and then moved up to Division I. These changes may have been good for the program in the long run, but the changing focus put the UD coaches into a much more competitive recruiting situation.

In 1984, the last season in Division II, Dayton hosted the NCAA's first round games. The Flyers defeated Northwest Missouri State and St. Cloud State to advance to the semi-finals in Springfield, Massachusetts, where the Division II men's tournament was played.

Virginia Union defeated the UD team 71-59, and while it wasn't immediately evident, the program was in for rough going in Division I the following season. With the move, Dayton joined the North Star Conference and posted a 17-11 record. Theresa Yingling, Michele Kruty and Mary Byers were the top performers.

At the end of the season, Makowski departed to become head coach at George Washington and was replaced by Sue Ramsey. In Ramsey's third season, the women found themselves in the Midwestern Collegiate Conference, a step taken in tandem with the men's program.

The MCC affiliation lifted the Flyers into another level of competition which became even more difficult with a subsequent move into the now defunct Great Midwest.

Ramsey's seven seasons found the program struggling to stay over the .500 level. Tobette Pleasant led the UD women with 16.5 and 16.9 scoring averages (1988-89), after which the individual leaders dropped below 15 points, indicating the struggle. The only post-season appearances were in the MCC tournament. That event was held in Dayton in 1990 and 1991 and in both years the women lost to Notre Dame.

After the 8-19 season in 1994, Ramsey was dismissed and the administration made a pledge to new coach Clemette Haskins to rebuild the program with a larger recruiting budget, the full quota of 15 scholarships and a concentrated effort for greater media exposure.

Coach Haskins is the daughter of Clem Haskins, the head coach at Minnesota who sent his Western Kentucky teams against the Flyers before his Big Ten opportunity developed.

"We will be back," declared administrator Dreidame in giving Clemette a vote of confidence.

The Lady Raiders

The women's basketball program at Wright State had an even less conspicuous beginning than the men's.

Two years after John Ross found himself swamped by a turnout of 87 male candidates for the Raiders in the fall of 1969, Arnelle Jackson was hardly swamped by the nine girls who responded to her call in 1971.

Jackson, like Ross at first, was a part-time coach hired out of the Dayton school system. It was her job to put together a team of girls who had only modest success at the high school level.

"It was a very meager beginning," recalled Ms. Jackson, who was coaching at Fairview High School. "Our first group of girls wasn't large enough to have an effective scrimmage that first year. I think the girls who did come out looked on it as something like intramural competition. We were no way prepared for the schedule we played. But we did win our very first game over Rio Grande, but then we lost the next 13."

There was no effort at recruiting other than what Ms. Jackson did on her own limited time as she remained on the Fairview faculty. There were more candidates the second year and the record went up to 4-10 and by the third season, the women actually had a winning record at 9-8. Kim Hill, Jeanne Keister and Margie Coats were mainstays in those first years.

"By that time, the university wanted to improve the program and they wanted a full-time coach," Ms. Jackson explained. "I had enjoyed my experience, but I was thinking of the financial security I had going through the state system and passed up the offer."

Peg Wynkoop, who had come to WSU as the women's volleyball coach and stayed on to advance to her present position as Assistant Athletic Director, explained the university's plans for women.

"The school joined the state AIWA (Association of Intercollegiate Athletics for Women) in 1976. The league included Ohio Dominican, Wilmington, Cedarville, Dayton, Mount St. Joseph, Cincinnati and Capital in addition to Wright State," she explained.

The odd assortment of schools from huge Cincinnati to tiny Ohio Dominican in that grouping offers testimony to the uncertain status of women's programs.

With that league affiliation, Pam Davis became the first full-time women's basketball coach, hired out of the Kettering system where she coached Barnes Junior High. After going 5-12 and 10-10 in her first two seasons, Davis managed to get her team into the state OAIAW tournament where it lost twice and settled for 10-13.

By then scholarship money for all women's programs was becoming available. Without a football team, WSU has been able to finance its grants program up to NCAA limits in most cases.

"Our first impact player was Jodi Martin," Wynkoop maintains, referring to one of the early scholarship prizes. "She came out of Columbus and was a center-forward at 5-feet-10."

Martin was voted MVP of the women's team all four years she played (1980-81-82-83) and the team had winning records her first three seasons.

WSU's best record to that point came in the 1980-81 season when they posted a 15-10 record, ending with a loss to the Dayton Flyers. Despite the fact the WSU and UD men weren't playing each other, the women's teams were meeting every year.

The WSU lineup that season included Jeanne Bierman, Christi Hill, Lois Gebhart and, of course, Martin.

Ms. Martin wound up as the all-time leading scorer to date with 2,055 points and going into the 1995-96 season held the record well ahead of runner-up Jenny Horn, who was the MVP in 1985-86.

The Raider women moved up to Division II NCAA standards in the early 1980s and built toward their finest year ever when they went 24-6 in the 1986-87 season and made it to their first NCAA tournament.

Lois Warburg, the center and to that point the tallest player, was a mainstay along with Janet Emerson (MVP), Tammy Stover, Dana Whitesel and Shawna Moffitt, along with first year player Kristin King.

The program began to skid a bit the next season and collapsed to a 3-25 record in the 1989-90 season. The fact the Raiders went into Division I elevated the level of competition. In that 25-loss season, WSU was put down by the likes of Louisville, South Carolina, Vanderbilt, LaSalle and Cincinnati among others.

Following Davis' resignation, Terry Hall was named the third WSU coach April 20, 1990. Hall was returning to coaching after being out of it for three years. Prior to that she had a seven year regime as head coach at the University of Kentucky.

The Raiders started off 4-24 under the new coach. From there the rebuilding has been slow but steady, moving up to 8-20, 9-18 and 11-16 seasons.

A concern developed for and around coach Hall in the summer of 1993 when a physical examination revealed an ovarian cancer. Ms. Hall has continued to coach while gamely fighting the disease. She underwent a successful bone marrow transplant in December of 1944, missing a stretch of games during which assistant Lisa Fitch filled in.

Her prognosis going into the 1995-96 season is good and her players, the WSU administration and the community have been very supportive.

Central State Women

The Central State women's basketball team has enjoyed great success after Teresa Check took over the program going into the 1984-85 season. In her first 11 seasons, the Lady Marauders posted a 232-69 record in NAIA Division I competition.

Check is even prouder, she says, that she can point to a 100 per cent graduation rate among the players who played out their eligibility.

Check grew up in Cedarville, one of five girls in an athletic family that pioneered in girls competition at the high school there. She enrolled at Adelphi University in New York State and played there before transferring to CSU for her senior season.

She later coached in the early years of Alter High School's girls program before becoming head coach at Western Illinois University. Her coming to CSU coincided with the school's intention to give stronger financial and other support to the women's program in accordance with Title IX.

Many of her players are recruited from the area. Co-captain Janice Tillman, who came from Cedarville, spoke about the togetherness taught by the coach.

"We go out together, go to movies and stuff like that. We look out for each other," Tillman said.

"It's important to demand the best, that's the way you earn their respect," the coach said of her philosophy.

Sinclair Community College has fielded a successful women's basketball program dating back to 1975 when Charlene Gomer, the first coach, posted a tryout notice on the bulletin boards around campus.

Operating at the two-year level, nearly all the players came out of area high school programs and still do. There are no scholarships and few amenities; and many of the players have had to support themselves with jobs while going to school.

Linda O'Keefe succeeded Gomer in the 1978-79 season and was in her 18th year as this material was being compiled.

"At this level, as much as anything, we're teaching life," O'Keefe was quoted by *Dayton Daily News* columnist Tom Archdeacon.

Typical of the women athletes are Tina Tucker and Angele Williamson, who came from Akron Ellet High School to the Dayton campus. They share an apartment (there is no on-campus housing) and work to support themselves.

Another member of the 1995-96 team is forward Angie Folkerth, whose three-year-old daughter sometimes attends practice, and who works full-time at a Dayton machine shop.

Despite the quick turnover which is not a problem for four-year schools, O'Keefe had compiled a 238-185 overall record going into the 1995-96 campaign.

19

The High School Game

Unlike football, there can be no research into high school basketball prior to the turn of the 20th century because the game itself did not come into being until the last decade of the 19th Century. The Big Ten did not have a collegiate basketball season until 1905-06.

Dr. James A. Naismith created the game when he was physical activities director of the YMCA in Springfield, Massachusetts with this explanation, "we decided there should be a game that could be played indoors and in the evenings."

Steele High School, then the oldest Dayton high school, was the first to field a basketball team. The early records are hazy but the first Steele-Stivers game was played in 1909 with Steele winning 16-10.

Emerson H. Landis, who captained the 1910-1911 Steele team and later became superintendent of the Dayton city schools, offered to provide historical material in 1975 to the author, then sports editor of the *Dayton Journal Herald*. Portions of his letters follow:

Dayton's population was approximately 80,000 people (in 1910) and there were two high schools, Steele and Stivers.

It was difficult to conduct athletics because of the lack of transportation. Trains, traction cars, streetcars and horse drawn vehicles were our only means of getting to out-of-town games.

Steele did not have its own gym and it was necessary to practice and play whereever we could get a gym. It was often necessary to walk to the different places to either practice or play.

Steele practiced at the St. Marys Institute gym and incidentally we had many practice games against the St. Marys Cadets. My man (to guard) was Harry Solimano. A second gym used was Turners gym which was just across the Third

Street bridge. Ted and Pete Hughes, Eddie Graef, Carl Pfhal and others were on the Turners team. Ted Hughes gave us help to practice there.

What we considered our floor was Lakeside Park Skating Rink. The street car service was irregular and on many occasions the team had to hoof it up the hill through snow to get to the daily drill.

Dr. Ward McCally and Sam Cohen (the stars of the 1909 team) had graduated. The remaining three, Clarence Shively, "Monk" Pierce and Ralph Wright formed the nucleus of the 1910 team. Emerson H. Landis became the new center and D. G. Boyd the other forward. The substitutes were Raymond Aull and Clarence Fox.

Steele played 9 games and won all but one. Steele edged their oldest opponent, Hamilton, 23-22. Early in the season Steele won over Piqua twice, 33-16 and 26-18. The latter game was at Piqua. Plain City, one of the strongest teams in the state was beaten 35-15.

Landis went on to describe the two wins over Stivers, referring to the 29-23 game as for the city championship.

Steele's longest trip found the Lions travelling to Granville where they defeated Doan Academy (prep school for Denison University) 28-23. Dave Reese of Dayton Triangle fame was Landis' opposing center.

The last game was at the Lakeside rink and a crowd of 1,000 people watched West Milton edge Steele 22-21 with many of the fans skating before the game. Landis described the games as "very rough with close guarding" paying attention to his personal battle with Hamilton's Campbell Graf, who went on to play three years on the Ohio State football team.

In 1911 Landis was the only returning starter for the Lions but got plenty of help for another successful season. Among the highlights was a 61-9 rout of Troy High School, a very high score for the time.

The return of Landis vs. Graf in Hamilton's visit to Dayton ended with future Buckeye star Graf going out with a fractured collar bone. Landis described their personal duel as "quite a spectacle."

Steele and Stivers wound up playing three times that year, splitting the first two games, but the Tigers came on to win their first city championship by a 27-18 score in a game played at Lakeside. Carl "Dutch" Thiele, better remembered as a Triangles football standout, led the way.

Stivers was about to embark on a remarkable two decades in which the Tigers dominated the state in a way no other school ever has. The Tigers won eight state championships starting in 1916 and ending in 1930. The climax came in the 1928-29-30 seasons when Stivers won three straight, a record that has never been duplicated.

It needs to be noted that the Ohio High School Athletic Association started to designate state champions in 1923. Prior to that, an invitational tournament was sponsored by Ohio Wesleyan University in Delaware, the winner of which was recognized as the state basketball champion.

The earlier Stivers state championship seasons are not recognized by the state association. Even though OHSAA does not recognize the Delaware Invitational as a state championship event, most observers and newspapers at the time accepted the tournament as just that. The 1928-29-30 Stivers state titles are the only ones recognized by the OHSAA.

The OHSAA came into being in 1909, emerging from annual meetings of the Western Ohio Superintendents' and Principals' Round Table, which had been discussing drafting rules to govern athletic competition.

George R. Eastman of Dayton was chairman of the committee to draw up the rules for a statewide control body. Eastman's committee was formed at a round table meeting in Dayton in 1906. When the OHSAA came into being there were 84 member schools.

The first four Stivers championships came out of the invitational affair called the Buckeye Interscholastic Tournament played in Edwards Gym on the Ohio Wesleyan campus in Delaware. At the time, Ohio Wesleyan was a power in state collegiate athletic circles.

In 1916, Stivers went 12-2 in the regular season and rolled through the six-game event, spaced out over two weekends in Delaware. Teams had to play two games on Saturday to decide the title, Stivers defeating Marietta, 30-16, in the morning and downing East Liverpool, 45-31, for the title.

Newspaper reports of the day did not include first names, and the Stivers names in the box score included captain Lightner, Mumma, Carmony, Marsteller, Patterson and Eberling.

Mumma scored 11 and 9 field goals in the two games and Lightner 7 and 2. The goals were scored by the men in the offensive end with the defenders playing behind the center line. Center Carmony controlled the tap, a very important phase of play since the teams jumped center after every basket.

Clyde Mumma won the mile and half mile runs for the Tigers in the 1917 state track meet to go along with his basketball and later golf heroics. Willard Marquardt coached that 1916 team as well as the 1919 team which started a run of three straight championships in the Delaware tourney.

The 1919 team lost its opener to Tipp City and then went undefeated the rest of the way piling up awesome totals such as 93-8 over Sidney, 55-4 over McGuffey and 62-8 over North High. The Tigers had a tough time beating Cleveland East Tech for the title, 25-22, with Jake Matusoff scoring the final two goals. The Schwab twins, Harry and Harvey, were standouts in their sophomore season.

Marquardt having started his administrative career, Earl Brandenburg coached the 1920 team to a 15-2 regular season record and again a six game sweep at Delaware with a 29-19 win over Akron Central in the title game. They accepted an invitation to a national tournament in Chicago where they lost to Wingate, Indiana in the second round.

That Wingate team, claiming the national championship, was on the 1921 schedule when the Tigers, under new coach Guy Early, won their third straight state title. They went through what was described as "a gruelling schedule" of 23 games without a loss. The 17-game regular season was featured by a 34-24 win over the Indiana team that had beaten them the year before.

The Stivers overall record in those three unofficial state championship seasons was 58-3.

Harry and Harvey Schwab earned all-state honors with Herman Poock and Ralph Stevenson receiving honorable mention. The Schwabs were standouts in four sports, football, basketball, baseball and track. A third Schwab brother, Vernon, followed the twins at Stivers.

Harry Schwab went into pro baseball upon graduation and worked his way up to spring training tryouts with both the Pittsburgh Pirates and Cincinnati Reds. He later became an outstanding game official in both football and basketball and his career in golf is covered in the golf section of this book.

Harry Wilhelm was coaching both football and basketball when the Tigers won their fifth state basketball title in the spring of 1924 and a few months later, his football team went 10-0-1 and claimed a national championship in that sport.

The OHSAA took over sponsorship of the tournament in 1923 and divided the schools into two divisions, larger schools class A and smaller one as B. Prior to that time, there had been no divisions and the Delaware tournament was open to all if their record justified an invitation

Stivers captured the title game, 30-16, over Columbus East. Lee Fenner, better remembered for his long football career with the Dayton Triangles, was selected to the all-tournament team. Other key players included Joe Cox, Fuzzy Evans, center Bus Trautwein and Hawk English. Although the Tigers had winning years the next three seasons, it was their three successive championship years in 1928-29-30 that brands them as one of Ohio's finest teams ever.

Floyd Stahl had taken over the coaching in the 1926-27 season and his first team was a good one, going 18-2, but the real glory was just ahead. Bob Lively was the senior captain of the 1928 team and Bill Hosket provided the necessary big man at center. Hosket was only 6-4, but at the time, a six-footer was regarded as tall.

Lively, Bobby Colburn and Larry McAfee were the forwards, Herb Brown, Marv Farrier, Bob Payne and Bob Albright rounded out the squad. Those seven and Hosket were the only ones taken to the tournament.

The Tigers went to Columbus by train and stayed at the Deshler-Wallick hotel, at the time the center of everything in Columbus at Broad and High. Most hotel rooms had a view of the state capital across the intersection.

Although Colburn is the only survivor as this was being written, several the other players were interviewed in a 1987 reunion.

"Going into the tournament, Fremont was favored," Lively recalled. "Stahl and I got our heads together and decided that after the center jump, I'd just plant myself under the basket not planning to shoot, but waiting to find Hosket open and drop off the ball to him."

The strategy apparently worked as Hosket scored 22 points to knock off Fremont, 36-20. It was an eight team tournament and Stivers went on beat Akron South, 26-15, before the championship showdown with Canton McKinley, which the Tigers won, 25-20.

Although Hosket scored only four foul shots in this win, he was the tournament top scorer with 39 and was named to the All-State team for the first of three successive years. Lively and Payne tied for the game's high-scoring honors with 6, Colburn added 5 and Hosket and McAfee four each. The Tigers were invited to the national tournament in Chicago and bowed out to a team from St. George, Utah.

With so much talent returning, much was expected of the 1929 team and it lived up to expectations but fell just short of the winning that national tournament in Chicago.

"We were expected to win 30 games," recalled Herb Brown who moved into the starting lineup at guard. They almost did, the streak of 29 victories being finally stopped in Chicago by Cicero Morton High, the Illinois state champs.

Six members of the 1929 team went on to play on conference champions in college. Hosket, Colburn and Brown were on Ohio State's 1933 team which shared the Big Ten championship with Northwestern. Sam Andrews and Bob Albright led Otterbein to an Ohio Conference crown while McAfee was on a championship team at Wittenberg.

Stahl's Stivers team went to Columbus by automobile this time but again stayed in the Deshler-Wallick hotel, the best address in the city.

"We dressed in our rooms at the hotel," Colburn said. "You put on your sweat clothes, stuff a couple of towels in a bag and take a cab to the Coliseum. The locker room in the Coliseum was cold and dirty."

The "Orange Crush" as their fans called them, breezed through three opponents, Akron Garfield, Columbus Central and finally Dover in the 36-22 championship game that was never close. Hosket scored 14 points and Colburn backed him with 11. Then it was on to Chicago for the only loss that ended a 29-1 season.

Testimony to Hosket's dominance as the only returning starter and Stahl's coaching ability, is that despite the graduation loss of five college-bound players off the 1929 team, the 1930 team did have a perfect season at 27-0. But that group didn't play in Chicago as that national tournament had been abandoned.

Max Padlow and Tom Denny moved in at forward while Marty Armbruster and Bob McConnell took over at guards. There was more of a defensive emphasis on this team evidenced in the state tournament when the Tigers held Findlay to 16 points, Canton McKinley to 18 before winning the championship game, 18-16.

Colburn, Andrews and Brown remained active in the Dayton sports scene after their playing days were over. McAfee, Albright and Hosket went into the business world. Hosket sired a son we will meet later who followed in his father's footsteps. Young Hosket played and starred on a state high school championship team and also at Ohio State.

Andrews coached football at Wilbur Wright and Oakwood in his time. Colburn had a varied background as a coach and administrator at several schools and was also a top-notch football and basketball official. Brown coached the Dayton Metropolitans, the last local top level pro basketball team immediately after World War II, and was in the real estate business here until his death in 1994.

Stivers had a number of winning basketball teams while it remained a high school, but none were of state championship caliber.

Nelson And The Teddies

The unofficial formation of the Big Six league began in the early 1930s and the Roosevelt Teddies became the first team to break the domination of Steele and Stivers as city champions.

Although situated in what is now called predominantly black West Dayton, the area around Roosevelt High School when it came into being in the late 1920s was generally a white, ethnic area. The facilities in the school were segregated in many ways including separate swimming pools, but not when it came to basketball. Thus Al Tucker was one of the stars of the Roosevelt team that became Dayton's second school to capture a state high school basketball championship in 1934.

Coach Paul "Putty" Nelson was in the early stages of a long career at the West Third Street school and coached both football and basketball.

The starting unit found Maynard Brixey, the 6-5 "giant" at center with Jim Armpriester, Charles Turley, Don Watkins and Tucker rounding it out. The other members included Jim Horn, Ray Midlam, Ortho Marko, Joe Sakal and Willard Sessler.

They suffered two regular season road losses at Hamilton and Middletown but won the city championship with a great come from behind victory over Steele. The Lions held a 14-6 half-time lead, but the Teddies turned it on in the second half to win it, 30-20.

At a 60th anniversary reunion in 1994, the eight survivors met but couldn't agree if they went to Columbus by train or car. But all remembered the 39-32 upset of Toledo Central, the 38-25 win over Youngstown Rayen and the 46-30 conquest of Portsmouth in the championship game.

Tucker was high scorer with 10 in the Toledo game but Brixey led in the next two games with 17 and 13. Tucker went on to play with the Harlem Globetrotters and later back in Dayton was active as a player and coach in industrial basketball. Brixey, who died in 1971, was also very active in amateur sports over the years.

Ben And The Hirsch Brothers

Northridge competed in the 1930s in what was known as the Montgomery County League, it being situated just north of the city limits at the time. Over the years since, it has been affiliated with several different area high school leagues. But the Polar Bears became Dayton's first class B (small school) state champions during an amazingly successful run of three straight seasons at the end of World War II.

Ben Ankney graduated from Miami University in 1940 and his first coaching job was at Northridge, where he was involved in all the varsity sports.

Doubling as head man in both football and basketball, he hit the jackpot in the latter sport when talented brothers, Bob and Walt Hirsch, came on the scene to join a number of senior veterans.

Bob, a year older, was a junior and lefthanded Walt a sophomore in 1945 when the team won the state championship, losing once during the regular season to Eaton and finishing at 28-1. The brothers complemented each other well, taking advantage of Bob's right-handed shots and Walter's skills from the left side.

Other members of the team that defeated Columbiana, 51-42, in the title game were Ray Lowery, Sam Armstrong, Jack Scrafield, Carl Driscoll and Ed Hardin.

"We were expected to repeat in 1946," Ankney recalled, "and we might have had not Bob Hirsch suffered a badly sprained ankle at tournament time. He played, but he wasn't up to his ability and we lost to Bradford in the regional."

The school enrollment was going up, forcing Northridge to advance to the A level in Walt Hirsch's senior year. Playing a tougher schedule, the team finished with a 17-4 record but bowed out in the regional tournament in Dayton with a double overtime loss to Middletown, on its way to the state championship. Walt Hirsch forced that game to overtime by sinking two free throws after time had expired.

He was a brilliant athlete in basketball and baseball, good enough to be a starter on Adolph Rupp's University of Kentucky Wildcats. Unfortunately, he was involved along with Bill Spivey in a point-shaving scandal that cost him his last year of eligibility and a chance to play pro basketball.

Ankney left Northridge to become a member of Miami's football staff, having posted an 111-16 record with the basketball team. He later returned to high school coaching.

The Roosevelt Powerhouse

As it happened in football, the population explosion that followed World War II changed the basketball map in the area as well, but it wasn't until 1960 that another state champion emerged from the immediate Dayton area. Roosevelt's championship was followed by three more Dayton teams in the next decade involving first timers Belmont and Chaminade.

John Woolums was putting together strong teams year after year at Roosevelt, winning city titles in 1952 and 1954 before launching a string of six straight (1957-62) that included the state champions.

Followers of the Teds thought that 1954 team that had Norm Lee, Uriah Holland and Anthony Steele would get to Columbus but it didn't. But there was no stopping the 1960 team that posted a 27-0 record and was hardly challenged during the regular season schedule.

The lineup included Ray Brown, voted the Ohio's top player, the multi-talented L. C. Snow, John Henderson, Buford Davis and John Shehee, the elusive 5-11 dribbling whiz who triggered the fast break that delighted Roosevelt partisans.

Snow and Henderson starred on the Roosevelt football team with the latter going to Michigan as a pass receiver.

Perhaps the most enjoyable moment for Woolums came in the first game of the regional tournament played in the Cincinnati Gardens when his team smashed Middletown in an amazing scoring orgy, 95-63.

It was the most points ever scored against a Paul Walker-coached team. Walker, the winningest high school coach in Ohio history, and his Middies had been tormenting the Roosevelt mentor and had a 14-5 edge over him going into that tournament game.

Brown erupted for 34 points, Snow backed him with 22 and Davis scored 17 as the tall Teddies swept the boards. It was no surprise that the Teddies cooled down against Cincinnati Western Hills for the right to make it to Columbus. The Cincinnati team wanted to slow the tempo and it did, but Roosevelt won, 66-56.

That made Roosevelt the first city team to make it to the state tournament since Fairview got there in 1939 and 1940 under the colorful Raymond (Doc) Pumphrey. But the Bulldogs, led by Ken Huddleston, never quite reached the title game.

Foul problems came close to thwarting the Teds in their battle against Toledo Scott. Starters Davis, Henderson and Brown all picked up four, with leading scorer Brown piling up his in the first half.

Reserves Gene Van Hoose, Joe Shaw and Henry Burlong all came off the bench to help keep things under control until Woolums could get his starting unit back intact during the final minutes to hang on to win, 62-58.

The win sent Roosevelt into the championship game against Cleveland East Tech, which had won the tournament the two previous years and was bidding to match the Stivers run of three straight titles 30 years earlier.

It was the first time all year that Roosevelt was dealing with a taller front line, but Snow and Henderson held their own on the boards and the Dayton team triumphed, 51-41. Brown led the scoring with 20 points, raising his career total to 1,197, the record at the time.

Burlong, a sophomore reserve, developed into a standout player the next two seasons, leading Woolums' teams to city titles. He enrolled at UD but academic problems eventually forced him out of the program.

The Dixie Greyhounds

Dixie High School in New Lebanon remained one of the old Montgomery County League schools that neither grew nor was absorbed into a bigger school. As such the Greyhounds remained a small school and captured Class A state titles in 1962 and 1966 under the colorful veteran coach Columbus Hines.

The 1962 team had an outstanding scorer in Al Peters, a 6-4 forward who was considered a big man at that time. Playmaker Gary Peffly directed the offense with Don Brunk and Milburn Kincaid helping Peters in the scoring.

The big victory in the 1962 semifinals in Columbus was an overtime 71-69 win over Ayersville, a perennial small school power that won the title the year before and had a 57-game winning streak. The win over Berlin Hiland for the crown was relatively easy, 74-62.

Dixie came back four seasons later with another Hines-coached champion that finished 25-2 overall. Adam Powell, Ken Staples, Mark McClendon, Ed Briggs and Jim Shimp made up the regular lineup. Shimp was the hero of a 49-48 semifinal win over Rayen, sinking six of eight free throws in the waning minutes.

Enter Ross, May, Hosket

John Ross, who was later to become the first coach at Wright State, was also a pioneer in developing a premier high school program.

Belmont High was opened to serve the southeastern edge of the city in 1956 and Ross was promoted from an elementary position to be assistant basketball coach under R. C. (Skip) LaRue. Ross became head coach in 1961 and won two city championships while building toward the 1964 powerhouse, starring two future All-Americans, on a team that ranks with the area's best ever.

Discipline was the key to Ross' theories. A Wilmington College graduate, he was a Marine radio operator in the Pacific in World War II. The future All-Americans were Bill Hosket, Jr. and Don May, a pair of big men who complemented each other on the boards and in the offense.

All through his high school career, young Hosket was plagued by people comparing him to his father, who had died without ever having had the privilege of enjoying his son's high school performance. The comparisons were not appropriate because the game had changed so much. Suffice it to say that both Hoskets rank among Dayton's best.

The 1964 Bison team ranks right up there with any before or since and, on the basis of their two one-sided victories in the state tournament, can be called one of the city's best teams. Belmont was not only big, it was especially balanced.

Harry Culbertson, at 6-6, was listed at center and was an efficient rebounder. May was always a force on the boards and became a great, if undersized, collegiate rebounder in his years with the Flyers. That big front line was augmented by classy guards Tim Kenner and Ray Ridenour and Ralph Jukkola was an excellent sixth man.

Belmont suffered only one defeat in the regular season, at the hands of Chaminade, and had its most serious tournament challenges from Fairview and Roth, teams it had handled during the season.

The Bisons clicked on all cylinders in the state tournament, smashing Canton McKinley, 80-56, and following that with an 89-60 romp over Cleveland East. In terms of scoring, May and Hosket each had 18 with Culbertson getting 16 against McKinley. In the championship game it was May (24), Hosket (23), Jukkola (14) and Culbertson (10).

May, Hosket and Culbertson made the all-tournament first team. May and Hosket made the first team AP All-Ohio. A member of the latter team was Larry Hisle of Portsmouth who went on to become a major league outfielder. During the regular season, Belmont made a rare overnight road visit to Portsmouth and defeated Hisle's team.

Hosket attained an additional distinction by being selected to play with the 1968 United States Olympic team which won the gold medal in Mexico City.

The two former Belmont stars, May and Hosket, who had gone their separate ways in college, were reunited as rookies in the NBA as they began successful professional careers with the New York Knicks.

Jim Turvene's Two Champs

Although Chaminade had won a city league title in 1946 under Joe DiMatteo, the Eagles didn't get into a dominant position in basketball until Jim Turvene's decade (1962-1972) during which Chaminade won the state in 1966 and 1970. Turvene's overall record was 154-46 and his 1966 powerhouse went 26-1, losing a regular season game to Dunbar.

The Gottschall twins, Jim and Jerry, along with Al Bertke from that team went on to play for the UD Flyers. Center Gary Arthur played college football as a tight end at Miami. Mike Bockrath, Jim Dichito, Steve Cooke, Jim Zweisler and Mike Duffy were the other players to see action.

"We were the first parochial school to win the big school (then AA) state championship," Turvene says in looking back. "We had a very real scare and a very real struggle to beat Toledo Libbey (55-52) in the championship game."

The Eagles had a tough tournament. They went in rated the No. 1 team in the state AP poll and made an inviting target. Getting by Warren Harding, 60-52, was a struggle but the championship game with Libbey was much more difficult.

"They played a very tenacious defense which forced us to try to run our offense further out than we wanted," Turvene explained. "That, plus our not shooting well, we had no scoring punch at all for three quarters."

Libbey held a 15-point lead going into the fourth quarter but in the last eight minutes, Chaminade outscored the Toledo team, 28-6, for a remarkable 67-64 victory after the coach pulled a Knute Rockne.

"In the time-out to start the fourth quarter, I told the kids that we weren't getting anything done with our offense," the coach explained. "So I told them to forget it, go out and have some fun and try to go down fighting, and by golly, they fought their way back into it."

In 1969, a young cast of Eagles got to the state but were totally wiped out in the semi-finals by Canton McKinley (72-48) in what Turvene looks back on as "my most embarrassing defeat ever."

The entire starting lineup was back for the senior year and that loss helped motivate them to an undefeated (27-0) season. Dan Gerhard was the

Ohio UPI Player of the Year. Terry Tyler went to Michigan, Ted Wuebben to Creighton and Mike Eifert to Kent State on basketball scholarships. Paul Kurpiel, nicknamed "The Mop" for his hair style, elected to go into baseball.

"They were great athletes, in that sense better than the '66 team," the coach says. "That 1966 bunch, however, was the smartest team with the best feel for the game that I ever coached."

The 1970 regular season game with Roth, featuring Donald Smith and Phil Lumpkin, who went on to fine college careers at UD and Miami respectively, sold out the 13,544 capacity UD Arena. The Eagles won the district by 15 points over Roth and went on to Columbus where they had an easier time of it, defeating Rockford, 69-47, with Tyler (20), Gerhard (17) and Wuebben (16) leading the way.

A year later, the previously all-boys Chaminade merged with Julienne, the parochial girls school, and the overall administration underwent drastic, and as it turned out, ridiculous changes.

In an obvious attempt to de-emphasize the importance of the school's athletic tradition, Turvene was dismissed because his disciplinary methods did not fit into the image of the new C-J. He got the news in a letter saying his contract would not be renewed.

Turvene went to West Carrollton, a school which had gone without winning a single game over the previous two seasons. It took him a while to turn things around, but he did. After seven years he resigned and was replaced as head coach there by Dan Gerhard, one of the stars of his 1970 champions.

Petrocelli"s Alter Knights

Archbishop Alter High School didn't graduate its first senior class until 1966, but the Knights wasted no time establishing a basketball dynasty under head coach Joe Petrocelli, also the only athletic director the school, located on David Road in Kettering, has had.

If Stivers dominated Dayton area basketball before World War II, Alter has come close to doing so against much heavier competition in the last quarter century.

Petrocelli's career record at the end of the 1994-1995 season was 550-157, and if he maintains his winning average, will definitely threaten Paul Walker's state career record of 695 victories.

"I have no plans to retire now," said the coach, who was 57 when interviewed for this book.

A native of Cincinnati, he played at Cincinnati Purcell and Xavier University and applied for and got the job with the new school in Dayton despite having only limited experience.

"When I started here, I couldn't dream of the kind of success we've enjoyed," he says. "In the beginning, all I thought of was beating Chaminade (the established parochial school) and winning a tournament game." As for winning tournament games, the Knights have captured 16 district championships, four regionals and the 1978 state AAA crown.

One of the more interesting aspects of Alter's success has been the steady flow of sons of former University of Dayton players who have contributed to the Alter cause.

The most prominent of these would be Jim and John Paxson, who went on respectively to UD and Notre Dame and the NBA. Jim Paxson, Sr. starred at Dayton in the 1950s and had a fling in the NBA. John Paxson, who stands second on Alter's all-time scoring list, made international headlines when his game-winning field goal with time running out gave the Chicago Bulls the third of their three straight NBA championships in 1993.

The list of sons of former Flyers also includes Bill Uhl, Jr., Bill Frericks, Greg and Dan Meineke, Doug and Ted Harris, Jack and Mike Zimmerman, Dan and Dave Bockhorn, Dan, Pete and Kevin Boyle, along with Pat, Matt, John, Mike and Tim Riazzi. Joe Siggins' father was an outstanding quarterback at UD.

Alter's current all-time scoring leader, the energetic Andy Meyer, started his senior year in UD uniform in the fall of 1995. Marc Molinski enjoyed a four-year career as a playmaking guard with Boston College in the Big East and was recognized as the senior scholar-athlete of the year in the conference.

"I'm very proud of the fact that over 50 of our former players have gone on to play college basketball," Petrocelli said.

The starters on the team that won the state championship in 1978 with a 68-52 win over Akron Central-Hower included Jim Paxson, Jr., Don Meineke, Pete Boyle, Andy Heher and Jack Zimmerman.

Although the Knights have enjoyed 25 straight winning seasons, they have never gone undefeated. The 1974-75-78 and 1985 teams each lost only one game.

Mike Haley's Four-Peat

Mike Haley grew up in Portsmouth down on the Ohio River and as a player helped lead his team to the state class AA championship in 1961. He went on to play for Jim Snyder at Ohio University and helped the Bobcats capture two MidAmerican Conference championships and play in the NCAA. Haley helped the Bobcats defeat Kentucky in the 1964 tournament before losing to Michigan.

Haley was to coach four state championship teams and take another team to the title game before he ended his coaching career to move into administration. He became head coach at Roosevelt going into the 1973-74 season and in his next season (1975) went 20-2 before losing to state runner-up Stivers in the district tournament.

The decision to close Roosevelt that spring created chaos in coaching assignments and where the student athletes were going. Haley took over at Roth and, with the players who followed him, produced his first championship team in the AA level.

Dwight Anderson, who was to later play at the University of Kentucky, was one his key performers. Center Donald Nelson, Tony Peters, Mel Crafter and Jonathan Williams were the usual starters along with Anderson.

Haley's coaching philosophy centered on a run-and-gun fast break which called for bench depth and he often ran 10 or 11 men in and out, the concept being to wear down the opposition.

In their first tournament game, the Falcons beat Cincinnati Green Hills 64-58 with help from reserve guard Tony Harrell. Haley's theory worked perfectly in a 79-54 blasting of Wellsville, the running Falcons hit for 32 points in the final quarter.

The championship game was another matter, Roth edging Lorain Catholic 82-81 on a Paul Moore free throw. Haley said "our discipline held up and that was the most important factor."

Roth had moved up to the AAA (top level) bracket by 1981 when Mike's team went 26-1, paced by Fred Johnson, William Colston, Ike Thornton and football standout Keith Byars, who was also a very fine basketball talent.

The Falcons had their hands full in downing Sidney, 67-64, and edging Newark, 83-81. Newark's star player, 6-9 Mike Giomi, who went on to become a starter at Indiana, scored 39 points against Roth.

"But we wore him down," Haley said, paying tribute to Giomi's ability.

Colston was the tournament MVP and Haley became the first coach ever to win state titles at different levels.

Roth dropped back to AA because of declining enrollment the next season. Colston and Johnson had graduated but the Falcons were still playing mostly an AAA schedule and went 24-4. They won Haley's third state title under very unusual circumstances. While the Falcons were in Columbus in the state event, the Dayton Board of Education, which often seemed floating without a compass, voted to close Roth as a high school and return it to middle school status. Roth players and their followers were angry and took some of their frustration out by beating Youngstown Rayen, 68-56.

At the welcome home celebration Sunday afternoon at the school, the players had been introduced before school board member Virginia McNeal got up to speak. The team and many in the audience got up and walked out, making that their protest.

The decision once again created a coaching and player shuffle. Steve Smith transferred to Alter and later played at UD. Coach Haley took over at Dunbar where he promptly reeled off four more big winning seasons before what has to be considered his masterpiece.

His 1984 Dunbar team got back to Columbus, finishing 24-4 before losing in the final game in overtime to Canton McKinley. But the best was yet to come. Haley's 1987 team followed a familiar emotional sports scenario in the father-son picture. The star was Mike Haley, Jr., an agile 6-8 performer with a seemingly unlimited future.

Haley, Jr. at center was surrounded by a great guard tandem in senior Kirk Taylor and junior Mark Baker and two good forwards in Renaldo O'Neal and Troy Harris. Taylor went on to play at Michigan while Baker was a standout at Ohio State under Randy Ayers.

This team was so explosive that it was a disappointing night when it didn't crack the 100-point barrier. Sports columnist Gary Nuhn dubbed the Wolverines "Century City."

The highest scoring and perhaps the best basketball game in Dayton high school history was played in the UD Arena Jan. 31, 1987 when Dunbar and Alter collided. In double overtime, the final score was Dunbar 106, Alter 102.

Dunbar's Taylor, nicknamed "Ice T," finished with 38 points, hitting 17 of 27 field goal attempts. Alter's Jeff Graham had 36 in a gallant losing cause. Both Taylor and Graham were first team all-state selections. The 8,000 fans were left in a state of limp exhaustion.

The state tournament was shifted to the UD Arena that year giving Dunbar an added advantage, but this team was good enough not to need anything extra. The Wolverines qualified for the tournament by hammering Cincinnati Oak Hills 110-64 in the regional championship game.

Haley's 1-2-3 punch of Taylor, Baker and Mike, Jr. scored 31-23 and 16 respectively in the 94-80 win over Cleveland St. Joseph in the semi-finals. An unanticipated problem developed early in the championship game against Canton McKinley, the school that had beaten Dunbar in the 1984 title game.

With 2:45 left in the first quarter, Baker went down with a twisted ankle and sophomore Mike Garrison rose to the occasion taking his place. Taylor carried the scoring burden, finishing with 31. Haley, helped by O'Neal and Harris, managed to work the boards well.

In the late going, Coach Haley asked for and got more ball control than the Wolverines liked to play and it contributed to the 70-65 victory, the overall fifth state championship for Haley, Sr. as a player and coach.

Both Baker and Haley, Jr. had a delayed start to their college careers because their grades made them ineligible as freshmen under the NCAA Proposition 48 rule. Baker went on to three strong years at Ohio State but academic problems haunted young Haley at Wright State. He dropped out prior to his senior year.

Mike Haley, Sr., frustrated at not getting a head coaching opportunity at the collegiate level, retired from coaching and went back to his native Portsmouth in a key administrative position.

Scales And The Rest

Colonel White's Cougars were the last Dayton school to win a state championship, in 1990, coming through late in the season in a manner not even coach Tom Clements could have predicted.

The team was an under-achiever (13-7) during the regular season, not even winning the city league. But the Cougars got it going once the post-season tournament came along.

Key player was Jervaughn Scales, a 6-6 center who had both a great scoring touch and dominance on the boards. Scales, a native of New York, moved to Dayton with his mother when he was 15, and was a late bloomer.

The Cougars were a big team with 6-4 Ivan Patterson and Jeff Elder helping on the boards. Ricardo Hamilton, Ron Amerson and Will Watkins played the backcourt.

An important victory over C-J captured the sectional tournament. The Eagles had beaten the Cougars in the regular season. Scales picked off 20 rebounds in that game and then 16 against Cincinnati Roger Bacon. In Columbus the Cougars were awesome in pounding Canton South, 100-73, and then took the measure of Portsmouth, 71-57, for the AA crown.

Scales went to on enjoy a brilliant career at Southern University in Baton Rouge. In his senior season he finished third in NCAA Division I scoring and second in rebounding.

The Jefferson Broncos won the state AA title in 1979 under coach John Watkins in a 24-2 campaign. The scoring leader of the team was 6-6 forward Darrell Jackson, who went on play for Don Donoher at UD. It was a well balanced team with guard Joe Watkins a defensive standout. His running mate at guard was Michael Mayfield, who directed the offense. Alton Walker, Joe Harrison and Dave Williams rounded out the cast.

The Broncos had made it to Columbus two years earlier when Jackson and Mayfield, playing in a losing cause, were exposed to the pressures of playing in front of the huge crowds in St. John Arena.

In the title game, Cleveland Cathedral Latin went into a stall with a three point lead with 2:18 left. But two free throws by Harrison cut the lead to 63-62 with only 21 seconds to play. When Jefferson got the ball on a turnover junior forward Williams took the all-important shot giving Jefferson the lead. Latin's last bid resulted in a turnover.

Veterans Zawadzki And Holden

Although they have never taken their teams to the state tournament, two highly competent coaches with longevity and sensible programs are Ray Zawadzki and Larry Holden.

Zawadzki was headed into his 28th season at Vandalia-Butler going into the 1995-96 competition, making him second to Alter's Petrocelli in terms of longevity in the Dayton area. The onetime UD Flyer owns a 361-191 overall record and, among other things, had the pleasure of coaching two of his sons. His 1976-77 team went to the regional finals.

Holden has a 306-130 record over his 16 years at Beavercreek, where his 1986-87 team wound up with a 22-2 record.

Boy's City Basketball Champions

1930 - 31	Steele	1967 - 68	Dunbar
1931 - 32	Stivers	1968 - 69	Roth
1932 - 33	Stivers	1969 - 70	Roth
1933 - 34	Roosevelt*	1970 - 71	Dunbar
1934 - 35	Roosevelt	1971 - 72	Meadowdale
1935 - 36	Stivers		Roth
1936 - 37	Roosevelt*	1972 - 73	Roth
1937 - 38	Fairview	1973 - 74	Dunbar
1938 - 39	Roosevelt*		Roth
	Stivers		Fairview
1939 - 40	Roosevelt	1974 - 75	Roosevelt
1940 - 41	Fairview	1975 - 76	Fairview
1941 - 42	Roosevelt	1976 - 77	Meadowdale
1941 - 43	Fairview		Roth
	Roosevelt	1977 - 78	Colonel White
	Wilbur Wright		Meadowdale
1943 - 44	Stivers	1978 - 79	Meadowdale
1944 - 45	Wilbur Wright		Roth
1945 - 46	Stivers	1979 - 80	Dunbar
1946 - 47	Stivers	1980 - 81	Roth
1947 - 48	Wilbur Wright	1981 - 82	Meadowdale
1948 - 49	Dunbar	1982 - 83	Dunbar
1949 - 50	Dunbar	1983 - 84	Dunbar**
1950 - 51	Stivers	1984 - 85	Dunbar
1951 - 52	Roosevelt	1985 - 86	Dunbar
1952 - 53	Stivers	1986 - 87	Dunbar
1953 - 54	Roosevelt	1987 - 88	Dunbar
1954 - 55	Dunbar	1988 - 89	Dunbar
	Wilbur Wright	1989 - 90	Meadowdale
1955 - 56	Kiser	1990 - 91	Dunbar
1956 - 57	Roosevelt	1991 - 92	Dunbar
1957 - 58	Roosevelt	1992 - 93	Meadowdale
1958 - 59	Roosevelt*	1993 - 94	Dunbar
1959 - 60	Roosevelt		Colonel White
1960 - 61	Roosevelt	1994 - 95	Patterson
1961 - 62	Roosevelt		
1962 - 63	Belmont		
1963 - 64	Belmont*	* State Champs	
1964 - 65	Dunbar	** State Runners/Up	
1965 - 66	Roosevelt		
	Roth		
1966 - 67	Roosevelt		

Coach Mike Haley, with an unprecedented four state titles, celebrates a victory (above, left); Alter powerhouse coach Joe Petrocelli in typical form (center) and Bill Hosket, Stivers, OSU and Olympic standout (right). The Dayton Metropolitans (below) featured Sweetwater Clifton (standing, third from right) in 1946-47.

20

Elwood, Mickey and the Pros

Dayton has had several flings at professional basketball, but for varying reasons it never took root.

In the late stages of World War II, a strong delegation of top level former collegiate basketball players was assembled at Wright Field by the recreation division and travelled around to play teams from other bases in the midwest.

Standout athlete of the group was Bruce Hale, who had played at Santa Clara and would later become a national figure involved in the maturing NBA as well as the ABA. Among the others were Dwight Edelman (Illinois), Al Negratti (Seton Hall), John Mahnken (Illinois) and Chris Hansen (Bradley).

In the spring of 1945, promoter Elwood Parsons secured the backing of Acme Aluminum and entered a team of the Wright Field players in a tournament in Chicago. That tournament, to determine the national pro champion, was sponsored by the *Chicago American* newspaper.

The Dayton Acmes, coached by Bobby Colburn, lost in their first game to the Fort Wayne Zollner Pistons of the old NBL, the team that won the tournament.

Although the war was over going into the 1945-46 winter, most of the airmen were still at Wright Field and Parsons put together the Dayton Mickeys to play an independent pro schedule in the Fairgounds Coliseum.

Hale was the star of the team which also included Negratti, Hansen and Mahnken plus Beryl Drummond, one of the Waterloo Wonders, John Schick from Ohio State and Rex Gardecki, a Miamisburg athlete, father and namesake of the Dayton Flyer star 25 years later. The 1946 Mickeys were sponsored by Mickey McCrossen, who operated a popular tavern on West Third Street in the vicinity of the Inland manufacturing plant known as Mickey's Grill.

Later, there was another Dayton Mickeys, sponsored by Milton (Little Mickey) Friedman.

Typical of the unregulated pro game of the time, on Sunday, Jan. 13, 1946, the Mickeys defeated the Chicago Monarchs in the afternoon in Dayton. The Monarchs, featuring Sonny Boswell and Pop Gates, jumped into their cars and drove to Columbus where they defeated a team of former Ohio State players that night.

The Metropolitan Clothing Co. gave the team its most solid financial backing the next year. The team had a new look with all the military players except Hansen gone. Parsons beefed up the team by signing two black players, Sonny Boswell and Roscoe (Duke) Cumberland, who had played with different teams, most notably the New York Renaissance.

For years the Rens, along with the original New York Celtics, had been the two most successful barnstorming pro teams. With the NBL, forerunner of the NBA, getting a foothold, the sport was getting stronger and the days of the barnstormers were fading fast.

On Jan. 12, 1947, the Rens came to Dayton and defeated the Mets 46-35. The account in the *Dayton Journal* referred to a Clifton Nathaniel, the center of the Rens, as the star of the game.

Parsons promptly signed the player, established his correct name as Nathaniel (Sweetwater) Clifton and the Mets suddenly had a team capable of beating many of the league foes that came into Dayton to play the Sunday exhibitions.

Promoter Parsons had many sellouts. "The fire department was there every week shutting the doors," he said. The official capacity was 2,800 but on several occasions more than 3,000 people were there.

A year later, the 6-7 Sweetwater Clifton returned to Dayton in baseball uniform as the first baseman of the Dayton Indians. That winter he advanced into the big time with the New York Knicks in the NBA. He had a 12-year basketball career before going back to his native Chicago where he worked as a taxi driver before his death in 1993.

Although the Mets played another year, the party was over and Parsons became the victim of the same fate that befell other and wealthier black promoters.

"When Jackie Robinson broke down the barriers, it started the downfall and eventual elimination of black baseball and basketball," said Parsons, who was 84 years old when interviewed for this book. He died in 1995.

In 1949-50, Dayton's General Motors plants sponsored the Air-Gems, a team entered in the National AAU league. Playing their games in the then new UD Fieldhouse, the Air-Gems brought in such top-flight amateur teams as the Phillips 66ers, Peoria Caterpillar Tractors, the Akron Goodyears and others stocked with former college players.

Wayne Morse, then a recent graduate of the University of Michigan, was hired to run the front office.

The players recruited for the team, hired by different Dayton GM plants to conform to AAU rules, included Hal Morrell and Don McIntosh of Michigan, Wally Salovich and Chet Tomczyk from Minnesota, Chet Giermack of William and Mary and Rip Gish of Western Kentucky.

Joe DiMatteo, then athletic director at Inland, was the first coach and Al Volkman of Delco handled the team in its third and last season. A later playing addition was George King, who went on to college coaching and became athletic director at Purdue.

"We never won the league title, but we had winning records and brought quality basketball to Dayton," recalls Morse, who married TV personality Betty Rogge and stayed in Dayton in the advertising business, ending up with his own firm.

But industrial basketball was also fading away in competition with the NBA which was paying higher salaries to the players coming out of college. The Air-Gems were also hurt by the coinciding rise of the Dayton Flyers, who almost overnight generated great community excitement.

Mickey Friedman's Mickey's, born in 1961 as members of the minor league Midwest Professional Basketball League, played their home games at Stebbins High School.

R. E. (Ira) Price, with Butch Sedam as assistant, was the coach of the Mickeys. Both had been highly successful in the city's top amateur leagues. The personnel was a mixture of area players: Bill Cramsey, Phil Dubensky and Chuck Grigsby of UD fame; Jim Morgan who had starred at Louisville; ex-Stebbins player Gene Millard, who had captained the Ohio State team and Jack Harner, then the all-time scoring leader at Wilmington College.

Success on the court did not translate into success at the box office and after two years and lots of red ink, Friedman gave it up.

That same fate befell Milt Kantor's Dayton Wings, who entered the short-lived World Basketball League. The Wings, coached by Pat Haley, had the most spacious and attractive home floor of any of the Dayton pro teams in the Ervin J. Nutter Center on the Wright State campus.

The Wings won the league championship in their first year in 1992, but were deep in red ink. Even that might not have stopped sports enthusiast Kantor's involvement had not the whole league fallen apart in 1993 despite, or perhaps because of, a summer schedule.

Troy Lewis, an All-Big Ten player at Purdue, stayed on in Dayton and is with Kantor's Victory Wholesale Grocery business. The leading scorer was Alfrederick Hughes, husky 6-5 forward who had tormented the UD Flyers during his playing days at Chicago Loyola.

AUTOMOBILE
RACING

Typical action at the Dayton Speedway in the 1970s (left and above); Indy cars raced here after World War II.

General manager Lefty McFadden points to backstretch (below).

21

The Dayton Speedway

The Dayton area has long been a hotbed of automobile racing interest, our proximity to Indianapolis likely having something to do with that.

It might be difficult for the younger breed of race fans watching the various forms of bigtime racing on television in the 1990s to realize that the long gone Dayton Speedway once had this community in the big leagues of the sport.

This was particularly true in the decade that followed World War II, but it dates back to the late 1930s when the best known drivers in this country came to drive at the Dayton Speedway.

This city was also the headquarters of a racing association that was a rival of the AAA (American Automobile Association) before that group dropped out of racing back in 1956, bowing to criticism that an organization stressing driving safety shouldn't be involved in promoting racing.

The rival was the CSRA (Central States Racing Association) of which Dr. H. K. Bailey, a Brown street physician, was president and chief investor. Norm Witte, who was involved in the layout of the Dayton Speedway, was the secretary and chief operating officer of the CSRA. That group sanctioned racing at a number of tracks mostly in the midwest at the same time auto racing in general was starting to grow in the aftermath of the World War I.

Dr. Bailey was an investor in the original group that was put together in 1932 to build the Dayton track. The makeup of the original group was an odd mixture. Sgt. J. E. Aldredge, a Dayton motorcycle policeman, was one of the pushers. He got Paul Ackerman, longtime head of the AAA in Dayton, interested. The farm land selected for the site was owned by J. H. Dorgan, who became a member of the original group. Others identified in newspaper clippings included Charles and Louis Sucher, Ed Thum and Charles Shell.

The farmland that became the Dayton Speedway was once part of a landfill and had a gently sloping terrain. The track was laid out below the wooden grandstand which was built on the higher level. The backside of the track had a railing over which a car could and sometimes did plunge down out of sight. The racing surface in the beginning was oiled dirt and not very smooth, a problem that persisted even after the track was paved.

Two area racing veterans who remember the first race at the Speedway and talked about it to the author were 87-year-old Russ Clendenen, longtime official with AAA racing, later USAC, and 80-year-old Mutt Anderson of Xenia, who has done it all as driver, mechanic and car owner.

The first race in the new Dayton Speedway was scheduled for June 3, 1934, one week after the Indianapolis 500 of that year.

In those Depression days, the top name drivers were interested in supporting anything like a new track that could mean more purse money and the entry list for that first Dayton race was a true all-star group that included Mauri Rose, Ted Horn, Rex Mays, Charley Van Acker, Babe Stapp and others.

Ken Fowler, a Dayton native then living in the east, had come out to Milwaukee and drove there in a Saturday afternoon race. After the race, he packed up his gear and with car in tow, drove to Dayton to see the Speedway debut before returning east.

He arrived after midnight and stopped in a downtown restaurant where race drivers and fans liked to hang out. His friends assumed he had come here to drive and when they learned he had no intention of entering, began to tease him about not wanting to go up against the classy field including Mays and Horn.

Fowler explained that he didn't have tires for his racer, but one of the track investors said he'd find the necessary tires and offered Fowler a $1,000 bonus if he won the race, never suspecting a guy who had just driven 400 miles with his car in tow would be up to it.

"We need a local boy in the race," was the plea. So Fowler took up the dare and driving on the borrowed tires made off with the $1,000 check plus his share of the purse.

Excitement had been building about the opening of the new Dayton track. Wild Bill Cummings, who lived in Indianapolis, had filed an entry. He was a surprise winner of the 500 mile classic and was too busy with immediate local public appearances to get ready to drive in Dayton. But he promised to make an appearance which Clendenen remembers well.

"He rode his Harley-Davidson motorcycle over on Sunday morning with his wife on the back end," Russ said. "He drove it around the track waving to the fans."

As for Fowler, he drove mostly on the boards and dirt tracks in the east but fulfilled an ambition to drive in the 500-miler in 1937, finishing in 19th place. He drove a second time at Indianapolis a decade later in 1947 and retired following a 15th place finish.

Fowler moved back to Dayton and served as a starter and track official at races all over the midwest, usually working AAA events with Clendenen. After retiring from his factory job at Frigidaire, he moved to Florida and unlike many of the drivers he rode against, died in bed and not on the track.

One of the local Dayton favorites in the pre-war years was Everett Saylor, a Darke County native, who was Mutt Anderson's first driver. Saylor won a number of times mostly on dirt tracks in the midwest including the Dayton track.

"He was really a fine man and good friend, at the same time very competitive on the track," Anderson recalled. "He was only 31 when he was killed at the end of the 1942 racing season out at Des Moines, Iowa. It was the last race of the season and really because of the war, the last racing for three years."

Saylor drove a yellow racer with the a big number 4 on its raised tail, and Anderson has a rebuilt replica of the car in his Xenia garage. He has attracted much interest putting the replica on display at race events in recent years. The replica looks ready to turn up good speed.

The Xenia garage where Anderson worked on cars for A. J. Foyt, Roger McCluskey, Johnny Rutherford and Bobby Unser in their early years, is a virtual racing museum. He has two other rebuilt sprint cars and the walls are lined with pictures.

His most success as an owner after the war was with Mike Nazaruk as his driver. Nazaruk, a Long Island native, was a tough guy on the track. He was killed in 1955 at Langhorne, the Pennsylvania track that was once one of the top sprint car courses.

"He wasn't driving for me then," Anderson said. "No driver who ever drove for me spent a night in the hospital."

Another pioneer in Dayton's auto history was Johnny Vance Sr., who was a designer, mechanic and owner. Vance was born in Tennessee in 1896 and moved to Dayton in 1913, the year of the flood, according to his son, also known now as Johnny Vance, Sr. and a current sprint car owner.

In his early years Vance was a team rider for Harley Davidson and rode motorcycles in racing competition around the midwest.

"The Harleys were made in Milwaukee and Dad hung around the tech shop when he was up there and picked up a lot about building an engine," the current Johnny, Sr. says. "He was different than most owners around here in that he built his own engines."

Vance's first garage was on Little York Road, but he had to give that up around 1930 when the Great Depression created money problems everywhere. He had a smaller garage on Louie Street Just west of the Fifth Street bridge in downtown Dayton. Later when he was doing well financially, he went into a bigger garage and tech shop on St. James Avenue.

Wilbur Shaw, another racing figure who went on to the top level at Indy, drove for Vance in the early 1930s. Another of Vance's early drivers was Mauri Rose, who later gained fame as the winner of the 1947 and 1948 Indianapolis 500. Rose, who was born in Columbus, is known to have spent some time living in Dayton in the 1930s.

The 1930s sprints, known as Vance Motors, raced all over the midwest.

"At that time there was only one big race, the one at Indy," the younger Vance recalled. "Everything else was a sprint with not much difference in the prize money."

Dayton natives Tom Wall and Bob Carey, also rode for Vance before World War II. Wall was a pattern maker and built the attractive wooden frames for the cars he drove, adding a little extra touch to the classy appearance of those early sprinters. After World War II, Duke Dinsmore and Spider Webb drove for him. He never entered a car in the 500.

"But he built excellent sprint car engines. He designed a 4-cylinder, overhead cam that was very similar to the Offenhuaser which became something of a standard for sprint cars in the 1940s and into the 1950s." said his son, who still is very active in the sprint car racing in the midwest.

Frank Funk, a dominant figure in big car racing in this part of the world, took over the Dayton Speedway in 1939 primarily by assuming the debts. It was Funk who rebuilt and paved the track and installed the high banks that made it such an exciting place.

Funk, who farmed just outside Winchester, Indiana, got into the racing business when he built the Winchester Speedway, the first track featuring the slanted high banks. He also opened the track at Salem, Indiana.

He was a canny businessman who didn't look the part. He was often visible at the races wearing bibb overalls and people who didn't know him would not assume he was the track owner.

When Funk took over the Dayton track, he brought along Joe Goodman, who worked for him on his Indiana farm. Goodman became the maintenance man and caretaker at the Speedway. Goodman lived in a small house on the property and stayed on after the ownership changed hands. He lived 41 years on the Speedway grounds even after it was falling down. He died at age 85 in 1981.

In the Speedway's early years, a number of Dayton drivers tested their skills there and three of them, Duke Dinsmore, Spider Webb and John Shackelford, were successful enough to aim at the Indianapolis 500 miler. Dinsmore and Webb made it. The Duke made the Indy field six times, his best finish being 10th in 1947. Webb also was in the starting field six times, his best finish being 19th in 1953.

A bit later another Dayton driver, Bud Tingelstad, made 10 starts in the most famous race of them all. Bud's best finish was sixth in the tragedy-marred 1964 race. He retired after finishing seventh in the 1971 race.

Joie Chitwood, who later toured the country with his daredevil thrill show, also raced at the Dayton Speedway before the war and also drove in the 500 mile race. Later, he returned to the Speedway with his thrill show several times. Another daredevil show to visit Dayton and other area tracks was headed by Lucky Teeter.

Tragedy On The High Banks

There is no doubt that the high banked tracks made for exciting racing, but they also may have been at least partly responsible for the six Dayton Speedway driver fatalities, incurred between 1936 and 1952 when sprint cars dominated the scene.

Dayton native Jimmy Kneisley was the first to die on the track in 1936. He was well known as an amateur boxer as well as a race driver. He grew up in what is now West Dayton and as a youngster hung out at Johnny Vance's garage. Vance gave him his first ride, and later, his last. He had a reputation as "a little on the wild side" and crashed through one of the billboard advertising signs on the wall. The other pre-war fatality was a driver named Tommy Legge.

Clendenen has good reason to remember the mishap that took the life of Elbert (Pappy) Booker in 1947. Booker was a Detroit native and well known sprint car driver around the midwest.

"Booker went airborne off the third turn, and darned if Spider (Webb) didn't drive right underneath him," Russ said. "Of course, Spider wasn't hurt at all. But when Booker's car stopped rolling down the hill, there wasn't much left."

Drivers had a tendency to flip off those banks if they went too high and Clendenen also remembers it happening to Rex Mays.

"He went upside down and fell out of the car, and didn't get a scratch," the veteran racing official recalled. "He should have been wearing a belt but he wasn't. Maybe that saved him that time."

John Shackelford, a local favorite who did it all in sprints and dirt tracks, never achieved his goal of driving at Indy, became the fourth driver to die on the Dayton track. On June 13, 1948, the Dayton native was running in second place, dueling with Ted Horn, when he lost control in the south turn, crashed through the fence and plunged some 40 feet down the embankment before his car came to rest.

Shackelford was driving the Iddings Special, the same car Lee Wallard had driven to seventh place in the Indy 500 two weeks earlier. He was rushed to St. Elizabeth Hospital where he lived two hours after being admitted with severe internal injuries and a crushed chest.

The most tragic day at the Dayton Speedway occurred April 20, 1952 in a highly advertised opening race of the season. Promoter Blair Ratliff had attracted a crowd of 14,000, believed to be the biggest ever, to a race that featured hot young driver Troy Ruttman, destined seven weeks later to become the youngest driver to ever win the 500.

John T. Stanko had become a prominent figure in Dayton sports after coming here with a Budweiser distributorship in the late 1940s. Stanko, who had grown up in eastern Ohio and played college football at North Carolina State, was promoting his beer business with sports sponsorships and a booming, outgoing personality.

He had gotten into an auto racing in partnership with Charley Engle, a veteran track figure who had been a driver, car designer and owner.

As driver of their Engle-Stanko car, they hired Gordon Reid, a 29-

year-old who was hoping to follow his friend and fellow Californian Ruttman to racing's big time. Reid was on the track in the first heat of the day with Joey James and Ruttman out there with him. Pressing hard to stay with the other two, he lost control coming into the north turn, skidded against the grandstand and then bounced off an abutment under the pedestrian bridge that carried people from the grandstand to the infield.

Reid's out-of-control car crashed into two 50-gallon drums of gray paint sending sprays of paint and other debris into the horrified spectators scrambling to get out of the way. It was a wild, unreal scene and the injured, some covered with the gray paint as well as blood, made for predictable chaos.

The final toll, in addition to the decapitated Reid, included a special policeman, who died trying to push people out of the way, and two spectators. More than 50 spectators were dispatched to area hospitals by all sorts of emergency vehicles that raced to the scene. Fortunately, most of the injuries were minor and only nine people were hospitalized overnight, none in serious condition.

When racing was resumed about 90 minutes after the tragedy, Joey James went on to edge Ruttman in the feature race. Six months later, James was killed in a racing accident in San Jose, California.

Car owner Stanko, who had been talking about building a team to get a car and driver capable of getting into the 500 miler, was shocked at the carnage around his wrecked car that awful day and his enthusiasm for racing was considerably diminished.

The last driver to die at the Speedway was veteran Jim Rigsby who died later that year. Rigsby was another who went over the wall as his car ended up in the "cabbage patch," a term for crops planted by prisoners in the adjacent Dayton workhouse.

Blair Ratliff And A New Look

Promoting auto racing when the sport resumed after the war was no difficult trick and Funk wasted no time going for the big names.

George Robson, winner of the 1946 Indianapolis race, appeared in Dayton at a sprint car race two weeks after the big one. Robson, who went out early in his two pre-war starts it Indy, didn't have long to enjoy his taste of glory, dying in a crash in Atlanta in September that same year.

Ted Horn never won the 500 but in a nine-year-span (1936-1948 interrupted by the war), he never finished lower than fourth in AAA point standings. He was defending AAA national champion enabling him to have the number 1 on his car when he raced for the last time in Dayton in mid-summer 1948. He was killed October 10 that year at DuQuoin, Illinois, one of the early mile length sprint tracks.

After the war, new stock car racing groups were popping up all over the country. With the installation of a lighting system, the Speedway began to offer weekly races featuring stocks, accurately known as junkers.

Some of the early drivers who attracted a following were Briar Johnson, Jack Farris, whose hometown gave him a poetic ring, Jack Farris of New Paris. Red Harvey, brothers Arnold and Levi Dunaway, Wayne Woodmansee, Chick Hale and Walt Scherer were other regular performers.

After promoter Blair Ratliff came along in 1949, he managed to get television station WLW-D, as it was known then, to do a one hour weekly show live from the Speedway featuring the junkers. Omar Williams, then very new in town, was the announcer and the show ended in time to make way for the 11 o'clock news.

One night, with that deadline a minute or two away, a junker went over the hill and plunged out of sight. Immediately, flames shot up visible to the cameras as Omar apologized for having to go off the air to make way for the news show.

Legend has it that the flames were from piles of hay into which the clunker had tumbled with engine turned off. The newspaper switchboards lit up for the next two hours wanting to learn the fate of the driver, who had taken the daredevil plunge. Legend further has it, he was enjoying a couple of beers from the bonus he was paid to be part of the show.

Buster Blackford later was a regular winner as the modified stocks took over in place of the candidates for the wrecking pile. Then came the late model stocks, the forerunners of today's ultra successful NASCAR circuit, which dates back to its southern beginnings.

Lee Petty, the father of the legendary Richard Petty, raced here under the banner of MARC (Marcum Auto Racing Circuit), owned and operated by promoter John Marcum. Curtis Turner and Jim Romine also drove with that group.

Then the late models came under another association ARCA (Auto Racing Club of America), which brought in the popular Iggy Katona, Benny Parsons (who got into the big money with NASCAR) plus Dayton drivers Dick Freeman, Dick Dunleavy and Harold Smith.

Turning back to the sprint cars, in 1949 Funk sold the track to a trio that included Blair Ratliff, Dayton business man George Geis and Bill Edmonds, a Hamilton businessman. Ratliff, a University of Kentucky graduate, was the front man and built a reputation as a colorful promoter.

Ratliff struck pay dirt when he made an early association with owner J. C. Agajanian, the colorful Californian who loved the spotlight and had two cars start in the 500 before he had Troy Ruttman under contract.

Ruttman was a genuine "boy wonder" in a sport in which teenagers start to build early reputations. He made his racing debut at age 15 driving his father's Model-A Ford in the Ash Can Derby for jalopies at San Bernadino. At age 17, he won the roadster championship of the Pacific Coast. He was lying about his age when entering sprint events, and was actually only 19 when he qualified Agajanian's car for the 1949 Indianapolis race and finished 12th.

Standing 6-4 and weighing 240, he was much taller than the average driver and with handsome good looks to go with it was an immediate fan favorite wherever he appeared. Ruttman was hard to beat on the midwest half mile tracks (including Dayton) and he wasn't competing against second rate talent.

Dayton's role as a racing power was illustrated in October of 1951 when the Midwest AAA Sprint Car Association held its annual awards dinner at the Miami hotel here. Ruttman was awarded a championship trophy and a check for $750. In the association point race, Ruttman's 481 was well ahead of Duane Carter's 389 points. Other drivers up in the point standings included Joey James, Mike Nazaruk, Jimmy Daywalt, Gordon Reid, George Lynch and Leroy Warriner.

The sprint opener here in the spring of 1952 was the race in which Reid and three others lost their lives at the Speedway.

Carter was another up-and-coming star who built up a following here. Duane drove in 11 of the 500 mile races, the first in 1948. He made his debut here the year before. Ratliff would bring in one or two of the star attractions for his upcoming races and manage to get television, radio and newspaper attention. Duane Carter was an excellent interview.

Eddie Sachs was another who became familiar to Dayton race followers through his races at the Speedway. Bob Sweikert, who won the 500 miler in 1955, was another regular competitor at the Dayton track.

Sachs was a regular in the Indy 500. Starting in 1957, he qualified every year through 1964 when he met a fiery and tragic end in full view of many of the 200,000-plus fans settling in after the start. Rookie Dave Mac-Donald went into the wall coming through turn four and his car bounced back across the track in flames.

Ruttman, trying to avoid the burning car, risked going by close to the wall and made it. Sachs, trying the other way, smashed into Mac-Donald's car and Eddie was immediately engulfed in flames. When the fire and rescue crews arrived, it was obvious Sachs had no chance and they directed their attention in a futile effort to pull MacDonald out. As it turned out, neither had a chance.

Ratliff meanwhile established the Dayton 100 as the Dayton Speedway race of the year.

Ruttman suffered a serious injury to his right arm the summer he won the 500 and wasn't able to drive at all through the 1953 season. But he came back strong in 1954, winning the Dayton feature and qualifying at Indy. With late relief from Duane Carter (because of the weakened arm) the car finished fourth.

The big Californian remained in competition through 1964. He was driving for Dayton-Walther when he was almost involved in the accident in which his friend Sachs perished. He announced his retirement late that summer.

A. J. Foyt, the rough and ready Texan, made numerous appearances in Dayton before he became one of the best known of them all. Foyt launched his incredible string of 35 consecutive starts in the Indy 500 in 1958, by which time he had taken the checkered flag here more than once.

Going into the 1960 racing season, the Speedway was sold to a group headed by Dayton businessman George Flanagan, who hired sports writer and radio voice Lefty McFadden to operate it, taking over Ratliff's role.

McFadden put in five years not only directing the Dayton track but also the New Bremen speedway. That track had been opened by Frank Dicke, a banker in that small Auglaize county community. The track, another half miler, did well with sprints and stocks, but Dicke died of a heart attack in 1960. A. J. Foyt was a frequent driver at both the New Bremen and Dayton tracks in that era.

McFadden was involved in racing through 1965 when he left to become general manager of the Dayton Gems hockey team, just being organized.

With USAC (United States Automobile Club) racing becoming

more popular across the country, the need for longer tracks put the half mile Dayton course on the skids as far as attracting top flight entries.

Harlan Fengler, who represented the Ford Motor Company in Dayton and had driven in the 1923 Indianapolis 500 miler, became one of the top track officials with USAC. For a while he served as racing director at the Dayton Speedway, but the deteriorating condition of the property continued to make it difficult to attract the top owners to compete here.

Earl Baltes, who has built the Eldora Speedway north of Greenville into the biggest racing operation in southwestern Ohio, leased the track in 1967. Baltes repaved the oval and brought in sprint cars again. But Baltes pulled out after a year and in 1970 the track was shut down.

Fengler, who started as a low level official at the Indianapolis track before the war, worked his way up through USAC to become chief steward, making him the man in command of the Indianapolis track which was expanding to accommodate the huge crowds.

Fengler's most controversial decision as chief steward came in the 1963 race when several owners and drivers complained that he should have blackflagged winner Parnelli Jones, whose car seemed to be leaking oil.

J. C. Agajanian, the owner of Parnelli's car, pointed out to Fengler that the oil wasn't coming from the engine, but from a small auxiliary side tank. The controversy carried into the awards dinner the night after the race when Jones and Sachs came to blows and Parnelli gave Eddie a black eye.

There were several attempts to reopen the Dayton track. One of the problems never overcome was the high cost of maintenance. The high banks made it difficult to pave and "soft holes" continued to crop up on the racing surface. The stands were finally levelled and the track closed.

There had been one other track operating in Dayton for a dozen years, the quarter-mile Forest Park Speedway located at what is now the Forest Park Shopping center. There had been a small amusement park known as Frankie's Forest Park which had flourished in the 1920s but ran into difficult times leading up to the second World War.

When the amusement park didn't reopen, the Speedway was put together by Carl Dice and Ade Hoff and ran junker stocks as well as motorcycle racing with modest success.

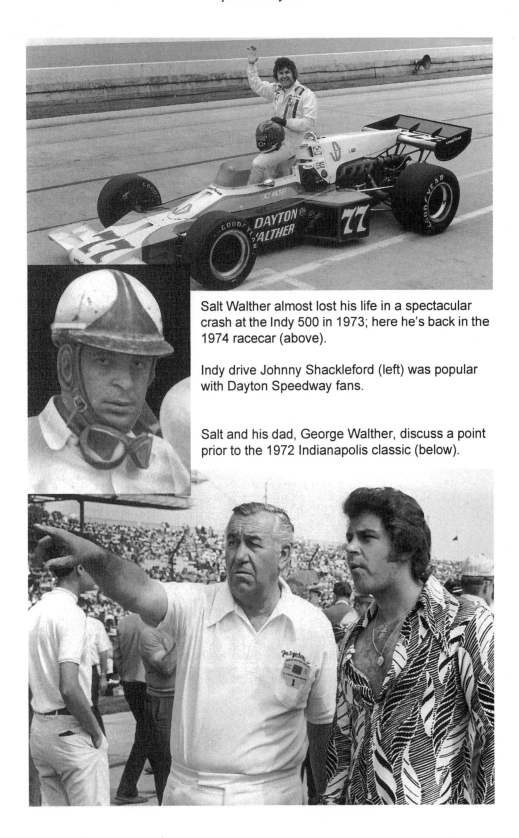

Salt Walther almost lost his life in a spectacular crash at the Indy 500 in 1973; here he's back in the 1974 racecar (above).

Indy drive Johnny Shackleford (left) was popular with Dayton Speedway fans.

Salt and his dad, George Walther, discuss a point prior to the 1972 Indianapolis classic (below).

22

The George and Salt Saga

The longest, costliest and most successful effort to bring an Indianapolis 500 race victory to Dayton is the one launched by George N. Walther, Jr. back in 1955.

George was then president and CEO of the family owned Dayton-Walther Corp, which was expanding its business of manufacturing wheels and other automobile parts into international markets.

Any memory of the Walther effort immediately centers on the horrible nine-car crash at the start of the 1973 race in which George's son, Salt, miraculously survived near fatal burns over 60 per cent of his body.

Salt, given name David, was only seven years old when his father entered his first car in the Indianapolis classic. The car was called the Dayton Steel Wheel special and was driven by Elmer George, who crashed it in his driver's test.

Elmer George's future at the Speedway didn't include a driving triumph but he became very much involved. After becoming track owner Tony Hulman's son-in-law, he became director of the Speedway Radio Network and later Vice-President of the corporation.

Coming back in 1956, the Walther racing group entered a dirt track car driven by Jim McWithey of Anderson, Indiana, that did not qualify. The idea of a dirt track car trying to make the Indy field nearly 40 years ago illustrates how far the computer-designed 200-mph plus cars have come in technical and cost advancement. To enter an Indy car in the 1990s has to be a seven figure investment.

In his third try, George Walther got his Kurtis Kraft vehicle into the field and rookie driver Mike Magill not only qualified to start in the 18th position, he finished 24th.

Walther made international headlines looking ahead to the 1958 race. He invited Juan Manuel Fangio, recognized as the No. 1 driver in the world on what is now known as the Formula One competition, to drive a new car. With great fanfare Fangio tested the car at Indianapolis and decided he didn't want to drive it.

Fangio didn't race at Indy, and the consensus opinion was that he didn't want to risk his reputation in a car that he couldn't get up to the desired speed. That put Magill back into the driver's seat and Mike managed to qualify in the last row and drove 136 laps. Magill had a new Sutton roadster in the 1959 race but crashed, fortunately without serious injury, on the 45th lap.

Then followed four costly years of not getting the Dayton entries in the race even though Walther had two cars entered in 1963. A year later Troy Ruttman, a former winner, and Bob Mathouser qualified both cars. Ruttman blew a tire and Mathouser finished 22nd.

The first rear engine Dayton-Walther car appeared in 1966 and rookie driver Carl Williams qualified it and finished 16th. For various reasons, the Walthers didn't succeed in getting anyone into the race until Salt came along as a rookie in 1972.

Carl Williams continued to have hard luck in that unproductive interval. In the 1971 race, he was sitting in 33rd spot with qualifying time about to expire. The cannon went off at 6 p.m. halting further attempts, but there was a car on the track that bumped the Dayton car.

Salt Walther was 24 years old when he attempted to qualify for the most challenging motor race of them all. His credentials as a big car driver seemed skimpy. He had cut his racing teeth in speedboats, at one time aiming at the Unlimited Hydroplane circuit.

Salt had been trying to qualify the second car in the stable, but Bud Tingelstad wasn't getting much out of the other one. Salt jumped into it, qualified it into the race in 27th position but went out early with engine problems.

It might seem logical to think that Salt would have been a popular figure on the Dayton sports scene. But a great many fellow drivers as well as racing fans looked upon him as a "spoiled rich kid" whose father bought him a toy to get him into the Indy 500 while more experienced drivers were around looking to catch on with an owner. Young Walther also had a reputation for fast living. There weren't many parties he missed and he had an eye for pretty girls in Dayton's night life.

The dramatic climax for Salt and the Dayton-Walther entry came to pass early in the 1973 race. This time he qualified number 77, the number that his father applied to his top cars, in 17th position in the middle of the sixth row.

When starter Seth Klein waved the green flag to start the race, there was a spectacular nine car crash before most of the field reached turn one. Young Walther was in the middle of it, his car crashing sideways into the retaining wall, overturning in flames and skidding down the main stretch in flames. Salt's feet were visible extending from the wreckage as the rescue crews reached him, battling to put out the flames.

He was pulled from the wreckage, obviously very badly burned, hustled in an ambulance to the track hospital where he was put into a heli-copter and quickly dispatched to Methodist Hospital. There is no way of being certain, but a majority of racing experts believe no other driver has ever survived a more disastrous accident.

His recovery was certainly against long odds. He twice was given last rites in the first week of his hospital stay and the long rehab to get his burned hands and arms to the strength required to hold a car in control at nearly 200 mph was an act of great determination and dedication.

"By all rights, I should be dead," he was quoted by *Dayton Daily News* columnist Tom Archdeacon in 1989.

Whatever anyone felt about Salt's life style or his lack of racing experience, no one will ever question his courage. His strong physical con-ditioning contributed to his recovery.

He made an incredible comeback to qualify another 77 car for the 1974 race and earned grudging respect from the gasoline alley fraternity by qualifying in 14th position. He was running even when engine failure caught up with him.

He did even better in 1975, qualifying ninth, the best ever for a Walther racer, but bad luck dogged his efforts as a broken supercharger took him out of the race early. Salt's best finish in the 500 came in the 1979 race when he started in 15th place and finished 12th, driving 191 laps in the last Dayton-Walther entry in 500 mile history.

Business problems forced George Walther to cut back on his racing operations in the 1980s and Salt lapsed into a trouble-filled decade in which he developed a drug problem that got him involved in several brushes with the law and sent him into rehab on several occasions.

Salt is destined to wear a glove on his left hand to cover the burned stubs of his fingers and the fingers on his scarred right hand seem to go off at odd angles. He attempted a racing comeback as late as 1989, but his story will remain forever in the "what might have been" category.

The problems that seem to haunt Salt from time to time in recent years do not belong in this historical study of sports. Suffice it to say the Walther father-son combination never generated a happy ending. But the Walther effort remains the dominant part of Dayton's involvement with the 500 mile race.

Shannons Find Their Niche

Bob and Gene Shannon grew up as red hot automobile racing enthusiasts who remember selling newspapers at the Dayton Speedway back in the 1930s.

Once they were established in the business world as owners of the successful Shannon Buick agency, they wanted to fulfill a lifelong ambition to get involved in racing as car owners.

In 1956 they owned the car that the veteran Duke Dinsmore qualified for the Indianapolis 500 and finished in 17th place.

"We took a look at the way costs were going up at Indy and decided we weren't in a position to continue in that direction," Bob Shannon said of their change in plans.

Turning their attention to the less expensive USAC midgets, they launched a successful 22-year run that landed them jointly into the AAA/USAC National Midget Auto Racing Hall of Fame.

In addition to winning the national championship in 1972, with Larry Rice as driver, they finished runners-up three other times in the national point standings.

Overall, they finished 12 times in the top ten point standings and enjoyed watching their various cars finish 143 times in 1-2-3 (43 feature first place wins, 57 second place finishes and 43 third place finishes.

"We got a lot more satisfaction out of the years we had good cars and good drivers than we possibly could have by trying to stay in the Indy competition," Gene Shannon puts it. Both Shannons are retired now, having sold the Buick agency and also retired from racing car operations.

The Shannons feel they went at it the right way. In 1964, they hired the late Bob Higman to run their operation as chief mechanic and he stayed with them through 1978, their last year.

The roster of drivers who drove for them, in addition to national champion driver Rice, includes Dave Strickland, Gene Force, Pancho Carter and Sam Sessions.

Midget racing began in 1933 and some of the biggest names in racing were involved in the early years including such Indy drivers as A. J. Foyt, Fred Agabashian, Henry Banks and Parnelli Jones.

The Kelleys And Cycles

Motorcycle racing in the Dayton area is a legacy of Harry Kelley Sr. and his son J. R. The Kelleys started the KK Motorcycle Supply Company, the wholesale operation that provides parts and accessories to the numerous franchised cycling dealers in southwestern Ohio.

The elder Kelley was born in the Oklahoma territory in 1899 before it became a state and in his early years joined the U.S. Cavalry while it was still an active military operation. In his case, combat duty was riding against bandits on the Mexican border in what was left of the wild west.

Harry started racing Indian-built motorcycles, one of the first manufacturer of the cycles. The Indians and Harley Davidsons were the two major cycle outfits through the 1920s and 1930s and both had teams of "company riders" trying to beat their rivals on the dirt tracks. Harry frequently rode against the first Johnny Vance.

Harry rode what was called an Indian-manufactured "Pea Shooter" and rode against the best. He was the first half-miler to break a mile-a-minute (60 mph) on the Winchester, Indiana track.

"When I was old enough to go along, we'd take the front wheel off (the motorcycle) and hitch the back wheel to the back of our car and take off," J. R. says of the early days. "We never stayed in a motel. You'd go where you'd have a shot at the top prize money. $75 was big money," he added.

Harry Kelley had the Indian dealership in Dayton before World War II, and his business was called Kelley Motors. They launched the wholesale phase of what is now KK in 1960, by which time the younger Kelley had come to the conclusion that being in business had more of a financial future than racing a cycle himself. He confined his racing interests after that to sponsoring some of the area's top riders.

J. R. Kelley was 15 in 1941 when the United States responded to Pearl Harbor by entering the war.

"People think I rode cycles when I was a kid, but in those days they didn't make small cycles like they do now and you had to grow up to ride one of those old Indian models," he said.

J. R. enlisted in the Marines and came dangerously close to not surviving the invasion of Iwo Jima, where he was a spectator to the famous photograph of the six Marines raising the American flag. That same day, a Japanese bullet entered his chest, damaged his lung and came perilously close to his heart.

"My dog tags were bent, and they told me the tags shielded my heart lining," he recalled.

The Indian company had been forced out of business by the war and there were no cycles available when both Kelleys went about rebuilding their business in early 1946.

"We got our first Indian Scout in bushel baskets, picking up pieces and parts here and there and put it together," J. R. recalled

Harry, Sr. managed to get a Triumph franchise and later became mid-central distributor for Berliner motors.

"That first year we were getting two cycles a month," J. R. continues his description. "We could have sold a hundred."

Harry's racing days were over but he was deeply involved with J. R.'s new career on the tracks. They had a good year in 1949 on the short tracks at county fairs and the two then new tracks here, the short-lived Forest Park Speedway off North Main and Kil-Kare over in Greene County.

"One year, I stayed back in Dayton when Dad took a driver he was sponsoring down to Daytona Beach and I sold 12 cycles while they were gone that week," J. R. said. "I said to myself, 'this can be better than racing,' and not long afterwards, I gave up the competition."

J. R. looks back on his seven year career with one regret. "I never won a 100-mile national race, but I came close a couple of times." J. R. eventually became influential at the national level of his sport, and served a term as president of the American Motorcycle Association.

In 1983, KK was the sponsor of a cross-county motorcycle ride as radio personality Steve Kirk and advertising executive Dwight Mitchell tried to make it from the Triborough Bridge in New York to the Golden Gate in San Francisco in 70 hours. That the pair of non-professional riders even attempted such a feat staggers the imagination, but the two of them did the 2,945 miles in 74 hours and 37 minutes, earning them a spot in cycling records.

One of J. R.'s ambitions was to fight the image of cyclists as bearded, wild riding hooligans of the Hell's Angels type. Along those lines, in 1971 he launched what has become the annual Old Time Newsies Charity race at the Montgomery County Fairgrounds, a track where both Kelleys raced in their careers.

The Newsies originally were a group of men who as youngsters had sold newspapers on the streets. Their purpose was to help others, and the current primary recipients of the more than $1 million raised at the races are the Big Brothers, Big Sisters of Dayton.

The annual event has brought some of the country's top riders to Dayton, and the rivalry between Gary Scott and Steve Morehead has drawn national attention. Scott won the race seven times, Morehead four.

Ronnie Rall won the first race in 1971 and Gary Scott won the first time a year later. George Roeder II strung together consecutive wins in 1991-92-93.

"When we went over the million dollar plateau with the 1995 race, I felt we (the motorcyclists) had made our point that we were good citizens," said J. R., who divides his time in retirement between North Carolina and Florida.

Among the earlier motorcycle racers from this area were Bill Boyce, once ranked 8th nationally, Doug Davis, Don Fry, Ted Heil, Tommy Heil, Bob Hinkle, Don Reese and Tommy Warden.

And All The Rest . . .

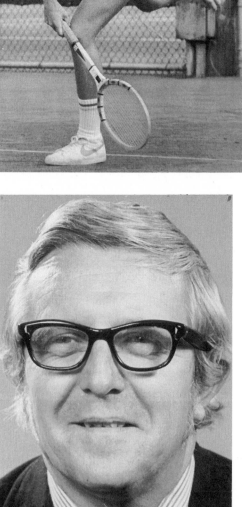

Bill O'Neill (above), named a "Player of the Century" in a 1995 poll.

Bob Kronauge (above right) won five straight county singles championships starting in 1977.

Newspaperman Jim Nichols (right) for whom tennis courts are named.

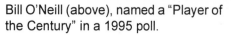

23

Tennis

The highly civilized sport of tennis can stake a claim to being involved in organized competition in Dayton before the more macho pursuits of football and basketball.

The 1995 Montgomery County Tennis championships were celebrated as the 100th anniversary of the first event.

For the last 67 of those years the tennis championships have been sponsored by the *Dayton Daily News*. Governor James M. Cox, publisher, began the sponsorship in 1928 and the tradition has since been maintained through a whole series of publishers and editors.

Nearly everyone who figures in the history of the sport in Dayton, including Davis Cupper Barry MacKay (1957-58-59), is listed among the champions.

The tournament has had four sites, beginning on the YMCA courts on Riverside Drive where the Riverside Terrace Apartments are located. It moved to the Dayton Country Club in 1929, which hosted it until the entry list grew to create scheduling problems.

It moved next to the city-owned Walnut Hills courts before shifting in 1958 to its present site, the Jim Nichols Tennis Center on Ridge Avenue just south of the Dayton Museum of Natural History.

The Nichols Center is named for longtime *Dayton Daily News* writer Jim Nichols, who covered tennis for the newspaper and took up the sport himself at an early age. He has been involved in promoting the sport in a volunteer role. The Nichols Center is not far from the original tournament site.

In the beginning the men's singles championship was the only division. The men's doubles weren't added until 1906.

The women's singles didn't come into the picture until 1931 and it was another two decades before women's doubles was added. Various age brackets in both men's and women's divisions and the mixed-doubles were later added.

George V. Pottle was the first men's champion in 1895. The youngest player in that first tournament was 17-year-old Jim Adamson, who captured the first of several championships at age 19 two years later. Adamson was one of the dominant early players, remaining competitive well into his 40s and he notched seven championships, the last in 1918 when he would have been 40.

Beginning in 1923, when Frank Kronauge, Jr. won the first of nine championships he was to win over an 11-year span, we can trace the *Who's Who* in Dayton tennis circles by frequent repeat winners - Bud Bickham, Billy O'Neill, Shaw Emmons, Jim Provines, Bob Kronauge (Frank's grandson) to R. J. Dunkle. Emmons, a six-time Montgomery County champion, was undefeated as a collegian at Denison University.

When the women's side was established in 1931, Naidyne Hall was seeded No. 1 with Evelyn Graul No. 2. Ms. Graul upset the top seed to become the first champion, but Ms. Hall gained her revenge by capturing the crown in the second women's event.

That set the stage for Virginia Hollinger to become the first dominant woman player by winning the title the next four years, 1933-34-35-36. Described in newspaper accounts as a "poker-faced little redhead girl" she was taught the game by her father on the old East Oakwood courts.

In 1938 she won the women's national indoor title, but tragedy was just around the corner. After her marriage to Wayne McCloud she was diagnosed with Parkinson's disease and she died in 1946. The Virginia Hollinger Tennis Club in Oakwood is named in her honor.

Mary Wilson captured the women's title for the first time in 1942 and went on to win six straight through 1948. There was no tournament in wartime 1944.

Mrs. Wilson, a school teacher by profession, was long involved in tennis after her competitive days were over as secretary of the women's association and an organizer of volunteers for the tournament.

In more recent women's competition, Nancy Janco rolled up four straight singles titles (1976-79) to go with an earlier one for five overall and Chris Burkhardt strung together three straight in 1986-87-88.

The Kronauge Dynsasty

Clearly the first family of Dayton tennis is Frank Kronauge, Jr. and his grandson Bob, who between them captured the Montgomery County men's singles championship 14 times.

The elder Kronauge is also listed as a 12-time winner in doubles competition, playing several times paired with Dr. Dave Reese, the one-time Denison and Dayton Triangles football standout who later became Commissioner of the Mid-American Conference.

Frank Kronauge, Sr. moved from St. Louis to Dayton with his family in 1904, when Frank, Jr. was three years old. He attended Holy Angels grade school and the University of Dayton prep school before graduating from UD where he captained the tennis team.

He took up tennis in 1913 when John H. Patterson of NCR fame built four courts at Main and L streets for NCR employees and offered racquets, shoes and balls to neighborhood youngsters willing to take up the game. The infamous 1913 flood intervened and the area of the tennis courts was converted into a tent city to house flood victims who had lost their homes. But the tennis courts were quickly restored.

Young Kronauge sharpened his skills when playing for UD, known then as St. Mary's Institute. He entered the county tourney for the first time in 1918 when he was only 17. Newspaper clippings are hazy, but he is listed as the doubles winner with a partner identified only as Pond.

Frank's son, Tom Kronauge, played tennis at Chaminade high school, but stayed at the game afterwards only in the recreational sense.

"He played every summer, but there was no place to play in the winter," Tom said of his father, who died of a heart attack in 1956, when he was only 55 years old.

Tom's son, Bob, took up where his grandfather left off in the county tournament, starting a string of five straight singles championships in 1977 by beating Bob Helmers, who had been one of his teachers.

Bob, who played high school tennis at Alter, starred at the University of Cincinnati, graduating in 1980. He qualified for the NCAA tennis tourney in three of his four college seasons. He was in college and at the top of his game when he was winning the county event.

After going into the family insurance business, Bob toned down his competitive efforts and has been in the tournament mostly in doubles since 1982.

Cathie, Billy Rated Tops

In conjunction with the 100th anniversary of the County Tournament in 1995, in setting up the celebration the committee took a poll that named Billy O'Neill and Cathie Gagel-Anderson as Dayton's Players of the Century.

O'Neill has captured 30 county titles in every men's division going up the age ladder while Gagel-Anderson owns seven county women's singles titles and 21 overall.

Cathie's honors in the sport go beyond the local. She has won tennis championships around the world and has been ranked as high as No. 2 internationally in her age group.

She grew up in Oakwood but spent her high school years at Chatham Hall, a boarding school in Virginia. She spent two years at Briar Cliff Junior College in Briar Cliff Manor, New York, and then two more at the NCAA level at the University of California-Berkeley where she competed and earned her degree.

While she wasn't spending much time in Dayton, she tried to keep her schedule open to come back for the county tournament. Her string of achievements includes singles trophies in 1962 and 1965 under her maiden name and then five more as Gagel-Anderson, the last in 1982. Add to that six doubles, seven mixed-doubles and an over-35 title and you have her record. She lives in California in the San Diego area and is still active in age group amateur events.

O'Neill's name has popped up more often than anyone else in the history of the tournament. The now retired O'Neill first entered in 1942 when he was only 13 years old. He believes he got started because the tournament was being played at Walnut Hills in the area where he grew up.

His trophies include six open singles championships and a string of age group titles in both singles and doubles. He was still competitive in the recent 65-or-over category as this was written.

The Vinnie Westendorf Story

The story of tennis in Dayton isn't complete without looking at Vinnie Westendorf, a legendary participant who led a very unusual life.

Westendorf was born in East Dayton at the turn of the 20th century and his early years were those of an active boy growing up doing the things active boys did before there were organized sports activities for pre-teens. In the summer of 1915, he was riding a borrowed motorcycle out on old Xenia Pike (now Linden Avenue) when he was thrown off, suffering a serious leg injury with a severed artery.

The injury was treated in a hospital stay, but there was permanent damage and he was told he would always walk with a limp. Moreover, the doctors warned him not to play football or any contact sport because a hard bump could reopen the repaired artery.

"A year after that accident, I borrowed a tennis racquet and played for the first time," he said in an interview a few months before he died in 1959. "I was told tennis would be all right because the ball, being softer than a baseball, wouldn't be a danger."

In the era following World War I, he played at the McKinley park courts and Community Country Club and had a job as a railroad clerk. He lost that job in the early days of the Great Depression and his leg continued to bother him.

But there was a more serious problem just ahead. He was having other health problems and the ailment was diagnosed as Parkinson's Disease. Vinnie took that news with the same calm approach he took when he learned of his first disability and determined to challenge it.

"I just didn't let it stop me," he said in the 1959 interview with his longtime friend, Jim Nichols. "They told me those who suffer from Parkinson's disease shouldn't be able to get out of bed after five years. But I kept playing tennis and it was then I started helping kids learn to play."

Most of the early lessons at the Walnut Hills courts were without compensation. But in 1946, the city hired him to be an instructor at those same courts where he took up the game. In 1958, the city renamed them the Westendorf courts. He was honored by the Agonis Club, the Optimist Club and the Knights of Columbus.

He helped Billy O'Neill and Barry MacKay in their pre-teen years. MacKay came back to Dayton from California to be present when the Walnut Hills courts were re-dedicated to Vinnie.

"I've had some great coaching from fellows like Jack Kramer and Billy Talbert," MacKay said at the dedication. "But during the Challenge Round (Davis Cup) in Australia, I thought back to things Vinnie had told me." Westendorf died Sept. 19, 1959 at age 59.

Barry, Tim And Beth

Barry MacKay was only the second Ohioan to be rated No. 1 in the country after he turned pro in the late 1950s. The other was Cincinnati native Tony Trabert.

MacKay was born in Cincinnati but grew up in Oakwood where he starred for coach Mack Hummon on the Lumberjacks high school team. He won two state championship singles titles for Oakwood. He went on to the University of Michigan on a scholarship that was considerably less generous than the full scholarships awarded under the NCAA rules today.

"The scholarship was for books and tuition," he said in a 1980 interview with Marc Katz of the *Dayton Daily News*. "I waited tables in the fraternity house, scraped ice in the (hockey) rink and sold programs for extra money."

It was in his days at Michigan that he began to think of making it big and turning pro. In his junior year, he beat Dick Savitt and Vic Seixas in an indoor tourney and in his senior year won the NCAA singles crown.

He was selected for the Davis Cup team in 1957 after winning the collegiate championship, the first of four years he competed for the USA against Australia. He was part of the winning American team in 1958 although he lost both of his singles matches.

A year later, he won his singles match against Rod Laver even though the Aussies regained the cup. Later, MacKay faced Laver in the semi-finals at Wimbledon before bowing in a tough five set match. The next year he beat Laver in the U. S. Open at Forest Hills.

Barry won 17 tournaments in 1960 as a touring pro and was ranked No. 1. The money wasn't all that great at the time, but the sport was the vehicle that Barry rode to success in later years. After his playing days were over, he served as a TV announcer and turned promoter, based in San Francisco, where he also was involved in other business ventures.

Barry wasn't the only member of his family to attain national distinction. His sister, Bonnie, joined with Elaine Lewicki of Hamtramck, Michigan, to win the national girls junior doubles.

The only other male player with a Dayton connection to make it to Wimbledon was Tim Gullikson, who early in his career fresh out of Northern Illinois University, took a job as teaching pro at the Kettering Tennis Center.

Tim and brother, Tom, turned out to be the most successful set of twins ever to pursue big time tennis. In the summer of 1983 they made it into the championship doubles match in the legendary British event. But they were beaten by fellow Americans John McEnroe and Peter Fleming. The Gulliksons are natives of LaCrosse, Wisconsin and played college basketball while at NIU.

Tim's arrival in Dayton was just before Tom Clark took over as KTC manager in the summer of 1974.

"He was not only a very good teacher, but a very likeable young man, and popular with the kids," said Clark, who had just gone into the tennis business after having been sent to Dayton 10 years earlier by the parent company to operate Dayton Outdoor Advertising.

In his three years in Dayton, Tim played in local and area tournaments while looking for a financial sponsor to get him started on tour. He also worked a lot with Hank Jungle, the military officer stationed at WPAFB who was an experienced and capable player. Jungle won the 1973 Montgomery County crown.

"I never thought Tim would go as far as he did," conceded Clark. "He was an excellent teacher for both young or older players. I know he helped my game and he had a lot of people in this town pulling for him once he got out on tour."

Both Gulliksons established themselves as world class players, and Tim later won the 35-and-over singles division title at Wimbledon. But his greatest achievement may eventually be recognized as the coach who helped Pete Sampras attain his No. 1 world ranking.

Unfortunately, Tim began to encounter serious physical problems in 1994, suffering what were described as two "minor strokes." He had to be hospitalized in Australia around the Christmas holidays when he was there with Sampras in the Australian Open.

He was flown back to the United States for observation for a possible brain tumor, but was well enough to be at the 1995 U. S. Open when Sampras regained his No. 1 ranking by defeating Andre Agassi in an outstanding match.

Beth Herr is the other player out of this area to make it to Wimbledon and travel around the world on the tennis circuit, now fueled with television revenue as are so many other sports.

Ms. Herr played her high school tennis at Centerville and went on to become a standout at the collegiate level at Southern California. At one time, Beth stood 31st in the world in the computer index system that decides the ratings.

In 1988 she won her first round singles match at Wimbledon and got to the third round in doubles competition. Herr turned professional after winning her NCAA singles crown at USC and in her first six years on the tour, earned $300,000 in prize money.

The Tour Comes To Dayton

Dayton was a stop on the pro tennis tour for seven years starting in 1973. The event staged in the Dayton Convention Center was known as the Dayton Pro Tennis Classic.

Jack Kramer, one of the top American players in the 1940s and 1950s, was one of the organizers of the ATP (Association of Tennis Professionals) in 1972. The aim of the ATP was to enlarge the pro tennis schedule by seeking more tournament sites.

In the beginning, the tour could be booked for a guaranteed $25,000 in prize money. Kramer contacted sports writer Jim Nichols to see if he could suggest a sponsor for a stop in Dayton. Nichols came up with Little Mickey Friedman, who was active in several sports promotion areas at the time. Friedman put up the money and the first tournament was a success.

"That seems remarkable now to think you could get eight legitimate pros by putting up only $25,000," Nichols said looking back. "But the tour was just getting going then."

Realizing the Dayton event would require steady upgrading in both prize money and promotion costs, Nichols asked Friedman to step aside for Foreman Industries. Foreman carried the event through 1980 when the soaring cost cycle was too much to stage a successful event in the limited spectator capacity of the Convention Center.

Charles (Bo) Foreman, then heading the construction business founded by his father, was a sports enthusiast who spent a lot of money in supporting various sports activities. The football stadium at his alma mater, Fairmont High School, is named Foreman field.

Foreman was a walk-on candidate for the Ohio State football team, but never won a letter. When Pete Ankney was available after being let out as UD football coach, Foreman hired him for his company and later made him director of the ATP. Ankney worked tirelessly to cajole enough of the top name pros to make an attractive field here.

In the early years, Ankney tried such gimmicks as matching Pete Rose and Bobby Riggs in an exhibition and a year later brought in daredevil Evel Kneivel and stuck a racquet in his hand.

But even increasing the prize list to $75,000 was not enough to make Ankney's job easy. With more and more tourneys coming up with bigger purses, Foreman saw the handwriting on the wall.

The winners of the DPTC in order of the seven years were Raul Ramirez, Brian Gottfried, Jaimie Fillol, Jeff Borowiack, Gottfried again, Butch Walts and Wojtek Fibak.

Dayton tennis fans still had a major treat coming when Dr. Jo Geiger, the executive director of AIM for the Handicapped, linked up with a tennis promotional group to stage the Borden Tennis Invitational in 1983-84-85-86.

Larry Ball, who had the Borden franchise in the Dayton area, got involved in the promotion which brought world class performers Bjorn Borg, Ivan Lendl, Jimmy Connors, Billy Jean King and Martina Navratilova to the UD Arena in one night exhibitions.

In the first tourney, Borg played Vitas Gerulaitis and Virginia Wade took on hometown standout Beth Herr in the women's match. A year later, the men's match was the same, Borg vs. Gerulaitis while King and Navratilova made up the women's match.

Connors, Sandy Mayer, Roscoe Tanner and Butch Walts came in with an expanded field in 1985 with Billy Jean King returning with Rosie Cassels on the women's side.

Oakwood's Long Regime

Tennis at the high school level in Dayton was long dominated by Oakwood in the years Mack Hummon was the coach.

Hummon's success in coaching tennis has a unique twist. He came to Oakwood in 1925 as a football and basketball coach. He graduated from Wittenberg in 1923, having played four sports there but not tennis.

Hummon was making a little money on the side playing pro football with the Dayton Triangles and with various semi-pro basketball teams. He had taken up tennis as a summer camp instructor and persuaded the school to let him start a tennis program.

By taking the tennis coaching job, and becoming an assistant in football and basketball, he had more time to pursue profitable sidelines in those sports. Eventually, he spent 35 years as an active whistle-blowing high school and college official in the two sports he started out to coach.

His tennis record speaks for itself. In his 38 seasons, he took players to the state championships 20 times. His players won the state singles championship three times, MacKay in 1952 and 1953 and Buzzy Pierce in 1964. The overall record was 277 team victories, 50 defeats and one tie. He retired from coaching in 1965 and died in 1992.

24

The Grand American

The sports event that annually brings in more visitors and pumps more money into the greater Dayton economy than any other is an activity unfamiliar to most area residents. It is also one that does not provide much in the way of excitement for spectators.

But as a participant sport, the 1995 Grand American attracted 6,500 of the best shooters from around the United States and Canada and more than a few competitors from around the world.

The Grand, as it is known to all serious shotgun enthusiasts, has been anchored since 1924 at the seemingly ever expanding ATA grounds in Vandalia, adjacent to the James M. Cox Dayton International airport.

In the most recent survey made by the Dayton Area Chamber of Commerce, the world trapshooting championships contribute $7.5 million to area business, most of it to service industries such as hotels and motels, restaurants, service stations and the like.

During most of the week before and during the Grand week itself, the ATA grounds are jammed with as many as 700 recreational vehicles, each of which is parked in a previously reserved and paid for space.

"Taking into consideration wives, children and friends, we have no accurate count of how many people are living on the grounds," says John Norris, the tournament director.

Whatever the number, the ATA grounds have gone through their maximum expansion. The longest firing line in the world consists of 100 trap fields, running side by side and covering 1.58 miles. Tractor-pulled wagons carry contestants back and forth along the line from the tournament center where they pick up their shells before heading to their assigned position.

Each of those 100 trap fields has a semi-underground shed from where the clay birds are mechanically sent into orbit at the command of the shooter. Each field accommodates a squad of five shooters. The line extends westward to the boundary of the airport and eastward to neighborhood streets and the E. J. Morton Middle School.

With the airport to the north and the old U. S. 40 "National Road" to the south, the grounds become a tightly knit small city unto themselves. And, like many cities, the traffic problem is sometimes close to gridlock.

The 1995 Grand American was the 96th, the first being contested June 12-15, 1900 at the Interstate Park in Queens, Long Island, New York, in an area relatively close to what is now LaGuardia airport.

The four-day shoot was to feature a 100-target championship at distances from 15 to 25 feet. The targets were live birds.

The first Grand American champion turned out to be a Daytonian, Rolla (Pop) Heikes. He broke 91 of 100 targets from 22 yards, beating out Hood Walters of Baltimore by two birds, and in this instance, he was firing at live birds. There were 74 shooters entered.

The entrance fee was $10 and the total purse was $714 of which Heikes, then a well recognized shooter, earned only $130.25.

Heikes was born on Christmas Day, 1856 on a farm in western Montgomery County. His family moved west to Nebraska when Rolla was 21. It was said that he had "weak lungs" and the move would be beneficial to his health.

He took up trapshooting before the clay pigeon was developed, when the shot was fired at glass balls, if not live pigeons. In the 1880s, he operated a ranch in Utah and became a deadly big game hunter at a time when the remnants of big game still roamed the west.

Moving back to Dayton in 1885, he was hired by the LeFever Gun Company and was the first shooting professional before that term came into use. He competed around the country as an "exclusive shooter."

Heikes had already won the world target championship when he was entered in the event now regarded as the first Grand. He was 44 when he won it. Heikes spent the rest of his life closely identified with the shooting profession. In 1918 he managed a Chicago gun club and was a subscription salesman for the pioneer outdoor sports magazine, *Sports Afield*.

He participated in 25 Grand Americans over the years and was an established legend in the sport. He died at the ripe old age of 79 in 1935 and, of course, was a charter member of the ATA Trapshoot Hall of Fame.

The second and third Grands were staged at the same Long Island shooting grounds. E. C. Griffith was the second winner and because live bird shooting was abandoned after the 1902 event, is down in history as the only man to win both clay target and live pigeon Grands.

The state and local associations that were involved in staging the championships put the event up for bids from cities to stage it, and it moved first to a Kansas City site in 1903 and then moved to Indianapolis for three years.

Columbus, Ohio was the site of the 1908 tournament and Fred Harlow of nearby Newark was the winner. Harlow was a state conservation officer and went on to win other national championships. He was a familiar figure in the rankings.

That Heikes was from Dayton was coincidental to the eventual decision to make this area the tournament's permanent site. Taking nothing away from Vandalia, the land provided to the ATA was financed by Dayton's business and civic leaders.

Dayton came into the picture in 1913 thanks to John H. Patterson, the founder of NCR and the man involved in so much of Dayton's history. Patterson had invited the shooters to come here and compete at the NCR Gun Club, located along the Great Miami River adjacent to the expanding NCR factories.

The plan almost didn't work because the great flood of 1913 did awesome damage to much of downtown Dayton. It also levelled the gun club building which was situated close to what is now Carillon Park.

Patterson, deeply involved in the cleanup of the flood damage, did not give up on hosting the shooters and the grounds were repaired in time for the June competition. Participation jumped to 501, the highest number to that time, and the NCR people turned out to be great hosts, providing many free services to the shooters.

An invitation to return to Dayton for 1914 was accepted and again NCR was the generous host. The star on the firing line was Woolfolk K. Henderson, known as the "Yellow-haired lad from Kentucky."

Henderson not only won the Grand itself by firing 98 of 100 from the 22-yard line, but he also captured the North American Clay Target championship with a 99, the doubles with 90 and the high overall and the high-all around. That's five major titles, something no shooter has ever duplicated. Henderson was the first Grand winner since Pop Heikes to do it from the maximum range.

The Grand kept rolling on during World War I, in fact the 1917 and 1918 shoots were held at the South Shore Country Club in Chicago. The Chicago Country Club hosted the 1923 tournament for the ninth and as it turned out, last time.

The event stands out in the history of the tournament because it was won by Mark Arie of Champaign, Illinois. Known as the "Little Dutchman," Arie was a popular figure in the sport and was in contention for the Grand and other events on the program for a decade before he won it.

The 1923 Grand was also the first for a man whose name became a legend in the world of trapshooting.

Jimmy Robinson, a Canadian by birth, a World War I veteran and a former minor league hockey and baseball player, joined the ATA as a statistician. For the rest of his life Robinson was the goodwill ambassador and press agent of both the Grand and trapshooting as a sport.

He joined the staff of *Sports Afield* magazine for his year-around occupation, but he was "Mr. Grand" at Vandalia. Hardly a shooter would see the stocky little guy with the ever present pipe sticking out of his mouth without saying hello.

Robinson wrote several books about trapshooting, one of which, *The Grand, A History of Trapshooting*, written in 1974 in conjunction with Jim Nichols, *Dayton Daily News* sports writer, was an invaluable source of information for this book. He had a big hand in creating the Trapshooting Hall of Fame and Ducks Unlimited and was a legend long before his death in 1986.

The ATA Drops Anchor

The Vandalia location as the permanent home of the ATA traces its roots back to John H. Patterson and NCR hosting the shoot in 1913-14.

When S. C. (Chick) Allyn became the top executive at NCR he was a prime mover in putting together the group that purchased the land, being used then as a cornfield. It was donated to the trapshoot group with a pledge that the championship would be contested there every year.

Fortunately for Dayton, Allyn and the others made a lasting contribution to the community in an economic as well as prestige sense. The names on the commemorative plaque at the entrance to the grounds, reads like a *Who's Who* of Dayton leadership in the first half of the 20th Century.

In addition to Allyn, there are James M. Cox, Sr., the publisher of the *Dayton Daily News* who ran for President of the United States in 1920, Col. E. A. Deeds and Charles F. Kettering of General Motors fame and Frederick Rike, the founder of the department store that bore the Rike name for so many years.

Others include Robert Dickey, Dr. W. A. Ewing, George Greene, O. L. Harrison, Dr. W. W. Herrman, Robert Houk, J. M. Huffman, Robert King, Irvin Kumler, James Markham, F. B. Patterson, George W. Shroyer, Frank Hill Smith, W. W. Sunderland and Nelson Talbott.

The clubhouse opened in 1924 and has been expanded many times. The current building was constructed around the original structure and houses the year-around offices of the ATA as well as the Hall of Fame.

Along the central area of the firing line on each side of the club-houses are the commercial shops where you'll find items of all the competing companies: Winchester, Remington, Federal and the rest. Bob Allen of Des Moines, Iowa, one of the nation's largest hunting and fishing clothiers, is well established on the line.

Contractor Frank Hill Smith raced the clock to get the grounds finished in time for the 1924 event.There were two preliminary days, with the Grand itself starting Aug. 25. Over the years, August has been Grand month, giving an opportunity for gunners to come to Vandalia with state championship trophies in their possession.

One of the legends of the Grand is that no shooter has ever repeated as champion, thus the fresh face at the trophy presentation.

H. C. Deck, a 65-year-old carpenter from Plymouth, Ohio, helped establish the mystique that even unknowns can have their moment of glory in the event. In its first year at Vandalia, Deck became the oldest man ever to win the event.

But the human interest aspect so often typical of Grand winners, is that he wasn't around for the preliminary events, showing up Friday morning to register for the main competition. Using a $16 rabbit gun he had purchased in 1912, Deck and three other shooters, including Dr. C. C. Hickman of Logansport, Indiana, who had won the 1915 Grand, ended in a deadlock at 97 of 100.

Deck, a small man with a handlebar mustache, broke 24 of 25 in the shootoff to put his name on the roster of champions.

The 1925 Grand attracted an entry list of 710 and the top prize broke the $1,000 barrier for the first time.

There was never a more popularly accepted Grand champion than

Charlie (Sparrow) Young of Springfield, who made history in 1926 by breaking all 100 targets from the 23 yard line. It was only the second perfect score ever, the earlier one by Riley Thompson from the 19-yard-line.

Young, who derived his nickname from the fact he was deadly shooting at live bird targets, had shot in every Grand since its inception in 1900. In the aftermath of his victory, he posed for a picture with Pop Heikes and E. C. Griffith, the first two winners.

Young continued to shoot in the Grand through 1950. He died the following May at age 85. His appearance on the firing line in later years always attracted a big gallery of spectators, not a common occurrence.

There were plenty of spectators jockeying for position for the shootoff of the 1930 championship. Fred King of Wichita Falls, Texas, one of the better shooters in the country, brought his 14-year-old son Rufus along. Rufus took a turn on the practice range and broke 23 of 25 targets.

There wasn't a Junior classification then in the Grand program and no one had ever tried to enter a 14-year-old before. But a family friend, Walter Warren of Chicago, urged the elder King to let Rufus enter the Grand. Warren even offered to pay the boy's entry fee.

Fred King relented and Rufus went to the firing line, shooting from the minimum distance of 16 yards. He broke 97 targets to finish in a tie with three Ohioans, including Lawrence Crampton who lived in Murlin Heights, a few miles south of the ATA grounds.

Nearly every shooter on the grounds tried to watch the shootoff and young Rufus, undaunted by the attention, broke 24 of 25 and went home with the title. He later ran a cattle ranch in his native state.

Rev. Garrison Roebuck continued the tradition of the unknowns the next year and the Grand has carried on to this day: no repeat winners.

For all the legend of the unknowns, it must be pointed out that every shooter who goes to the line has had some experience in the sport. No one unfamiliar with handling a gun could come out of nowhere to win. One reason there has never been a repeat winner in the Grand is that only amateurs are eligible. The professional shooters are not eligible.

Over the years, the complicated set of option wagering has raised the ante to a shooter who bets on himself and comes through.

The Grand has gone on every year, including the World War II years. Shotguns have never been much of a military weapon and there were no wartime restrictions.

It was during the war that Jasper Rogers became the first Daytonian to win the Grand since Pop Heikes. Rogers, a toolmaker by trade, had taken up trap only four years before and was able to shoot from the 18-yard line. He broke 97 in the regular race but was tied with five other shooters. He broke 24 of 25 to emerge from that group with the title.

The war did cut into the list of shooters, however. Only 810 competed, a number of them in military uniform. Hillsboro native Joe Hiestand, one of the top guns throughout the 1930s, was among them as an Air Force captain. His duties included that of shooting instructor at the Officers Candidate School in Boca Raton, Florida.

Hiestand had won the Clay Target championship, the second biggest event on the Grand program, in 1935-36 and again in 1938.

C. W. Brown became Dayton's third Grand champion, capturing it in 1956, a year in which the record number of shooters was up to 2,136. Bernard Bonn, Jr. of Fairborn was the 1969 winner. Pat Neff of Xenia was the most recent area shooter to capture the title in 1990.

Another Daytonian, Johnny Sternberger, achieved a unique distinction when he became the youngest shooter in the country to qualify for the maximum handicap yardage.

Stemberger, who was taught to shoot by his father, Gus, was 18 years old when he broke 95 targets on May 13, 1956 at the Crystal Lake Gun Club. He was also the first Ohioan to be rated at the 27 yard line and went on enjoy a long career in the sport.

The schedule of the 1995 Grand shows how many competitions have been expanded to give the shooters plenty of opportunity to score and practice for the big one as well as pick up a little prize money.

The official Grand didn't get underway until Monday, Aug. 14 but there were four days of preliminary shooting with 11 different events Aug. 10-11-12-13. On Monday, after opening ceremonies there was the singles championships. Included were such special pairings as husband-wife, father-son or grandson, brother-brother, brother-sister and sister-sister shootoffs.

Tuesday's feature is the President's Handicap. The ATA Clay Target Championship, formerly known as the North American Clay Target Championship, runs on Wednesday. Thursday's program, including the Budweiser Handicap, is headlined by Champion of Champions shootoff. If one enters all events, a shooter would have nine days of competitive firing.

The Trapshoot Hall of Fame was established in 1968, dedicated to the sport and not confined to shooters who have performed in Vandalia.

Annie Oakley, the girl from Greenville who became world famous as "Little Miss Sure Shot," is one of the charter members.

Lela Hall Frank dominated the women's side of trapshooting from 1934 through 1948 and was selected on Jimmy Robinson's All-American trapshoot team before he divided it into men and women's classes.

The giants of the sport, too many to mention here, are remembered in the Hall of Fame.

Hugh McKinley, a 1995 inductee, deserves special mention for his many contributions, including 13 years as general manager (1964-74) of the ATA. McKinley attended his first Grand in 1926 when he was 10 years old and hasn't missed one since although he didn't always shoot in his years in charge of the operation.

One of McKinley's memorable appearances on the firing line came in 1957 when he shot on a squad that included Roy Rogers, the television and movie cowboy. Rogers, a native Ohioan, was entertaining at the Ohio State Fair in Columbus, but drove down to Dayton for an afternoon of relaxed shooting.

The ATA grounds are also the site of the Ohio trapshoot championships, which are contested a few weeks ahead of the Grand and also contribute to the area economy.

There are numerous small gun clubs in southwest Ohio which afford Dayton marksmen an opportunity to keep their aim in focus while awaiting the annual big show in early August.

The ATA has a definite place in the history of the Dayton community and every effort needs to be made to keep it here.

25

Bowling

Back in the early 1950s before Dayton's blue collar industries the likes of NCR, Frigidaire, Inland, Delco and the others went into decline, there were more than 25,000 male competitors registered in a year with the Dayton Bowling Association.

Bowling continues to be one of the largest participation activities in the area, but the decline in numbers of bowlers coincides with the changing population and job base of the area.

For the 1994-95 season, the DBA had a registration list of 18,825 while the Dayton Women's Bowling Association had an enrollment of 8,729.

Although there were several small lanes around town in the early years of the 20th century, the history of the growth of the sport in Dayton to a large extent is the story of the Zavakos family.

Brothers George, Otto and Louie Zavakos were part of a family of 10 youngsters that emigrated from their native Greece to this country just before World War I and settled for the time being in Chicago.

Otto was the first to come into contact with bowling through his father-in-law who operated a small set of lanes on East Fifth street. In 1920, the three brothers went into business with the Royal lanes, situated in a building that now houses the Spaghetti Warehouse on West Fifth, a block away from the older lanes where Otto was first employed.

"There was a 30-table restaurant that stretched along a narrow aisle to the back of the building and they installed the first set of lanes right underneath that in the basement," explained Christ Zavakos, the son of Louie and the president of Zavakos Enterprises.

"By the time we lost our lease there in 1949, there were also lanes an the second and third floors," he concluded.

There was an interesting family split in the 1930s when George went off on his own and opened the Varsity Lanes, on the west side of the 700 block on North Main. George also went into the candy business and owned a restaurant not connected to the Varsity as well.

The story of the Varsity Lanes is connected with two of Dayton's most famous unsolved murders.

In the early hours of May 24, 1947, George K. Zavakos was gunned down in gangster style in front of his residence at 128 Rockwood in the lower Dayton View area. There were no witnesses and there was no indication of robbery as he had $1,100 in cash on his body. There was virtually no evidence available to the Dayton police.

Rumors of an underworld connection were rampant and the police investigators were convinced it was a professional "contract killing" but they never came close to developing a lead toward solving the crime.

Almost 30 years later, on March 7, 1977, George's son, Harry G. Zavakos, was murdered in the same manner in front of the same house. George's widow had lived there until she died a few weeks before the second killing. For the time being, Harry was occupying the house.

This time there was a witness. A neighbor lady told police she saw a man step out from behind a tree and fire from close range at his intended target. But the witness had no description of the man nor any other useful information or any idea how the gunman left the area.

The Varsity continued in operation for a number of years under the management of Harry's sister and co-owner, Mary Karas. But with the building of the 1-75 interstate highway, the neighborhood was greatly changed and the bowling operation went downhill and eventually closed.

The other side of the Zavakos family, with Louie and Otto as partners, expanded its bowling operations to the extent that at one time they had ties to 21 different establishments.

Louie Z. had the reputation of being a very sharp business man who kept to himself. The outgoing Otto was the more popular of the two and more directly involved in bowling itself.

The 1995-96 Dayton telephone directory lists 22 lanes in the immediate local call area. The six expanded and modernized Zavakos properties are all identified now as Royal Z houses: Belmont, Driftwood, Clayton, Miamisburg, Vandalia and Dayton, the last formerly known as McCook.

The other major bowling operation is also a family owned and operated group of houses.

Joseph T. Poelking came to the University of Dayton on a football scholarship in 1929. He married a local girl, Margaret Kroger, in 1932 and became a successful businessman and spent the rest of his life here.

Like the Zavakos family, Poelking had a modest beginning. He first owned a gas station and in 1939 built the original Pla-Mor lanes on Salem Avenue.

With his sons, Joe, Jr., Jim, Jerry and Jon, the elder Poelking expanded the holding to include the four establishments running in the 1990s. These include the 52 lane Poelking Marian and South, the Poelking Woodman and Poelking lanes on Wilmington.

The third generation is involved in the operations with Jim's, Joseph F. and Jerry's son Michael in management. Joseph T. was one of the founders of the Dayton Proprietors association and served as President and Treasurer of the Ohio Bowling Proprietors.

The Jefferson Clothiers

The most famous team bowling accomplishment in Dayton's history is that of the Jefferson Clothiers. They were the only Dayton group to capture the National ABC team championship, doing it in the 1932 tournament in Detroit.

They were rolling into contention on the final shift of the tournament and had strong first two games of 967 and 1,038. But going into the final frame of the third game, they were 100 pins behind the leading team out of Milwaukee.

Team leader Tommy Zavakos started the dramatic heroics by striking out, which means rolling three straight strikes to finish the scoring. Harry Rosenkranz also struck out. Howard Sanders took up the challenge and did the same thing. Curley Gaylor responded with three more.

That left it up to Hal Stewart. A split or a miss would cost them the title. He maintained that he deliberately stayed away from the headpin on his first ball and knocked down seven pins. He made his spare and then knocked down seven more pins on the last ball. The Jeffersons had knocked down 137 of a possible 150 pins and ended up with a third game of 1,123 for a 3,108 total and the victory.

The 1975 national ABC was held in Dayton as one of the first major sporting events in the then new Convention Center.

The ABC provides a tremendous economic boost for the host city as it brings in thousands of bowlers from across the country and runs from 12 to 14 weeks. The span in Dayton ran from Feb. 14 to May 4. The hotel and restaurant business enjoys a real run of custom during the event.

As if to celebrate having the ABC here, Dayton's Jim Setser captured the singles championship with a 756 series while Bob Metz and Steve Partlow were doubles champs at 1,360. Metz had 746 and Partlow 614.

The Hall Of Fame

Carl A. Copp and Carl E. Herbert were automatic choices as charter inductees when the DABC Hall of Fame was organized in 1964.

Copp, a General Motors executive with Frigidaire, became "Mr. Bowling" in the Dayton association and earned recognition at the state and national levels in the sport.

He attained his highest honor serving as president of the national ABC in 1959 after serving as president of the Ohio State Bowling Association. He was first elected president of the Dayton Association in 1938 and was unanimously re-elected year after year. He was also involved in setting up the national Junior ABC.

The cities that host an ABC tournament need a convention center or arena much larger than the largest individual alley to stage the tournament. Copp "cashed in" his good will chips with the ABC when the new downtown Convention Center became available to host that 1975 tournament.

Copp died in 1978, a widely respected man, having been involved in many civic and philanthropic activities.

Carl Herbert was an officer in the DABC for 48 years, the first 13 as treasurer and the last 35 as secretary.

Beyond that, he was a very good active bowler and at the ABC tournament in Indianapolis in 1974, he was presented a plaque recognizing his 50th appearance as a competitor in the tournament.

His string of ABC participations began in 1922 when he was a fill-in for a sick member of an NCR team going to the tournament in Toledo. He never missed another tournament, even in the final year of his life. The ABC was not held during World War II or he would have his 50 year pin a bit sooner.

In his peak years, Herbert carried a 205 average and he was still bowling in two leagues a week in 1976, the year he died at age 78.

Charles A. Schneider, one of the early inductees into the Hall, told of beginning to bowl in 1907 with a wooden two-finger ball with no thumb hole. He rolled a 651 series at the ABC in 1911 in St. Louis and it was the high singles score for several weeks. He ultimately finished fourth, the first Daytonian to get attention in the national tournament.

Another early inductee into the Hall was Nick Manos, who was very popular with bowlers even though he managed several local alleys in the Zavakos operation. He was born in Chicago (his mother was a Zavakos) and came to Dayton in 1934 and spent the rest of his life here.

Manos had a gruff sense of humor that made him a good will ambassador for the sport.

The Dayton women's association was organized before the DABC and was to mark its 75th anniversary in the spring of 1996.

The DABC Hall of Fame

Regular Selection

Carl A. Copp	1964	Thurman "Tommy" Vogel	1978
Carl E. Herbert	1964	Dale Whisler	1978
Harry Phelps	1965	William "Bill" Gaines	1979
Gene Swindler	1965	Hollis Peterson	1979
Robert Zimmerle	1966	Howard "Bud" Ekberg	1980
Otto Zavakos	1966	Ted Porumb	1980
Nick Manos	1967	Ray Harden	1981
Charles A. Schneider	1967	Bud Tufts, Jr.	1981
Arthur M. Schreier	1968	Roy Schroeder	1982
John P. May	1968	Don Howard	1983
Floyd Weymouth	1969	Robert Herby	1984
Don Fairchild	1969	Thomas Marshall	1985
Harry Rosenkranz	1970	Robert Kwolek	1987
Charles Stonebarger	1970	Glen McConnell	1990
Hal Badders	1971	Del Wick	1990
George "Corky" Wilson	1971	George Belme	1991
Harold J. Dodson	1972	John F. Grubb	1991
Emil Ring	1972	Barney J. Bernat	1992

William D. DeHaven	1973	Odell Attaway	1992
Charles Pingle	1973	Lou Durko	1993
Paul Chambliss	1974	Jack Dyer	1993
Bob Ruth	1975	George "Bud" Orsi	1994
Virgil Shroyer	1975	James F. Poelking	1994
William Nolan	1976	Chuck Blair	1995
Robert Tucker	1976	Herbert Hines	1995
Robert F. Metz	1977		

Veterans Selection

Samuel Karpf	1975	G. "Buck" Buchanon	1984
George Klockson	1975	Ralph Marshall	1984
Lou Gaylor	1975	Orion Frei	1985
Hal Stewart	1975	Forest Ward	1985
Howard Sanders	1975	Robert Brodbeck	1986
Tommy Zavakos	1975	W. W. "Bud" Schueller	1986
William Breidenbach	1976	Leonard Wilson	1987
Henry Hager	1976	Clark "Curley" Powell	1987
G. W. "Jack" Moore	1977	John A. Henehan	1988
George T. Wilson	1977	George George	1989
William "Bill" Grosse	1978	Chet Reed	1990
Mike Redelle	1978	Robert Pollard	1991
Joseph T. Poelking, Sr.,	1979	George E. Sutton	1991
Louis K. Zavakos	1979	Joe J. Kucharsky	1992
Charles Gadker	1980	Pete Zavakos	1992
Cliff O'Ryon	1980	Taylor Cardwell	1993
John Herby	1981	John Carrell	1993
Albert Kelly	1981	Dave Atkins	1994
Earl Gallimore	1982	Harry Hoefler	1994
Steve Vargo	1982	Merlin "Lefty" Baker	1995
Harold Allesse	1983	J. C. Smith	1995
Gordon Nein	1983		

The DWBA Hall of Fame

Margaret Armpreister	Mary Hardin	Ella Reiser*
Agnes Baker*	Hattie Henton	Mary Ryan

Bowling

Frieda Barger
Roberta Becker
Susan J. Behr
Jeri Blair
Dottie Remick-Bohl
Joanne Borkenhagen
Lois Caylor
Cele Clark*
Betsy Corrigan
Sally Coughlin
Edith Deeter
Karen Dunlap
Emma Folino
Mary Margaret Fortener
Lona Getter*
Edna Greer*
Martha Haines
Ruth Hamburger*

Beatrice Houdieshell*
Eleanor Huelsman
Debbie Jessup
Edith Johnson*
Kathy Kan
Linda Kelly
Helen Kier
Rita Lawhorn
Eileen Lee
Shirley Levine
Amber McBee*
B. Jean MacGee
Barbara McKinney
Natalie McMorris*
Medrith Maxton*
Louise Moore*
Lois Parks
Maggie Parks

Shirley Sadow
Alicia Sanford*
Eleanor Schlorman
Helen Schneider*
Alvina Schoch
Mary Schopler*
Jan Schroeder
Margaret Schueller
Donna Sipniewski
Emma Smales*
Catherine Smith
Lois Spiller
Sandra Wallick
Lila Swaney
Ruby Whited
Emma Wilson*
Bernadette Zavakos*
Agnes Zimmerle
Bernadette Zimmerle*

*Deceased

This is the 1946 Golden Gloves championship team, sponsored by the *Dayton Daily News*: (left to right) Bruce Malsa, Jack Chambers, Gates Thruston, Jesse Gooden, Charles Frazier, Richard Armstrong, Bob Galey, Lewis Logan and coach Joe Sekyra, Dayton's top boxer.

Carl Copp, charter member of DABA's Hall of Fame, with a 30-year ABC award (left); the lanes are inspected by Carl Herbert (above, right) and Belmont manager Nick Manos after a 300-game by Moon Mullins.

26

Boxing and Wrestling

Dayton had a reputation as a "good fight town" especially in the first half of the 20th century and even before that.

But the history of boxing is very tricky to research because there was never a record-keeping function of the longgone Montgomery County Boxing Commission, or in the files of the *Dayton Daily News* or the Dayton and Montgomery County Library.

For a number of years, the newspaper sponsored the Golden Gloves here and sent its amateur champions to Chicago for the national tournament. Hardly any history of the paper's involvement is available.

There were both pro and amateur fights staged almost weekly through the 1920s and 1930s when boxers were plentiful and the ticket prices were low. But whatever historical interest there may be seems to be tucked away in the minds of the surviving participants and spectators or perhaps in family scrapbooks.

The boxing Hall of Fame, located in the Dayton Gym Club, is loosely run by the Dayton Old Time Boxers club, a volunteer organization which also lacks any organized historical records.

George Freiberger, a onetime fighter who was the force behind the Hall of Fame project, runs the boxers group which has an annual induction banquet.

Three men who held the heavyweight championship have appeared in Dayton rings in action against opponents. Two of them, Jack Dempsey and Joe Louis, disposed of opponents here on their way to the top.

Muhammad Ali boxed three opponents in an exhibition in Welcome Stadium in the summer of 1971, during the period he was protesting American involvement in the Vietnam War.

Rocky Marciano made several appearances here in non-fistic situations because of his close friendship with Dayton jeweler Jack M. Werst.

Jack Dempsey's five round knockout of Terry Kellar on July 27, 1918, caused considerable excitement. Dempsey had been fighting for at least five years in relative obscurity in the west prior to that time and not even the *Ring Record Book*, the acknowledged source of accurate boxing records, has his full early record.

Dempsey, expertly handled by his legendary manager, Jack (Doc) Kearns toward his historic championship fight against Jess Willard a year later, was running through a string of one-round knockouts of obviously unqualified opponents through most of the year.

His appearance in Dayton against Terry Kellar was his 14th main event of 1918. Three weeks before coming here, he had a one-round knockout of Fred Fulton, a fighter of some reputation, in Baltimore. Dempsey had fought Kellar twice, winning 10 round decisions in Ogden, Utah and Ely, Nevada in 1916.

Dempsey and Kearns arrived in Dayton by train on Thursday, two days before the Saturday night fight and registered into the Holden Hotel just around the corner from Union Station at Fifth and Wilkinson Streets. The fight was staged in Westwood Park (later Sucher Park) and drew a capacity crowd of 2,500.

The account of the fight in the *Dayton Daily News* was under the byline of "Jerry." Jerry was city editor Jerry Conner who didn't use his last name when he wrote sports stories.

Jerry's version of the fight saw it as an exciting legitimate fifth round knockout. There were also two curious references to Kellar as a "local boy."

Whatever, there was a close relationship between Dempsey and Kellar as the two met in a four round exhibition in Washington D. C., March 1, 1919 and Kellar was one of Dempsey's sparring partners leading up to the July Fourth battle in Toledo when Jack savagely battered Jess Willard to win the title.

There are boxing figures and sports writers who have gone to their graves believing Kearns had slipped moistened plaster-of-paris into Dempsey's gloves to turn them into almost lethal weapons.

The appearance of Joe Louis on April 22, 1934 against Biff Benton in Memorial Hall didn't generate that degree of excitement. Louis was only

20 years old and in his second year as a pro fighter. But his awesome knockout punch was very much in evidence as he put Benton away in the second round of their fight.

Cincinnati native Freddie Miller, who won the featherweight championship in 1933, earned a 10-round decision over Willy Davies in Dayton, Sept. 20, 1935. Memorial Hall was used for boxing and wrestling for years before it was converted into a cultural center.

Joe Sekyra - The Best

There is general agreement that the best fighter to come out of Dayton was Joe Sekyra, a light heavyweight out of North Dayton's ethnic community who fought main events in Madison Square Garden in New York.

Sekyra was born in Dayton in 1907 and attended both Steele and Stivers High Schools. He got into boxing at an early age. In his era many boxers carried ethnic nicknames that today would be considered offensive. Sekyra's name appeared on the boxing posters that you'd spot on telephone poles or store windows as the "Bohemian Bearcat."

His biggest fight in New York was a losing decision in a 10-rounder to Max Schmeling Jan. 4, 1929, a year before the German fighter won the heavyweight title.

Although a lightheavy, Sekyra fought the best heavyweights of his time, twice winning decisions over James J. Braddock. Although Braddock went on to win the championship, no title was at stake in his meetings with Sekyra.

Sekyra had two fights with Tommy Loughran, one of the top light heavyweights of the era, the first ending in a draw. Loughran won a close decision in the second bout in New York.

Sekyra retired after being knocked out by Red Burman in a bout in Memorial Hall in 1935. After his retirement, Sekyra worked in the office of County Auditor Charlie Pfeiffer and served as coach of the team of Dayton Golden Gloves champions which went to Chicago for the nationals.

He moved to California in the mid-1950s and following a stroke, died in a Los Angeles suburban hospital Sept. 17, 1985.

Two other Daytonians who rose to the top in the 1930s were heavyweight Buddy Knox and lightweight Joe Marinelli.

Knox missed out on a shot at a title fight with Joe Louis when Billy Conn knocked him out in the eighth round May 26, 1941.

Barely five weeks later, Conn stunned the boxing world by being ahead on points against Louis into the 13th round before the Brown Bomber knocked him out.

Marinelli, turned pro after winning the Golden Gloves as a featherweight. His biggest victory in Dayton was a 10-round decision over Joey Archibald in the Patterson Boulevard Arena Aug. 2, 1940. Archibald had lost the world featherweight title via 15-round decision to Harry Jeffra in Baltimore on May 20 and had not fought again before coming to Dayton.

The boxing fans of the time weren't greatly enamored of Marinelli because of his style as a counter puncher rather than wielding a knockout punch. His victory over Archibald was by the narrowest of margins.

Manager Al Weill, who later managed Rocky Marciano, protested the verdict. The referee was Joe Sekyra, who voted 51-49 for the hometown boxer. Judge Art Rathgaber voted it even at 50-50 while judge Dave Hall voted 51-49 for Marinelli.

Dave Hall later became mayor of Dayton and is the father of Olympic diving medalist Sam Hall. Another son, Tony, was a standout college football player at Denison and later U. S. Representative from this area.

Action At North Side

It was only natural that North Side Field, known for its role in Dayton's baseball history, would have a boxing history as well.

From the time it opened in 1922, the park was the scene of frequent boxing cards of both the amateur and pro variety in the summer months.

Joe Sekyra was a frequent main event fighter early in his career, and his 1927 bout with Johnny Risko, advertised as the "Cleveland Baker Boy," is one of the best remembered.

The usually stylish Sekyra and Risko wound up in a slugfest at the end of their 10-rounder which was scored a draw. Once Sekrya started to climb in the national rankings, he had to pass up his home town for the big money in New York and other big cities.

In the early 1920s, lightweights Blockie Richards and Young Webb fought two memorable all-out battles. The first was a 12-round draw; Richards won the 15-round return battle. Later on, Frankie Bob, another local battler out of North Dayton, knocked Richards out, signalling the end of Blockie's hopes to work up to a title bout.

In his history of North Side Field, Roland Larke described Syd

Cohen as "a Jewish lad from England who moved to Canada and later to Dayton, who became a headliner at North Side Field." Cohen earned good paydays against fighters from the Italian community having two action-packed battles with Shifty Dando.

Other Daytonians who headlined programs at North Side Field were Joey Lawrence, Joe Delaney and Tommy Herman.

After The War

Although the boxing boom of the years between the two World Wars was long gone, bigtime boxing hung on for a while. Promoters like Jack Laken and Don Elbaum with national connections moved in and out of Dayton staging cards from time to time.

One well-remembered Memorial Hall battle involving a pair of name fighters took place on Dec. 7, 1949 between lightheavies Harold Johnson and Bert Lytell.

Johnson was only 21 with a record of 28 wins in 29 professional starts and on his way to the world championship at his weight. A crowd of 1,865 fans paid to see Johnson earn a 10-round decision over the more experienced Lytell. Lytell lived here for a while and was referred to being from Dayton.

One of the more interesting fighters from this part of the world was Springfield native Davey Moore, who turned pro after being a member of the 1952 U. S. Olympic team.

Moore eventually won the featherweight championship. He fought two main eventers in Dayton on his way up. He knocked out Eddie Cooper in the third round Nov. 20, 1953. A year later he kayoed Dick Armstrong in the sixth round of a Memorial Hall battle.

Davey won his world title in 1959, knocking out Hogan (Kid) Bassey. He lost his title and his life when he was knocked out by Sugar Ramos in the tenth round of their championship fight in Los Angeles, March 21, 1963. He died of brain injuries two days later at the age of 29.

The Hall Of Fame

The members of the boxing Hall of Fame are or were dues-paying members of the Old Time Boxers Club. They are listed with pictures (when available) on the wall of the main social room at the Dayton Gym Club.

Sekyra, Knox and Marinelli could be called charter members. The others, in no particular order on the gym club wall, are Allen Menachof, Jackie Dugan, Hack Wilson, Marion Condi, Buck Carroll, Tommy Devlin, Watson Woolam and Tish Kishner.

Also Johnny Lucas, Bobby Kraft, Reach Devlin, Pete Manley, Eddie Miller, Buddy Dillon, George (Sugar) Costner, Luther Morgan, Jeff Zenni, Carmen Ryan, George Mitchell, Bobby Vales and Roger Blosser.

Also Pat Aiello, Phil Flint, Al Poffenberger, Ray Dillon, Richard Branch, Mike Mantia, Clifford Six, Morris Moss, Babe Dare, Robert Tschudi, William Woodie, Ralph Dillon, Robert Neria, Lou Barney, Eddie Brant, Claude Waldon and Dick Vest.

The name of George (Sugar) Costner deserves mention. Costner is a Cincinnati native who, while he never held a championship, fought the best middleweights in the country in a career that began prior to World War II. He was twice knocked out by Sugar Ray Robinson and once by Jake Lamotta.

Costner went blind because of his boxing injuries, the problem starting with a detached retina. Later he was a member of the Ohio Civil Rights commission. He lived in Dayton for 15 years before moving back to Cincinnati

One of the most recent popular pro boxers out of North Dayton was Eddie Brant, a colorful lightweight (real name Roy Call) who came on the scene in the late 1940s when Dominic (Dee) Mantia and Lee Hammond were promoting fights under the banner of the Northern AC.

The unpredictable Brant won 103 of 137 professional fights which carried him around the country. He retired in 1959, but has been a judge and referee whenever local club fights have sprung up.

The Pro Wrestling Era

Contrary to the sensationally staged blood and guts matches involving caricature athletes on television today, professional wrestling was once an honest, legitimate sport.

There is no precise year to measure when it began to become more show business than man-to-man competition and it would be impossible to pin down either on the national or local levels.

Wrestling matches were frequently staged in Dayton before John W. Collins came onto the scene as a promoter in 1928. Collins, who had come to Dayton as a sports writer for the *Dayton Herald* in 1916 was clearly ahead of his time as a promoter.

Starting with his first effort in March, 1928 at the Eagles Hall near downtown on South Main Street, the Quality Athletic Club, which was the corporate name of the business was involved in staging weekly events on Tuesday night.

The shows at various outdoor sites in the summer months and indoors in the winter were still going regularly in 1968 when Collins retired and Little Mickey Friedman popped up in still another promotional capacity.

Collins was associated with Al Haft of Columbus, who set up the booking network which provided the wrestlers who appeared regularly here as well as Toledo and Columbus and occasionally in other Ohio cities. Collins referred to Haft's operation as "the territory," meaning that when headliners like Bobo Brazil or Don Eagle were in the area, they would be working three or four nights a week in different towns. Haft provided the wrestlers for Collins' first Dayton promotional event in McCabe's Athletic Club which had a capacity of 800.

"I thought Al was off his rocker," Collins was quoted in a story at the time of his retirement. "He made us give away several thousand free tickets. Well, the night of the show was place was packed. We took in only $89 but the next week it was packed again with no free tickets."

In the 1930s the top names in the country, Jim Londos, John Pasek, Jim Browning, the Dusek brothers and the others appeared in Dayton. Londos was generally recognized as world champion. A Dayton favorite was "Gentle John" Kilonis, one of the early villains who got the crowds worked up to a peak of excitement.

One of the legends of Dayton's wrestling is that the original Gorgeous George made his debut here. The story is that Collins persuaded Marj Heyduck, the feature columnist of the *Dayton Herald*, to do a column about the wrestler getting his permanent wave in a local beauty parlor.

Although several Gorgeous Georges have appeared over the years, the original was George Wagner. He entered the ring wearing a gorgeous golden gown, carrying flowers and attended by a valet. The valet, of course, worked into the act from the corner.

One of Collins' masterpieces of hype involved Gorgeous George. On an August night in 1950, George was going against one of the notorious villains of the time. Oregon McDonald entered the ring at the old arena on

Perry street (where the RTA bus garages are located now) wearing an outfit of burlap sacks stitched together and clinging to a bouquet of dead flowers which he flung at the gorgeous one. The confrontation started before the opening bell.

Marj Heyduck's role in Dayton journalism covering wrestling was unique. Even though she was a featured columnist on what was then called "the Modern Living section," Heyduck covered the weekly Tuesday night bouts and wrote columns in the Wednesday afternoon paper under the byline of Kid Heyduck.

The winter wrestling shows were held in Memorial Hall before it was converted from a multi-purpose arena into the concert hall it is today. Collins had a number of outdoor locations, the last of which was Sucher Park at the intersection of Western (now James H. McGee boulevard) and Rosedale avenue in West Dayton.

Collins was a native of Portsmouth and worked for the *Portsmouth Times* before coming to Dayton. He was the first paid publicity man for the Grand American Handicap before Jimmy Robinson came on the scene with that group.

Collins and Al Clark, the sports editor of the Dayton Herald, also staged an outdoor show called Annie Oakley Days on the ATA trapshoot grounds. But it was his 40 years of wrestling promotions that secure him his place in Dayton sports history.

Most of the time the eight or ten wrestlers on the Tuesday card would drive down from Columbus in two cars and go back up old Route 40 after the events were over. Haft owned a motel on that highway on the East side of Columbus.

Today, the contestants are more colorfully outfitted and given the star television treatment, but the antics in the ring look familiar to anyone remembering the Haft-Collins years.

27

Horses

There were brief attempts to stage thoroughbred racing at the Montgomery County Fairgrounds in the early 1930s, but a combination of low quality horses and unruly spectator conduct, to say nothing of the Great Depression, led to the Fair Board cancelling the last lease. Besides, there was no state regulated pari-mutual wagering.

Present Fair Board members and management could not verify the reports of such unruliness, nor have they any record of the thoroughbred racing itself.

Since World War II Dayton racing fans, and there are many, have regularly trekked to Cincinnati's River Downs, Northern Kentucky's Latonia or Beulah Park near Columbus to satisfy their betting urges.

The standardbreds still pull their sulkies during the Montgomery County Fair every year but only during that brief time.

A number of standardbred owners do stable their horses on the grounds and the horses and riders frequently can be seen riding exercise rounds, especially in the spring at the start of the season.

A number of Dayton residents are owners of thoroughbreds and two prominent names pop out in linking our town to horse racing. Interestingly both started their careers highly regarded in a different sport.

George A. Smith was once talked about by Ohio State golf coach Bob Kepler as a potential star on the PGA tour the same way the Buckeye coach was talking about Jack Nicklaus a few years later. Smith is now a successful owner and breeder.

Jim Morgan, who starred in high school basketball at Stivers and later at the University of Louisville when that school was building to national prominence, is currently one of the nation's top trainers.

Smith grew up in East Dayton and dabbled around in several sports at Stivers High School.

"I was a pretty small kid at the time," he recalled, laughing about growing up to be a 6-foot-2, 180-pound golfer who captained the Buckeye golf team to the Big Ten championship.

When he graduated from OSU in June of 1954, he had been in ROTC and went into active duty in the army as a second lieutenant. A year later in July of 1955, his life was changed when he became victim of a severe case of polio a few years before the vaccine came into being.

"I had big dreams of a career in pro golf, but all those died during the year I spent in an army hospital,'" he said.

It was a long and frustrating year, the medical attempt to restore full use of his legs was a losing cause.

"I had a lot of time to think, and it was discouraging to realize I could never play golf or compete in any physical sport," he said. "I thought about what I wanted to do and the idea came to me to get a real estate license."

That decision paid huge dividends as Smith found himself in the right time and place going into business in the Centerville area, just turning from a sleepy village into the booming economic area it is today.

George credits the late Dr. Robert Austin, an OSU graduate and longtime friend, with getting him interested in racing. Meanwhile, Smith was investing in some of that rapidly appreciating land on his own.

"Dr. Austin was enjoying some success with his horses, and I started going to the tracks," he said. "He was a marvelous man who did many things for me in many different ways."

In 1959, George went into partnership with George Zimmerman, a former golfing buddy, to purchase their first horse. The four year old gelding, named *Pineapple*, turned into an excellent investment, earning over $100,000 in purses racing at tracks in Florida, Chicago and Atlantic City.

Another influence on Smith's conversion to racing was Al Polk, who had owned racing stock for a number of years. Testimony to Smith's regard for Austin and Polk is the fact George's son, now active with him in real estate and racing, is named Austin Kepler Smith. His daughter is named Amy Polk Smith.

Through the 1960s, Dr. Wilbur Johnston, another of George's friends, became partners with him in several horses. It turned out to be a fateful partnership as the dentist went with Smith into the establishment of

Woodburn Farm in 1970. It was the first breeding farm for thoroughbred racers in southeastern Montgomery County. A number of standardbred owners have bred their horses in the area.

In 1977, Jim Morgan opened Wendover, where some outstanding racing stock has been bred and trained. Before that Tal Piper had opened Green Meadows Farm, just across Nutt Road from Morgan's dream farm. Wendover and Green Meadows shared a water source, pumping it into a small lake from an underground well.

After Piper's death in 1981, his racing operation went by the boards and Sam Morgan, Jim's brother, acquired most of the land for housing and condo development.

Two years after it opened, Woodburn's equine roster included 39 mares, 18 with yearling foals at their side, three stallions, 11 yearlings and a pair of two year olds.

Much of Woodburn's reputation as a successful breeding farm can be traced to Al Polk's *Grand Central*, who dominated the farm for two decades. In 1983, when *Grand Central* was nearing the end of his reign at age 22, the Ohio Thoroughbred Breeding Association credited him with having sired winners of 768 races with purses in excess of $4 million.

One of his better known sons was the aptly named *Grand Action*, co-owned by restaurant partners Joe Kiss and brother-in-law Joe Samu, who earned $275,296 in his career. Trained by Morgan, *Grand Action* captured the first running of the $50,000 Ohio Lottery Millionaire Stakes at Thistledown in 1974.

The Kiss-Samu partnership had another winner in *Grand Dandy*, foaled a year after *Grand Action*, who earned $150,343 before he had to be destroyed after a leg infection. Joe Kiss was involved in getting Jim Morgan started when the latter took the risky gamble going from successful high school coach to training horses.

Another Woodburn sire was *My Hope*, whose son, *Commissioner Gabe* earned $220,000 in his lifetime. The horse was named for Dr. L. J. Gabel, the Dayton veterinarian who was at one time chairman of the state racing commission.

"We're proud of the horses we have bred for a lot of owners in this area," Smith said, speaking for himself and Dr. Johnston.

"*Sweet Audrey* was the best filly in the state of Ohio for the last 30 years," he said. Smith may be a mite prejudiced in that he and Johnston owned the filly themselves.

"She proved herself when she won the $55,000 Falls City Handicap in the Fall meeting at Churchill Downs in 1980," George counters. "She was running against some of the top fillies in the country."

Smith was in the stands watching the $50,000 Criterion Handicap in Florida's Tropical Park when the *Frogman* was the winner in 1994 and *Classic Invitation* in 1995. Both colts were foaled at Woodburn.

The most recent pride and joy from Woodburn is *Franchise Player*, a colt that won the $100,000 Red Smith Handicap at Aqueduct in November, 1994. The horse is owned by Austin Smith. The young Smith, who is known as Kep to his friends, calls that victory "my claim to fame."

If horses that came into the world on Woodburn Farm have made their mark in the major leagues of racing, the same is definitely true of trainer Morgan as well as his Wendover farm, two miles east of Woodburn.

The Morgan family migrated north to Dayton from a poverty-stricken hamlet in Leslie County, deep in the Kentucky mountains.

Jim came to Dayton in the fourth grade and grew up into a backcourt standout on Stivers basketball teams that won city league championships in his sophomore and senior seasons in the early 1950s under coach Skip Larue.

Heavily recruited by the University of Dayton, he turned them down to enroll at the University of Louisville at a time when coach Peck Hickman's team was an archrival of UD.

His introduction to horse racing came during his years at UL. He worked as an usher at Churchill Downs during the spring meetings, climaxed by the running of the Kentucky Derby.

"Churchill Downs was another world for me, all that pageantry and beauty," he said looking back. His first year working at the track was 1953 when long shot *Dark Star* paid $51.80 on a $2 ticket by upsetting the favored *Northern Dancer*.

Morgan was drafted by the Syracuse Nats in 1957 but the salaries in the pro league weren't that attractive and he wound up coming back to Dayton and taking a job as head basketball coach at Stebbins, a new suburban school. He started with a contract for $5,700, just about what he could have made as first year pro.

Morgan posted a 109-57 record over eight seasons at Stebbins, but racing was in his blood. He had gone to Stivers with the two Georges -- Smith and Zimmerman -- and he had gone to the tracks with them frequently in the summers. He made his first monetary investment in 1959, putting up $1,000 to share ownership in a filly with Dr. Wilbur Johnston. By 1966, he made the dramatic, risky move.

"It was something I had to do," he explained. "I knew I would never be happy until I tried."

He made arrangements for his wife, Barbara, to control their $4,500 in savings and the family car. Leaving Barbara and his two children, he headed for Florida to begin at the bottom, as a groom.

Sleeping in a barn at the tracks and eating at fast food outlets, he hung on awaiting an opening, for someone to give him a horse to train.

Brother Sam Morgan, who at the time had not yet advanced in the business world to the solid position he enjoys today, went to restaurant owner Kiss, a sports follower and very generous man, who had advanced Jim some cash to start. Kiss came through a second time.

"Without Joe, I would never have made it," Morgan told everyone at the time Kiss died early in 1995.

Morgan's early success as a trainer was at Ohio tracks, particularly River Downs and Thistledown. He saddled his first winner in April, 1967, at Beulah, having acquired *Dames Red Boy* as a $1,500 claimer. The horse won his first five starts and Morgan was on his way.

His breakthrough into higher quality horses came that same year at Keeneland when he sent Al Polk's *Grand Central*, the horse destined to become such an exceptional sire, into the winner's circle.

Over the years, Morgan has never missed a spring meeting at Keeneland. Jim is a sentimental man with a deep love for Kentucky and his roots.

Dr. Austin turned a colt named *Federal Street* over to Morgan and the horse won over $200,000 in his career. In the 1972 meet at Thistledown, Jim saddled 11 stakes winners.

His horses have been winners in the two richest races staged at River Downs, the Cincinnati track adjacent to the former Coney Island amusement park. He won the $200,000 Miller High Life Cradle Stakes with *Wild Brigade*. His *Rose of Wendover* won the $187,000 Basinet, the richest filly event at the Downs.

He's sent 11 winners to the post in the $100,000 Governors Buckeye Cup at Beulah.

When he invested heavily in establishing the Wendover Farm in 1977, he was paying tribute to his remote birthplace. Wendover isn't on Kentucky maps but the hamlet exists and Jim likes to think of the farm named for his birthplace as his base of operations although he has a home in Florida.

One of his horses was named for Bill Monroe, the legendary blue grass fiddler. *Bill Monroe* the colt turned out to be good enough to earn Ohio Horse of the Year honors in 1981, just as *Grand Action* had nearly a decade earlier

Earlier, he won the 1975 Ohio Derby with *Brent's Prince*, a 15-to-1 choice at the bettor windows.

He has bred horses at Wendover named after Skip Larue, his Stivers basketball coach as well as Peck Hickman, his college coach, assistant John Dromo, who succeeded Hickman, and Frank Camp, the UL football coach when he was there.

He has saddled stakes winners for Dayton owner/partners George Zimmerman and Charles Zwiesler, Daytonians who have had considerable success with their equine interests.

But Morgan's success hasn't been confined to this area. He's well-known in Florida, Arkansas, Louisiana and at east coast tracks.

Morgan had to survive a life-threatening heart attack in 1993, but he bounced back and headed for the track the day he checked out of the hospital. The trainer, who turned 61 in 1995, maintains a heavy schedule still, but he is considering putting Wendover up for sale.

Whatever the outcome, Woodburn owners Smith and Johnston intend to keep going and hope that Wendover will remain a breeding farm in what horse owners like to think of a "Little Lexington" corner of southeast Montgomery County.

Woodburn Farm founders Dr. Wilbur Johnston (above, left) and George Smith with *Sweet Audrey*, once described as the best filly in Ohio.

Jim Morgan, one of the top trainers in the nation, gave up a promising NBA career for the track sport, investing in Wendover Farm. The jockey is Tommy Meyers.

28

Hockey

Ice hockey was introduced to the Miami Valley when the Troy Bruins made their debut in the International Hockey League going into the 1951-52 season.

Playing in the then-new Hobart Arena, the Bruins participated eight seasons in the league. Ken Wilson, who had been sent in by the IHL to organize the team as the general manager, continued with the team through its existence.

Julius Swick, Julian (Dad) Sawchuck, Norm McAtee, Guy LeClerc, Bill Murphy, Jim Campbell and Fred Evans came to Troy to play with the Bruins and all settled in the city after their playing careers.

The Bruins enjoyed a reasonable degree of success in the beginning, but as larger cities joined the IHL, operating costs kept going up. The Hobart Brothers Corporation, which had built the Arena and was underwriting the hockey losses, pulled the plug after the 1958-59 season.

Until the privately-financed Hara Arena became a reality, there was no ice surface in a large enough building available for professional hockey in Dayton. So there would be a five-winter gap before the sport surfaced again in this immediate area.

Aware that the new building in Dayton could accommodate an IHL franchise, commissioner Andy Mulligan, Ken Ullyot, longtime owner-coach of the Fort Wayne Komets and Ken Wilson, then with the league, believed a Dayton team would help the IHL. They went to work seeking financial backing from Canadian hockey friends for a Dayton franchise.

Enter Lefty McFadden, former sports writer, who for the previous five years operated the Dayton and New Bremen auto racing plants.

"There was a meeting at which the Dayton sports editors and television sports anchors were invited to hear the proposition from the league,"

McFadden said in recalling the start. "I assumed I was there because I was doing a radio sports show on WONE.

"Wilson, Ullyot and Mulligan took me aside and said they thought I was the guy who could get the franchise going. The problem was there was no Canadian money. The deal was, I would have five weeks to come up with $44,000 which would get Dayton into the IHL."

McFadden's plan was to sell 44 shares at $1,000 each to 44 different businessmen and sports figures.

"I didn't want anyone to have more than one share of the stock," he said. "Somehow, we made it with two days to spare," McFadden said. "Now I had a franchise, but no coach, no players and no experience in the sport."

That's how the Dayton Gems were born.

Some of the investors made up the officers of the corporation. George Flanagan was chairman of the board. Jack Reeder was president, Dr. Art Bok, vice president, J. Ramsey McGregor, treasurer and Barbara Brigner, executive secretary.

"Mulligan and Ullyot suggested I go after Warren Back to be our player-coach, and that turned out to be a great move," McFadden said.

Back, a native of Medicine Hat, Alberta, had come through Canada's structured youth hockey development system. Although only 27 when he came to Dayton, had spent seven seasons in the IHL, three at Louisville and four at Muskegon.

"Warren was and is a deeply religious, good family man and just the kind of a man we needed," McFadden put it. "We got a bonus because he had tried out twice with the Boston Bruins of the NHL and Lynn Patrick, the general manager, knew and respected him.

"That's how we got tied into the Boston farm system and it worked out so well," McFadden said, admitting he was a little taken aback at coming to the franchise with so little knowledge of the sport.

There had been another major problem in the rush to finish construction of the Hara Arena, named for the owner-brothers Harold and Ralph Wampler. A nearly disastrous accident occurred when a natural gas line into the offices at the front of the building had not been turned off.

The cigar-smoking Harold was on a stepladder doing some minor repair near the line. The resulting explosion blew off the front the building. It was something of a miracle that neither Harold nor anyone else was seriously injured.

"We played our first game with plastic covering the front of the building," McFadden recalled. "The Wamplers really went all out to make it possible for us to play."

A few things were missing when the first on-ice practice was called just two weeks before the season. The two goals and nets had not arrived, there were no goalie pads and there were only three pucks, one of which split in two during the workout.

Somehow Back put together a lineup that produced a 5-2 opening night victory over the Port Huron Flags. A crowd of 2,871 watched the game the night of Nov. 1, 1964.

The first goal was slapped into the net by center Al Cleary midway through the first period. Guy Trottier, who was to become a longtime hockey figure here and in 1995 an assistant coach with the Dayton Bombers, scored the second goal almost immediately.

Coach Back played center on the first line and the defense was anchored by Ted Lebioda, a grizzled veteran who had broken into the IHL with the Troy Bruins back in the 1952-53 season. Ludger Doucet, who was to get unwanted national attention several weeks later and is something of a legend in the history of the Gems, had in excellent night in the nets. He had 18 saves in a sizzling third period.

Doucet was a 21-year-old French Canadian who played without a face mask as did the majority of goaltenders up to the 1960s. In one of the early Gems games he took a sizzling shot squarely on the bridge of his nose. The result was two enormous black eyes which made him look like a comic cartoon character. A picture of Doucet's distorted face was sent out over the Associated Press wirephoto network and ran in many newspapers across the country. Playing behind a not-so-solid defense, that shot wasn't the only thing to mar Ludger's youthful countenance.

"He wound up with 111 stitches that season," Lefty said.

When Pat Rupp joined the Gems in mid-season, he took Ludger's job and wore a mask.

"Ludger's face was still swollen when I got here," Rupp said, aware that oldtimers liked to taunt a goalie with a mask. But Pat wisely wanted no part of proving himself a macho man that way.

General manager McFadden's biggest coup of the first season was persuading the IHL to lift the suspension of Bob Bailey. Bailey, playing with the Fort Wayne Komets, had been suspended after assaulting a game official 22 games into 1963-64 season. Bailey had 20 years of pro hockey experience all over the map including the Cleveland Barons of the AHL, the Toronto Maple Leafs, Detroit Red Wings and San Francisco Seals.

The Gems needed help and that may have influenced Andy Mulligan's decision to provide the team with a gate attraction. In that respect Bailey didn't disappoint. A brawler by nature, he put some fire into the team and managed to display his "bad boy" reputation by drawing a number of fines and suspension for badgering the whistle blowers.

"We had three teams that first year," Back recalled. "We had one coming, one playing and one going."

This was a reference to the constant shuffling of personnel. While many of the players coming in weren't solid additions, goalkeeper Rupp was an invaluable exception.

A native American, he had played on the 1964 U. S. Olympic team at a time when this country had never fared well in the Games. He belonged to the Philadelphia team of the Eastern League and wasn't happy there. The Gems purchased his contract.

Although no one has ever researched the numbers, McFadden believes that Rupp played more games as a Gem than any other player. He finished the 1964-65 season here and became the No. 1 man at a time the unfortunate Doucet had a good following among Dayton fans.

"The biggest thing we managed to do that first year is something Lefty and I talked about during the season, trying not to finish in last place," coach Back said.

The Gems finished fifth in the six team league, one point ahead of Muskegon. The Gems made legitimate solid strides the second year, winning 33 games (10 more than the first season) and making the playoffs.

Trottier and Bailey tied for the team scoring lead with 132 points, each man just one point short of Fort Wayne's Bob Rivard, the IHL leader. Rupp was in the nets for 69 of the 70 games.

The Gems upset Fort Wayne in the first round of the playoffs but lost to Port Huron for the championship.

The Gems were building a solid team following, thanks to their performance on the ice, McFadden's promotion and the exciting radio coverage they were getting from Lyle Steig, who had broken into broadcasting in his native Port Huron and understood the game.

John Huffman, a Dayton high school teacher who later worked for the Gems in several capacities, was an enthusiastic supporter and statistician.

"In our first year, between us, John and I appeared at 200 meetings, from the Rotary club to the PTA, talking hockey," McFadden recalled.

In their third season, the Gems won the regular season championship, finishing 10 points ahead of Fort Wayne with Trottier again making a strong bid for the league scoring title.

Before moving up to a higher classification, Trottier was the first Gem to be honored on the official All-Star team. He was named second team at right wing in the 1965 and 1966 selections before making the first team in 1967. He was joined on that first team by Moe Benoit on defense.

Back had taken himself off the playing roster and made himself a bench coach in that third season.

"We were getting enough good players by then," he said, referring to the arrival of Bob Regis, Sid Garant, Gerry Moore, Pat Donnelly and Gerry McMillan.

Thinking of the future, Back had become associated with Price Brothers. a major Dayton manufacturer of building materials.

"I knew if I stayed in hockey, I would be moving on," Back said. "Going into what was my fourth season, I wasn't thinking any further down the road than two years. I never did like the travel and being away from my family. As it turned out, I had the opportunity to join Price Brothers and I went ahead and took it."

By 1995, Back was associated with Woolpert, an engineering consulting firm. He and Mary Rose have raised their family of four, a son and three daughters. He looks back on his years with the Gems as a positive achievement in helping popularize the sport.

His last team finished second to Muskegon in the regular season and missed the Turner Cup, beaten 4 games to 1 by the powerful Mohawks. During the season, McFadden had made a trade for right wing Don Westbrooke, a very beneficial move.

With Back stepping aside, McFadden felt he had a team capable of going all the way and on the advice of his friends in the Boston organization, offered the coaching job to Larry Wilson, a veteran center who had a long career in the American Hockey League.

Wilson's two seasons with the Gems are looked back upon as the Golden Age of hockey in Dayton. The 1968-69 season was a clean sweep for the Gems. Wilson's men won the regular season title by a single point over Toledo and then roared through the playoffs for the Turner Cup with nine straight victories, an IHL record that still stands.

Westbrooke won the league scoring title with 118 points, a comfortable 14 over second place Bert Fizzell of Columbus. The left wingman on the line with Westbrooke was Duncan Rousseau, who was fifth in league scoring with 99 points.

Defenseman Al Beaule was a first team All-Star and the team had two fine goalies in John Adams and Rupp. Adams had come on in the 1968-69 year when Rupp had left the Gems to play a second time with the U. S. Olympic team.

Other regulars on the Turner Cup champs were Cliff Bristow, Moe Benoit, Sid Garant, Gerry Macmillan, Gordy Malinoski, Barry Merrell, Gerry Mazur, Lorne Weighhill, Duke Asmudsen and Mike Corbett.

A year later the IHL was split into North and South Divisions. The Gems won the South regular season title then captured their second Turner Cup with playoff victories over Muskegon, 4-2, and Port Huron, 4-3.

Westbrooke again won the league scoring title with 121 points, again beating out the Columbus star, Fizzell. Barry Merrell was ninth in the league scoring stats with Mike Dumas the No. I goalie.

This time the playoffs were more of a challenge with the Gems surviving a tough six game series over Muskegon, which won the Northern Division title. Then came a seven game battle to hold off Port Huron.

"This was a very exciting time for all of us," Rupp said. "There was a lot of excitement not only at the games but in the community. I don't think any of us dreamed there would be money problems down the road."

Rupp retired after the 1972 season, stayed in Dayton as a financial consultant and was still operating his own financial business as this was being written.

Wilson had an opportunity to move up, offered the coaching job with the Providence Reds in the American Hockey League.

McFadden selected Garry Moore from the playing ranks to replace him and the Gems continued to win the next two seasons, finishing third in both of Moore's two years.

Jim Anderson replaced Moore and the financial concerns begin to mount. The operating costs kept climbing.

"We paid a dividend in nine of the 10 years I was in charge," McFadden said. "But you could see the problems ahead."

McFadden left to join the Washington Capitals of the NHL, taking advantage of the opportunity to reach the major league. Whether it was Lefty's departure or not, things were never the same with the Gems.

Tom McVie, who had a stormy playing career, had been hired in the dual capacity of general manager-coach going into the 1973-74 season, McFadden's last. McVie didn't like front office work. Automobile dealer Jack Walker, who had become president of the team, offered the front office job to Bucky Albers, who had been covering the team for the *Journal Herald*.

While McVie wanted out of the GM responsibilities, he didn't like taking orders from Albers. Front office turmoil quickly developed when the coach formed an alliance with majority stockholder Ralph Skilken, Sr. to ignore having to work with the former sports writer.

Jack Walker resigned as president and Carroll Studebaker was named to succeed him. Albers resigned at the end of a stormy season. Ed Ralph, the public relations director, did most of the front office work the next year as McVie resumed the title of general manager.

The Gems captured their third and last Turner Cup in the 1975-76 season. McVie had an opportunity to take over the coaching job with the Caps in the NHL and departed in mid-season. Ivan Prediger coached the team through the playoffs.

The colorful Jim Pettie, who was headed to the NHL, manned the nets and was the last of the Gems with a strong personal following. Other standouts on the team included Jim Bannatyne, Larry Bolonchuk, Stan Jonathan, Gordy Lane, Brian Kinsella, Mike Powers and Bill Riley.

Despite the Turner Cup, the franchise was submerging into a sea of red ink. The Gems were losers on the ice for the first time in 11 years in the 1976-77 season and did not operate the next two seasons. An attempted revival in the 1979-90 season ended with the team finishing 11th in the 11-team league.

Hockey made a successful return to Dayton in the 1991-92 season when the Dayton Bombers made their debut in the East Coast Hockey League, an entry level professional operation.

The man who put the team into Dayton is Bud Gingher, who operates a successful mechanical contracting business in Peoria, Illinois. Gingher became a hockey fan watching the game in his home town. Although he was never an investor in the Peoria Rivermen, who play in the IHL, he became friendly with the owners there who advised him on the potential of filling the hockey void in Dayton.

Gingher contacted a close friend from college days at Bradley University, Arnold Johnson, who joined him in the ownership of the new Dayton franchise. Gingher is President/Governor and Johnson is general manager.

The Bombers are now in their fifth season and the attendance curve has been steadily going up. The ECHL pay scale is less than the IHL and the only problem with that is the better athletes are anxious to move up and are likely to play only one year with the Bombers.

Despite the shifting personnel, the Bombers have built a solid core of supporters. They attracted 132,699 fans to Hara in their first season, and it was up to 146,239 for the fourth year.

Claude Noel coached the team to regular season winning records in its first two seasons but the team was eliminated both times in the first round of playoffs. Jim Playfair was into his third season as coach starting the 1995-96 campaign, and the previous year got his team past the first round of the playoffs.

29

Soccer

In the rest of the world they call it football.

In the United States the game, played with the black-and-white round ball with an emphasis on footwork, is known as soccer.

It is a late blooming development on the local sports scene, and one with wide participation, but a controversial limited popularity as a spectator sport.

The frustrating aspect for the true soccer fan comes from the fact that thousands of boys and girls have played soccer in the CYO (Catholic Youth Organization) and the other programs for youngsters, mostly in the suburban communities. Yet few of them seem to develop an interest in following the game after their playing days are over.

The earliest visible soccer in the community was between ethnic group clubs, the best known being the Edelweiss, who were taking on club teams of Middle-European ancestry from cities such as Columbus, Cincinnati, Fort Wayne, Louisville and Indianapolis back in the 1920s.

The Edelweiss club was formed specifically as a men's soccer club. William Stegmeier, active in the club at this writing, is the German-American community's representative on the board of the annual World Affair held in the Dayton Convention Center. He says the club was chartered in 1926.

"The German immigrants in the club raised the money to purchase the 24-acre Edelweiss park, located on Wenger Road, and build one large playing field and one smaller practice field," Stegmeier explained.

At that time, Wenger Road was out in the country from downtown Dayton and the land was cheap. Today it is an oasis of valuable green space surrounded by the still developing Englewood community.

John Wagenbach, who helped reorganize the Edelweiss program

after World War II, believes soccer was being played in Dayton prior to 1926. Wagenbach has documents which list the names of the original Edelweiss players, none of whom survive.

That roster includes Fritz Bergman, Hans Bucheld, Karl Burbe, Hugo Behleu, Herman Glase, Fred Fisher, Ludwig Hofman, Fred Mang, Josef Marzluft, Joel Dieterman, Karl Greiner, Emil Schelwatt and Alfred Weber.

"The club's soccer program was inactive during World War II because of obvious anti-German feelings," Stegmeier says.

But it came back strong after the war with a new era of players. The zenith came in 1952 with the formation of the Ohio-Indiana Soccer League. It was made up of clubs from Cincinnati, Indianapolis, Fort Wayne, Columbus, Toledo and Dayton.

The key players in the 1950s included Pat Smith, the first coach at the University of Dayton when that program became a varsity sport in 1957. Paul Scheurmann, another Edelweiss standout, followed Smith as coach of the Flyers.

With the growing soccer youth programs, as well as those at high school and collegiate levels, the younger soccer players eventually had no need of the club and the Edelweiss teams began to weaken for a shortage of participants.

The club still exists today but mostly as a social group. The soccer played on the grounds today is, as Stegmeier puts it, "an old man's club with much passing and not much running."

University Of Dayton

The UD men's soccer program dates back to 1957 when the on-campus soccer club was granted varsity status. Coach Pat Smith, playing with Edelweis at the time, was a soccer enthusiast who became a collegiate level referee and has long been associated with the sport. He lives in Florida after his retirement.

The UD soccer program has never achieved NCAA post-season tournament level, but has built up a good student support level and represents the school well.

The most successful years were successive 11-3 years in 1975 and 1976 under coach Bob Richardson. A few years earlier coach John Schleppi's Flyers were 8-2-1 (1967) and 9-1-1 (1968).

Players Pat Obiaya and Bob Rohrback are in the UD athletic Hall of Fame.

The UD women's soccer team attained varsity status in 1984 at a time the university was moving to comply with the requirements of the Federal Title IX regulations governing women's sports.

The program got off to a very good beginning under coach Tom Schindler, who was the head coach for eight seasons. His second team went 15-5-1 in 1985 and a year later a shade better at 16-5 1.

Karen Kazmier, who played on those two winning teams, is the all-time goals leader in the program with 56. Standout players who followed include Lori Davis, Diane Coleman, Jenny Smith and Jenny Malloy.

Wright State

Men's soccer was the very first varsity sport on the agenda at the then new school across the Greene County line in Fairborn.

Under coach Bela Wollner, the Raiders played a 1968 schedule against small area colleges such as Wilberforce, Cedarville, the WPAFB club team and various junior varsity teams and posted an 8-3-2 record.

The schedule was upgraded to varsity level a year later and the Raider record dipped to 2-7-2.

The sport was discontinued for five seasons (1973-1977) but was resumed when the Raiders were planning ahead to play at the Division I level and join a league.

Greg Andrulis completed his 11th season as head coach in 1995, compiling an impressive overall record of 113-66-25. Two of his assistants, Brian Kohen and John Burgmeier played pro soccer with the Dayton Dynamo. The third helper is WSU grad Scott Rodgers, whose fulltime job is head of Soccer Centerville, a youth program in that community.

The alltime scoring leader list is headed by Rob Campbell (140), Manuel Baltres (107), Dan Durbin (107) and Bob Collins (102).

Defender Hilton Dayes was the MVP all four of the seasons he played (1982-1985) and later coached the women's team for seven seasons.

The women's program became a varsity sport in 1985, coached by Maggie Brandon.

Northmont

At the high school level, suburban schools Northmont, Centerville and Alter have accomplished considerable success, each of the three winning state championships in both boys and girls competition.

The sport has taken root very slowly in the inner city and the Dayton city schools have been far behind in both participation and enthusiasm.

George Demetriades is the coach who launched the boys program at Northmont in 1968 at a time it was a club sport.

Demetriades learned to play the sport at Salonika in his native Greece and played a year as a semi-pro before coming to this country upon earning an academic scholarship at the confusingly named Indiana University in Indiana, Pennsylvania.

He played for a while at the college level but his work load in class and at jobs to support himself caused him to give it up. He graduated in 1962 and eventually came to Northmont as a science teacher.

Since soccer became a varsity sport in 1976, Demetriades compiled a 289-47-21 record before his retirement after the 1992 season. His team captured the state championship in 1978 and 1988, the latter team going 25-0 and was ranked third in the nation.

His teams captured the league championship 10 out of 17 years of competition in the GMVC (Greater Miami Valley Conference). Fifteen of his former players have become high school or college coaches including Steve Spirk, head coach at Wilmington, and George Sherer at Marshall University.

After retirement from Northmont, Demetriades became an assistant coach at the University of Dayton where he aids UD varsity coach Roy Craig. Walter Slade, who played at Northmont, is the other Flyer assistant.

Bill Krintzline coached the Northmont girls to four state championships in the six seasons he was on the job. Joe Reed had started the Northmont program in 1980 when it was still a club sport.

Krintzline, who was never on the Northmont faculty, coached the program on a volunteer basis (1985-90), having gotten into soccer when his daughters were involved in the SAY, the soccer youth program in the area.

The championship years were 1985, 1986, 1988 and 1989. The 1986 group went 24-0 and the key players were Jean Klosterman, Lori Davis, who went on to be an All-American at UD, Karen Heil, Missy Mazzone and Debbie Krintzline, the coach's eldest daughter.

The 23-0-1 team in 1988 featured Kelly Klaus, Joy Tilly, Jenny Lewis, Dawn McGraw and Melissa Krintzline plus holdovers Davis and Heil.

Centerville

Gary Avedikian was building the Elks program at the same time Northmont was making a strong impression. The fact the two rivals were at opposite ends of Montgomery County helped focus attention on the sport.

Avedikian moved up from the prep ranks to become head coach at Ohio State, finishing his ninth season directing the Buckeyes in the 1995 campaign. A native of West Hartford, Connecticut, Gary is a graduate of Springfield, Massachusetts College, one of the nation's top physical education schools. He spent 10 years coaching in Connecticut high schools before coming to Centerville in 1973, just at the time soccer was elevated to the varsity level.

In his 14 seasons with the Elks, his record is an impressive 228-33-23 which led to his advance into the Big Ten. In addition to the 1984 state championship, his Centerville teams were state finalists on four other occasions. The Elks completely dominated the Western Ohio League, racking up the championship 11 straight years after the WOL adopted soccer.

An enthusiastic promoter of the sport, he is co-founder of the Ohio Scholastic Coaches Association, a three-time vice president and 1994 president of the National Soccer Coaches Association of America. As a soccer consultant with Nike, Inc., he is involved as a lecturer at soccer clinics and camps in this country and overseas.

"The 1981 state semi-final match we played against Northmont drew 8,500 people into Welcome Stadium on a cold, windy night," Avedikian recalls. "It was an electric atmosphere and I think it opened a lot of people's eyes as to how exciting the game can be."

The key players on Centerville's 1984 state champions were Sean Cox, captain Scott DeCuir, Mark Freidenmaker, Greg Harlow, Paul Howard, John Johannes, Dave Kinderdine, Kevin Konen, Jeff Miller, Dee Vaugh, Phil Wafford, captain of the defense, and Todd Young. Eight of those players went on to play college soccer.

The longest soccer game in Ohio history involved Centerville and Carroll High School in 1977. The game took three days to complete. At the time there was no overtime shootout and under the prevailing international rules, teams played until a game-winning goal was scored. The game started at 7:30 p.m. on Tuesday evening. With the teams tied at midnight, the game was halted and the exhausted players given the next day off.

When the game was resumed Thursday evening, Centerville finally won, 2-1, in the 25th overtime period. The completion of the game attracted a crowd of 6,000 and national interest.

The Centerville girls program developed much later, but Coach Don Skelton has directed it to the same level of area dominance enjoyed by the boys. Skelton, who operates a sporting goods store, started as a volunteer and is the only coach the girls squad has had. In his 13 seasons, the overall record is 234-26-25.

The Centerville girls had been runners-up in the state tournament on four occasions, coming close to matching their male counterparts. The standout girls who made headlines include Anne Sherow, who went on to star at North Carolina where she was MVP on a team that went to the NCAA tournament final round.

Emily Courtney is the alltime leading scorer with 93 goals. Cara Eichenlaub, Diane Coleman and Hollie Young led the team at different times.

Alter

The Knights' program came of age slightly behind the other two suburban powers but the boys captured state championships in 1987 in Class AAA and again a year later in Class AA.

The coach was Roy Bohaboy. The current Alter head coach is Bob Ellis, who was an assistant in the championship years.

The 1987 team had 19 seniors on the roster and went 31-3-2 in setting all kinds of school records.

Striker Tom Muzechuk scored the winning goal in the championship victory over Walsh Jesuit. The goalie was Mark Reichman backed by Ben Pickrel. Other senior standouts were Mark Schuermann and Dan O'Brien.

The 1988 team went 17-3-4. The captain was Ethan Cox, who had played a key role as a junior the year before. The others included Andy Gerdeman, Matt Bonanno, Josh Elmer and Scott Zimmerman.

As head coach, Ellis has guided his teams into the state semis on two occasions.

The Alter girls made the state semis for the first time in 1994 under coach Bob Kinderman.

The Dynamo

The ill-fated Dayton Dynamo came into being when Jerry Butcher, the owner and operator of the Englewood Indoor Soccer Arena, took the plunge of financing the project and putting the team together.

Butcher had played collegiate soccer at Wright State and later coached at Central State and the University of Dayton. He had a winning record in three of his four seasons with the Flyers (1980-83).

The Dynamo were put together to compete in what was called the American Indoor Soccer Association Challenge Cup in February of 1988, and they moved into the regular AISA season the next year.

"We finished dead last and naturally lost a lot of money," Butcher described it.

The Dynamo had been put together with a strong influx of local talent including Jeff Popp, Greg Ayers, Brian Kohen, Carl Powell, Eddie Ruff, John Bergmeier, John Luksic and Scott Molsenter.

In the first season they were overmatched and Butcher had to bring in talent from outside, including Tony Bono, the midfielder from Philadelphia who developed a strong personal following, and goalie Carlos Pena.

In their second season, the Dynamo won their division and in 1991 went into the stronger National Indoor Soccer League. But it was a losing financial proposition for Butcher, who went into bankruptcy at the end of the 1991 season and turned the team over to attorneys Dick Chernesky and Ed Kress.

The home court shifted from Hara Arena to the downtown Convention Center, but attendance didn't keep pace with rising expenses and the franchise moved to Cincinnati in 1994.

Fairmont High School and Ohio State championship diver Sam Hall won a silver medal in the 1960 Rome Olympics.His specialty was the 3-meter board.

Exercise guru and swimming teacher Lou Cox in training session with Tom Gompf, Stivers and OSU standout in 10-meter diving (below). Gompf won the bronze medal in the 1964 Tokyo Olympics. Hall and Gompf trained with Cox, preparing for a marathon run at age 75 (below, right)

30

Lou, Sam and Tom

Dayton has produced two diving champions who captured Olympic medals in a sport that has flourished here over the years mainly through the Dayton and Kettering YMCAs and private swim clubs.

Sam Hall and Tom Gompf are Olympians trained by Lou Cox, a legend in Dayton's sports history, who is remembered as a longtime champion of physical fitness.

Hundreds of Dayton men recall him as the man who taught them how to swim when the old downtown YMCA offered the only public indoor pool in the community.

Cox was born in 1907 in Yokahama, Japan to an American father and a Japanese mother. The family moved to Honolulu where Lou graduated from the high school operated by the Society of Mary, the religious order which founded and operates the University of Dayton.

That Marianist school directed a number of football players and other Hawaiian students to UD. Cox was among the latter, coming here and graduating in 1930 with a degree in mechanical engineering.

He never used that degree, finding employment difficult to come by in the Great Depression years. He was a strong swimmer and started off in a low-paying job as a swimming instructor with the YMCA, which was located then in what is now the City building at Third and Ludlow.

He stayed with the YMCA, moving with it to its present location on Monument Avenue as its first director of physical education and spent all but a few years of his working life there. He took time out in 1949 to do graduate study at the nation's best known school of physical education, the Springfield, Massachusetts College.

Cox had a personal regimen calling for running three miles a day. He did it in the streets of Oakwood, where he lived, in the summer time and around the YMCA indoor track in the winter. That dedication to conditioning allowed him to be in shape to run the full 26.5 mile Honolulu marathon in 1980 at age 73.

At the time of his retirement he said, "My career has been as rewarding as anything I could have wanted out of life. I can't imagine having spent my life in a place more attractive in so many ways than Dayton."

Cox developed a brain tumor in the summer of 1987 and died September 19th of that year, two months short of what would have been his 80th birthday.

Future Olympians Hall and Gompf were among the hundreds of young Dayton boy swimmers taught by Cox in odd-hours scheduling. Members of the YMCA swim teams in those years started their day with 6 a. m. workouts before they went off to their regular schools. Later in the day, pool time was limited to regular members and events.

In recent years, the Kettering YMCA with its sizeable indoor pool has been the development facility for later generations of men and women swimming competitors.

Not many Daytonians had ever paid much attention to water sports before Sam Hall came home from the 1960 Rome Olympics with a silver medal in the three-meter division, climaxing a brilliant career in collegiate and AAU diving competition.

Hall was 23 at the time of his first moment on the world stage. He is one of three brothers who made names for themselves in sports and later in the "real world."

Sam's younger brother, Tony, starred as a football player at Denison University and was honored at the national NCAA Convention in 1991 with a Silver Anniversary medal. The Silver Anniversary team honors athletes who have distinguished themselves in other areas.

Tony Hall has earned world-wide recognition for his campaign to eradicate world hunger as one of his primary interests as a member of the U. S. House of Representatives.

Other brother, Mike, was also a football player and has been a successful coach and teacher at the high school level in Ohio. The three are sons of Dave Hall, a successful business man and sports enthusiast, who was active in Republican party politics and served as mayor of Dayton in the 1960s.

Tony broke with his family along political lines by joining the Democratic party and was in his eighth term in Congress at this writing.

Sam was an all-around athlete when he entered Fairmont High School in the fall of 1952 but going into his junior year, gave up the other sports to concentrate on his diving.

At Ohio State, he was co-captain of the diving team through his last three seasons and racked up steady victories in the Big Ten. He was the conference champion at different times in the 1-meter and 3-meter boards.

Although his early success was on the 1-meter board, Hall began to concentrate on the 3-meter because the lower board was not on the Olympic schedule. As Big Ten and NCAA 3-meter champion in the spring of his senior year, his eyes were on Rome.

His family was in the stands as he qualified for the Olympics in Detroit and they went on to watch his fine showing in Rome.

Teammate Gary Tobian of UCLA, an experienced diver who had captured a silver medal in platform in 1956, won the 3-meter, edging Hall. Sam, in turn, edged out Ohio State teammate Juan Botella, diving for his native Mexico. Hall had to execute a difficult 2 1/2 somersault with a tuck to move past Botella on the 10th and final dive.

On his return to the U. S., Hall entered the political process by running for a seat in the state legislature as a Republican. At age 25 he found himself in the state house in Columbus long before brother Tony made his move into the political world in the other party.

At that point in time, Sam's future seemed to lie along conventional lines, but his career took an unexpected turn that eventually made a lot more headlines on the world stage than his Olympic achievement.

Sam was too restless or ambitious -- take your choice -- to follow in the footsteps of his wealthy father as a real estate developer. After failing to get interested in several business ventures, he began to get deeply involved in taking a stand against world communism.

He dropped out of sight in Dayton, eventually becoming a soldier of fortune. Sam floated in and out of a shadowy world of life as a mercenary and literally turned up in various corners of the world, Israel and Africa among them.

Anyone interested in the details of his convoluted adventure can read the book *Counter Terrorist*, which he wrote in 1987 after he spent seven weeks in prison in Nicaragua. He was captured fighting with a contra rebel detachment against the Sandanista government, which was delighted to show off the brother of a U. S. Congressman fighting the dirty little war in that Central American country.

Sam's release was obtained by American officials including brother Tony, and on his return to this country he appeared on numerous national television news shows including an interview on *60 Minutes*. He is out of the headlines in retirement in Florida as this was being written.

Tom Gompf grew up in East Dayton, graduating from Stivers High School, and followed Sam to Columbus on a diving scholarship. Unlike Sam, with whom he trained at the Y, Gompf developed as a platform (10 meter) diver, the phase of the sport calling for the ultimate in courage and body control. He was also a gymnast at Ohio State and earned All-American recognition in both sports.

He captured his bronze in the 1964 Games in Tokyo with an amazing comeback through the 10 dives in the championship round. He was in 18th place at one stage in the qualifying round, making it to seventh to survive. He started the final round and was consistent enough to climb into third to earn the medal.

By the time he won his Olympic medal., Gompf was competing for the Air Force, having also won his wings as a pilot.

The bronze medal was only the beginning of Gompf's involvement in the Olympics. He became active in the then newly established U. S. Diving Federation and was able to balance his role with that group to coincide with his regular work as a pilot for Pan American World Airways based in Miami.

He turned up as a judge in diving at the Munich Olympics in 1972 and was manager of the U. S. Diving team at the Montreal Games in 1976.

Kent Vosler, a native of Eaton, and like Hall and Gompf an Ohio State athlete, barely missed a medal off the platform in Montreal. Vosler, working off the 10-meter board, was nosed out for third place on the 10th and final dive by a Soviet.

The gold medal in platform was taken for the third straight time by veteran Italian diver, Klaus Dibiasi who was competing in his fourth Olympics. He had finished second ahead of Gompf in the Tokyo Games in his initial appearance.

The major development from the American point of view in Montreal was the appearance of 16-year-old Greg Louganis, who won the silver medal. Louganis went on to become a diving legend in later Olympics. A superb athlete, he is perhaps the greatest American athletic performer to "come out of the closet" as an admitted homosexual. He is currently following an acting career.

Vosler became diving coach at Florida, finished his medical training and followed his father's footsteps into optical medicine.

Gompf missed the 1980 Moscow Olympics when the United States boycotted them but was at Los Angeles in 1984 again as team manager. He was also chairman of the International Committee of the U. S. Diving Federation which dispatches teams to international events around the world. In that capacity, he has previously been with the divers at Pan American Games in Venezuela, Puerto Rico, Mexico and Columbia.

Renee Laravie was only 17 when she qualified for the U. S. Olympic women's swim team for the Montreal Games. The Alter High graduate competed but didn't qualify for the championship round.

Laravie went on to enjoy a standout career in NCAA competition at the University of Florida where she set a national record in the 100-yard breast stroke in 1979.

She also competed in the 100-yard and 200-yard individual medleys and swam with the school's freestyle 400 and 800 yard relays. Laravie had hoped to make the 1980 Olympic team, but missed out in the Trials and retired from competitive swimming.

31

Softball

Softball enthusiasts make a logical claim that their sport has the largest number of participants in the Dayton area.

Bowling aficionados challenge that claim, but they'll never make a believer out of Lou DeSaro.

DeSaro -- alias Mr. Softball -- is metro commissioner of this region for the ASA (American Softball Association) and maintains that 36,000 participants took swings in the spring and summer of 1995 at the under-hand-delivered pitches in men's and women's fast and slow pitch leagues.

There is no way of being positive as to the number of individuals, as the registration with the ASA is by teams. DeSaro pegs the number of teams at 2,000 in Montgomery County which adds up to a horde of players regardless of the number (maximum 18) on a team.

The ASA also sanctions the umpires, who have four area associations of their own.

Every weekend, there are anywhere from 15 to 20 open tournaments staged by independent promoters or team managers in the immediate Dayton area in addition to the regularly scheduled midweek leagues.

Sanford Thurman, Jr. directs the leagues utilizing the facilities of the City of Dayton Parks and Recreation department and had 411 teams registered in the summer of 1995.

The others in the ASA and DeSaro's domain include Montgomery County recreation department supervised leagues and those in Kettering, Moraine, West Carrollton, Miamisburg, Vandalia, Trotwood, Union and Phillipsburg.

Softball as a sport celebrated its 100th anniversary in 1987. It had a humble beginning, dating back to when a man named George Hancock devised a set of rules for the game, conceived as a a first cousin to baseball but with a less dangerous ball and smaller playing fields. At that time, the game started as "kitten ball" and a bit later "mush ball" with the term softball not coming into use until well into the 20th century.

Nearly all of the competition up to World War II was the fast pitch variety, but the growth of slow pitch in the 1940s was rapid.

The game was first played on City of Dayton playgrounds in the early 1920s, first using a 9-inch and then a 12-inch outseam ball. Only the first baseman and catcher wore gloves and baseball spikes were prohibited. About 1928 the 9-inch ball was dropped from the program and the 12-inch ball no longer had outseams.

The first lighted softball diamond was Edgemont Elms, located just south of the St. Elizabeth Hospital grounds.

Later Sucher Packing Company installed lights at its park on Western Avenue and the first lights at the Kettering Field complex were on diamond four.

In 1929, the Dayton Amateur Softball Commission was formed with Leslie Diehl as president, a position he held through 1947.

The Secretary-Treasurer position of the DASC automatically went to the City of Dayton athletic director because he was responsible for assigning the field and scheduling game times. Mike Solomon was the first municipal AD followed in order by Ellsworth Baer, John Somers, Ray Neff, Bob Anderson, Tom Taylor and Ed Knox.

In 1981, the job description of athletic director was abolished in a restructuring of the Divisions of Parks and Recreation into a single unit.

Jim Boyles, who made his mark in several different sports from his role as athletic director at Wright-Patterson Air Force Base, was the prime mover in the establishment of the Men's Fast Pitch Hall of Fame in 1965. Eight years later, Larry Chambers organized the Slow Pitch Hall.

Boyles came back as the organizer of the Women's Hall of Fame which includes both the fast and slow pitch versions.

Dayton is host to one national tournament each year that benefits the local economy to at least $2 million. That is the National Police Tournament in which lawmen from all over the country let their hair down and have a lot of fun while providing three days of non-stop action at the Kettering complex.

DeSaro says the economic benefits may be difficult to define, but a national regional tournament in September drew teams from nine different states and provided another $2 million boost to the Dayton economy. This tournament like the police tournament, and all softball activity, is open to spectators at no charge.

The softball fraternity holds an annual winter Snowball Tournament which raises $20,000 for the March of Dimes.

The Halls of Fame honor players, managers and nonplayers such as sponsors, umpires, scorekeepers and supervisors. As an example, the charter class in 1965 honored three fast pitch standout players in Maynard Brixey, Bertram "Toby" Leap and Talmadge "Ace" McKinney with Clarence "Shorty" Minzler as the honorary selectee. Minzler was one of the first umpires and founded that group's association. Over the years, he trained hundreds of umpires.

Softball Hall Of Fame

Year	Men's Fast Pitch	Men's Slow Pitch
1965	Maynard Brixey	
	Bertram "Toby" Leap	
	Talmadge "Ace" McKinney	
	Clarence "Shorty" Minzler*	
1966	Cloyd Carter	
	Ralph "Jock" Vogel	
	Basil "Rip" Zolman	
	Vic Lyons	
1967	Carl Clause	
	Margaret "Chuzz" Armpriester	
	Bill "Flub" McNay	
	Jim Boyles*	
1968	Tom Stahl	
	Jack Hulls	
	Jackie Fields	
	Bill Johnson*	
1969	Moxey Armpriester	
	Kenny Fox	
	Bob Shoemaker	
	Claude Schindler*	
1970	Mark Butts	
	John Arnold	
	Bill Early	

1971	Orville "Babe" Perkins	
	Leo McNees	
	Jack Miller	
1972	Bob Dineen	Ed Tate
	Jerry Reynolds	Everette Gray
	Hilby Silver	Bob Reed
	Homer Leisz*	
1973	Orville Smith	Dick Willis
	Olin "Lum" Jackson	Steve Iles
	Elwood "Sod" Sorrell	Jim Gift
1974	Mac Bulko	Vic Lyons
	Robert "Rip" Mayfield	Bill Troute
	Virgil "Jug" Zolman	Don Sponsler
	Jim Schwartz*	
1975	Bill Troute	Rex Warner
	Francis Gebhart	Jim Ruff
	Eugene Reed	Jerry Raiff
1976	Charles C. Childers	Jerry Sharritts
	Jim Ellis	Bob McMichael
	Loren "Pete" Murphy	Don Pierce
	Ray Counceller*	
1977	Charles Barlow	Ron Pohl
	Fred Pottenger	Ben Hardin
	Ernie Powell	Joe Tamaska
1978	Ed Sharp	Jim Boyles
	Martin "Moe" Spalding	Jim Turner
	George Williams	Norm Sharp
	Russ Willoughby*	
1979	Gil Ginter	Larry Chambers
	Stan Scott	Ron Brown
	Don Warner	Dan Rauch
1980	Herb "Grandpappy" Conley	Jack Jones
	Buford "Buff" Greer	Ed Kruskamp
	Charles P. Hicks	Jack Quick
1981	Harry Hively	Gary Butts
	Lowell Meyers	Bill Siekierka
	Steve Grant	Ray Zawadski

1982	Robert Caulfield	George Barnett
	Joe Gemza	Carel Cosby
	Bob Stewart	Ed McDonald
1983	Gerald Hamp	Dave Haeseker
	Donald A. Hutton	Jim Flanery
	Jess L. Waymer	Jim Collins
1984	Paul Johnson	Ed Vaughn
	Dewey Strine	Laverne Bailey
	Cal Calloway	Frank Seer
		George Cuny*
1985	Elmer C. Burns	Bob Vogelmann
	Gale Demaree	Don Wilson
	Ralph Palmer	Gary Barnes
		Neil Coleman*
1986	Stan Kavy	Jim Zink
	Denny Lewis	Chuck Nowlin
	John Pierce	Jerry Ward
1987	Melvin L. Easton	Bill Aldrich
	Mel Ramby	Don Maus
		"Dugan" Joyce*
1988	Emmett L. Hunt	Ken Alexander
	William R. Montgomery	Charles E. Barlow
	Robert E. Simison	Don Griever
		Carl T. Hines*
1989	Bob Jenkins	Terry Smith
	Chuck Nowlin	Jim True
	Bobby Haines	Jim Wessel
		Homer Leisz*
		Louis A. DeSaro*
1990	Walt Peck	Ed Beane
	Bill Skelton	Denny Braun
	Charles Turley	Knute Montgomery
		Clyde Brewer, Sr.
1991	Stephen "Butch" Macpherson	Jerry Booher
	Lawrence "Mickey" McNeal	Roger Clay
	Tom Wical	Bobby Harrison
		Mike O'Neal
		Joe Wannamaker*

1992	Charles D. Fearing	Jerry Powers
	Richard Heiser	Bruce Terry
		Dave Wood
		Timmy Pritchard*
		Falcon Club**
1993	Donald A. Weber	No Inductees
1994	Michael F. Gallagher	Kenny "Red" Booher
	Kenny Robinett	Merle "Don" Brunner
		Ray Huss
		Everett "Jess" Weidner
		Buck Erwin*
1995	No Inductees	Gary Pefley
		Bob Barlett
		C & L Carpet**

Women's Hall of Fame

	Women's Fast Pitch	Women's Slow Pitch
1977	Cecelia "Cele" Clark	
	Libby Smith	
	Ruby Wise	
	Margaret "Chuzz" Armpriester	
1978	Marilyn "Beno" Jackson	
	Elizabeth Medisch	
	Gert Reynolds	
	Russ Lyle*	
1979	Evelyn Hodgson	
	Natalie "Gerry" McMorris	
	Shirley Levine	
	Mickey McCroson*	
1980	Glenna "Lefty" Meyer	
	Rosalie "Rody" Sierschula	
	Joanne "Jo" Stewart	
	Ed Bausman*	
1981	Janice A. Heiser	
	Lois J. Hucke	
	Wilma Kies	
	Betty J. Palmer	

1982	Barbara Bowersock	
	Eleanor Huelsman	
	Sarah Hanby	
	Julia Carr	
1983	Betty Doughman Dillahunt	
	Evelyn Heiser	
1984	Barbara Smiley	
	Jerry Kroger	
	Beverly Weng	
	Vern Steck*	
1985	Barbara "Bobbie" Kymer	
1986	Clara Cochran	
	Carrie Jones	
1987	Claudine Woodruff	
	Lois Connaughton	
	Loretta Bowers	
1988	No Inductees	Clara Cochran
		Connie Jo McCarroll
		Ron King*
1989	No Inductees	Marilyn Lovett
		Maria Ferraro
		Karen Adams
		Ron Brown*
1990	No Inductees	Carrie Jones
		Lucy McClain
		Judy Peele
1991	No Inductees	No Inductees
1992	No Inductees	Kay Thomas
		Andrea D. Gray
		Doris F. Black
		Tonya L. Willhide
		Gary Smith*
1993	Cathy Conners	Cathy Conner Thompson
		Christina Sacksteder
		Debbie Milhause
		Barbara Balata
		Sandra Payne*

1994	Annie Stockes		Gloria Caldwell
			Terri Smith
			Kathy Staggs
1995	Dee Dull		Julie Caughey
	Beau Townsend**		Jan Deters
			Nancy Hittepole

*Honorary member
**Honorary Sponsor

Past Presidents, Dayton Amateur Softball Commission

1929-1947	Leslie Diehl	1967-1968	Jim Boyles
1948-1949	Hank Malloy	1969-1970	Ron Brown
1950-1951	Dan Wagner	1971-1972	Russ Willoughby
1952-1953	John F. McGee	1973-1974	Larry Chambers
1954	Clarence Minzler	1975-1976	Tom Griffin
1955	Hank Malloy	1977	Jim Strathopoulos
1956	Jim Schwartz	1978-1980	Clyde Brewer
1957	Ray Gillaugh	1981	Jerry McConnell
1958	Les Pointer	1982	George Cuny
1959-1960	Vic Lyons	1983-1984	Neil Coleman
1961	Ray Gillaugh	1985-1986	Bev Weng
1962	Hugh Turvene	1987-1988	Dick Burgmeier
1963	Dick Clark	1989	Denny Martin
1964	Jim Gift	1990-1993	Clyde Brewer
1965	Harry Bradbury	1994	Dick Burgmeier
1966	Ken Amick	1995	Clyde Brewer

Afterword

At Wright State and the University of Dayton they are referred to as "non-revenue" sports.

Those such as wrestling, volleyball, swimming, cross country, judo and field hockey are among other sports which have participants and a following and deserve some passing mention.

But they are either too recently on the scene in the historical sense or do not have sufficiently broad appeal to warrant the kind of research that went into this project on more popular athletic pursuits.

Likewise, youth programs such as Pee-Wee football and basketball may excite parents and friends, but the kids will have to mature and perform at higher levels to fit into the historical record.

And when they do, perhaps a writer in the next millennium may expand a similar study to included more activities.

The "Faces in the Crowd" segment in *Sports Illustrated* may be the metaphor to explain bringing this study to a close with a passing salute to thousands of faces in the crowd who participate in Dayton's sporting scene but do not make headlines.

In the last four years, the state high school wrestling championships have been grappled at the Nutter Center on the Wright State campus. Making it to the tournament on the merits of their qualifying triumphs is a major moment in the lives of the young wrestlers. Perhaps one of them will win an NCAA championship or even the ultimate dream of an Olympic medal. But until one does, he will have to savor his success while receiving limited recognition from school, family and friends.

Interestingly, the two top women administrators in the athletic departments of WSU and UD compiled impressive coaching records in non-revenue competition.

Peggy Wynkoop started the women's volleyball program at Wright State in 1973 and in 14 years as head coach compiled a 367-215-5 record for a .627 percentage.

Wynkoop, an Ohio University graduate, was in her 21st year on the Raider staff in the fall of 1995 and serves as associate athletic director overseeing six women's sports. Perhaps her most important role is serving as compliance officer for the overall program to conform to the numerous NCAA rules and eligibility regulations.

Her counterpart with the Flyers, R. Elaine Dreidame, whose title is senior associate director, coached the volleyball team there 10 seasons with an impressive 309-95 record.

Wright State has produced some quality swimmers. On the men's side, distance swimmer Scott Troutwine was team MVP all four seasons (1985-88) he competed. Sprinter Scott Gregory followed with (1990-91-92) three MVPs.

Various forms of martial arts have come into the picture in recent years. Y. C. Kim opened the first Tae Kwon Do school here and has two flourishing schools in Kettering and Centerville.

There were 29 martial arts schools listed in the 1995 Ameritech Yellow Pages including one operated by Luong Pham, the young Vietnamese student of Y. C. Kim who competed at the world class level and in the 1988 Olympics in Seoul.

Pham, who graduated from Fairmont High School, nearly lost his life in a match in the national championships in Indianapolis in 1987. He won his match but suffered a ruptured kidney from an opponent's kick and underwent emergency surgery to stop the internal bleeding.

His Olympic moment came when he was only 20 years old. He lost a close match to a Korean opponent rated No. 1 in the world in the Daytonian's weight class.

Earlier, Grace Jividen, piled up points in national competition in judo. Ms. Jividen was a student at Carroll High School when she won the Ohio AAU Junior Olympiad in 1980 and then finished fourth in the senior AAU championships. She won a gold medal in the Pan American Games in 1983. Later she spent time in the U. S. Olympic Training Center in Colorado Springs and competed in numerous judo events outside the USA.

Larry Pacifico has held the title of world champion power lifter nine times in a long career in that sport.

Pacifico won his early titles with 200 pounds packed on his stocky 5-foot, 6-inch body. As competition got stronger, he started using steroids, bulking up to 250 pounds before beginning to suffer side effects serious enough to require medical treatment.

He became a spokesman against the use of the drugs as he continued to train and develop other power lifters in the Dayton area.

Afterword

The Media World

Dayton has always had strong media sports coverage. At the end of World War II, there were three daily newspapers here, the morning *Journal* and the afternoon *Herald* and *Daily News*.

In 1949, James M. Cox, who had founded the *Daily News* in 1909, purchased the *Journal* and *Herald* and combined them into a single morning newspaper. Eventually, the *Journal Herald* was absorbed into operation of the *Daily News* and in 1986, lost its identity as the *Daily News,* following the national trend in the industry, became a morning paper.

The author of this book has the distinction of having served as Sports Editor for all three newspapers.

The legends of sports journalism in this community included such bylines from the past as Si Burick, Ben Garlikov, Jim Nichols, Bob Husted, Jake Froug, Harry Kennedy, Sr., M. Carl Finke, Ralph Morrow and Bob Smith to name a few. Other bylines from the more recent past no longer seen include those of Jim Ferguson, Clem Hamilton, Jim Zofkie, Jim Taylor, Marty Williams, Graham Justus and Joe Cunningham.

The *Daily News* heads into the future with a highly regarded veteran staff destined to take their places in future historical records. Included are Hal McCoy (Cincinnati Reds), Leal Beattie (auto racing), Dave Long (high schools) and Marc Katz (Ohio State). Senior staff writer Bucky Albers has made a name for himself and earned a following in covering the Reds, Bengals, the University of Dayton and golf.

Only two writers from a non-major league city have ever been inducted into the Writer's Wing of the Baseball Hall of Fame. Burick was the first and the author of this book was the second.

Burick was also a pioneer in radio sports journalism, having a nightly 15-minute sports round-up on WHIO following the news.

Today, television plays a dominant role in sports coverage with the sports anchors Omar Williams, Mike Hartsock and Don Brown familiar recognized "faces" at area events.

The first regular radio coverage of the Dayton Flyers included such voices as Lou Tschudi, Bill Kehl, Carl Brumbaugh and Charlie Hinkle. Tom Hamlin came to Dayton in 1960 to become the radio and TV voice of the Flyers but left broadcasting to go into the real estate business. Larry Hansgen and Bucky Bockhorn were paired into their 15th season as Flyer voices going into the 1995-96 campaign.

Greg Gahris was the pioneer voice of the Wright State Raiders. Gahris, with his booming voice, was the only play-by-play announcer the Raiders had until his untimely death on June 29, 1995. The fun-loving Gahris had completed his 15th season and was liked and respected by people who knew him on campus as well as with Raider followers. Tom Michaels replaced him as play-by-play man with Ron Coleman continuing as the analyst.

The enthusiastic broadcasting support from Lyle Steig played a part in developing the fan interest in the Dayton Bombers.

The Agonis Club

This is the community's major sports group not attached to an individual school or sport.

Founded in 1933, it was in the beginning basically a club of former football players with a strong UD influence.

No Agonis member can tell you what the word means or where it came from. It is not a secret code name from a ritual. It would be nice to think it was from a classical Greek word with relevance to the original Olympian.

There are Agonis clubs in Columbus and Canton but there is no link or interchange between the three.

Mostly, the Agonians are a sports-minded group who get together Mondays at noon nine months of the year (no summer sessions) to have fun and listen to a guest speaker from the sports world. They have several night meetings each year when they bring in nationally known speakers.

Starting in 1954, the club began to select and honor "Athletes of the Year." The trophies are all memorial awards named for former club members.

The top athlete at UD earns the Joe Gavin/Joe Quinn award. The top high school honoree is given the Beno Keiter/Russ Guerra trophy. The Wright State selectee gets the Dr. Dave Reese award and the outstanding Dayton athlete attending a college outside the Dayton area gets the award in memory of Dave Hall.

The list of speakers at Awards Night dinners has included Bear Bryant, Adolph Rupp, Fred Taylor, Joe Kuharich, Rev. Bob Richards, Don Shula, Bart Starr, Ara Parseghian, Bo Schembechler, Sam Huff, Tom Osborne, Dick Schultz and Rocky Bleier.

The greatest single collection of national celebrities to appear in Dayton came during the period in the 1970s and 1980s when the Laughter Corporation was hosting the Bogie Busters, a two-day golf outing in which the golfers played more for fun than anything else.

Bob Knight, Don Shula, Eddie Arcaro, Paul Brown, Bud Wilkinson, Otto Graham, Jack Twyman and dozens of others from the sports world came to play. But the celebrities from the business, entertainment and government fields were just as impressive.

Gerald Ford played in Dayton after his term in the White House was over and George Bush was a Bogie Buster before he was elected President in 1988. The Bogie Busters was launched by D. R. (Bob) Laughter but it was his son, Cy Laughter, who made it go by establishing friendships and personal contact.

Jesse Philips And *Charisma*

The late Jesse Philips came to Dayton as a youth from his New England birthplace and through hard work and skilled business acumen founded a small company which he nursed into industrial giant, Philips Industries.

Philips became an exceptionally generous philanthropist in the Dayton community, his primary interest was in providing educational opportunities for deserving youngsters. The annual scholarships provided by the Philips Foundation get a number of the brightest Montgomery County high school graduates on their way to a college education. He is remembered for his generosity toward the University of Dayton and a campus research building is known as Jesse Philips Humanities Center.

Relatively late in life, Philips became interested in yacht racing and quickly advanced from local lakes to Lake Erie and then to world class ocean racing.

He owned and raced his yacht *Charisma* in international waters with success in two of the top world events, the SORC (Southern Ocean Racing Conference) in Caribbean waters and the Admirals Cup, a five-race competition based at Cowes on the Isle of Wight off the southern coast of Great Britain.

The Admirals Cup, second only in importance to the Americas Cup in yacht racing, is run in odd-numbered years. Philips competed in 1973, 1975 and 1977, each time with a new boat named *Charisma*.

It was a rare privilege for the author to sail aboard *Charisma* in practice races in the English channel and North Atlantic with Jesse in his first venture in the Admirals Cup. Anyone with the notion that sailing is a "genteel pastime" has a lot to learn about the back-breaking duties of the crews.

The Admirals Cup field consists of three-boat teams representing each participating nation and 48 national flags were on display representing the teams in the 1973 racing. One of the other American boats was skippered by Ted Turner, who went on to win in Americas Cup competition later. The U. S. team won the Admirals Cup two of the three times *Charisma* raced.

In the 1992 Olympic Games, Steve Bourdow, a Stebbins High School graduate, earned a silver medal in the Flying Dutchman Class. Bourdow, who was living in New Orleans as this was written, sailed with Texan Paul Foerster on the two-person small yachts.

Amazingly, for a city as far removed from ample sailing water as Dayton, there is a considerable interest in boating.

Dayton small boat sailors share Eastwood Lake with powerboaters; others sail competitively on Kiser Lake, Indian Lake, Lake St. Mary's and even Lake Erie. Powerboaters make use of the Ohio River and the facilities at Cincinnati.

Beginning and advanced instruction in boat handling, rules and even navigation are taught by such groups as the U. S. Coast Guard Auxiliary and the U. S. Power Squadron, both of which have sizeable membership locally. Even the Red Cross teaches boating safety.

The Dayton Canoe Club had its beginnings in 1912, spearheaded by Charles W. Schaeffer who had been a charter member of the Stillwater Canoe Club.

What Schaeffer had in mind was a more active group interested in staging regattas and other events. Ground was broken in December, 1912 for a clubhouse on Stillwater Avenue, now known as Riverside Drive, just below Helena Street.

Despite the infamous 1913 flood which inundated the site, the building was completed June 13, 1913. An addition was built two years later.

The formal opening on July 12, 1913 found hundreds of people watching the city's first regatta. This became an annual event that lasted well into the 1930s.

On Labor Day weekend, 1914, the club staged a program of rowboat and canoe racing and swimming events. NCR provided bleachers for the spectators.

Harry Wimmers introduced canoe sailing races in 1936, a time when the club was at its zenith of activities.

The club still exists and the officers were talking of a 1996 revival of boating events on the Great Miami.

Newest boating group in the Dayton area is the Greater Dayton Rowing Association, formed in 1992 under the leadership of Dr. Todd Sobol. The objective of this club is to teach, promote and develop crew racing as practiced in major collegiate regattas and the Olympics.

The GDRA built a clubhouse in Island Park to store the shells (racing boats) of club members. The shells come in eight-person, four-person, pairs and individuals. Members vary from recreational rowers to highly competitive racing crews.

"It's an excellent exercise for health and physical fitness," Dr. Sobol puts it.

Picture Credits:
National Baseball Hall of Fame, front cover, right.
University of Dayton, front cover, left; page 58, upper left; page 92, upper left; page 228, top.
Wright State University, page 136, bottom; page 228, center and bottom.
All other photographs courtesy of Dayton Newspapers, Inc.

Index

Index

Herbstreit, Kirk 65, 107
Herman, Billy 143
Herman, Tommy 321
Hermann, Sam 95
Herr, Beth 295
Herr, Mike 217
Herriman, Delme 226
Herrman, Dr. W. W. 303
Hershey, Mike 99
Hess, Eddie 73
Heyduck, Marj 323
Hickey, Gene 198
Hiestand, Joe 305
Higman, Bob 282
Hildreth, Bob 103
Hill, Bro. Matthew 76
Hill, Christi 238
Hill, Kim 237
Hill, Lofton 101
Hill, Van F. 75
Hills and Dales 19
Hinchman, Lew 65
Hinkle, Bob 285
Hinkle, Charlie 363
Hipa, Sam 77
Hirsch, Walt 156
Hoare, Willie 18, 29
Hockett, Oris 133
Hoerner, Dr. Tish 95
Hoff, Ade 277
Hogan, Ben 30
Hogue, Cal 134
Hoke, John D. 104
Holden, Larry 258
Hollinger, Virginia 290
Hollon, Jack 109
Holmes, Howard E. (Ducky) 133, 139, 145
Holsinger, Joe 79, 195
Holsinger, Mrs. Joseph 229
Holzapfel, Tom 219
Hooper, Bobby Joe 207
Hoover, Bill 81
Hoover, Jim 103
Hoppe, Dick 104
Horan, John 199
Horn, Jenny 238
Horn, Ted 268, 273
Horne, Berly 133
Hornsby, Rogers 124
Hortman, Roy 97
Horvath, Joe 97
Hosket, Bill, Sr 245
Houk, Robert 303
Houlgate, Deke 75
Howard, Dan 21
Howell, Fredrick W. 146, 153
Hoyt, Waite 125
Huffman, J. M. 303
Huffman, John 334
Hughes, Alfrederick 264
Hughes, Brian 25
Hughes, Ted and Pete 242

Hummon, J. Mack 69, 297
Hungling, Bernie 133
Hungling, Don (Doke) 71
Hunter, Stan 108
Husted, Bob 363

I
Industrial Recreation Association Dayton 153
Irons, Jim 104

J
Jackson, Arnelle 237
Jackson, Darrell 258
Jackson, Joe 150, 223
Jackson, Marcus 216
Jackson, Rev. Lloyd 162
Jacoby, Bob 203
James, Joey 273
Janco, Nancy 290
Jauron, Bob 73
Jeremiah, Maryalyce 234
Jividen, Grace 362
Johnson, Chris 25
Johnson, Dick 95, 134
Johnson, Fred 86
Johnson, Harold 321
Johnson, Jim 100
Johnson, Julie 234
Johnson, Russ 82, 97
Johnson, S. D. 101
Johnson, Sandy 233
Johnston, Dr. Wilbur 326
Jones, Charles (Benny) 24, 197
Jones, Dave 90
Jones, Robert Tyre (Bobby) 20, 34
Jordan, Keith 88
Joseph, Gene 197
Joy, Tyrone 223
Jungle, Hank 295

K
Kain, Eddie 108
Kane, Deirdre 232
Kantor, Milt 264
Karas, Emil 84
Karas, Mary 310
Katcavage, Jim 59, 83
Katona, Iggy 274
Katz, Marc 363
Kavanaugh, Bob 195
Kazmier, Karen 341
Keck, Charles 105
Keefe, Linda 233
Keefer, Jack 95
Keeler, O. B. 34
Kehl, Bill 363
Keister, Jeanne 237
Keiter, Beno 80
Kellar, George 100
Kellar, Terry 318
Keller, Joe 97
Kelley, Harry 283

Kelley, J. R. 283
Kelley, Roosevelt 102
Kelly, John 108
Kelly, Mike 87, 88, 90
Kennedy, Carl 155
Kennedy, Sr., Harry 363
Kepler, Bob 43
Kern, Rex 64
Kerr, Bud 83
Kettering, Charles F. 21, 67, 303
Keyes, William A. 21, 78
Kidd, Norm 21
Kidder, Walter and Georgeana 20
Kilbane, Fran 82
Kilgore, Frank 180
Kim, Y. C. 362
Kinderdine, George (Hobby) 68
Kinderman, Bob 345
King, Betsy 41
King, George 263
King, Kristin 238
King, Robert 303
Kirk, Steve 284
Kiser Panthers 71
Kiss, Joe 327
Kissell, Ted 214
Kittyhawk Golf Center 24
Klaus, Gene 207
Klee, Ollie 65, 95, 133
Klein, Bob 100
Kneisley, Jimmy 271
Knight, Negele 212
Knisley, Bill 196
Knox, Buddy 319
Koepnick, Robert 65, 73
Kohen, Brian 341
Korutz, Bill 84
Kosins, Gary 85
Kostka, Stan 147
Kramer Winery and Pleasure Garden 18
Kramer, Jack 296
Kramer, Kyle 104
Kramer, Tony 73, 82
Kress, Bernie 85
Krintzline, Bill 342
Kroemer, William 76
Kroll, Ted 36
Kronauge, Bob 290
Kronauge, Jr., Frank 290, 291
Kruty, Michele 236
Kumle, Bill 25
Kumler, Irvin 303
Kuntz, Martin 194

L
Lackner, Bro. Elmer 75, 206
Laffoon, Ky 35
Lammers, Carol 234
Landis, Emerson H. 241
Lane, Don 203
Lange, Bill 85
Langley, Pat 99